Death in the Community

DL BORG EL CAPELAÑ DEL CRVCFISO
CON LI FRATELLI DE DITTA CŌPANIA
SE ABOTER QVI AL ORET AMARA
ESCNPORÑ DL MORBO EGNDE ABISSO
DEMORBO NELLANO

Death in the Community

MEMORIALIZATION AND CONFRATERNITIES IN AN ITALIAN COMMUNE IN THE LATE MIDDLE AGES

James R. Banker

The University of Georgia Press
ATHENS AND LONDON

Athens, Georgia 30602

Set in Bembo
The paper in this book meets the guidelines for permanence and durability of the Committee on Production Guidelines for Book Longevity of the Council on Library Resources.

Printed in the United States of America
92 91 90 89 88 5 4 3 2 1

Library of Congress Cataloging in Publication Data

Banker, James R.
Death in the community.

Bibliography: p.
Includes index.
1. Confraternities—Italy—Sansepolcro—History.
2. Death—Religious aspects—Catholic Church—History of doctrines—Middle Ages, 600-1500. 3. Sansepolcro (Italy)—Church history. I. Title.
BX808.5.I8B36 1988 248'.06'04551 87-34320
ISBN 0-8203-1034-4 (alk. paper)

British Library Cataloging in Publication Data available

Frontispiece: Plague Victim at San Sepolcro, Italian School, Sixteenth Century (SCALA/Art Resource, N.Y.)

For Maureen

Contents

Appendixes: Statutes and Testaments

Maps

Tables

Acknowledgments

In undertaking this study I have had the aid and encouragement of many individuals and institutions. They are too numerous to name here, but I do wish to record publicly my gratitude to several of them and to recall that each has no responsibility for any errors or infelicities of fact, style, or method. These are my own.

Several institutions have contributed to my research, including the Research and Professional Development Fund of North Carolina State University, the American Council of Learned Societies, and the National Endowment for the Humanities. Without their support my research could not have been undertaken, and I hope this acknowledgment will contribute in some small way to maintaining aid for scholars from these and other granting agencies. I wish also to thank the librarians of the Biblioteca Laurenziana and the Biblioteca Nazionale Centrale and the archivists of the Archivio di Stato in Florence for their assistance. The Interlibrary Loan staff at North Carolina State University, especially Margaret Suggs and Ann Baker Ward, sought the locations of my obscure sources, and they deserve particular mention in this account of those who contributed to my scholarly enterprise.

The days that I had the privilege of studying in the Archivio Comunale in San Sepolcro were some of the most pleasurable and intense of my life. For this, I wish to thank Nilde Mercati, Carla Maccarti, Annamaria Ricci, Franco Franceschini, and Adamo Gnignori. To the director of the Archivio and Biblioteca Comunale, Dr. Francesco Comanducci, I am particularly indebted. I owe him my gratitude as much for his willingness to honor my troublesome requests as for the elegance of his character. I wish also to thank Luigi Andreini, Giovanni Gorizi, and Giuseppe Monti, recently deceased, for their graceful introduction to their families and the rich cultural resources of San Sepolcro. The memory of their guidance through the streets of San

Sepolcro in search of a *porta del morto* remains vividly etched in my mind as a symbol of our common project of reconstructing a history of their medieval ancestors.

My colleagues at North Carolina State University have contributed to my research in both subtle and tangible ways. I wish to thank Joseph Hobbs and John Riddle and to remember Stan Suval for their encouragement and criticism of my ideas and writing. Alexander De-Grand took my manuscript at a critical moment and compelled me to recognize several problems of style and organization. I trust I have met some of his criticisms. For their introductions to the art of word processing, I wish to thank Bill Beezley and Jon Ocko; for their typing, I am in debt to Janice Mitchell, Amy Hosokawa, and Miriam Pond. Others, in places distant from Raleigh, made helpful criticisms at different stages of my writing. I express my thanks to Robert Brentano, Ronald Weissman, Margery Ganz, and John Henderson. Marvin B. Becker has contributed to this book in too many areas to be recounted here. He first stimulated my interest in late medieval Italian history and has always demanded through his restless intellect that the historian probe beyond the appearances of things. He is in my mind a model historian.

Maureen Banker and our children, Peri and Heather, have contributed to my research in ways that go beyond any possible acknowledgment. Maureen has been artist, mother, wife, encourager, and critic. I wish to express my gratitude for her love and support as we pursued our shared passion for Italian art and history.

Death in the Community

Introduction

This study begins with the assumption that one of man's primary needs is to die in the presence of other human beings and with their remembrance. Humans throughout history have participated in the reconstruction of social systems of death. Thus most deaths are in some manner socialized, despite the claims of those who speak of individualized death in the modern era. The individual's desire for the participation of larger social groups in his death and remembrance draws all the living from their daily routine to an involvement in the needs and aspirations of the dying and those already in the grave. Communities organized to meet the individual's demand for aid at the deathbed, honor at burial, and memorialization thereafter form the primary focus of this study. It is conventional wisdom that such communities were intimately linked to religion and were influenced by politics and economics. More pertinent to this study is the reality that these communities, organized around the interests of the dead, structured the social relationships of power and production that served life.

The dying individual, particularly as a testator, can for a moment transcend his customary calculations of self and family interests and take the opportunity to balance the future needs of his family with his longing for eternal life and wider social remembrance.[1] This desire for commemoration that transcends family and neighborhood raises the dying individual from his immediate social setting and makes him a participant in a religious or cultural drama. These more complex schemata promise eternal and social rewards after death in exchange for a portion of the deceased's patrimony or some service. The cultural systems of death and the communities that support them change and are transformed over time; therefore, they are likely subjects of historical analysis.

From the early thirteenth century through the eighteenth century, lay men and women of western Europe organized several thousand voluntaristic corporations that socialized death. In most instances, these corporations—confraternities—performed social and liturgical services for the parish or larger community, including expiation of sin, relief from disaster, praise of the divine, burial of the dead, and charity to the poor, aged, pilgrim, sick, and imprisoned. Though there existed a multitude of forms, the members of the confraternities usually elected lay leaders with limited terms of office, attended administrative meetings and liturgical services, rewarded priests for their liturgical acts, and often performed duties of a priestly nature, which included preaching, receiving "confessions," and chastising fellow members for improprieties. Some confraternities fostered a lay devotion to the person of Jesus Christ, especially his passion, that required attendance at numerous confraternal services, private prayers, and a rigorous code of behavior for the individual. Despite repetitious admonitions regarding personal behavior and subtle techniques for compelling adherence to confraternal statutes, most of the confraternities sought to exempt noncompliance with the statutes from being considered a sin. If noncompliance were a sin, clerical authority and otherworldly punishment would be required. The confraternities stimulated an intensive devotion in the form of voluntary prohibitions and charitable acts that constituted a stratum of watched personal and social behavior well beyond that the church expected of laypeople.

In this book the rise of confraternities will be studied in the context of the individual's concern for his death, forms of remembrance, the ultimate destination of his soul, and the disposal of his patrimony in this world. In the High and Late Middle Ages the lay confraternities appropriated several monastic practices, some that had been performed by and for monks and others provided by the monastic orders to enable members of the laity to memorialize themselves and to assure that their intentions were fulfilled after their deaths. The extending of the period of time in which prayers could be offered for the well-being of souls led to a novel set of problems surrounding death and memorialization. The lay leadership of confraternities assumed the greater part of the responsibility for mediating between the dead and the living. This mediation became increasingly problematical after 1200 because the dead became objectified as beings existing in an identifiable place. Because the dead were conceived as existing in an afterlife, their problems had to be addressed directly. The confraternities, along with the clergy, who were the traditional mediators between this world and the next, served the dead by representing their interests in the temporal world.[2]

The term *confraternitas* was frequently used before the thirteenth century to designate a union of prayers by which two monasteries agreed to pray for each others' departed souls or to indicate an association of individuals, lay or clerical, with a monastery. The chancellors of the monasteries entered the names of the associates in their books of co-brothers and at death in the books of the dead. The monasteries thereby gave remembrance to associated members of the laity and clergy, granted many of them formal burial with habits in their chapel cemeteries, and recited prayers at designated intervals, including, for some, perpetual prayers. Though practices varied from monastery to monastery, the co-brother usually made a gift of money or property to the monastic corporation, which gave him the right of burial and remembrance identical to that of the order's members.[3]

In the course of the thirteenth century the laity of western Europe borrowed these practices, though also using the intermediate forms of the mendicants and the penitents and a few precocious pre-1200 lay confraternities. In imitation of the monks, the laity appropriated not only their practices but also an underlying authority and virtue. This appropriation was necessary for laypeople to give each other meaningful remembrance in this world and place a claim on God's assistance in the next. Certainly part of laypeople's authority derived from the clerical assistance they received, including grants of indulgences from their bishops, but many confraternities existed for decades without the sanction of a bishop or the encouragement of indulgences. The lay confraternities gained the authority to give remembrance in the thirteenth century by joining together two fundamental acts that earlier had been primarily in the hands of the regular clergy: giving charity to the poor and efficacious care to the dead. The confraternal impulse could be turned to a variety of purposes from building bridges to providing a lavish table with convivial companions, and the authority of the confraternity could be grounded upon a rigorous code of personal behavior or purgation of the body. In the thirteenth century, however, most confraternities built their authority on serving the poor of Christ.

The advent of the lay confraternities can best be understood in relation to several analogous movements in religion and to changes in attitudes about death. In the thirteenth century medieval Christianity was enriched by lay participation in penitential movements and by the appearance of the mendicant orders with their mission to the recently urbanized and their zeal to construct lay confraternities. In addition, many small orders, preachers, and holy men addressed the laity more directly with an appeal to turn away from the sins of urban society toward the apostolic life. Other than seeing confraternities as a logical result of mendicant preaching, the relationship between these fundamental changes in medieval Christianity and the rise of confraternities has been overlooked. Several researchers, however, have formulated critically important interpretations from the perspectives of the history of religion and death in the High Middle Ages.[4] Arsenio Frugoni in 1957 analyzed death themes in a northern Italian fresco and accepted as self-evident that medieval men and women had little concern for their own death. The destiny of all mankind stirred the medieval imagination; life was considered a brief pilgrimage and death subordinated to an intense concern for the afterlife and fear of eternal darkness. In time, society created more institutions, joys, wealth, and activities than could be subsumed under medieval universalistic conceptions linked directly to the supernatural. By the fifteenth century history had become individualized, though death, hell, paradise, and judgment remained important; the principal problem, according to Frugoni, had become the salvation of one's own soul with its fate being decided in a singular moment of judgment.[5]

Raffaello Morghen believed that eleventh-century men rejected the earlier medieval emphasis on flight from the world and the reform of universal institutions. Eventually, a European spiritual crisis in the thirteenth and fourteenth centuries was resolved by abandoning hopes for a reform of society. By the fourteenth century, belief in renewal could be sustained only when conceived as the renewing of the interior man. The humanist Francesco Petrarca best represents this internalized renewal. Morghen also held that after 1300 commitment to universal and collective salvation weakened as the church became accepted as possessing exclusive authority over the treasury of merits, the sacraments, and the instituting of corporate religious groups. The church compelled an outward conformity, which encouraged the individual to construct a separate freedom of the spirit. Content with this inward form, the individual became concerned with death only at the end of life.[6]

Building on these earlier interpretations, Philippe Ariès popularized ideas of a transformation of attitudes on death that occurred in the twelfth and thirteenth centuries. With Frugoni and Morghen, he saw the basic question to be corporate and individual attitudes toward death. Death visited early medieval society so often that men and women accepted it as a part of life, as indeed they ignored the ancient prohibitions against and suspicion about burying the dead within the walls of the city. The moments before death were not particularly troublesome or emotional because the individual performed simple rituals that both expressed and contained a measure of sorrow. As was true of all God's creation, men and women lived a season and died; death meant a sleep of the soul followed by corporate judgment and paradise. Although this pattern prevailed for centuries for the vast majority of people, the privileged few—the nobles, high clerics, and rich merchants—had by the thirteenth century constructed a new pattern of death, which expressed their own individual strivings and achievements. Death became problematic for these few as each individual sought fulfillment and some sign that his or her deeds would satisfy the divine Judge's eternal law. The act of dying became invested with an emotional intensity unknown in the earlier period. Individual death or "one's own death" required personalized forms of memorialization and hence individual graves, epitaphs, and effigies.[7]

Lester Little, following Georges Duby's interpretation of the profound importance of gift-giving in early medieval society, hypothesizes that the triumph of money exchange had disastrous consequences for religious practices formerly based on gift exchange. Marvin Becker, also influenced by Duby's works, argues that as gift exchanges were replaced by money exchanges in the High Middle Ages, human society became more solidified, so secure that the individual could invest it with trust. Although money destabilized most personal and institutional relationships earlier based on gifts, the increasing coherence of society stimulated a trust in the solidity of human relationships.[8] Human society perceived as sempiternal provided a solid foundation upon which the individual could build his aspirations for immortality. Hence the High Middle Ages witnessed the rapid diffusion of the practice of writing testaments and of perpetual prayers administered by lay confraternities. Contemporaneous with the consolidation of temporal and social relationships was an analogous materializing of the afterlife. Jacques Le Goff has demonstrated that about 1200 purgatory became conceived as a geographic entity. No longer faintly imagined as a transitory state, purgatory became a place to which the souls of most Christians had to go for a period of cleansing.[9] This new concept no doubt was based on a changing sense of time and space relationships but also derived from the desire of western Europeans to enhance their ability to influence the conditions of their family members in the afterlife. The lay confraternities linked care for the dead to several practices, particularly charity, that were beneficial to society, simultaneously contributing to the dignity of temporal relationships and drawing from these services merit to memorialize the dead.

Jacques Chiffoleau, who has studied several thousand testaments in the area of Marseille and Avignon from the Late Middle Ages, has discovered two patterns of reaction to death in these years, one learned-clerical and the other popular or folk.[10] The first absorbed and gave coherence to the second over time, thereby integrating folk and marginally Christian elements into orthodox belief. Participants in popular religion viewed death as a process that ended in the mourning at the anniversary of the individual's death. This logic has the appearance of being universal or at least widespread; it is based on the anthropological studies of Robert Hertz and Arnold van Gennep.[11] Mourning continues in the year after death, contemporaneous with the soul's completion of its journey to its rest. In this process mourners are reintegrated into society and the soul enters the world of the dead. The flight of the soul is a return to one's forebears; and if the dying are too far from their ancestral tomb, they seek the proxy family of the mendicant orders. The successful flight to one's ancestors required a "price of passage," which was paid to various groups of priests and monks. Only after 1350 did the people of Chiffoleau's research area bestow substantial sums upon the confraternities. The priests performed essentially propitiatory rites to facilitate the passage to the next world, though the family and other social groups continued to participate in mourning. Finally, Chiffoleau finds that these folk funerals concentrated prayers for the soul of the deceased in the time immediately bounded by the anniversary masses, whereas the clerical-savant tradition emphasized perpetual or repetitive masses that indicate a judgment of the soul after the end of history. This long period before the repose of the dead provides the foundation for the idea of purgatory, though the term itself was not commonly used. After 1350 these two patterns of prayer for the soul merged to bring about a fundamental Christianization of the folk culture of death.

Chiffoleau's substantial achievement is marred only by the conceptual problem of separating several practices surrounding death and then designating these practices as folk. They may have been folk and non-Christian at some earlier period, but by 1300 these practices—propitiatory rites, for example—were integrated within Christian rituals and theology. There is little evidence, structural or empirical, to indicate that the people of the region of Avignon perceived or understood themselves to be participating in two different cultures of death. Though the records of death for this period seldom contain personal reflections on death, the contemporaries' understanding of the meaning of their rituals must have precedence over explanations of behavior drawn from some archaic past.[12]

The question whether a folk or popular culture of religion existed in the Middle Ages has stimulated an important historiographical debate.[13] Frequently those who aver the existence of a folk religion find social relationships to be more fundamental or defining of the remainder of culture and society than intellectual traditions or clerical institutions. Religion, whether as belief or practice, is defined as originating in other social processes or in a more basic popular attitude or behavior. Defenders of the concept of a folk religion usually see the historians who oppose their views as defenders of the medieval church. And all too often in the past those who denied the existence of a separate folk culture defended an autonomous learned clerical tradition.

These opposing orientations are manifest in two recent works on Italian confraternities. Gilles Meersseman's magisterial three-volume study, the result of five decades of research, places the history of lay confraternities in the unfolding of Christian revelation.[14] He views the confraternities as part of a larger mendicant and penitential movement that swept through western Europe in the High Middle Ages. The men of the confraternities labored to acquire a lay spirituality modeled on that of the Franciscans and Dominicans. The acquisition of this spirituality represented a logical extension and fulfillment of Christian doctrine, and in Meersseman's study this phenomenon required no explanation outside itself. Ronald Weissman's researches are based on a close reading of statutes and statistical studies of membership in several confraternities of Florence.[15] He avoids the reduction of religion to society or politics implicit in several of his assumptions and demonstrates that relationships initiated in acquiring or exercising economic and political power, social relationships generally, replicated themselves in the Florentine confraternities. He shows how a coalescing elite altered the forms and rituals of the confraternities for their benefit. Meersseman accepts the confraternities on their own terms; Weissman often views the activity of the lay groups as symbols of deeper social unities and conflicts. Each strives to integrate elements from the diametrically opposed perspective. Meersseman, for example, examines the social origins of the members of several confraternities, and Weissman describes eloquently the activities of brotherhoods based on Christian doctrine as part of a pacification of Florentine society.

No one has succeeded in explaining the existence of the extraordinary number of confraternities in northern and central Italy—not to mention much of western Europe—beginning in the thirteenth century. Meersseman is correct that the confraternities helped deepen Christian spirituality among the laity, and Weissman's point is equally valid, that they united disparate and often aggressive individuals into brotherhoods capable of acting beyond their self-interest. These are significant, but not sufficient, explanations of the extraordinary number and qualities of the confraternities in Italy. Moreover, any interpretation has to address the reality that small towns and even villages with relatively little wealth and economic differentiation gave birth to confraternal forms identical to those of the largest urban centers. Already in the fourteenth century, each type of human settlement in northern and central Italy supported confraternities. There were, for example, three confraternities in the Tuscan village of Linari with a population of approximately five hundred inhabitants, fourteen in the Tuscan town of San Sepolcro with a population of approximately five thousand, and nearly one hundred in Florence with a population of approximately one hundred thousand. The ubiquity of the confraternities casts into doubt explanations that they were based on specific social relationships characteristic only of large urban areas.[16] The rapid diffusion of confraternities into all sizes and types of Italian urban groupings in the hundred years from 1250 to 1350 points to a social or cultural gene whose ancestor existed in every form of social organization.

This study of San Sepolcro steers a middle course between those who see religious ideas and practices as descending from a learned-clerical tradition and those who view social practices as anterior to or in some way more defining than religion. Religion need not be conceived as supernatural to recognize that it is not just another social reality. It is grounded in recurring individual relationships but is perceived by participants as that and, more fundamentally, as beyond mundane reality. The desire to transcend this world and to articulate the significance of human existence constitutes a dynamic but permanent element in man's consciousness. Religion and historical consideration of it remain social projects of profound significance. If a popular or folk culture existed in San Sepolcro in the Late Middle Ages, it was not pagan or heretical, but a lay culture concerned with achieving social esteem at death and remembrance thereafter within a general Christian framework. The functional acts of giving to the less fortunate of the community and praying reciprocally for each other constituted the core of lay religion and concurrently served to bond together the local society.

Death and charity were linked throughout the period under study here. In the social world a sense of community, though ever in transformation, involved individuals in the lives of their neighbors and led them to aid the less fortunate. In the divine economy charity conferred eternal merit on the contributing community and the individual. The sense of community doubtless underlay the individual's view that charity obtained merit, and ecclesiastical indulgences for charity confirmed the individual's intuition that he accomplished worthy goals in giving to the poor and weak. Charity, however, is not a necessary or "natural" consequence of community; minimally, different communities foster various forms of charity. Community is constructed and destroyed through the acts of its members. Charity has too often been studied as an autonomous phenomenon but is best analyzed in conjunction with the acts and beliefs of the historical participants who bring community into being. The practice of aiding the poor will be discussed in detail, but this study does not view charity as self-generated.

Death is onc of several possible foci for the study of confraternities. It will be my focus because ceremonies surrounding death provide one of the foundations of community and because it is only in the context of these ceremonies that the role of charity can be comprehended. Several scholars of the confraternities have noted the central place of death and mortuary ceremonies in the life of the confraternities. Gennaro Monti, the first scholar of Italian confraternities, began his history of lay confraternities with an examination of Roman burial societies. Recognizing that the confraternities served various purposes, he stated that burial functions were such an integral part of all confraternities that their death rituals required little discussion. More recently, Meersseman commenced his study by discussing the monastic prayers and services for the dead. He does distinguish "unions of prayers" from confraternities but only on the technical grounds that the former were not "organic societies" with statutes and periodic meetings under their own leaders. He recognizes that confraternities and unions of prayers have at their core the members' sense of their own sin, their terror of the supreme Judge, their desire to redeem the dead from the punishments of the other world, and their practice of celebrating for them propitiatory and anniversary masses. And Giuseppina de Sandre Gasparini has stated in regard to the confraternities of Padua that death "is the center of meditation and occupies a large space in the mental horizon of the adherents of the confraternities."[17]

This book integrates the perspectives of the studies of death with those of lay spirituality. In addition, Jack Goody's discussion of the central importance of social groups that mediate between the dead and the living has contributed one of the principal ideas on the role of confraternities in medieval western Europe.[18] Underlying the activities of the confraternities in the High Middle Ages were the individual's desire for remembrance at and after death and his aspiration that his patrimony be administered efficiently for the benefit of his soul and his descendants. The realization of these goals required a socialized form of resolution. The evidence presented in this study from a hillside town in the Upper Tiber Valley points to an intense socialization of death already in place when documentation becomes relatively full in the second half of the thirteenth century. In some periods, such as our own, this socialization precedes the moment of death with intensive means and extraordinary attempts to delay and prepare for the physical deterioration that accompanies the onset of death. Other societies construct for the actors in the death drama elaborate ceremonies after the body has lost its breath. The citizens of San Sepolcro participated in a series of rituals revolving around death that resemble the baroque socialization of death discussed by Michel Vovelle in France in the seventeenth and eighteenth centuries, but the thirteenth-century pattern is defined more fully by its differences. Whereas Vovelle finds a large number of hired mourners, monks, priests, and prayers in France, the central theme in Italy is the memorialization of the deceased by fellow laymen, who achieved a claim on the divine through their corporate charity. This broad participation in death extended the concern for the deceased from the family and neighborhood to society.[19] In the thirteenth century vast numbers of the townspeople exchanged prayers, thereby expressing and intensifying a growing sense of lay community. In the fourteenth century, however, the Fraternity of San Bartolomeo, which had served to express and had supervised the wide memorialization of the deceased at the time of the individual's burial, began to serve the memorialization needs of the few. The intensity of mourning at death could be perpetuated only in small units, in confraternities of praise and discipline.

This study does not presume any particular cogency or persuasiveness in the teaching of the regular and secular clergy of San Sepolcro. The clergy appear here as they presented themselves in documents of the lay institutions. They served as instruments of lay society performing mass, hearing confessions, receiving bequests for the exercising of sacred rites, entering monasteries and convents from the families of the laity, and occasionally asserting ecclesiastical rights. The relative passivity of the clergy and the clerical hierarchy may have derived from the region's jurisdictional arrangements. The bishop of the nearby town of Città di Castello exercised spiritual authority outside the walls of the town, and the abbot of the Camaldolese monastery in the center of San Sepolcro possessed spiritual authority within the walls. Bitter conflict occurred frequently between the towns of San Sepolcro and Città di Castello, between secular clergymen subject to the bishop but within San Sepolcro and under the abbot's authority, between the laity and the abbot over the latter's secular authority in the town, and between the abbot and the bishop of Città di Castello over rightful spiritual jurisdiction in San Sepolcro. Each conflict made more difficult an assertive and unified clerical dominance over the religious life of the town. The laity by no means ignored monastic spirituality or mendicant preaching; both had a profound influence on the religious life of the people. But by the fourteenth century the lay confraternities had assumed so many clerical functions that most of the day-to-day religious acts occurred under lay supervision or sponsorship, albeit with priests administering the sacraments and, though not evident in the documents, instructing in the faith. The supervision of sacred acts by the laity led to some conflicts with the clerical hierarchy, but the documents from lay institutions do not show these conflicts to be especially sharp or enduring. Conflict frequently reveals the nature of historical institutions, but the medieval church has too often been viewed either as a harmonious whole or as ripped by competing factions. Neither orientation can define the church and religion in the High and Late Middle Ages, and neither is an effective means of organizing knowledge of medieval religion.

The records from San Sepolcro may overemphasize the role of the laity in the religious life of the town, but because so many historical studies have been based on clerical documents, this one should redress the balance. In addition, the documentation questions Ariès's influential interpretation of death in the High Middle Ages. The number and intensity of monastic rituals point to a profound socialization of the preparation for death. To accomplish what Ariès called "tamed death," the fear on the part of the living had to be contained through rituals of dying and through prayers perpetuated over time. Ariès was aware of the intensive rituals surrounding death in the Early Middle Ages; he concluded that they necessarily achieved release from a fear of death, which permitted early medieval men blithely to accept the obliteration of their being as part of a rhythmic natural cycle. But Ariès's evidence, primarily drawn from sources on the rituals of death, did not permit him to make judgments on the consciousness of his subjects. The literary sources that he employed were written largely in the twelfth century, which he believed was the period when the older pattern of tamed death was breaking down. The opposite problem weakens his interpretation of the High and Late Middle Ages, when the rich and powerful became more concerned and fearful about death, and death became a more individualistic experience. For this period Ariès ignored those sources that in the Early Middle Ages he had held up as definitive. He failed to recognize the profound socialization of death implicit in indulgences, family tombs, perpetual prayers, and other mortuary practices that he saw as evidence of one's own death. These rituals can be seen as distributing fear of death outward into society as easily as those of the Early Middle Ages.

This study of religion and confraternities in San Sepolcro demonstrates that a profound transformation of practices surrounding death occurred in the period from 1250 to 1450. This was not simply a change from corporate to individual because throughout the period the individual required the aid of social institutions. Chapter 1 assesses the nature of the Christian church and clerical corporations in San Sepolcro in the thirteenth century. It will show that the clergy controlled charity in the form of hospitals and that there were relatively few clerics, especially secular priests, in San Sepolcro in the thirteenth century.

The second chapter examines lay institutions of death and charity in San Sepolcro in the second half of the thirteenth century. The large lay Fraternity of San Bartolomeo provides significant sources for assessing patterns surrounding the death of practically everyone of the town. Whether patterns of death and charity found in San Sepolcro were typical can be proved only after several more local studies are completed. It is evident, however, that this town on the border of Tuscany and Umbria shared many of the same religious enthusiasms, institutional forms, and social conflicts of much of northern and central Italy in the thirteenth and fourteenth centuries.

The dissolution of the corporate unity and the lay memorialization practiced by the Fraternity of San Bartolomeo occurred contemporaneously with several fundamental changes concerning death practices. The decline of the fraternity in the first half of the fourteenth century, discussed in Chapter 3, accompanied the rise of more intensive forms of piety expressed in smaller, exclusive confraternities and the rapid increase in the number of individuals who wrote wills. Together these changes constitute a fundamental transformation of attitudes and practices surrounding death. Important in this transformation was the exclusion of females from active participation in the confraternities expressing the new forms of piety.

Chapter 4 addresses this transformation through an analysis of one of the newer types of confraternities of the fourteenth century. This chapter surveys the rise and bureaucratization of the Confraternity of Santa Maria della Notte that early linked praising of God and giving charity but in time became a corporation for the administration of testaments and charity. In Chapter 5 confraternities of discipline are examined as another expression of intense piety; members identified with the passion of Christ by flagellating themselves. This mortification of the flesh presented a purged identity on the part of the confraternal member and constituted his merit to a greater degree than participation in large-scale contributions to the poor or administration of charity. As such, the flagellants represented a particularly committed portion of Christian society, which saw the requirement of taking upon themselves the salvation of self and society. In San Sepolcro, however, a high proportion of male adults were flagellants.

San Sepolcro was chosen for study because of the extraordinarily complete documentation on confraternities and the religious life of the laity from the perspective of death. The statutes of the Fraternity of San Bartolomeo, one of the earliest and still unpublished of the statutes of confraternities in western Europe, contain a detailed description of the activities of this large communitywide lay association. The fraternity left behind its thirteenth-century lists of several thousand members and its necrology of over two thousand of its dead. Beginning in 1377, it maintained daily records of each death in the town; these are among the earliest of such books of the dead in Italy and western Europe and are substantially complete for 350 years. Statutes of the two other types of confraternities existing in San Sepolcro are extant from the fourteenth and fifteenth centuries. An abundant number of testaments from the early fourteenth century provides the basis for examining the attitudes toward death and the citizens' loyalty to the confraternities and other religious corporations. If we add the abstracts of more than seventeen hundred bequests to two confraternities from the mid-thirteenth century to 1437, we see a convergence of documents for the period 1250 to 1450 that enables us to gain a rare detailed portrait of how charity and death evolved in a community in the Late Middle Ages.

Yet even more important than these documents in choosing San Sepolcro as the object of historical inquiry is the existence of a fifteenth-century manuscript with the title "Specchio." Its author, Francesco de Largi, intended this "mirror" as a book of instruction for subsequent confraternal leaders. He served as notary (*scrivano*) of one of the town's two most important confraternities from 1415 to his death around 1447 as well as several times as prior of the Fraternity of San Bartolomeo. During his first term in 1414–15 he perused the fraternity's fourteenth-century documents and extracted important memorials for himself and subsequent priors. Most important, in his third term as prior in 1437–38, he wrote his "Specchio," the fruit of his careful examination of the corporation's records that includes his extracts of over one thousand testamentary bequests. In addition, he estimated income and meditated on the fraternity's practices and well-being. Seeing the confraternities through the mind of a fifteenth-century confraternal executive gives us an insight into the religious piety of a specific participant. This study begins with the appearance of the first lay confraternity in San Sepolcro around 1250 and concludes about 1450 soon after Largi provided his abstracts and historical meditation on the preceding two centuries of lay devotion. From a variety of perspectives, the middle of the fifteenth century is a logical terminus of this study. It permits us to view an extended period of lay piety that early expressed itself in several innovative institutions; it also gives sufficient time for the innovations to work out their logical implications. Moreover, in 1441 Florence assumed political control of San Sepolcro and destroyed that town's political autonomy.

In referring to the pious organizations of the laity, I have usually employed the term *confraternity* as a translation of the Latin *confraternitas* and the Italian *compagnia*. I have avoided translating the latter as *company* because that term is fixed in the modern mind as an economic entity. The documents of the period always specify the brotherhood of San Bartolomeo as a *fraternitas;* therefore, when wishing to indicate it, I use the translation *fraternity*. In various documents of the Middle Ages, the town under study here was designated as *Borgo, San Sepolcro,* and *Borgo San Sepolcro*. I have adopted the modern usage and in the text refer to the town as San Sepolcro.

CHAPTER ONE

The Topography of Worship: Religious Corporations and the Paucity of Clerics in San Sepolcro

This chapter locates the reader within the town of San Sepolcro and its numerous clerical corporations to set the context for analyzing religious devotion. This discussion of the clerical corporations will reveal that in the hundred years before the demographic catastrophes of the mid-fourteenth century, the town supported a small number of clerics and its ecclesiastical institutions were not systemically organized. Therefore, the laity performed several functions that conventionally are associated with the clergy. Such a finding should not be interpreted to signify a crisis in the church or a failing of one or more of the clerical corporations; rather, the prominent role of the laity should be understood as a complement to the recent discoveries that the medieval clergy played minor roles in performance of marriages and funerals.[1]

This evidence suggests that the clergy may have aided but not dominated the local societies. Clericalization of important social activities and rituals in the late Middle Ages and in post-Tridentine Europe has hidden the vital role of the laity in religion in the earlier period. The argument of this study, however, does not turn on the character or behavior of the clergy. Nor does it turn on the number of clergy and the ratio of clergy to laypeople, although the large number of females in convents at the beginning of the fourteenth century suggests that male ecclesiastical institutions could have been equally and substantially enlarged. We should ascribe greater significance to the lay religious corporations, whose number jumped from three to approximately twenty in the years from 1300 to 1350, while the number of clerical corporations declined. The newly founded lay corporations served the town by memorializing the dead and by performing acts of

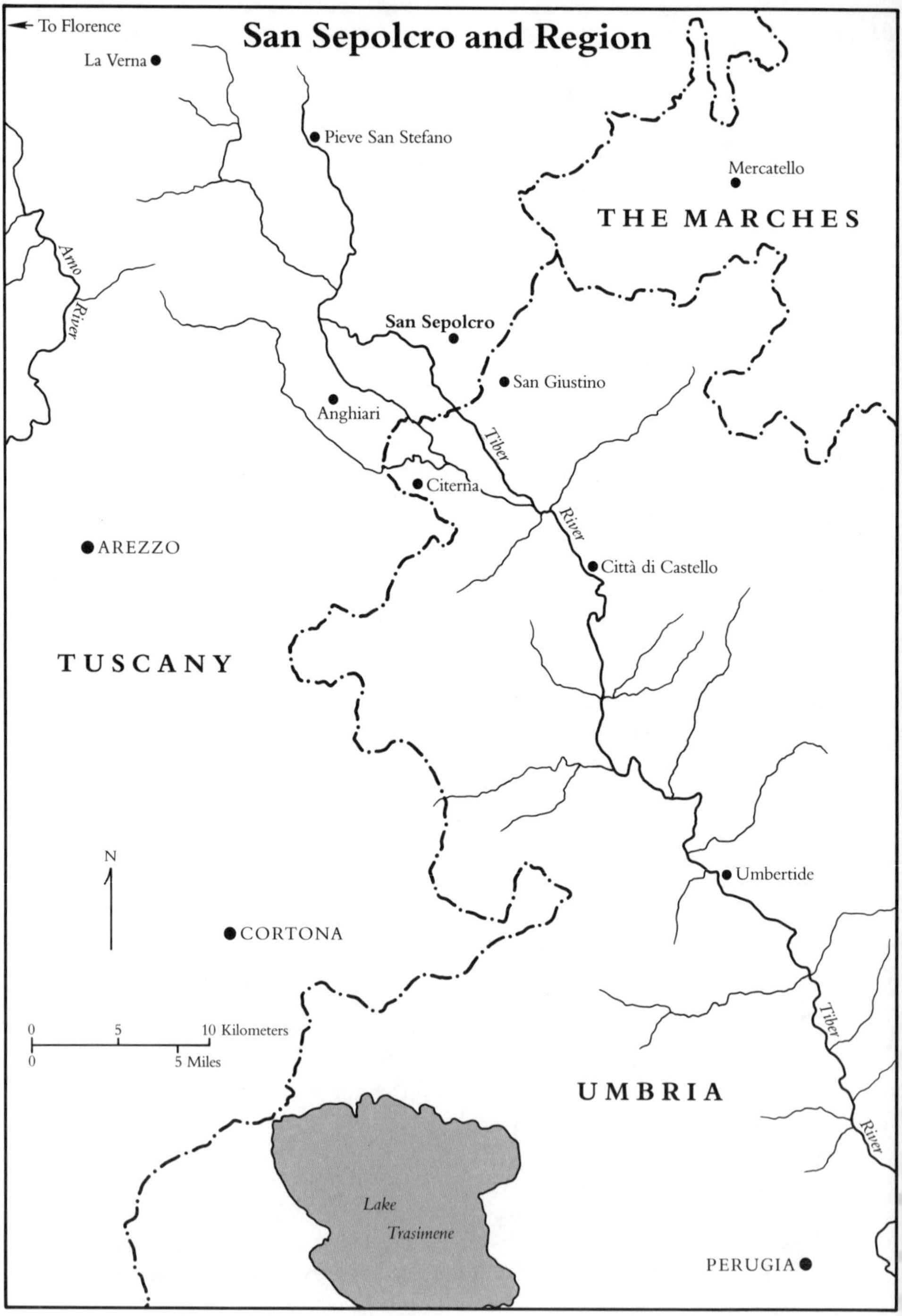
San Sepolcro and Region
To Florence
La Verna
Pieve San Stefano
Mercatello
THE MARCHES
Arno River
San Sepolcro
San Giustino
Anghiari
Tiber River
Citerna
AREZZO
Città di Castello
TUSCANY
N
Umbertide
CORTONA
0 5 10 Kilometers
0 5 Miles
Tiber River
UMBRIA
Lake Trasimene
PERUGIA

charity. The confraternities' appropriation of functions formerly performed by the family, clergy, or other social group appears to have been largely independent of the quality or quantity of the clergy. In the period from 1250 to 1350 the laity gained political authority, became more specialized economically and constructed a guild system, and took responsibility for death and charity. Through the performance of acts associated with death, charity, and the afterlife, the laity in the confraternities acquired a near sacred character.

There is little evidence to indicate that a parish system existed either to encourage or to block the enlarged role of the laity in religion in San Sepolcro. Elsewhere in Italy, and in Christendom generally, parish organization varied substantially from town to town. In the best study of parish structures to date, Jean Coste has linked the development of parishes to the willingness of the ecclesiastical superior, whether the bishop, the prior of a monastery or a collegial chapter, to permit other churches and chapels within his jurisdiction to perform the sacred rites associated with the care of souls (*cura animarum*).[2] Coste believed that the ecclesiastical superior's ready yielding of his monopoly over the care of souls and an attentive supervision fostered the rapid development of strong and viable parishes, though bodies of clerics often performed the sacraments for their lay constituencies before receiving ecclesiastical approval. In some towns, London and Cologne for example, parish organization was completed by the late twelfth century and, despite continued population growth for another century, only a few parishes were added until the early modern period. Elsewhere, the cathedral maintained an effective monopoly over the care of souls with no parishes until the twentieth century.[3]

In San Sepolcro the problem of parish development was complicated by the conflict over spiritual jurisdiction between the bishop of Città di Castello and the abbot of the monastery of San Giovanni in San Sepolcro. The bishop and the abbot at times delayed construction of churches, thereby blocking or delaying the clerics in the proposed churches from performing the sacraments for the residents of the area around their churches. Parish organization in San Sepolcro appears to have been closer to that of Padua than London or Cologne because in Padua and San Sepolcro churches exercised quasi-parish functions without formal recognition for a long period of time. Coste largely ignores mendicants and baptismal churches; the introduction of the Franciscans, the Servants of Mary (Servi di Santa Maria), and the Augustinians into San Sepolcro complicated the systematic organization of parishes. As a result, San Sepolcro did not have a discernible parish structure in the period under study. This lack permitted and encouraged the laity, in cooperation with the existing clerical bodies, to undertake the construction of institutions to aid and console the town's inhabitants through the vicissitudes of their lives. The existence of these lay organizations probably delayed systematic organization of parishes.

San Sepolcro from Its Founding through 1200

Legend holds that San Sepolcro was founded in the tenth century, when two pilgrims, returning from the Holy Land with relics of the Holy Sepulcher, received a divine commandment to construct an oratory for the relics on the site of the present-day town. The families of the surrounding hillsides, attracted by the relics and the exemplary devotion of the pilgrims, established their homes around the oratory named in honor of San Leonardo. The settlement enlarged in the course of the eleventh century, leading to the construction of a monastery next to the oratory. Both monastery and oratory came under the authority of the Benedictine order. The abbot of the monastery exercised full spiritual authority over the people of the town, despite the claims of the bishop of nearby Città di Castello, whose spiritual jurisdiction encircled San Sepolcro. By 1100 and perhaps earlier, the Benedictines possessed a spiritual monopoly in the town for no other clerical corporation existed within its walls. The presence of the Benedictines, the coming of new religious corporations, and waves of religious enthusiasm structured the acts and beliefs of the laity of this hillside town in the years from 1100 to 1300 (see the map of religious corporations).

At the beginning of this period, the Benedictines were concentrated near the pilgrims' fount at the church and monastery of San Giovanni, which had surpassed the chapel of San Leonardo as the center of worship in the settlement. The monks supervised the hospital of San Niccolò, which was at the side of the monastery. The abbot also had authority over three hermitages located along the town's walls. To baptize their children, the townspeople, for some unknown reason, exited from San Sepolcro to the rural baptismal fount at Pieve Boccognana in Melello to the west. Here the secular clergymen administered the sacrament to the children of the town and surrounding area.[4] Men under the rule of St. Augustine possessed an oratory or small church outside the walls to the southwest. Despite the existence of these two small groups of non-Benedictines, we may assume that the majority of

The Religious Corporations of San Sepolcro

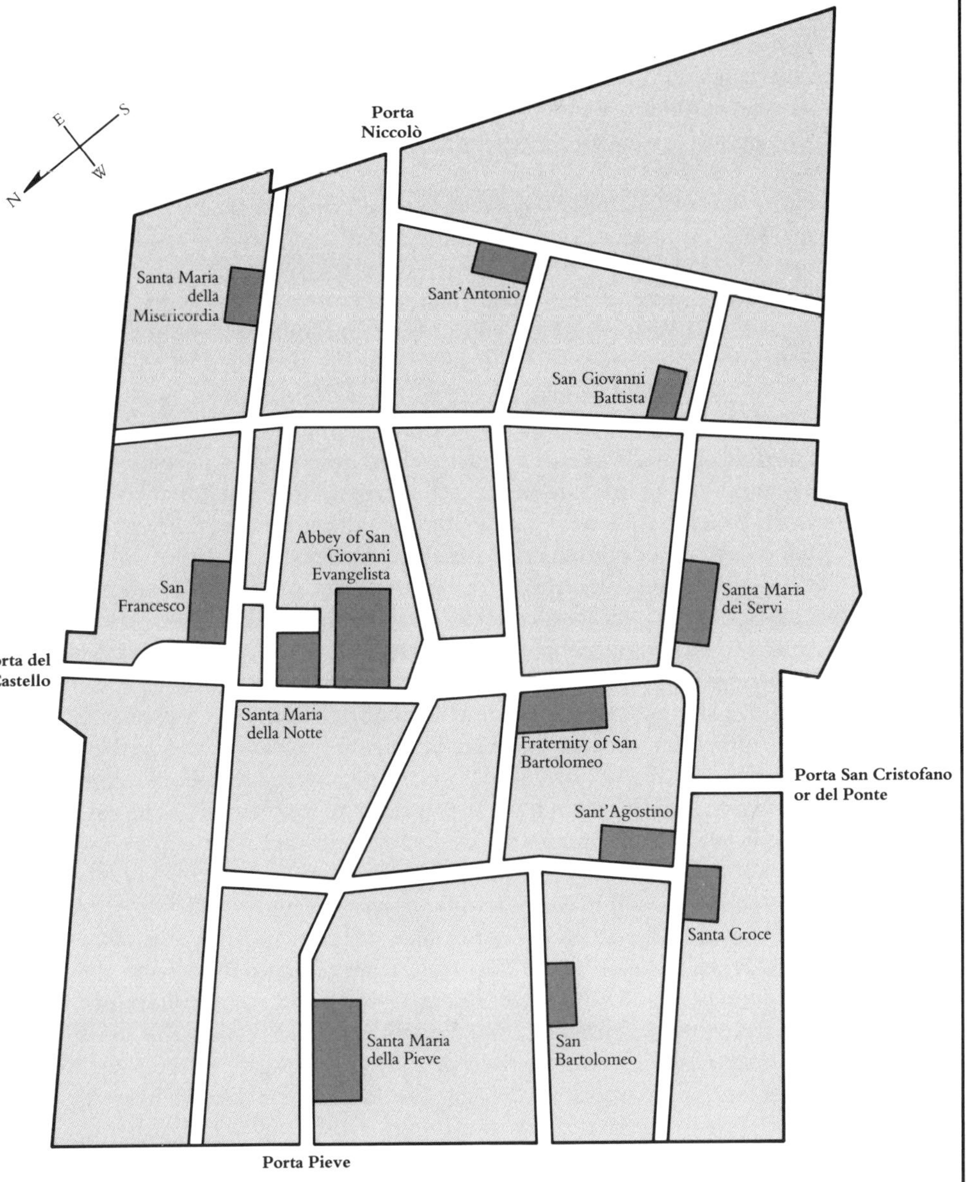

townspeople worshiped with the Benedictines in the great abbey church of San Giovanni and supported the Benedictine monastery and hermitages with gifts of food, property, and their children. In return, the townspeople gained the monks' prayers, liturgical services, and burial within their cemetery.[5]

The exclusive control or supervision of the religious life of the citizens of San Sepolcro passed from the Benedictines to the stricter Camaldolese order in the course of the twelfth century. By 1137 the Camaldolese monks who followed the reforms of San Romualdo had entered the town. In a tortuous encounter the two monastic orders battled for control of the town. The conflict ended definitively by 1198, as is evident from a bull of Pope Innocent III, in which the abbey of San Giovanni is listed as a Camaldolese possession. The white-cloaked Camaldolese monks appear to have displaced completely the Benedictines in their churches, hermitages, and monasteries within and around the walls of San Sepolcro with the exception of the extramural monasteries of San Benedetto for men and San Lorenzo for women. From the abbey of San Giovanni in the center of the town, the Camaldolese abbot commanded the spiritual lives of the citizens. The Camaldolese monks confirmed and married the youth, administered the masses, heard the confessions, and assigned public and private penances to the townspeople. The Camaldolese brothers buried the townspeople in their cemetery across the great piazza in front of San Giovanni, perhaps near the present-day Museo Civico, and probably shared with their greatest benefactors the holy ground under their chapel of San Leonardo for burial.[6] The monks served the people from the eastern half of the town from their priory of San Niccolò. The sole non-Benedictine challenge to the exclusive control of the town by the Camaldolese derived from the Augustinian friars, who probably administered the church of San Cristofano near the south wall.[7]

The Camaldolese order also controlled the hospitals of San Sepolcro in 1200. From its position outside the northern Porta del Castello, the female monastery of San Leone, referred to as San Leo by contemporaries, served the pilgrims passing through the Tiber Valley. But most of the hospitals were concentrated near the eastern gate of the town. Outside the eastern Porta San Niccolò, the small Camaldolese hospice of San Baroncio served the sick, the dying, and the traveler.[8] Further to the east, at the Castello di Baldignano, the nuns of San Bartolomeo held the leprosarium of San Lazzaro. Later located closer to the walls of San Sepolcro at a site named Doglio, this was probably the "Casa di lebbrosi" to which St. Francis was taken when he fell ill near San Sepolcro.[9]

In the course of the twelfth century the abbot of the monastery of San Giovanni gained control of the secular government in San Sepolcro. That acquisition was completed only after conflicts with the local nobility, an interim period of imperial control, and successive imperial and papal grants of authority to the abbot. By 1200 the town and surrounding feudal lords recognized the abbot's superior authority, although he delegated the exercise of power to representatives of the townspeople. In common with many Italian towns and cities of the period, a legislative council—the Council of Twenty-four—made law, and day-to-day administration was lodged in the hands of consuls and, for at least a time, a *podestà*. The abbot retained the right to certify the men selected by the townspeople. Later, in the thirteenth century, this right led to increasingly bitter conflicts between the abbot and the townspeople.[10]

Secular Clergy and Mendicants in the Thirteenth Century

The townspeople of San Sepolcro witnessed and participated in substantial changes in their religious worship in the course of the thirteenth century. An aspect of this transformation is the dramatic increase in the number of clerical corporations with novel devotions practiced by the townspeople; new clerical corporations supplemented the Camaldolese and thereby eliminated the monopoly of that order over the spiritual life of the citizens. The secular clergy under the bishop of Città di Castello was the first new group of clerics introduced to the town. The protracted conflict between the Benedictines and the Camaldolese had provided the opportunity and the expansion of the town's population out to the west beyond the then existing walls offered a rationale for the bishop of Città di Castello to introduce his authority into San Sepolcro. It was the first encroachment of the bishop and his secular clergy on the spiritual hegemony of the Camaldolese over the townspeople. The populated area was for a time outside the walls but later became enclosed within new walls. The presence of the secular clergy within the town walls initiated a prolonged conflict that raged for three centuries.

In the first years of the thirteenth century the secular clergy constructed a large new church with the name of San Bartolomeo just outside the walls to the southwest of the town. At the same time,

Bishop Ranieri of Città di Castello began negotiations with the town government for permission to build another church just outside the walls to the west of the town. In 1203 they agreed to move the site of the baptismal fount of the townspeople from Melello to this new church closer to the urban settlement. Perhaps Bishop Ranieri recognized that the western suburbs would soon be enclosed within new walls. He and his secular clergy would then have a substantial enclave within the enlarged town and thereby could diminish the ecclesiastical authority of the Camaldolese abbot of San Giovanni.[11] There is no evidence, however, to indicate whether Bishop Ranieri or the people of the area initiated the process of church construction.

The implantation of the two churches demonstrates the awareness of contemporaries that a substantial portion of the population of the town lacked a nearby church or oratory. The area in which the two churches were built represents nearly one-half of the territory enclosed within the walls in the 1220s. Bishop Ranieri and the town councillors persuaded the Camaldolese abbot to accept the second church within the soon-to-be-constructed walls on the condition that it and San Bartolomeo would be the only churches under the authority of the bishop and the secular clergy in the town. The abbot permitted the new church to be led by an archpriest, who was termed a *pievano* because his church served as the site for baptisms in the town. In addition, the archpriest administered the baptismal church and possessed all rights traditionally associated with the office of an archpriest, including the privilege of having his own house and subordinate clergy. The customary rights of the archpriest included those associated with *cura animarum,* the most important of which was the administering of the sacraments. The secular clergy named Mary the patroness of the new church, and it was by the name of Santa Maria della Pieve, or simply the Pieve, that the church became known.[12]

Despite the persistent efforts of the archpriest's superior, the bishop of Città di Castello, to enlarge the spiritual authority of the secular clergy in San Sepolcro, neither the church of Santa Maria della Pieve nor the house of the archpriest became a center of the religious life of the town. The town government did enlarge the walls in 1226 and 1228, enclosing the area around the two churches administered by the secular clergy. The secular priests addressed the needs of the townspeople of this western half of San Sepolcro, and all the town's children were baptized at Santa Maria della Pieve after 1205. The number of secular priests remained minuscule, never passing, in all likelihood, the seven who welcomed Pope Pius II to Città di Castello in 1460. The archpriest of Santa Maria della Pieve added the church of San Giovanni d'Afra to his jurisdiction by 1348 and supervised thirty to forty churches in the countryside, but within the walls his authority was limited. Only a few secular clergymen actively served the people of the town.[13] In the early thirteenth century the town possessed two ecclesiastical focal points: the church of the archpriest for baptism and the abbey as the source of spiritual authority.

Substantial changes in the religious practices occurred with the arrival of three orders of clerics after 1250. Two mendicant orders and the Augustinian friars founded churches and convents just inside the new walls in the second half of the thirteenth century. The success of the three clerical groups in constructing spacious churches and in persuading individuals from San Sepolcro to enter their orders demonstrates the willingness of the laity of San Sepolcro to adopt the new forms of devotion. Emphasizing penitence and charity, the mendicants and the Augustinian friars exhorted the laity to a more active piety.

The Franciscans were the first of the mendicants to construct a church in San Sepolcro. St. Francis of Assisi in or around 1213 preached in the town's central piazza in front of the abbey of San Giovanni and thereafter passed through the town on several occasions, always drawing large crowds into his presence.[14] After his death in 1226, however, his immediate followers did not found a house in the town, though his friars continued to occupy the small hermitage of Monte Casale to the northeast of San Sepolcro. In 1250 the Camaldolese abbot invited a Franciscan friar, Andrea Cacciolo da Spello, to preach from the pulpit of San Giovanni. Contemporaries reported that he preached with great zeal against male and female sinners, reducing many of them to penitence. So moved were the citizens that they offered the Franciscans a site to build a church. Fra Andrea refused this offer, but soon a group of friars built a place of worship just outside the walls near the eastern portal of San Niccolò.

These events in San Sepolcro confirm Luigi Pellegrini's general theory of the development of the Franciscans in Italy. He finds that in the initial stage the Franciscans were content with interchangeability of roles, transitory "places" of habitation, and generally "precarious and provisionary" conditions. Even in the second stage of "itinerancy," which in San Sepolcro can be associated with the 1250s, the Franciscans resisted a fixed site for a church and stable habitation within the city, preferring more remote locales. Pellegrini proposes as a third stage an acceptance on the part of the friars of a church and convent within the walls of the towns. This occurred in San Sepolcro in 1258, when the Franciscans began construction of the church and priory of San Francesco at its present location.[15] This site, only a few meters north of the Camaldolese abbey, was just within the northern walls in a section called the Giunte, which had been added in the expansion of the 1220s. Though the date of completion of construction is unknown, San Francesco served as a center of worship by the 1290s, when one of the friars was termed the priest of the parish. Despite the use of the term, there exists no other evidence to indicate that the town had been divided into parishes or that any group of clerics had exclusive rights in an area of the town. We may assume that the Franciscans had completed the principal portion of the church's construction and had taken the responsibility of ministering to the spiritual needs of the people of the Giunte. Though some of the people of this area may have worshiped in the Camaldolese abbey, in the Giunte itself there were no other male clerics. With a large garden and facing on a grand piazza, the church and priory became a new focal point for religion in the town. The church has a large nave and could contain a considerable number of worshipers. The available evidence indicates that the Franciscans made up the largest group of male clerics in San Sepolcro. The only known document on the number of Franciscan friars records ten of them in a chapter meeting in their sacristy in 1378.[16] Since chapter meetings required a quorum of two-thirds of the members, we may state that the Franciscan priory in the fourteenth century housed from ten to fifteen Franciscan brothers.

The presence of the Franciscans in San Sepolcro extended beyond this church and priory. When the friars moved into town in 1258, a group of women living in common without a rule took the friars' building at Pozzuolo. In 1266 Bishop Niccolò of Città di Castello permitted the women to adopt the rule of Santa Chiara, which had been approved by Pope Innocent IV in 1253. They were also given the right to choose their own prioress. The townspeople built a small church or oratory for the fifteen or twenty Clarian nuns there, which Bishop Niccolò consecrated in 1268.[17] Later this convent received a large number of females, housing thirty-three in 1317 and thirty in 1343. Membership declined slightly after mid-century to twenty-one in 1364 and nineteen in 1378.[18]

In the decade of the founding of the female house of San Francesco another female monastery was dedicated to Franciscan devotion in the same northeast corner of San Sepolcro. Located outside the eastern Porta San Niccolò, this female house was named Santa Maria della Strada because it was located on the road to the Franciscan hermitage of Monte Casale. In 1267–68 the nuns resisted Bishop Niccolò's attempt to submit them to his authority. After he excommunicated them, however, their Prioress, Cecilia, conceded in 1268 that the monastery of Santa Maria della Strada was under episcopal jurisdiction. In the following year Bishop Niccolò, after having received the submission of the nuns to his authority, exempted Santa Maria della Strada from his episcopal authority, excepting the rights of dedicating the church, consecrating altars, bestowing benediction on the nuns, and consecrating their robes. He also compelled them to follow the rule of Santa Chiara.[19]

The monastery of Santa Maria della Strada attracted the daughters of the local nobility and greater merchants. For example, in 1356 the prioress of the convent, Catherine Gnoli, could trace her descent to the noble Pichi family. Doubtless there were women in the priory who were daughters of the less affluent and influential in the local society, but the great family names of Bercordati, Graziani, and Carsidoni recur as do the names of notaries and doctors.[20] Moreover, these women frequently received substantial bequests from their families and their family friends. Though extant examples are from the fourteenth century, bonds between the families and their daughters in the thirteenth century must have been similar to the examples from the 1360s of Sister Francischina of the Graziani family who received five lire annually for life and Sister Johanna, granddaughter of a physician, who received fifty lire from her mother.[21] These bequests were given to daughters after they had entered the monastic life. Such support was justified by the families on the grounds that financial grants served the necessities of the individuals and required the nuns to perform specific religious acts for the family. In most cases the nuns prayed for the souls of family members or conducted vigils for the testator and recommended his soul to God.[22] On the basis of his research on the central Italian town of Rieti, Robert Brentano has hypothesized that women, similar to the poor and those in hospitals, were conceived to be powerless and poor and that, therefore, their prayers were regarded as particularly efficacious before God.[23]

A large number of fathers regarded these spiritual labors for their family and material well-being for their daughters as sufficient reasons to send their daughters to Santa Maria della Strada. Already in 1269 seventeen nuns followed the rule of Santa Chiara. By 1317 this convent housed the remarkably large number of thirty-one females.[24] The number of nuns in the convent dropped only slightly after the scourge of the plague in 1348 and the earthquake of 1352, although the original convent and church were destroyed by the earthquake. In 1356 and 1358 twenty-four and twenty-seven females lived in the reconstructed Santa Maria della Strada.[25]

The dedication of the families of the town to Franciscan piety did not exhaust itself in the dispatching of their daughters and widows to these two convents. San Sepolcro supported an additional female convent dedicated to Franciscan piety. The female house of San Leo passed from Camaldolese to Franciscan rule at some point before 1300. Located outside the northern walls, this convent contained the largest number of individuals in a religious house in the town. Thirty-seven females lived in the convent of San Leo in 1317. Again the demographic disasters of the mid-fourteenth century did not destroy the conditions under which families sent or females elected to go to monastic houses. The number of females in San Leo, as in the other convents, remained relatively constant. In 1380 a total of twenty-nine nuns lived within its walls.[26]

In the female houses of San Francesco and San Leo, the names of the women are not usually recognizable as belonging to the local elite, but they performed functions identical to those of the women in Santa Maria della Strada and likewise maintained close ties with their families. Such was the honor accorded the Franciscans in San Sepolcro that a total of 101 females lived in the three Franciscan convents in 1317. In this town of approximately 5,000 individuals and 1,000 hearths, one out of every ten families on average sent a daughter or a widow to a house of Franciscan devotion. After mid-century the figures are not as precise, but in the period 1356–80 at least 75 nuns lived within the walls of the three convents.[27] Their large numbers indicate the durability of the extraordinary devotion of the citizens to the Franciscans.

We should not, however, conclude that this radical expansion of the number of Franciscan female convents was limited to San Sepolcro. In nearby Città di Castello four female houses under the rule of Santa Chiara were founded in the middle of the thirteenth century. The extraordinary expansion of female houses, usually associated with the mendicants though often local ecclesiastical superiors substituted more traditional monastic orders for the women seeking mendicant auspices, was common to all of central Italy at this time. Bishop Niccolò appears to have been particularly concerned with regularizing groups of religious individuals in his diocese of Città di Castello. Niccolò's efforts were probably linked to the general papal attempt to move women from houses of spontaneous devotions to recognized monastic houses in the second half of the thirteenth century. Since

Niccolò gave the rule of Santa Chiara to a large number of female houses, he probably possessed a strong attachment to the Franciscan and Clarian orders.[28]

A second clerical corporation of mendicants began to address the spiritual and charitable needs of the people of San Sepolcro in the 1250s. The Servi di Santa Maria had originated in Florence in the 1230s with its earliest advocates exhorting an eremitic withdrawal from the city and a fervent devotion to Mary. In the 1250s the Servites turned to a more active form of devotion supported by Pope Alexander IV's grant of privileges, which were identical to those of the Franciscans and Dominicans. The Servites preached, celebrated the divine offices, brought the laity to their innovative Saturday masses in honor of Mary, and buried laymen in their cemeteries when the local bishops permitted these activities.[29] When the Servites became a mendicant order serving in the world, representatives of the order obtained permission from the bishop of Città di Castello to build a *locus,* presumably a priory with a chapel, outside the walls of San Sepolcro.[30] After four decades of wrangling between the Servites, bishops, and Camaldolese abbots, the Servites received the abbot's consent to build a church, named Santa Maria dei Servi, within the walls.[31] Construction of the church continued for nearly a century; until its completion in 1382, the Servites ministered to the lay men and women from a priory within the walls.[32] Documents of the late thirteenth century indicate that the number of Servites varied between seven and twelve; at the beginning of the fourteenth century fully three-fourths of these friars were recruited from San Sepolcro.[33]

These ten or twelve brothers of Santa Maria dei Servi served the people of San Sepolcro who lived along the south wall. Through a century of construction, the Servites appealed for aid, and the people of this area and other townspeople as well responded with gifts. Though the Camaldolese abbot had initially forbidden the Servites the privilege of burying any of the townspeople except the brothers' family members, this restriction was removed or forgotten in the course of the fourteenth century. The Servites were recipients of numerous testamentary bequests, and in exchange the friars buried these testators and offered up prayers and masses for their souls.[34] The Servites also obtained an important concession that empowered them to receive money and property from those testators who feared their usurious or extorsive behavior would jeopardize the orderly disposition of their testaments and their liberation from purgatory. The extraordinary example of Francesco, scion of the local noble family of Dotti, illustrates the Servites' role as a recipient and distributor of ill-gotten gains. Francesco defrauded seventy-five individuals and pious corporations, including the Servites. In his testament of 1365 he provided for the restitution of one thousand florins and placed his mother and the Servite prior in charge of restoring these usurious and fraudulent gains to the seventy-five individuals and corporations.[35]

The Augustinians were the third group of clerics who established a church within the walls in the second half of the thirteenth century. Earlier they had possessed a house and the church of San Cristofano outside the Porta del Ponte along the southern wall of the town. In the war of 1281 between Arezzo and San Sepolcro, the army of Arezzo destroyed the house and church of the Augustinians. Soon thereafter the Augustinian friars entered the walls and built a large church and priory named Sant'Agostino in the southwest corner of San Sepolcro. The number of friars in San Sepolcro was never substantial. The seven friars who witnessed a testament in 1328 represent the approximate total of clerics in the Augustinian priory under study here. Of these seven in 1328, four originated in San Sepolcro.[36]

Each of the three orders of St. Francis, the Servites, and St. Augustine established a priory and a church within the walls of San Sepolcro between the years 1258 and 1295. Their respective presence on the north, south, and southwest sides, each close to the walls, complemented the abbey church of the Camaldolese in the center of the town and Santa Maria della Pieve and San Bartolomeo of the secular clergy on the west side of San Sepolcro. This configuration of mendicants, monks, and secular clergy is an important variant of the pattern that Jacques Le Goff and others have analyzed elsewhere. Le Goff has hypothesized, and demonstrated in several areas, that the mendicants settled on the outer rims and suburbs of the towns and cities that enlarged with the population growth of the twelfth and thirteenth centuries. Near the rural areas that earlier monastic orders sought to escape the evils of the cities, and yet close to concentrated masses of people within the walls, the mendicants retained the virtues of corporate life relatively safe from the temptations of urban life and could still serve the manifold needs of the urban populace. The mendicants in the thirteenth century implanted priories and churches on both sides of the walls of towns where rural immigrants had settled and, according to Le Goff, created a piety particularly adapted to these uprooted rural peoples.[37]

In San Sepolcro the secular clergy anticipated the ministry of the mendicants, when the bishop of Città di Castello established the churches of San Bartolomeo and Santa Maria della Pieve around 1200.

Because the Camaldolese regular clergy occupied the center of the town and refused to permit the secular clergy free choice of the location of their churches, the latter were compelled to build on the fringes of San Sepolcro. Though the exact nature of the ministry of the secular clergy in San Sepolcro is unknown, it is clear that the recent settlers on the western side of the town worshiped in the large churches of Santa Maria della Pieve and San Bartolomeo. The secular clergy employed St. Mary as the advocate in one church and permitted, or perhaps encouraged, the founding of an early confraternity in the other church. The friars in the course of the thirteenth century followed the example of the secular clergy and formed a semicircle of churches, hospitals, and convents to the south, east, and north of the center of the town where the Camaldolese were concentrated. Here in the periphery the friars and the secular clergy encouraged the recent immigrants to worship through their innovative piety that elevated Mary to a mediator between man and God. They preached, established hospitals, and provided burial places for those uprooted peoples whose migrations had separated them from their ancestral graves.[38]

The growth of the town's population supported as well a large number of smaller religious corporations after 1260 in addition to the male and female mendicant houses. There were two types of monastic houses for males and females in San Sepolcro at this time. The monastery or convent could house a significant number of men or women and with an approved rule, as occurred in several of the Franciscan houses. The organization was cenobitic and oriented toward the secular world. The second type housed hermits, though in San Sepolcro the hermitages were not a great distance from the walls of the town. The small *carcera* for women and *carcero* for men housed from two to six individuals and required of their members a more restrictive discipline and withdrawal from secular society and its values. Hermits in San Sepolcro were said to have been "buried alive for God."[39] The women were often termed *incarcerate* as a means of emphasizing their renunciation of the world. By the late thirteenth century there were four cenobitic houses and five hermitages of women in and around the town. In addition to the Camaldolese monks at the abbey of San Giovanni and the nearby priory of San Niccolò, for men there was only one monastery—San Benedetto—and two *carceri*.

The Camaldolese convent of Santa Caterina comes into historical light in 1281, though it had been in existence for several years. The convent housed only a few nuns, four in the only listing extant today, but it was never referred to as a *carcera*.[40] In 1284 the nuns of Santa

Caterina sought permission to obtain the church of San Cristofano just outside the southern walls from the Camaldolese abbot. The nuns apparently gained the abbot's permission and remained at the church until the 1340s, when they moved to the town's center. In their new location near the priory of San Niccolò, the nuns of St. Catherine built a church and cloisters. The building project received the support of several bishops in Avignon who each granted an indulgence to those assisting the nuns in constructing the church. In addition, the prior general of the Camaldolese order granted participation in the spiritual benefits of the order to all who supported the building project.[41]

Less is known of the nuns in the convent of Santa Margarita, which was located outside the eastern gate of San Niccolò. They were under the authority of the Camaldolese abbot and perhaps assisted in the leprosarium of San Lazzaro. They did constitute a separate ecclesiastical corporation and received testamentary bequests in their own name, but the number of nuns in the house was exceedingly small.[42]

A wave of reformed Benedictinism, which passed through central Italy in the late thirteenth century, decisively transformed two female houses in San Sepolcro. The reform began in Gubbio, when a man named Sperandio left his wife and became a Benedictine monk. Because of his pious life and his attempted reform of a Benedictine monastery in Gubbio, this monk became known as Beato Sperandio. A woman of Gubbio, Santuccia, was so moved by his exemplary life that she followed him into a monastic vocation. She established a house of nuns in Gubbio based on Sperandio's reform of the Benedictine rule. By 1271 Santuccia had become the abbess of a house in San Sepolcro with a group of women devoted to Sperandio's rule. In that year Santuccia submitted to Bishop Niccolò's authority and agreed to give him a small gift of wax. Her followers were named Santuccie after her, and in San Sepolcro they occupied a building near the Benedictine convent of San Lorenzo. They took Santa Maria Maddalena as their patroness, and the convent was named in her honor. In 1305 and in the 1340s the number of nuns in this convent varied between five and six.[43] By 1290 a second group of Santuccie lived west of the city on the old site of the baptismal fount at Melello. This *carcera* served to close off two or three women from the world under a male friar of unknown affiliation. In 1307 and 1316 the guardian of the Santuccie bequeathed this hermitage with house and cloister to the Fraternity of San Bartolomeo on the condition that the lay corporation was not to alter the hermitage or its purpose. The small complex was to be preserved to assure that the hermitage would remain a place where women served God through their perpetual praise of Him.[44] After the demographic crises of the mid-fourteenth century, however, the corporation of nuns was moved first to San Cristofano and then in 1364 to the ruined monastery of San Lorenzo.[45] Thus in the area outside the western gate of Porta Pieve, there were two groups of Santuccie—the Santuccie of Santa Maria Maddalena and the Santuccie of San Lorenzo—with approximately ten nuns in total.

As several scholars have noted, several forms of religious life were open to women in the early fourteenth century. Female religious devotion remained innovative and open to experiment, despite the efforts of the thirteenth-century popes and, in the diocese of Città di Castello, of Bishop Niccolò to regularize women living in common and submit them to a rule and episcopal supervision.[46] The fluidity of female religious life is evident in the reference to the female house at Melello. If it was a house of Santuccie, it had an established rule. It is, however, referred to as a *carcera,* which implies that it was a voluntary exile from the world and not under any particular rule.

There were, however, five houses of enclosed women that were referred to as *carcere* in this period of the late thirteenth and early fourteenth centuries. These small houses lacked an established rule and were often dependent upon the holiness of one member and the willingness of a patron or patrons to give financial support. These houses usually survived for a limited time, and, therefore, it is difficult to be precise about their nature or size. The *carcera* named Bona is an exception to the short-lived nature of the *carcere.* In 1228 Guido di Orlandino Magalotti bequeathed land in Petrognano outside San Sepolcro to the sisters Bona and Bontadose and to anyone else who desired to imitate the lives of the sisters. On this land a house with two cells was to be built; bequests into the fourteenth century signal the continued existence of this house.[47] A second *carcera* existed along the southern walls of San Sepolcro at Cerreto by 1277, when the four nuns there sought the death benefits of the fraternity. Another house was known as the "Carcera sororis Anne." Its location is not known. The final two female houses include the one identified by its location at the Porta San Niccolò and another named the "Carcera de filii Mucius sodi extra Porta Castello." Bequests to these five houses of sequestered women through the mid-fourteenth century attest to their continued presence in the town. Thereafter, however, one seldom finds bequests to the female *carcere* (or male *carceri*); this appears to be true throughout central Italy, where the *carcere* and *carceri* had been concentrated.[48]

The town of San Sepolcro gave birth to only two houses of sequestered males. The *carcero* of "the brothers Lando and Baroncio" and the *carcero* of "Porta nova of Borghetto Pieve" housed an unknown number of enclosed men. The paucity of information about them points to their limited influence and size.

There were five houses of enclosed females and two of enclosed males. For no house, excluding the female *carcera* of Cerreto, can a definite number of individuals be determined. Cerreto housed four nuns, and if we assume that the other *carceri* and *carcere* contained a like number, this would yield a total of eight males and twenty females. The pattern of more female than male houses of sequestered individuals repeats the ratio of female convents to male monasteries. Among these larger monastic corporations, and disregarding the female and male mendicants for the moment, there were four female convents and three male monasteries, including in the latter group the Camaldolese abbey of San Giovanni, the Camaldolese priory of San Niccolò, and the Benedictine monastery of San Benedetto. There were more male mendicant priories than female mendicant convents, four to three, but the number of mendicant women vastly surpassed that of mendicant men.

The townspeople of San Sepolcro in the late thirteenth century also supported eight hospitals, six of which were administered by clerics. By 1300 the hospitals rimmed the town along the walls and were concentrated outside the gates. The hospitals outside the eastern portal of San Niccolò were those of the Franciscans at Santa Maria della Strada, the Camaldolese at the leprosarium of San Lazzaro, the Camaldolese at Santa Margarita, and just inside the gate, the Camaldolese hospital of San Niccolò. The hospitals outside the western portal of the Pieve were those of the Santuccie in the Borghetto of San Lorenzo and of the Fraternity of San Bartolomeo at the Ospedale Nuovo. Outside the northern portal del Castello the Franciscans administered the hospital of San Leo, and in the southeast corner of San Sepolcro the layman Jacomo de Domenico founded the Casa della Misericordia.[49]

The Dearth of Male Clergy

This survey of ecclesiastical corporations in San Sepolcro yields several striking features of the religious life of the town in the late thirteenth and early fourteenth centuries. There were relatively few male clergymen in the town, despite the growth of population and the number of clerical corporations in the thirteenth century. Of equal importance is the dearth of secular clerics in San Sepolcro in the early fourteenth century. To comprehend the significance of the number of clerics in San Sepolcro around 1300, it is necessary to estimate how many people resided in the town. Yet the ratio between the number of clerics and the number of townspeople will not necessarily reveal whether there were sufficient clergymen to perform the necessary church functions. No one knows for this period what constituted a sufficient number of clergymen for these functions. A comparison of the ratios of clergy to population in other times or places, however, will permit us to conjecture whether the same percentage of clergy were present in San Sepolcro. More important, this study will demonstrate that alternate means existed of performing the services conventionally viewed as properly performed by clergymen.

Several decades ago Amintore Fanfani estimated that the population of San Sepolcro in the thirteenth and fourteenth centuries never surpassed 4,000.[50] This estimate was based on his analysis of the number of deaths per year and space within the walls of the town. A document from the 1440s and a more complete knowledge of population changes in the Late Middle Ages and early modern period provide means of estimating more closely the population of San Sepolcro in the period of this study. The document of the 1440s—perhaps from the hand of Francesco de Largi—estimates the population of San Sepolcro at 4,397.[51] From studies of several other Italian towns, it is known that population grew steadily from at least 1000 to 1300 and perhaps through the 1340s, fell dramatically in the 1340s, remained relatively low for nearly a century, and revived after 1430 or 1440 with growth then sustained through the sixteenth century.[52] Assuming that the population of San Sepolcro followed an analogous path, it is evident that the figure of 4,397 in the 1440s represents the results of an initial upswing from a plague in 1425 when approximately 1,200 individuals died.[53] Thus Fanfani's conjecture of 4,000 is an underestimate and also fails to specify population changes over time.

By the end of the thirteenth century approximately 5,000 individuals lived within the walls of San Sepolcro. This conservative estimate is obtained by projecting the 4,397 figure for the 1440s back to 1300 along a curve derived from known figures for other central and northern Italian towns. Population surveys of San Sepolcro from the sixteenth and seventeenth centuries confirm my hypothesis that its demographic history replicates those of other Italian towns (see Table 1.1). The exact population curve of this later period cannot be determined because the totals in the table do not consistently employ iden-

TABLE 1.1
Population of San Sepolcro, 1200–1672

Year	*Inhabitants*	*Hearths*
1200	3,000*	–
1340	5,000*	–
ca. 1450	4,397	–
1551	6,211	1,158
1606	4,076 (4,376)†	977
1622	6,943‡	–
1642	3,486	877
1672	3,528	–

Sources: See, for ea. 1450, ASF, CRS, San Sepolcro, L.XX.27, fol. 68 bis; for 1551, ASF, "Manoscritti," 182, fol. 79v; for 1606, AC, SS, cl. 2, reg. 24, fol. 89r; for 1622, Florence, Biblioteca Nazionale Centrale, II.I.240, "Descrizione dell'anime della Città e Contado di Firenze," unfol., see under San Sepolcro; for 1642, ASF, "Cart. Strozz.," I, 24, fol. 120r; for 1672, ibid., fol. 148r.

*Estimate.

†Number in parenthesis includes clerics.

‡Includes some persons from outside the walls.

tical categories of persons or boundaries, but it is clear that within the walls of San Sepolcro the number of hearths varied from 877 to 1,158 and the population from 3,468 to 6,211 from the mid-fifteenth century to 1672. These data reveal that the population of San Sepolcro remained relatively stable from the thirteenth through the seventeenth centuries. In summary, an estimated 4,000 townspeople in 1250, 5,000 in 1300 through the 1330s, demographic disaster in 1348 and 1352 with perhaps 2,500 survivors, partial recovery limited by recurring plagues, relapse to 3,000 in 1425, and growth to 4,397 in the 1440s would ascribe to San Sepolcro a demographic history analogous to those of other, more thoroughly documented, Italian towns.

Approximately fifty male clerics served the devotional and sacramental needs and aspirations of the 4,000–5,000 inhabitants of San Sepolcro in the period from 1250 to 1348. At most, ten secular clergymen administered the sacraments in the churches under the archpriest at Santa Maria della Pieve. Mendicants were more plentiful. The proportion of clerics in San Sepolcro confirms the thesis that the mendicants ministered to the newly enlarged towns in the thirteenth century when the traditional orders and secular clergy failed or had been unable to respond to the urban populations.[54] Even the number of male mendicants is modest, however. The number varied in the years between 1250 and 1350, but available documentation indicates that at most seven Augustinians, thirteen Servites, and fifteen Franciscans served the townspeople at any one time.[55] The labor of mendicants among the laypeople of San Sepolcro, much more than that of the secular clergy, displaced the six or seven Camaldolese monks whose predecessors had possessed a near monopoly over sacramental and priestly services to the townspeople. Including the several males under Benedictine rule in the small monastery of San Benedetto, the total in the town could not have surpassed ten monks.

By contrast, the number of females in houses of varying degrees of confinement approached 150 at least in the period after 1300. This total is based on the 101 females in the three Franciscan houses, 10 nuns in the two Camaldolese convents, and 30 women in the two Santuccie houses and six *carcere*. Though no evidence exists to indicate the number of women in religious houses in 1250, the number would have been considerably lower, based on the limited number of female houses, perhaps two or three, in San Sepolcro. The 150 women in religious houses after 1300 may reflect the growing number of widows or a higher percentage of women in the population of the town. Nevertheless, the exclusion of women from certain novel religious corporations and several religious activities suggests that a reorientation of the fundamental roles of women in religion was occurring around 1300.[56]

The reorientation of the place of women was doubtless an aspect of the restructuring of the roles of several constitutive groups in medieval religion. One of these aspects is the limited number of clergymen serving the churches and altars of San Sepolcro. The circumscribed influence of the male clergy is emphasized in the realization that some unknown proportion of the fifty clergymen were priests. Hence even fewer carried on the essential sacramental duties. The limited number of male clerics in San Sepolcro in the period 1250–1348 takes on added significance through a comparison with the number of clerics in eighteenth-century Tuscany and San Sepolcro. In 1745 the secular and regular clergy of both sexes constituted 3.25 percent of the population of Tuscany and 4.7 percent in San Sepolcro.[57] In the early fourteenth century the secular and regular clergy constituted 5 percent of the population in San Sepolcro. Nuns or sequestered females made up 3.75 percent of the population. Precision is not possible because my figures for clerics and population represent totals taken at different years within the period.[58] If we compare the percentage of male clerics in the population of eighteenth-century San Sepolcro with that in early fourteenth-century San Sepolcro, we can judge the relative presence of clerics in the late medieval society. (The lower population figure for the early fourteenth century of 4,000 rather than 5,000 individuals is used to compensate for possible errors that would magnify the already extraordinary results.) In 1751 male clerics made up 2.9 percent of the total population in San Sepolcro (388 of 13,514).[59] In the early fourteenth century, male clerics constituted only 1.25 percent (50 of 4,000). Even more striking is the paucity of secular clergy in San Sepolcro in the early fourteenth century. In 1751 the secular clergy made up 2 percent of the population of the town (292 of 13,514) but only .025 percent in the early fourteenth century (10 of 4,000). Some scholars have claimed that more clergymen than laity died in the plague of 1348, leading to a shortage of clergymen in late medieval society. The statistics for San Sepolcro indicate that even before 1348, clergymen made up a small percentage of the population.

San Sepolcro was probably not the only town or city with a minimum of secular clergy and a large percentage of females in convents. David Herlihy has noted the small number of clergy in Pistoia. Though his judgment is based on data a century later than that for San Sepolcro, he found an "acute shortage" of parish priests in that Tuscan town. Robert Brentano has noted the large number of female convents in Rieti in the fourteenth century, and others have commented on the high percentage of females in the cloistered state in Florence in the fifteenth and early sixteenth centuries.[60]

The paucity of clergymen in San Sepolcro in the early fourteenth century should not necessarily be read as a crisis in the church or a change from earlier decades. Excluding natural disasters, the occasional cleric charged with simony or heresy, and conflicts over ecclesiastical offices and privileges, the sources from San Sepolcro do not hint at a crisis in the church that several studies of the church have indicated in other parts of Europe.[61] Religion in thirteenth- and fourteenth-century San Sepolcro was characterized by the extraordinary number of women in monastic houses, in which one out of every seven families placed a member, the small number and percentage of male clerics, and the large number of males in confraternities.

Giovanna Casagrande and Antonio Rigon have found in Città di

Castello and Padua, respectively, a large number of lay associations and religious groups in the thirteenth century.[62] Oblates, lay brothers (*conversi*), syndics, and male and female penitents gathered near the clerical, and especially mendicant, orders in these towns. The lack of notarial documents for San Sepolcro does not permit a secure judgment of whether analogous groups existed there in the thirteenth century. The clerical houses of San Sepolcro certainly required a host of syndics and procurators. Though I am inclined to hypothesize that San Sepolcro had its lay brothers and penitents, the largest number of the laity in thirteenth-century San Sepolcro participated in the church through membership in the Fraternity of San Bartolomeo. This and other confraternities provide the institutional base for the remainder of this study.

CHAPTER TWO

The Fraternity of San Bartolomeo and Commemoration of the Dead in San Sepolcro in the Thirteenth Century

In the thirteenth century the growth of population in San Sepolcro had accompanied expansion and increased complexity in the economic system, which derived from the ever more skilled laborers as well as from the natural resources and geographic position of the town and its hinterland. Founded on the eastern hillside of the Tiber Valley at the point where the valley opens up into a large plain, San Sepolcro by the middle of the thirteenth century served as the market for the peasants and landlords of the valley, for exchanges of local goods, and as the region's market for more distant trade. Because it was located on the crossing of north-south and east-west trade routes, San Sepolcro drew merchants from Perugia and towns farther to the south, from Pieve San Stefano to the north at the headwaters of the Tiber River up to the Romagna, from Tuscany to the west, and from towns along the Adriatic Sea to the east. This trade involved mainly exchanges of agricultural tools and products, but the merchants of the town also exported cloth to nearby villages. In addition, they sold *guado,* the woad plant, from which cloth manufacturers of northern and central Italy extracted a vibrant blue dye. Emigrants from surrounding villages found homes and employment in the market town. Under these favorable conditions, population growth continued into the early fourteenth century.[1]

The growth of population and the increasing complexity of the town's economy made the Camaldolese abbot's lordship over San Sepolcro more tenuous in each succeeding decade of the thirteenth century. The townspeople regularly attempted to limit or eliminate the abbot's jurisdiction over secular affairs. The first crisis began in 1224, when the Council of Twenty-Four selected a *podestà* without first gaining Abbot Omodeo's consent. The town government also constructed a communal palace on the site of a Camaldolese cemetery, destroying a wall of one of the order's churches. The citizens asserted theoretical dominance as well; the town government attempted to coerce Abbot Omodeo into renouncing his feudal rights over San Sepolcro and moved all legal cases between the abbot and the townspeople and between the abbot and the archpriest of Santa Maria della Pieve to the town's secular courts. After Abbot Omodeo's excommunications of the town's political leaders failed to bring their compliance, Pope Gregory IX, angered by what he termed the citizens' "spirit of rebellion," reaffirmed the abbot's authority over San Sepolcro, and by the 1230s the abbot had regained his political and judicial primacy over the town.[2]

A second crisis in the 1250s again involved the abbot's privilege of approving each incoming *podestà* and a new official, the captain of the people. According to the excellent local historian of San Sepolcro, Ercole Agnoletti, the townspeople retaliated by removing a hospital from the abbot's authority and placing it under a lay institution, the Fraternity of San Bartolomeo. Papal intervention again brought the townspeople to heel. Another dispute between the abbot and the citizens over unknown issues in the 1260s was resolved through the intervention of the bishop of Città di Castello.[3]

The citizens of San Sepolcro exercised their independence of the abbot in 1269, when they declared war against the towns of the Upper Tiber without his consent. After San Sepolcro defeated these towns, Arezzo, which claimed rights over the region of the Upper Tiber, compelled San Sepolcro through threat of war to relinquish control over this area. Furthermore, Arezzo forced the town government of San Sepolcro to send a *pallium* on the feast day of San Donato, Arezzo's protector-saint, to serve as a token of submission. The decision to go to war and the treaty with Arezzo appear to have been undertaken without the abbot's consent. More important, submission to Arezzo virtually eliminated the abbot's secular authority in San Sepolcro. Although the exact relationship between Arezzo and San Sepolcro cannot be defined, Arezzo's dominance continued in some fashion through the 1290s.[4]

Political life in San Sepolcro was further complicated by the introduction of the first signory into the town in 1290. As lord of Arezzo and count of Pietramala, Bishop Guido Tarlati acquired lordship over San Sepolcro. Either through a defeat of the bishop's faction by Florence in 1298 or in Arezzo in 1301, the abbot was able to regain his authority in San Sepolcro.[5] The abbot's possession of secular authority proved, however, to be temporary.

Though the feudal rights of the Camaldolese abbot over San Sepolcro had been granted and confirmed by the empire and the papacy, his ability to influence events in San Sepolcro waned in the second half of the thirteenth century, as the empire declined and the papacy failed to maintain the abbot's privileges in the town. Within the walls the *podestà* and the Council of Twenty-Four exercised authority year after year by making and enforcing laws. Constant challenges to the abbot's authority led him to offer to sell his feudal rights over the town in exchange for a few pieces of property. Eventually, the abbot renounced his rights in favor of the town.

Politics and the Rise of the Fraternity of San Bartolomeo

During the period of rapid economic expansion and political upheaval, the laypeople of San Sepolcro placed their solidarity and achievement in a divine perspective. This assertiveness was exemplified in the contemporaneous emergence of the Fraternity of San Bartolomeo, an expression of lay religious idealism, and the laity's assault on the political overlordship of the Camaldolese abbot. Lay political assertiveness grew together with the fraternity in the second half of the thirteenth century. By 1300 the communal government had charged the priors of the fraternity with supervision of the poor; subsequently, the priors were charged, or took responsibility for, nearly every problem concerning death. The size of the fraternity, its vast membership, its charitable work throughout the town and the countryside, and its close relationship with the communal government established it as the expression of lay religious solidarity in San Sepolcro. This was not a simple matter of the lay confraternity rationalizing or justifying the laity's drive to political power. The assumption of control over the collection and distribution of charity and the success in wresting political power from the abbot required the laity to enter into acts and rituals formerly reserved for the clergy. The enlargement of lay achievement and responsibility required a divine validation. The fraternity gained a place in a divine system of meaning by feeding the poor of Christ and commemorating the lay achievements of the citizens at their death.

Although there were elements of a conflict between clergy and laity, the traditional interpretation does not fully encompass the struggle of the laity to extract eternal significance from day-to-day life. The conflict between the abbot and the town over political power did not involve overt religious questions, though the parties may have possessed differing views of authority within a divine commonwealth. Nor is the more recent trend of viewing religious practices in the Late Middle Ages as requiring a second conversion of marginal Christians a sufficient explanation of the events taking place in San Sepolcro.[6] Such a theory presumes a necessary or modern definition of what constitutes "proper" Christianity and deflects our vision from the behaviors of groups of believers as they labored to interpret their lives and deaths within a social and political world in rapid transformation. Changes in production, assertions of power, and the relationships of individuals required, or perhaps enabled, a profound alteration of acts and beliefs concerned with the individual's and the society's relationship to supernatural powers.

De Sandre Gasparini has found an analogous process in a small village, Villa del Bosco, located in the low plains southeast of Padua. Though many of the terms of her analysis differ from those of this study, in part because Villa del Bosco had only one or two dozen families and the process occurred there two centuries later than in San Sepolcro, nevertheless, in both instances confraternities served to express the solidarity of the laity as it achieved economic viability and political community. In Villa del Bosco the laymen of the village founded the Confraternity of San Rocco in 1478 after a lengthy process of reclamation of agricultural land. De Sandre Gasparini also demonstrates that, even though a specific cleric may have played an important role in the founding of the confraternity, the lay community had in the two previous decades fought to assure for itself a regular order of divine services. There is no evidence that an outsider or an alien and superior culture or exploitive clergymen foisted the confraternity on a naive laity; rather, the new families of an agrarian renaissance sought an agency through which they could aid pilgrims and the less fortunate of the village through gifts of charity. Lacking sufficient "organs of representation" and with the ecclesiastical system in disorder in the middle of the fifteenth century, the laity thereafter sought to provide the agrarian community with access to a correct religious life. The villagers were most attentive in demanding that the sacraments be available at the crucial moments of life. De Sandre Gasparini asserts that the families of Villa del Bosco were most concerned by the failure of their priest to provide funerals for the dead of the village.[7]

In San Sepolcro as well, the laymen wanted assurance of divine presence and social participation at their death and commemoration thereafter. Apart from clerical sources, documentary evidence on the layman's relationship to God in thirteenth- and fourteenth-century Europe is scarce. San Sepolcro is an exception to this general rule because it offers extant documents on precisely this question. Not by accident have the documents survived; the Fraternity of San Bartolomeo that produced them survived into the modern world because it focused on the persistent problems of the layman at and after death. These documents point us in the direction of one critical problem, the individual's and social group's relationship with the divine at the moment of death. Two registers, both of which are unique for the period under consideration, provide the evidence for the study of man confronting his God at the end of life.

After having been in existence for several decades, the Fraternity of San Bartolomeo in the late 1260s reorganized and recorded its practices and membership. The fraternity corporately also determined to list its incoming members and to maintain a necrology. The resulting documents have survived in one register begun at the time of these proposals. Composed of three sections, the register begins with the fraternity's statutes, probably written in 1269 or somewhat earlier, followed by lists of members as of 1268–69, entrants from 1269 to 1309, and a necrology of deceased members from 1269 to 1309.[8]

The second unique document is the "Specchio" of Francesco de Largi. Though he lived in the fifteenth century, Largi scrutinized documents, some extant and others lost, for the two hundred years from 1240 to 1440, wrote on the fraternity's purposes, members, and finances, and analyzed the causes of its decline. These documents have survived with extensive financial records that were once in the fraternity's chancellery. Now in the Communal Archive in San Sepolcro, these registers provide documentation for an analysis of the fraternity's purposes and activities.

Origins of the Fraternity of San Bartolomeo

The Fraternity of San Bartolomeo was founded in the first half of the thirteenth century, though the exact circumstances and date are unknown. An examination of the historiography of the early period of the fraternity and the available evidence is instructive. St. Francis has often been credited with founding the fraternity. Seventeenth- and eighteenth-century historians tended to inflate the role of the mendicants in the history of the medieval confraternities. Nor have modern historians escaped the lure of attributing the existence of confraternities to St. Francis, St. Dominic, and their most spiritual followers. The early seventeenth-century historian of San Sepolcro, Francesco Bercordati, placed the fraternity's beginning early in the thirteenth century, when a Bishop Giovanni held the episcopal chair in Città di Castello. Bercordati's purpose in dating the foundation to that period becomes apparent when he explains that Bishop Giovanni had been moved to grant the fraternity an indulgence because St. Francis had contributed to the brotherhood's founding. In his mind, the fraternity gained spiritual grandeur through its association with the esteemed mendicant saint. In the eighteenth century Pietro Farulli and subsequent modern historians followed Bercordati in attributing the fraternity's origin to St. Francis.[9] Bercordati's probable source, the "Specchio" of Francesco de Largi, is far more cautious about St. Francis's role. Largi wrote that the chronicles did not record the establishment of the fraternity, though succeeding generations had passed the account to his time. He cautiously attributed his account to oral sources, according to which it pleased God to renew His body and passion in St. Francis and in his friars, who "created great devotion for him in the hearts of the Borghesi." Within his lifetime, the citizens of San Sepolcro built a priory outside the walls for St. Francis and his followers.

> Many devoted men had wanted to leave their property to those friars but because, according to the rule, they are not able to hold property, neither as individuals nor in common . . . [the devoted laymen donate] only for the necessities of the infirm; and for clothing are the other brothers able to have solicitous care according to the place and time and the frigid regions only through the hands of their spiritual friends, the ministers and custodians. Hence, these brothers, having counseled with the Holy Spirit, encouraged the devotion of the Borghesi to institute the devout and charitable fraternity, and those, who desirous of bequeathing to them, they counseled them to bequeath to this fraternity and through the hands of the rectors of it, as spiritual rule, charitable subvention to the poor friars according to their need. ("Specchio,"4v–5r)

The organization, Largi continued, was named a Fraternity "for the brothers who were thus the cause of it" and because all should be brothers in Jesus Christ.

The account of the founding of the fraternity has no corroborating evidence and contains elements that betray its late formulation. For example, Largi drew from the oral tradition to link St. Francis and the founding of a Franciscan priory outside the walls of San Sepolcro. But the Franciscan priory at Pozzuolo was founded in the mid-1250s, three decades after Francis's death. In addition, Largi links the Franciscans and the fraternity, but the fraternity of San Bartolomeo congregated in the church of San Bartolomeo officiated by the secular clergy and located in the southwest corner of San Sepolcro. The Franciscan church, priory, and convents were along the east and north side of the town. Also, in its early years the fraternity received several indulgences from the bishops of Città di Castello, the ecclesiastical superior of the secular clergy in San Sepolcro. The Franciscans failed to acknowledge the fraternity until 1281, when the order granted members of the fraternity full participation in its spiritual benefits ("Specchio," 7r). Finally, according to Largi's own reckoning, the first bequest from the laymen to the fraternity was given in 1247, decades after the death of Francis. This evidence demonstrates that the proposed link between St. Francis and the fraternity has no foundation in fact and that the center of fraternal activity was located far from the Franciscans. The fraternity's location and the indulgences suggest its association with the secular clergy.

The documentation relative to the founding of the fraternity appears in Largi's "Specchio" in a series of privileges that he abstracted from documents held by the fraternity in 1437. On April 13, 1244, Bishop Azzo of Città di Castello granted ecclesiastical recognition to the Fraternity of San Bartolomeo and conceded forty days of "imputed penitence" to anyone in his diocese who gave charity to the fraternity ("Specchio," 6v). The indulgence assumes an already existing institution, which tends to confirm Largi's claim that Bishop Giovanni of Città di Castello granted the first ecclesiastical recognition of the brotherhood. This would place the founding of the fraternity in the years from 1210 to 1227.[10] The laymen may have started the fraternity in the 1210s or 1220s, well before 1244, when Bishop Azzo "confirmed and approved" it.

The bishop's granting of an indulgence of forty days to the benefactors of the fraternity was not unusual in the thirteenth century; such indulgences were customarily given to encourage the faithful to contribute to building projects and to support the clergy. Successive bishops of Città di Castello confirmed this indulgence and added others that more fully illuminate the relationship between older forms of penance and the purposes of the fraternity.

Bishop Pietro of Città di Castello permitted the members of the fraternity to substitute their fraternal participation for one of the more traditional penalties for sin. Fasting one day a week on bread and water had been, and continued to be, applied by priests for small and large sins, or an individual could take a vow of voluntary fasting for extended periods of time. Bishop Pietro absolved anyone in his diocese from a vow of fasting of up to two years if he or she gave charity to the fraternity. It does not appear that Bishop Pietro granted individuals release from penance imposed for confessed sins. A voluntary gift to the fraternity substituted for a voluntary vow of penance. In both imposed and voluntary penance, merit accrued to the individual, but in the case of charity, the corporation served as agent for the individual ("Specchio," 6v).

Bishop Pietro bestowed on the rectors, who acted as the fraternity's executive officers, a privilege that again substituted fraternal activity for a traditional form of penance. The fraternity possessed more than one thousand members, and the rectors had numerous burdensome responsibilities because they were the only administrative officers until 1371. Recognizing the rectors' labor, Bishop Pietro granted them an indulgence equivalent to a pilgrimage to the famed shrine of St. James at Santiago de Compostela ("Specchio," 6v).

The bishops of Città di Castello, though not necessarily undermining the penances of fasting and making pilgrimages, found correspondence between these penances and donating or administering charity for the benefit of the poor. If self- or clerically imposed deprivation is the basis of penance, then the equivalence that underlies the bishop's concession may have been derived from the fraternal members' donation of material goods and the rectors' donation of time and labor. Part of the attraction of these substitute methods of achieving merit consisted in the possibility of donating money or labor without weakening a commitment to one's own profession or occupation and without absence from family and shop.

In 1266 Bishop Niccolò again recognized the fraternity, conceded forty days of pardon to its benefactors, and confirmed his predecessors' substitution of gifts of alms to the fraternity for fulfilling a vow of fasting. Moreover, the bishop exhorted everyone in his diocese to make donations to the sodality in San Sepolcro. He added the pardon of one hundred days to anyone who attended the meeting of the fraternity on the first Sunday of the month in the church of San Bartolomeo. The rectors of the fraternity received from Bishop Niccolò the benefit of a pilgrimage to St. James at Santiago de Compostela. More extraordinary is the grant of a plenary indulgence, which the bishop had already conferred upon the rectors in 1265. If the rectors distributed the charity of the fraternity to the poor and did so in a "confessed" condition, they were to receive a plenary indulgence, a "full remission of all their sins."[11]

Taken together, the indulgences of the bishops of Città di Castello in the middle of the thirteenth century gave an ecclesiastical imprimatur to charitable work and attendance at services for the memorialization of the dead. By substituting charity to the poor and respect for the dead for pilgrimages and penitential fasting, the bishops encouraged laymen to turn from individual acts of penance to corporate acts of Christian charity through the agency of the fraternity.[12]

Of a different nature was a privilege conceded to the rectors of the fraternity by Bishop Pietro in 1257. He granted them the right to collect from any person the accounts, confiscated goods, and bequests to the fraternity. Largi lists this as an "ancient privilege" of paramount importance because of the ambiguous character of the property of the dead. Bishop Pietro here acknowledged that the fraternity had to be recognized as a sacred institution in order to receive bequests of money or property that were intended for the benefit of the testator's soul and were distributed to the poor of Christ. To aid the dying individual in extracting wealth from his family's patrimony, bishops and town governments in the thirteenth and fourteenth centuries elevated confraternities above other secular corporations. The fraternity had to be confirmed as functioning in a sacred economy of salvation.[13]

Selection and Responsibilities of the Rectors

In the thirteenth century the fraternity placed all of its administrative responsibilities in the hands of its three rectors. Before 1257 the members apparently elected the rectors, but in that year Bishop Pietro granted the outgoing rectors the privilege of selecting their successors ("Specchio," 6v). This co-optation of new rectors occurred in the presence of the "good men" of the fraternity, and candidates for the office were to be "spiritual, wise, and solicitous in the exercise of the said office" (lines 1–5). In practice, however, the outgoing rectors limited their selections by unwritten constraints. They never selected one of their own members to a successive year in office; occasionally an individual held office a second time but not until several years had passed. From the thirteenth through the fifteenth centuries, the fraternity was never headed by a cleric, despite the presence of both regular and secular clerics among its members.[14] The outgoing rectors in the century after 1268 chose their successors from a wide spectrum of the society of this market town.

Co-optation of incoming rectors continued until 1430, when Pope Martin V took control of the town and required the election of the administrative heads of the brotherhood. This arrangement proved unsatisfactory, perhaps because of the problem of finding members, and, when Florence gained political dominance in the town in 1441, the administrative heads were selected by lot ("Specchio," 4r). The rectors held office for one year from July 25, the day of their selection.

By analyzing the responsibilities of the rectors as found in the statutes of 1269, we can gain an understanding of the fraternity's role in death and charity in thirteenth-century San Sepolcro. The rectors gathered food, money, and property and distributed this food and money to the "shame-faced poor especially and others, and religious and pious places."[15] The rectors collected dues from members, who promised to give varying amounts by the week or year. The names of new members were entered in a book of matriculation. The mode of collection of these dues and other income of the brotherhood is one of the two activities of the rectors minutely described in the statutes. After tierce (about 9:00 A.M.) each Saturday, which was market day in San Sepolcro, the rectors were to go "through the land, especially through the streets and highways where the artisans and good men and those who are of the fraternity, asking for the pennies of God. One of them carries the *thefama* [bag or box] and then all who promised to give pennies every Saturday, and even many who are not of the fraternity, place their pennies in the *thefama*" (lines 17–23). The members of the fraternity congregated with nonmembers on the first Sunday of each month in the church of San Bartolomeo. While they assembled, the rectors walked among the worshipers, seeking and then repeating the names of those members who had died in the previous month. Upon entering the fraternity, members were encouraged to obligate themselves to pay one denaro, in addition to regular gifts, on the occasion of the death of fellow members. While repeating the names of the dead of the fraternity, the rectors carried the bag in which self-obligated members offered their denaro for each member deceased in the previous month. A portion of the members offered sums "according to their will"; others, especially women, donated eggs and bread (line 31).

The rectors distributed the accumulated wealth of the fraternity on each Thursday and on one Sunday a month. On Thursday they gathered up the available bread and cooked food, including beef and pork. Each rector carried a bag of bread and was accompanied by a servant with a box of the meats and other foods. "Together they go through all the streets of the land, offering to the poor and the religious places and nunneries, the charity of bread and meat by measuring to each according to what they judge to be proper and to other poor they offer their charitable gifts through the recommendation of persons" (lines 43–51). While the three rectors and their servants walked the narrow streets, distributing bread from their bags and meat from the boxes, the women of San Sepolcro donated additional bread and eggs to be given to the poor and infirm (lines 50–51). A century and a half after the statutes were written, Largi explained more fully this exchange of bread between the rectors and the women members. The rectors passed out loaves of bread to the poor and also smaller loaves to members, which the rectors or their representatives had sanctified. While the rectors distributed these small holy loaves, which Largi calls "pane di Dio," they took from members larger loaves. These larger loaves were then distributed by the agents of the fraternity to the poor and needy of the town and countryside ("Specchio," 6r).

Within the walls of San Sepolcro the three rectors acted in concert, but when they exited through the town gates, they divided the countryside into three sections. Each rector, exercising responsibility for the poor of his third of the town's rural area, possessed "a purse in which he always carries the pennies of the Fraternity from which . . . he provides for the poor of his area, chiefly the shame-faced and needy, giving pennies, bread, meat, chickens, and fowl, and other foods to the infirm and the needy poor."[16] In distributing charity, the rector judged the needs of the poor and the infirm, though, as within the town walls, he consulted with neighbors and nearby priests. The individual rector had authority to give up to twelve denari, although for substantial handouts to those in the countryside with unusually large needs, the rector was required to consult with his peers (lines 62–69). On the first Sunday of the month the rectors retraced their steps through the town and countryside. Having gathered together the contributions of food and money in the church of San Bartolomeo, the rectors immediately distributed them to the poor and the religious houses of San Sepolcro (lines 62–69).

The fraternity's charity to the poor included clothing. The rectors distributed wool clothing around All Saints Day, when the weather turned cold and damp in San Sepolcro, and linen at the beginning of summer (lines 51–52). In all the charity of the fraternity, religious houses and individual clerics appear as prominent recipients. Monasteries, nunneries, and churches may have continued to serve as distribution centers, and the clerics acted as middlemen, as they had in earlier centuries. The thirteenth-century documents from San Sepolcro, however, show that charity flowed from laypeople to clerics. The lay members of the fraternity contributed alms, the rectors accumulated and distributed them, and the poor, including the clerics, accepted the charity. In recognition of their preeminent role, the town government enacted a law that empowered the rectors to act as the representatives of the poor. In this period local bishops usually assumed such a role. Whether the bishop of Città di Castello objected to the new office for the rectors is not known; perhaps the peculiar jurisdictional situation of San Sepolcro, where spiritual and temporal authority was in the hands of the Camaldolese abbot, permitted the rectors to attain this office. The communal government named the rectors "the General Administrators of the Poor" and charged them to defend and assist the poor and to maintain them in all their rights (lines 68–71). This law was passed around 1269; for five centuries the Fraternity of San Bartolomeo carried out this charge and in the process brought under its authority a vast number of activities, many of them unforeseen by the communal lawmakers.

Commemoration of the Dead

If we assume that detail of instruction in the statutes indicates degree of importance, then we may judge that equally important to charity in the minds of the legislators was memorialization of the dead. The service in honor of the dead included two distinct phases and three categories of persons. The service of commemoration of the dead was intimately involved with the accumulation of money and food for the poor. Charity for the poor and aid to the dead traditionally were regarded as two of the seven acts of mercy. In supervising these fundamental acts of Christian charity, the fraternity played an important role in socially integrating its members and the townspeople as well.

The first phase of the service of commemoration was part of the monthly Sunday service in the church of San Bartolomeo. The rectors passed among the congregation accepting alms, seeking the names of members who had died in the past month, and then informing other members of their departed brothers. In a large brotherhood and in a period of limited communications, these interchanges between rectors and members must have often been the first notice many of the living received of the deaths of fellow members. The second phase of memorialization focused on the ritual of calling aloud the names of the dead before God. This practice has had a long history, but in the West it has been most often associated with the communities of monks, who held up the names of their deceased brothers before God and requested their souls' well-being throughout eternity.

In the monthly memorial service of the fraternity, another official led the community of members in recalling to their minds the deceased of the previous month. Selected by the outgoing rectors, this official held office for a year and took the name *prior.* The prior had to be a priest and could hold no other benefice (line 40). The prior-priest intoned the names of each brother or sister, noting that he or she had died. The remaining portion of the community beseeched God for the soul of the dead. Each deceased member's name was announced in turn, and the fraternity prayed to God for the safety of the individual soul (lines 35–38). Any nonmember who bequeathed a gift to the fraternity received the identical formalized remembrance, including the statement that the benefactor belonged to the fraternity. This category of individual was analogous to the monastic "knocker at the door," who, after a life in the lay state, entered the monastery just before death to gain the benefits of monastic burial and memorialization.

The Fraternity of San Bartolomeo, however, did not simply confer social remembrance and beseech the divine for the souls of members and those who gave property or money. The fraternity possessed confidence in its ability to gain divine favor for all categories of persons, whether they had membership or not, property to give or not. They viewed their corporate virtue as so grand and their beseeching of God so eloquent that the statute writers permitted the name of any deceased individual to be announced by the prior of the fraternity to God (lines 38–39).

This service for the departed of the fraternity and the community of San Sepolcro occurred within a series of acts and rituals that are not found in the confraternal sources. Doubtless the memorialized individuals had already received family remembrance with a procession to the burial place and perhaps a death mass on the day of burial. It is not clear whether the prior-priest of the fraternity gave an office for the dead in the monthly service in the church of San Bartolomeo. It is clear that the ritual of memorialization occurred "before the preacher gets up to preach" (lines 40–41). There is no mention of candles or money to purchase them. Nor do we find the statutes requiring members to say Our Fathers or Hail Marys for the deceased brothers and sisters. Rather, the corporate voice of the fraternity had the authority to move the mind of the divine in favor of the dead soul. The model for this ritual derives from monastic culture in which the community of monks prays corporately for each deceased brother. The fraternity members did not have a merit identical to that of the monks, who had withdrawn from the world. Sufficient merit to gain the capacity to persuade the divine could only have been based on the charitable work of the fraternity. The amount of that charity and the size of the fraternity must have also persuaded the confraternal members that their prayers for the dead would be efficacious. The fraternity's membership surpassed one thousand, enabling members and contemporaries to conceive that its supplications emanated from the town itself. The remembrance of the deceased of the community of San Sepolcro brings into focus almost every activity of the fraternity.

The Social Composition of the Fraternity

Between meetings, the rectors required a written memorandum of the names of the dead to assure that a member did not lose his or her right to remembrance. Out of this necessity was born the book of the dead, which followed in the tradition of the monastic books of the dead. The fraternity also had to list those men and women who associated with the corporation by promising regular gifts to the brotherhood. This matricula of entrants and the book of the dead resembled the monastic *Libri vitae* and the *Libri memoriales*. The monastic *Libri vitae,* at times titled *Libri confraternitatum,* recorded the names of those associated with the monasteries, who thereby received the benefits of the prayers of the monks and burial within their monastery. At death the names of the associated individuals were entered in the *Libri memoriales* to provide the monks with the names for whom they owed varying types of commemoration. These monastic books of the living and the dead, in turn, were derived from the early Christian practice of entering the names of the great spiritual heroes and bishops on ivory diptychs that occupied a prominent place on the altars of the late Roman basilicas.[17]

In San Sepolcro the matricula of entrants and the book of the dead preserved the names and years of entrance of more than four thousand individuals and a lesser number of names and dates of the dead. The rectors occasionally included the occupation or status of the member and gifts to the brotherhood in the list of members or deathbook. Often the names include the place of residence, if outside the walls of

San Sepolcro. From these documents we can sketch a social portrait of the membership and understand the fraternity's ability to attract members from outside San Sepolcro across the forty-year period from 1269 to 1309.

Studies of the social composition of specific confraternities have been limited in number and success. Medieval notaries habitually recorded the occupation or status of some individuals but neglected to record that of others. Researchers have been forced to assume that those lacking an indication of occupation or status had social roles in the same percentage as those for whom the notaries provided such information. The notarial practice limits all studies of the social composition of the medieval confraternities, including my own and an earlier study of the Fraternity of San Bartolomeo by Fanfani. Analyzing more than one thousand individuals who made bequests to the fraternity from the 1240s to the 1430s, Fanfani assumed that it drew from all the "social classes" of the town and the Upper Tiber Valley and that 75 percent of the benefactors resided in San Sepolcro.[18]

Documentation that records the entire membership of the fraternity makes possible a fairly precise definition of the social composition of this brotherhood.[19] The basic categories were determined by the statutes of 1269, which state that all new members should be inscribed in "a book of the fraternity, males in one part of the book and females in another, and they are to be set down with the year of our Lord and in the time of the rectors under whom they entered" (lines 9–12). The hand of the writer of the book of entrants changes in late July or by August 1 in conformity with the date, July 25, that the new rectors took office. The year in San Sepolcro changed on December 25, but the writers of the lists of entrants seldom note the change in years. For males, the rectors recorded the name of the entrant with his city, town, or district, though the amount of information fluctuates from name to name and year to year. In years for which residency is recorded for many individuals, the village or castle of other entrants is missing; in these instances it is assumed, following Fanfani's example, that these members resided within the walls of San Sepolcro. For female entrants, the rectors usually recorded their civil state and their male guardian (*mundualdus*). For some years it is possible to gain a relatively complete knowledge of the number and percentage of widows, servants, daughters, married, and unmarried women who entered the fraternity.

An analysis of the social composition of the fraternity reveals that individuals from nearly every occupation and status of the Upper Tiber Valley were enrolled. Its capacity to transcend boundaries of wealth and status demonstrates that the fraternity represented the town's corporate solidarity in matters relating to death and charity. The analysis of the social composition of the fraternity is based on a sample drawn from the 184 male entrants in the years 1285 to 1289 and the 176 female entrants from 1274 to 1275.[20]

Among the 184 men in the sample, the status or *arte* of an entrant or his father was recorded in fifty-one instances, or 27 percent of the entrants. The recorded social statuses and activities were typical of the small towns and villages of the Italian Middle Ages. Clerics of the church of the Upper Tiber Valley represented 4 percent of the membership of the fraternity. The Camaldolese abbots of the monastery of San Giovanni, who possessed feudal rights over San Sepolcro, joined the brotherhood. Abbot Zeno, for example, entered in 1279. In 1286 Bishop Jacopo of Città di Castello matriculated and donated one hundred soldi to the fraternity. He died, according to the book of the dead, under the corporation's protection.[21] Bishop Jacopo may have viewed his membership in the fraternity as related to his conflict with the Camaldolese abbots for ecclesiastical control of San Sepolcro; in any event, within a year of taking office Jacopo affiliated with the fraternity. Among those enrolling in this period from 1285 to 1289 were four priests, two of whom served in the rural parishes of Monte Giovio and Sant'Andrea. There were also two friars, the priest administering the leprosarium of San Lazzaro, and a pilgrim bound for Rome.

The lay members ranged from the nobility and judges through the basic craftsmen serving the small agriculturally oriented town. The count of Monteferetto, Montefelitanus, joined the fraternity in the year 1287–88 and received its benefits at his death in February 1288.[22] Twelve additional noblemen, 7 percent of the male entrants, matriculated between 1285 and 1289. As with the clergy, these percentages are probably an accurate indication of their membership because the notary would not have failed to record the statuses and offices of these luminaries of the Upper Tiber Valley. The professional and merchant social groups found the fraternity an appropriate expression of their desire to participate in corporate charity and for prayers for their souls; four merchants including a mercer, four notaries and judges, and four other men with the title of *magister* joined the fraternity in the years 1285–89. These merchants and professionals constituted 7 percent of all members and 21 percent of those whose status or occupation was noted. A large number of small shopkeepers—ten—affiliated with the fraternity, including tailors, oil sellers, bakers, and shoemakers; they made up 5 percent of the entering male members and 18 percent of those for whom status or occupation is indicated. Craftsmen with a variety of skills joined the brotherhood; they included an ironworker (*feranius*), blacksmith, turner, woolworker, miller, and silversmith (*argentini*), together constituting 7 percent of the men entering in this period and 21 percent of those with occupation or status indicated.

The women who entered in 1274–75 were less likely to have their status or occupation, or that of their husbands, sons, or guardians, recorded in the lists of entrants. Occupations were noted for less than 18 percent of the female entrants, but the social pattern is nearly identical to that of the men with one important exception. Among the male entrants from 1285 to 1289, there was only one servant. Among the females, there were ten, and they were the largest group with occupation or status noted. Servants constituted 6 percent of the females who entered in the sample year and fully one-third of those with status or occupation indicated. The other female entrants followed the same distribution as the male entrants, though the presence of two wives of *fabri*—ironworkers or blacksmiths—reminds us that this craft often appears in the fraternity's records in the thirteenth century.

The names in the fraternity's book of the dead yield a pattern identical to the one in the entrance records. Servants, priests, craftsmen, and merchants typical of a small town constantly reappear. In addition to the crafts mentioned above, there were town criers, soldiers, drapers, leatherworkers, locksmiths, butchers, wall or bricklayers, and hospital workers as well as the names of the great families of San Sepolcro: the Tarlati, Bercordati, and Abarbaliati.

On the basis of the crafts and statuses recorded in these documents, we may judge the Fraternity of San Bartolomeo to be an inclusive institution, which absorbed all but the poorest social groups of San Sepolcro and the surrounding villages. Within the walls of the town, beggars, indigent widows, and the recipients of the lowest wages were least likely to enter the brotherhood. The statutes of 1269 had exhorted the rectors to seek donations for the poor in areas where the "craftsmen and goodmen" of the fraternity lived (lines 18–23).

But did the inclusiveness of the lay corporation extend to the peasants of the town and its countryside as well as into the villages under the political authority of other towns and lords? There was considerable social and economic differentiation among those who worked the land, but the documents of the fraternity do not show it—the entrance and death records omit occupational categories for those who tilled the land. The peasants probably constituted a substantial proportion of the 69 percent of the entrants for whom the rectors entered no status or occupation, but the evidence is largely indirect. First, a proportion of the agricultural laborers, tenants, and owners of agricultural land lived within the walls and walked to their fields each morning. Thus failure of the documents to mention residency and occupation does not necessarily imply that the person was an urban craftsman or merchant. Largi asserted, admittedly writing in 1437, that the *terrazani* belonged to the fraternity. Though the context indicates that he meant by this term agricultural landowners, these landowners were unmentioned in the thirteenth-century records of the fraternity, as were the peasants. Therefore, peasants were as likely to have been members as the *terrazani* mentioned by Largi ("Specchio," 5v). Second, the entrance of sixteen women in 1273–74 from the small agricultural village of San Giustino, where there would have been little economic differentiation, indicates probable agrarian membership in the fraternity from this village of peasants and, by extension, from the Upper Tiber Valley. For the agricultural laborers and wage earners, many of whom barely kept themselves above the subsistence level, there is no specific evidence. Some doubtless received charity from the rectors when they dispensed food and money in the countryside, but the presence of a large number of names of members in the fraternity's records from the villages and castles of the Upper Tiber Valley and its hillsides indicates that some of the workers of the land took membership in the fraternity. Clearly the thirteenth-century fraternity drew its large membership from all or nearly all the social statuses and economic categories. Largi ignored individuals of lesser social status so as to elevate the dignity of the fraternity, though he conveys its spirit of inclusiveness when he states that many abbots, bishops, friars, monks, preachers, doctors, landowners, noblemen, and noblewomen entered and an individual "did not seem to be a good Christian who was not inscribed in this glorious fraternity" ("Specchio," 5v).

An examination of the social status of the rectors demonstrates that the leadership represented the same broad spectrum of the town's social groups. The scribes of the fraternity failed to record the social status or occupation in listing the names of nearly 80 percent of the rectors in the period from 1269 to 1309. Of the approximately 120 rectors in this forty-year period, only 26 were given an identifying characteristic. Seven rectors were drawn from six great urban or noble families; a Carsidoni, Cipolli, Befolci, Mazzetti, Dominus Raynerius, and two members of the Pichi family made up this relatively small group. The other rectors identified in the documents were men of occupations of low or little honor. Five notaries made up the largest single occupational group, followed by three shoemakers and three ironworkers. There were also a physician, a university graduate, the operator of an oil press, a butcher, and a money changer. No one individual or occupation dominated the office, nor were there more than one or two men reelected to office. And neither priest nor monk gained elevation to this honor. The men and women of the fraternity reciprocated prayers and accepted the leadership of shoemakers, blacksmiths, and notaries. Membership in the social elite or an elevated professional status did not aid one in being selected to lead the fraternity.

In addition to recruiting members from nearly all the occupational and professional groups of San Sepolcro, the fraternity attracted numerous men and women to its membership, though not its leadership, from a large geographic area, which included most of central Italy. The nucleus of the incoming members resided within the walls of the town. An examination of the male members in the years from 1285 to 1289 yields an image of concentric circles with the highest concentration drawn from within the inner circle of the town's walls. Of the 184 matriculating into the fraternity in these years, 114, or 62 percent, resided in San Sepolcro.[23] The next concentric circle from the walls to an outer rim twenty kilometers from the town contained a highly concentrated number of villages and towns, from which approximately 30 percent of the male members originated. Seeking inscription in the fraternity were men from the villages of Aboca, Anghiari, Gricignano, Citerna, Soyara, and many others as well as from the two towns of Città di Castello and Pieve San Stefano. In a broader circle skewed to the west, the fraternity drew members from the Arno Valley and, to a lesser extent, from over the Apennines to the east of San Sepolcro in the territory of Massa Trabaria. Even men from the Tuscan cities of Florence, Arezzo, and Siena sought the protection of the association.

This broad geographic appeal demonstrates that the recruitment of the fraternity did not conform to either ecclesiastical or political jurisdictions. Despite being an association of the town of San Sepolcro and distributing alms only within its territory, the fraternity succeeded in acquiring members from distant cities and towns. This lack of symmetry between the area of recruitment of members and the distribution of money and food can best be explained by analogy to the monastic practice of association. From at least the eighth century, individual monks, laymen, corporate groups of a monastery, or a lord with his vassals sought associations with a monastery, by which, in exchange for a gift of property or money, the individual or group received benefits of membership in the body of monks. Such benefits included inscription in the book of life, burial in the monastic habit and cemetery, and a variety of prayers and masses for the associated brother's soul. Associated brothers ranged from Bede, who sought inclusion in the *Album* of the religious community at Lindisfarne, to the layman Gudinus, who gave his daughter and servant to the monastery at Remiremont in exchange for inclusion in the great book of life, a mass, and probably burial near the chapel of the monastery.[24]

The Fraternity of San Bartolomeo represented the corporate community of San Sepolcro that was responsible for the poor and the needy of the town's territory. Individuals from outside the boundaries of the town, however, could gain access to the accumulated virtue of the fraternity by being placed on the matricula and pledging periodic gifts. The disjunction between the area of distribution of alms and the larger area of recruitment demonstrates the desire of thirteenth-century men and women to transcend customary social and material interests and local identifications. The fraternity encouraged these laypeople to believe that they could contribute to the well-being of the poor and to deceased members through their prayers. Their participation would bring them social remembrance at death and their souls' commendation to God by the fraternity. This exchange system linked one generation to the next and integrated men and women from vastly diverse social and geographical origins.

The Fraternity of San Bartolomeo was not, however, immune to profound changes in its character. This large brotherhood, in common with other corporate confraternities of the thirteenth century, did not survive the overwhelming demographic and social disasters of the fourteenth century without profound transformations. By 1400 the nature of the membership had been decisively altered.

Other studies of the social composition of medieval confraternities demonstrate that this organization could be adapted to a variety of social groups and might at times mix men of vastly different occupations and statuses. Meersseman examined the Confraternity of St. Maurice of tenth-century Tours. Its sacramentary contains the names of 168 men and women who contributed six denari for a single member and twelve (occasionally twenty-four) denari for a married couple. This urban confraternity recruited from the "modest people" and those of "humble social condition": carpenters, cooks, millers, washerwomen, male and female servants, and other craftspeople of an urban center lacking significant commerce and manufacturing. But here too a large proportion of the names lacks any indication of occupation or status.[25]

Charles de la Roncière has offered an explanation of the origin and existence of several confraternities in the towns and villages of the valley of the Elsa in the Florentine countryside in the late thirteenth and fourteenth centuries. Though maintaining that a pious organization has religious motivations at its core, he finds the existence of these confraternities in this period linked to demographic decline, economic regression, and the loss of political autonomy of this part of the Florentine countryside. The "crisis" of the fortified towns in the fourteenth century destroyed the social cohesion of these "micro-urban societies"; the confraternities served to reestablish at the spiritual level a social solidarity threatened by daily ruin, death, and disappointments. Moreover, he holds that, despite the presence of a wide variety of occupations, the numerous confraternities in his study drew essentially on the average bourgeoisie—the merchant, landowner, and professional of these micro-urban societies.[26]

The evidence drawn from San Sepolcro from 1269 to 1309 points in a radically different direction. The Fraternity of San Bartolomeo grew to approximately one thousand members and recruited from various social groups, including the craftsmen and nobility of the Tiber Valley that De la Roncière found of minimal importance in the confraternities of the Florentine countryside. The Fraternity of San Bartolomeo prospered in the decades in which San Sepolcro became the major market for the Upper Tiber Valley; the town grew in population, and the laity seized control of its political destiny from the Camaldolese abbots. San Sepolcro was outside the persistent economic and political dominion of any large city, unlike the towns of the valley of the Elsa examined by De la Roncière, where Florence established its political and economic authority in these years. On a much smaller scale, San Sepolcro in the Upper Tiber Valley functioned in a manner similar to Florence in the Arno Valley: each brought within its walls a portion of the population, buyers, and products of the smaller towns and villages and eventually drew these towns and villages into its political orbit. Differences between De la Roncière's research and my own may occur because we have examined two different types of towns and focus on different centuries. From the perspective of San Sepolcro and the Fraternity of San Bartolomeo, I find that this pious society primarily assured its members of memorialization in their community in this world and before God in the next world. De la Roncière discovers or relates the impulse to form or join a confraternity in the infelicities of daily life from the late thirteenth to the late fourteenth centuries. Though not denying the importance of the darker side of human existence or a broader social awareness of it with the higher incidence of death, loss of self-government, and economic problems of this period, I find that the Fraternity of San Bartolomeo grew and prospered with the steady growth and prosperity of San Sepolcro. This fraternity's founding predated the general western European crisis of population and economy, and it declined or stagnated before the general decline of the middle of the fourteenth century.

The research on Florence by Ronald Weissman, supported by refined statistical methods, likewise demonstrates the diversity of participation in Florentine confraternities. Though he recognizes the importance of the large Florentine confraternities such as Or San Michele, the Bigallo, and the Misericordia—similar in size and function to the Fraternity of San Bartolomeo in San Sepolcro—he focuses on two types of brotherhoods, the *laudesi* and the flagellants. Both drew widely from the middle ranges of Florentine society. Weissman discovered two fundamental distinctions between the brotherhoods in the fifteenth century: the moment in the individual's life at which he begins to participate and the geographical extent of the confraternity's recruitment. The *laudesi* brotherhoods in Florence tended to orient around churches that served districts—areas larger than parishes but not citywide—and recruited mature men with families who anticipated the confraternity's death benefits. In contrast, the flagellant confraternities attracted younger men before their marriages, a significant proportion of whom were drawn from each quarter of the city. Weissman also sees these brotherhoods as forums in which tensions and aggressions created by the competitive political and economic world of Florence could be released.[27]

Though the thirteenth-century Fraternity of San Bartolomeo existed in a social world of agonistic relationships and frequent violence similar to that of Florence, it fostered a sense of community by focusing on charity for the poor and the religious as well as enabling each adult to realize his yearning for broad remembrance. Drawing together all the social groups of the town and countryside, the fraternity could speak for the corporate body of Christians and invest its prayers with the weight of number and unity.

The Corporate Voice and Body of the Fraternity

The fraternity in its commemoration services implicitly claimed the authority to engage the mind of God for the aid of its dead members. The laity's capacity to influence the divine in the interest of the souls of

TABLE 2.1

Entrants to the Fraternity of San Bartolomeo, 1269–1309

	Females		*Males*			*Totals*	
Year	*Entrants*	*Percent Female in Decade*	*Entrants*	*Estimated Number*	*Percent Male in Decade*	*Yearly Totals*	*Extrapolated Totals for Decade*
1269–70	44					44	
1270–71	30					30	
1271–72	38					38	
1272–73	27					27	
1273–74	169					169	
1274–75	176					176	
1275–76	110					110	
1276–77	81					81	
1277–78	99					99	
1278–79	137		73 (partial)			210	
	911		73	(756)*		984	(1667)
1279–80	64		69			133	
1280–81	13		16			29	
1281–82	39		20			59	
1282–83	45		39			84	
1283–84	19		25			44	
1284–85	85		160			245	
1285–86	30		17			47	
1286–87	35		59			94	
1287–88	58		54			112	
1288–89	78		54			132	
	466	48	513		52	979	

TABLE 2.1 *(Continued)*

	Females		Males			Totals	
Year	*Entrants*	*Percent Female in Decade*	*Entrants*	*Estimated Number*	*Percent Male in Decade*	*Yearly Totals*	*Extrapolated Totals for Decade*
1289–90	29		27			56	
1290–91	34		27			61	
1291–92	20		26			46	
1292–93	14		24			38	
1293–94	57		75			132	
1294–95	36		48			84	
1295–96	42		79			121	
1296–97	62		66			128	
1297–98	87		83			170	
1298–99	99		21			120	
Totals	480	50	476		50	956	
1299–1300	58		41			99	
1300–01	42			(37)†		42	(79)
1301–02	67		48			115	
1302–03	58			(37)†		58	(95)
1303–04	37		19			56	
1304–05	117		76			193	
1305–06	50		17			67	
1306–07	29		43			72	
1307–08	78		31			109	
1308–09	38		17			55	
Totals	574	66 (61)	292	(366)	34 (39)	866	(940)

Source: AC, SS, 32, reg. 159.

*This figure was gained by taking the ratio of males to females in the decade of the 1280s and, assuming that the same ratio would be found in the 1270s, computing the total number of males for the decade of the 1270s from its ratio to the known female total for that decade. I have removed the recruitment year of 1284–85 for males and females when estimating the decade of the 1270s and the males in the fraternity in 1269 because the high recruitment was an anomaly, and in a trial computation the results differed markedly from Largi's totals for this period.

†Based on yearly average of eight years of males of decade 1299–1309.

the dead was by the thirteenth century long established. St. Augustine had argued that God could not but be moved by the prayers of pious Christians, lay or cleric. His authority was most often cited as the basis for these prayers.[28] The effectiveness of the prayers of the fraternity was, in all likelihood, founded upon its size and the charity distributed to the poor. When it corporately appealed for the safety of its deceased members, it did so with a thousand voices. The amount of food and clothing given to the poor must have been considerable. Though this amount cannot be estimated, it is important to realize that food was distributed weekly and varied according to season. Thus the charity of the fraternity appears as a regular Thursday distribution followed by a monthly distribution on Sunday, rather than by the festivals of the liturgical year.

The two series of entrants and deaths from 1269 to 1309 provide the basis for estimating the size of the fraternity. We can know the minimal number of men and women for whom the rectors and the prior spoke when they appealed to God for the well-being of a departed brother or sister. When the rectors implemented the requirement of the 1269 statutes to record the names of entrants and the monthly deaths, they began by inscribing all the members of the fraternity as of that date. The folios of the register containing the names of male members in 1269 and male entrants from 1269 to 1278 have been lost. The names of 694 females, however, were entered under the rubric "Book of the Females of the Aforementioned Fraternity." By applying the ratio of men to women in the first decade of extant statistics of entrants (the decade 1279–88) to the inscription year 1269 and the decade 1269–78, it is possible to fill the two lacunae in the male series.[29] This proportional computation produces a total of 572 males in the fraternity in 1269. Combining these males with the 694 females yields a total of 1,266 members in the fraternity in that year (see Tables 2.1 and 2.2).

The Fraternity of San Bartolomeo in 1269 constituted a powerful corporate presence in San Sepolcro. Though the church of San Bartolomeo had an ample nave, it is doubtful that the monthly Sunday services ever drew all these members together into that sanctuary. Nevertheless, the number of members was extraordinary for one corporation, and the members could well have expected that their corporate voice would rise to the heavens with as much authority as that of any clerical corporation of the age. This fraternity resembled most closely monasteries such as Reichnau and St. Gall in which the large body of monks prayed for thousands of associated laymen as well as for their deceased brothers.[30]

TABLE 2.2

Entrants to the Fraternity of San Bartolomeo, 1269–1309

	Females		Males			Totals	
Year	*Entrants*	*Percent Females*	*Entrants*	*Entrants Plus Extrapolation*	*Percent Male*	*Decade Totals*	*Extrapolated Decade Totals*
1269–79	911		73	(756)*		984	(1,667)
1279–89	466	48	513	513	52	979	979
1289–99	470	50	476	476	50	946	946
1299–1309	574	66 (61)	292	(366)	34 (39)	866	(940)
Totals	2,421	64	1,354		36	3,775	(4,532)

Source: AC, SS, 32, reg. 159.

*Extrapolation but not computing the 73 males because it is an unknown portion of the year 1278–79. For the method employed to arrive at the figure, see Table 2.1.

A large proportion of San Sepolcro's households were represented in the fraternity. If we take the calculation that approximately 62 percent of the male members in the years from 1285 to 1289 lived within the walls of the town and apply it to our total of 572 male members in 1269, we would estimate that 355 male members of the town belonged to the fraternity in 1269. San Sepolcro in the thirteenth century was made up of four to five thousand individuals inhabiting approximately one thousand hearths. Few children entered the fraternity; therefore, nearly all the 355 male members represented households. Employing the estimate of one thousand hearths, we may conclude that these 355 represented a like number of hearths or households. Thus in 1269 more than one-third of all the families of the town were represented by an adult male in the Fraternity of San Bartolomeo.

Applying this same calculation to females yields a total of 430 in the fraternity, or nearly half of the households of San Sepolcro. Doubtless some households were represented by both male and female members; as will be discussed below, however, in an examination of a sample year of male and female recruitment in which a total of 47 individuals joined, only one household was represented by both husband and wife. Though a husband and wife could have joined in separate years, this one example indicates that it was not necessarily the practice for both husband and wife to join. Moreover, 10 percent of the females joining the fraternity and 25 percent dying under its auspices were widows, many of whom headed their own households. The exact percentage of households represented in the fraternity cannot be determined, but it is clear at least that one adult in a majority of households and families was affiliated with the Fraternity of San Bartolomeo.[31]

Slightly over one-half of those who entered the fraternity died with its commemoration. In the forty-year period from 1269 to 1309, the names of 2,335 individuals were inscribed in the fraternal book of the dead (see Tables 2.3–2.5). The relative lack of names of the dead, when compared with the number of entrants, suggests that some members either failed to maintain their membership or their relatives failed to inform the rectors of their deaths.

Although only 52 percent of the members on the matricula are recorded in the book of the dead, the fraternity maintained the capacity to recruit large numbers of members into the fourteenth century. There were 3,785 individuals affiliated with the fraternity in the four decades from 1269 to 1309. Adding the 694 females already in the fraternity in the summer of 1269 to the 3,775 enrolled in that forty-year period yields the sum of 4,469 certain members. If we also add

TABLE 2.3

Deaths in the Fraternity of San Bartolomeo, 1269–1289 (in number and percentages)

Year	*Totals*	*Male*	*Female*	*Widows*	*Women with Husbands Alive*	*Sisters*	*Daughters*	*Servants*	*Nuns*	*Uncertain or Unattached*
1269–70	38	13	25		20	3				2
1270–71	35	22	13	6	2	2				3
1271–72	20	6	14		12	1				1
1272–73	33	15	18	1	8					9
1273–74	77*	19	58	3	23	1	1		1	29
1274–75	60	21	39	9	26		1	1		2
1275–76	63	32	31	15	10		4			2
1276–77	70	28	42	13	23				1	5
1277–78	71	37	34	18	9		4		1	2
1278–79	54	31	23	2	17	–	1	–	–	3
Totals	521	224 (43%)	297 (57%)	67 (23%†)	150 (51%†)	7 (2%†)	11 (4%†)	1 (.4%†)	3 (1%†)	58 (20%†)
1279–80	80	39	41	10	26		3		1	1
1280–81	74	32	42	20	15	1		1	1	4
1281–82	67	29	38	4	28		2	1	1	2
1282–83	53	27	26	10	15					1
1283–84	40	16	34	10	14		2			8
1284–85	86	34	52	14	25		1	2		10
1285–86	70	35	35	12	21		1		1	
1286–87	46	11	35	9	20	2				4
1287–88	51	23	28	11	13	2			1	1
1288–89	61	21	40	7	15	–	4	–	–	14
Totals	638	267 (42%)	371 (58%)	107 (29%†)	192 (52%†)	5 (1%†)	13 (4%†)	4 (1%†)	5 (1%†)	45 (12%†)

Source: AC, SS, 32, 159.

*For 1273–74 there are two series of deaths which are combined in this table.

†The percentages for the subcategories of females are percentages of females, not of the total deaths.

TABLE 2.4

Deaths in the Fraternity of San Bartolomeo, 1289–1309 (in number and percentages)

Year	*Totals*	*Male*	*Female*	*Widows*	*Women with Husbands Alive*	*Sisters*	*Daughters*	*Servants*	*Nuns*	*Uncertain or Unattached*
1289–90	87	36	51	15	31		1			4
1290–91	61	27	34	8	17	3	1		3	2
1291–92	64	31	33	17	14	2				
1292–93	43	18	25	6	15	2	1			1
1293–94	39	16	23	6	11	1	1		2	2
1294–95	44	18	26	2	19	1	1			3
1295–96	57	30	27	3	5		1			18
1296–97	44	15	29	6	13		1			9
1297–98	46	23	23	7	5					11
1298–99	51	19	32	9	14	2	2	–	–	5
Totals	536	233 (43%)	303 (57%)	79 (26%*)	144 (48%)	11 (4%)	9 (3%)		5 (1.5%)	55 (18%)
1299–1300	75	36	39	4	26	3	2		1	3
1300–01	56	26	30	7	13			1	1	8
1301–02	67	29	38	13	15		1			9
1302–03	54	25	29	11	14		3			1
1303–04	55	12	43	5	31	1				6
1304–05	45	17	28	1	16	1	1			9
1305–06	(59)†	(24)	(35)							
1306–07	(59)	(24)	(35)							
1307–08	62	31	31	3	2	1				25
1308–09	57	18	39	7	17	4	–	–	–	11
Totals	471 (589)	194 (41%) (242)	277 (59%) (347)	51 (18%)	134 (48%)	10 (4%)	7 (3%)	1	2	72 (26%)

Source: AC, SS, 32, 159.

*As in Table 2.3, the percentages for the subcategories of females are percent of females, not of total deaths.

†Numbers in parenthesis are derived from the average for the decade; those in totals include the two years 1305–6 plus the actual sums of the other years of the decade.

TABLE 2.5

Totals of Deaths in the Fraternity of San Bartolomeo, 1269–1309 (in number and percentages)

Years	*Totals*	*Male*	*Female*	*Widows*	*Women with Husbands Alive*	*Sisters*	*Daughters*	*Servants*	*Nuns*	*Uncertain or Unattached*
1269–79	521	224 (43%)	297 (57%)	67 (23%)	150 (51%)	7 (2%)	11 (4%)	1	3	58 (20%)
1279–89	638	267 (42%)	371 (58%)	107 (29%)	192 (52%)	5 (1%)	13 (4%)	4	5	45 (23%)
1289–99	536	233 (43%)	303 (57%)	79 (26%)	144 (48%)	11 (4%)	9 (3%)	0	5	55 (18%)
1299–1309	471	194 (41%)	277 (59%)	51 (18%)	134 (48%)	10 (4%)	7 (3%)	1	2	72 (25%)
	(589)	(242)	(347)							
Totals	2,166	918 (42%)	1,248 (58%)	304 (24%)	620 (50%)	33 (3%)	40 (3%)	6 (.5%)	15 (1%)	230 (18%)
	(2,284)	(966)	(1,318)							

the estimates for the lacunae in the entrance statistics for males, we find that just over 5,800 individuals associated themselves with the fraternity from about 1260 to 1309.

Members and Charity

The thousand and more members supported the fraternity in its charitable and commemorative activities. The size of the membership also contributed to the spirit of expansiveness and generosity; the rectors administered a corporation whose members were confident of the fraternity's ability to fulfill its purposes. As we have seen, the brotherhood permitted anyone to receive its commemorative benefits with no apparent diminishing of honor, even those who had not been members and who neglected to bequeath a gift to the fraternity. In the same mental universe is the practice of permitting members to promise gifts of varying values at the time of their entrance. There were no set "dues" for members. When an individual enrolled in the brotherhood, he determined the amount of what the statutes refer to as "charity." Other options cited as examples and not prescriptions in the statutes included annual gifts of five or ten soldi, one lire, and four and one-third soldi (explicitly one denaro on each Saturday of the year). But, again, the statutes state: "Some promise more, and others less." In addition, one could promise to pay one denaro for each deceased member when the rectors passed through the congregation in the commemorative service and two denari on All Saints Day (lines 12–17). These promises were not dues in the modern sense of the word; rather, the stated amounts constituted charity, which has its origin in the members' love of God. This charity could not be quantified or specifically mandated.

An examination of the promises of the incoming members in one year will demonstrate that there was no correlation between the amount of charity promised and the status or wealth of the individual. Of the fifty-four males entering in 1288–89, the status or craft of twenty-one is noted.[32] Of these twenty-one men, a lord and an operator of an oil press promised the smallest gift, a paltry one soldo a year. A merchant of an unknown product promised two to three soldi a year. Agreeing to give four soldi annually were ten men of diverse occupations: three lords, three oil merchants, an abbot, a barber-surgeon, a blacksmith, and a woolworker. A miller, another lord, and a *geriarius*(?) each promised five soldi, and another blacksmith promised to contribute six soldi annually. One individual alone, a lord, promised more—a *staio* (.73 of a bushel) of grain valued at approximately thirty soldi.[33] Nobles made from the lowest to the highest promises of gifts and were heavily represented in the middle of the range of gifts. Likewise one finds an oil merchant promising one soldo and a blacksmith agreeing to contribute the next to the largest charity.

The fullest expression of this generous impulse within the fraternity was for a member to decide spontaneously the amount of charity he wished to give from year to year. The statutes allude to this practice in describing the activities of the rectors in the monthly memorial service. When the rectors collected the one denaro for each deceased member and other gifts promised by members, they also collected from others who gave "according to their will" (lines 28–30). The statute writers were not simply describing capricious gifts. In the lists of those matriculating into the fraternity, individuals frequently promised no set amount; the writer of the register of entrants occasionally noted that the incoming member preferred to keep his future gift in his will.[34] Of those twenty-one male entrants whose craft or status was noted in 1288–89, three opted to decide the amount of their gifts year by year. These included a miller, a dressmaker, and a shoemaker named Tutius from San Sepolcro, who "promised that which he wanted to give." Thus the individual member could decide the degree of monetary participation without any discernible influence on his position or the benefits he received.

An examination of female recruitment and promises of gifts demonstrates the willingness of the fraternity to include groups whose financial support would have been minimal. Evidence taken from the matriculation year 1274–75 reveals that 176 women entered. Among these entrants, a notation of male guardian or some indication of civil status was given for all but 11.[35] The largest proportion of female entrants were married women; 67 percent of the 176 entrants were recorded as Donna ____ wife of ____. Another 10 percent were widows noted as the mother of a male or the wife once of a male. Adult unmarried daughters made up 11 percent and servants 6 percent of the entering females. In this particular year not one nun entered, but they often appear throughout the late thirteenth century.

The book of the dead yields a slightly different portrait because many of the women died late in life. Compared with the entrants, fewer females in the necrology were married at the time of death (approximately 50 percent from 1269 to 1299) (see Tables 2.3–2.5). The greatest difference is the higher percentage of widows in the death records; nearly 25 percent of women dying under the auspices of the fraternity in the period from 1269 to 1299 were widows. Daughters and servants appear less often in the book of the dead; many of them had married or entered some other status. Of those whose status can be determined, only 5 percent of the dead females were referred to as daughters and only 1 percent as servants.[36]

An examination of the pledges of gifts by females in the sample year 1274–75 confirms the judgment that the fraternity accepted women without regard to their willingness or ability to support the corporation with money. The female entrants of that year promised sums varying from nothing to five soldi a year. The only substantial gifts from the 176 women were from 2 individuals, each of whom promised one *staio* of grain annually. One-third of the female entrants (60 of 176), however, did not state an intention of contributing any sum to the fraternity. Perhaps a few conceived membership as being paid by their husbands or guardians. For example, in 1285 Benvenutus of the village of Sculokio promised five soldi yearly for himself and his wife. Membership of a husband brought rights of membership to his wife in several contemporary confraternities,[37] though this possibility was not mentioned in the statutes of the Fraternity of San Bartolomeo. In fact, a comparison of male and female matriculation lists in any particular year reveals few occasions when both husband and wife entered the fraternity. Given the subordination of women to men in contemporary documents, reflected in the fraternity's registers by the inclusion of the female's male guardian, one might assume that the husband's entrance conferred fraternal membership upon his wife. This assumption does not manifest itself in the lists of members.[38] The example of Benvenutus suggests that for an individual to be considered a member by virtue of the entrance of the spouse, it had to be so stated. Such a statement is seldom found and occurs as infrequently as husband and wife being listed as entering in the same year. In view of the value placed on the inscription of names in matriculation and death books, in all likelihood adults had to enter formally and have their names inscribed in the fraternal entrance lists.

In addition to the one-third of the women in 1274–75 who made no pledge to give the fraternity charity, another third promised only one to three soldi. The remaining third vowed to give four or five soldi or a *staio* or less of grain. Thus two-thirds of all female entrants pledged three soldi or less annually to the fraternity. The most humble among the female entrants made a high proportion of paltry donations; of the twenty-nine servants and daughters, only four could promise more than three soldi. It is clear that the rectors over an extended period of time did not closely scrutinize the pledges of female entrants to determine whether they could contribute to the material well-being of the fraternity. The total lack of fraternal documents recording dues paid by individuals in this period and the fourteenth century, when financial records become more common in this fraternity and other confraternities, suggests that the rectors did not believe it was necessary to require or supervise the yearly payment of pledges. Moreover, when Largi surveyed and cataloged the fraternal archives in 1437, he did not find any register devoted to recording the paying or failure to pay yearly charity ("Specchio," 18r–19v, 22v–24r).

Records of dues paid, however, became common in other confraternities in the fourteenth century. In Florence, for example, the Confraternity of San Frediano required its notary to record the names of those paying their dues in 1333. Reliance on dues as the source of finances for confraternities led to the practice of recording the names of those who failed to pay their dues. After a period of probation, the derelict member would be expelled from the confraternity, thereby losing all his confraternal benefits.[39] Inasmuch as the Fraternity of San Bartolomeo did not require members to pay dues, it never maintained records of those who failed to pay them. In the thirteenth century the fraternity fostered a devotion that deemphasized contributions; confident of its ability to recruit new members and to persuade God to aid its dead, the fraternity eschewed a close accounting of its income and expenses.

Recruitment and Decline of Membership

The fraternity maintained a large corporate presence in San Sepolcro in the second half of the thirteenth century, but in the first decade of the fourteenth century it suffered a devastating decline in male membership. Through an examination of the lists of entrants from 1269 to 1309, we can measure the well-being of the fraternity over this forty-year period.[40] It is assumed here that one means of gauging the health of a corporation providing charity to the poor and prayers for the dead is to determine whether the corporation maintained a steady flow of new members. In the decade 1269 to 1279, 911 females became associated with the fraternity; the years 1273 and 1274 marked the high point of recruitment for the decade and for the forty-year period of documentation, when 169 and 174 females respectively entered the corporation. In the following decade recruitment fell off dramatically; only 466 females joined, only 51 percent of the figure in the 1270s.[41] In the decade of the 1280s, 513 men affiliated with the brotherhood. If we employ the estimates for the decade 1269 to 1279 discussed above, we discover that male recruitment declined in the 1280s as well. The enrollment of 513 is only 68 percent of that recruited in the 1270s.

The decline of male recruitment of the 1280s continued in the 1290s. The fraternity succeeded in bringing only 476 males into membership in the 1290s, down from the 513 of the previous decade. While male membership was slipping, female membership increased slightly from 466 to 480 in the 1290s and continued to rise to 574 in the first decade of the fourteenth century. Of profound significance was the precipitous decline of male entrants after 1300. In the first decade of the fourteenth century only 292 males were recorded as entering the fraternity. This figure constituted only 59 percent of male enrollment in the 1290s. For two years of the decade the names of entrants are lacking in the register; if we assume that some males did enter in these two years and recruitment in the missing two years was equal to the average of the other eight years of the decade, then 366 males entered the fraternity from 1299 to 1309. Even with these estimates added to the totals, the male recruitment in the first decade of the fourteenth century was only 75 percent of that of the previous decade (see Tables 2.1–2.2).

One of the important findings of this analysis is the marked feminization of the membership of the fraternity in the period from 1279 to 1309. A comparison of male and female enrollment shows the relative decline in male recruitment after the 1280s. In that decade new male members made up 52 percent of the enrollment, but in the 1290s the male proportion slipped to 49.5 percent and in the decade from 1299 to 1309 to 39 percent.[42] The preponderance of women cannot be explained as simply as reflection of their preponderance in European populations generally because at the exact moment when the numerical superiority of females became manifest in the fraternity, two new types of confraternities limited to males were founded in San Sepolcro. The declining interest of males in the Fraternity of San Bartolomeo presaged the development of new forms of lay devotion.

In judging the place of the Fraternity of San Bartolomeo in the early history of the Italian confraternities, it is necessary to avoid two persuasive, though contradictory and ultimately misleading, interpretive strategies. It is tempting to view the fraternity as an example of medieval corporativism, in which its charity and concern for the dead of the town are seen as an expression of community. Later developments in the history of the fraternity and the town can then be seen as destructive and as shattering of the earlier bonds. Gabriele de Rosa, I believe, falls victim to this conventional interpretation when he views the charity of medieval confraternities as simply an expression of the corporative nature of society.[43] Equally misleading is the view that there was a gradual unfolding of charity and brotherly love so that by the fifteenth century the confraternal members expressed in deeds the *carità* and *humanità* praised by the humanists. The formulation is that of De la Roncière and is based in part on Meersseman's view that thirteenth-century confraternities were formed primarily to fight heresy and to express devotion to Mary. De la Roncière sees the Florentine confraternities in the period from 1350 to 1430 moving toward an ethic of assistance and concern for the common good based on love of neighbor. Thus there is a movement from the thirteenth-century confraternities concerned with heresy and devotion to charitable confraternities after 1350.[44] The extensive charitable activities of the Fraternity of San Bartolomeo in San Sepolcro should remind us that elsewhere several other confraternities with large memberships carried on extensive charity. In Florence, for example, the Confraternity of Or San Michele fostered a sense of citywide brotherhood through its distributions of charity to large numbers of the poor in the decades before the plague of 1348. As did its counterpart in San Sepolcro, the Florentine confraternity linked charitable activity to commemoration of the dead.[45]

The lay confraternity was a powerful and expressive social organization that could serve many psychological and social functions; as Meersseman and others have pointed out, the confraternities were marvelously adaptive to changing social needs and religious purposes.[46] Throughout much of the prosperous thirteenth century, the Fraternity of San Bartolomeo expressed the corporate concern of the town for its less fortunate and the members' desire to transcend their mundane pursuits, limited life expectancy, and punishment for sins. As this study demonstrates, these ends were accomplished through an organization that permitted or required a minimum of individual exertion or contribution. One could find assurance that his or her purposes in joining the fraternity would be realized by its corporate acts. This assurance was grounded in the charitable labor of its members. But the Fraternity of San Bartolomeo lost a large portion of its membership and standing before the great crises of the fourteenth century and became an administrative arm of the town government with its rectors performing many of the town's mortuary and charitable functions. Confidence in the corporate work of the fraternity broke down soon after 1300, leading to a different type of brotherhood. The new spirituality required individual effort and individual accounting that initially could be expressed only in smaller confraternities. In San Sepolcro these were brotherhoods of processional chanting and of discipline.

CHAPTER THREE

The Fraternity as Agent for the Poor, the Rich, and Dead Souls

Political authority in San Sepolcro underwent changes from 1301, when the citizens purchased feudal rights over the town from the Camaldolese abbot, to the end of this study in 1450. In that century and a half the citizens enjoyed communal autonomy for only short periods, as various greater powers and *signori* sought to bring the town under their authority. The Tarlati family of Pietramala, which had possessed some undefined power in San Sepolcro in the 1290s, established its rule once again by 1310. Led by Bishop Guido of Arezzo, the Tarlati family established its hegemony over the towns of the Upper Tiber Valley and the mountain castles from San Sepolcro to Arezzo. In 1335 Guido's brother and successor, Pier Saccone, lost control of San Sepolcro, and the town suffered through periods of brief autonomy, subordination to its archenemies in Città di Castello, and the attempts of the Tarlati to regain their predominance. The Black Death and the earthquake of 1352 were additional catastrophes for the people of the town. The early historians of San Sepolcro recount these two visitations of mortality as particularly devastating, though no evidence, other than mounds of brick and mortar within the town, today attests to the violence of the earthquake. The Visconti of Milan helped the Tarlati regain power after the great mortalities and contributed to the rebuilding of the town. Città di Castello maintained its military pressure, however, and succeeded in subordinating San Sepolcro to its rule in the late 1350s and 1360s.[1]

In 1370 Pope Urban V successfully asserted papal overlordship in San Sepolcro and in 1371 sold the town to the Malatesta for eighteen thousand florins.[2] The Malatesta family governed San Sepolcro from 1371 to 1430, though there were periods when the citizens attempted to regain their lost freedoms and other powers imposed their rule over the town. The early historians of San Sepolcro treat this period as a time of prosperity and grandeur. The Malatesta allocated resources for the restoration of the town's fortifications and the beautification of its buildings, particularly the communal palace. Under Carlo Malatesta, the forces of the town repeatedly defeated its traditional foes until 1416, when internal rebellions as well as the political and military ventures of the Visconti of Milan initiated more rapid alterations in political authority for the following twenty-five years. Through the support of the papacy, Carlo returned to power and retained it until his death in 1429.[3]

The papacy briefly exercised direct political control over San Sepolcro in the early 1430s. As part of a larger settlement, Pope Eugenius IV in 1432 conceded rule over the town to the military adventurer Niccolò Fortebraccio da Montone. Through his rebellion against the papacy, Niccolò initiated a series of conflicts in San Sepolcro that resulted in the triumph of forces led by Niccolò Piccinino and loyal to the Visconti. San Sepolcro thus became involved in a war against Florence and was defeated in the battle of Anghiari in 1440. The papacy recognized Florentine superiority in the Upper Tiber Valley when in 1441 Eugenius sold rights over San Sepolcro to Florence for twenty-five thousand ducats. Florence maintained its rule over the town into the modern era.[4]

Over this long period of political changes the purposes and membership of the Fraternity of San Bartolomeo were transformed. In the thirteenth century the fraternity recruited several thousand members from diverse social and geographical origins. In this first phase of its history, the fraternity served as the institution that linked citizens' concern for the well-being of the less fortunate of San Sepolcro with the members' desire for assistance at death and in the afterlife. Having gained responsibility for charity and memorialization by the beginning of the fourteenth century, the fraternity in its second phase from about 1310 to 1450 received massive amounts of money and property from individuals. This inflow continued until 1340, but thereafter the fraternity lost its ability to attract members or bequests.[5] This chapter will address both the pace of growth and the causes of the decline of popular support. These causes were linked to a transformation of services at death from memorialization of members to recorders of the deaths of all persons and to an increased reliance upon large benefactions. The rectors' labor on behalf of great benefactors is expressed in the numerous documents they or their notaries drafted in administering the benefactions in the testator's interest.

The documentation on members of the fraternity ends in 1309.

Thereafter, there are no extant records of entrance and only two years in which the dead were noted before 1377. Although Largi, writing in 1437, asserts that deaths were noted, he neither recorded entrance of new members, mentioned dues, nor mentioned members after those of 1282. Among the many ancient practices that he wanted to reclaim as means of restoring the fraternity to its former greatness, neither the recruitment of members nor imposing dues for the economic well-being of the fraternity struck him as useful.[6] By the middle of the fourteenth century, therefore, neither members nor dues provided the foundation of the fraternity.

Bequests to the Fraternity

The recruitment of the 1270s marked the apogee of the fraternity as it existed in the thirteenth century. The decline in the Rectors' ability to recruit new members, especially males after 1300, indicates a general faltering of the fraternity in its first phase. In 1437 Largi wrote with melancholy about the decay of the fraternity in his own day, but he was discussing a different lay corporation than that of the thirteenth century. He was clearly witnessing the decline of a second phase in the history of the Fraternity of San Bartolomeo. This second phase began soon after 1310 when income from bequests outpaced the charity promised by incoming members and when the administration of the property of the dead replaced memorialization of all the dead of the fraternity in the church of San Bartolomeo. An examination of the number of bequests to the fraternity over a period of 150 years will permit us to trace its fortunes in its second phase. The number and value of bequests jumped dramatically early in the fourteenth century but declined before the 1348 plague. After a sudden transfusion of gifts because of the great number of deaths in that year, the fraternity continued its slow decline to Largi's day.

Largi explained the development of the fraternity as a matter of testamentary bequests. He interpreted the piety stimulated by St. Francis in the laity of San Sepolcro as fundamentally concerned with property. Gifts of property intended for the Franciscan brothers, which they could not accept because of their vow of poverty, required that the fraternity be founded as a lay holding corporation until the property could be given to the poor or in support of the necessities of the friars ("Specchio," 5v). Largi assumed that the early role of the fraternity and its executives revolved around the legal acts of gaining, holding, and distributing the property of the dead. Actually, by his day, the fraternity primarily served the dead by administering their patrimony. He interpreted the broad membership and memorialization of the first phase of the fraternity's history in light of its role in 1437, as a quasi-state agency that distributed charity to the poor and executed the wills of the wealthy. In its first phase, the fraternity served as an institution of mediation between the living and the dead by concentrating upon memorialization and the distribution to the needy of money and food given by hundreds of members. In this way the fraternity served as an institution of mediation between the living and the dead.

In its second phase, the labor of the fraternity centered on administering the property of the dead. Bishop Pietro of Città di Castello in 1257 granted the rectors the right to collect and, by inference, to hold pious bequests. Largi recognized that this constituted a privilege that underlay the ability of the fraternity to pursue successfully the bequests from benefactors. The episcopal grant permitted the rectors of the fraternity "to collect from every person the accounts, the judged goods [*beni guiditii*], and bequests and everything that one bequeaths to the fraternity" ("Specchio," 6v). Already in 1247 a benefactor had instituted the fraternity as his heir of some goods of an unknown value ("Specchio," 25r). Bishop Pietro's privilege was of little importance before 1300, but thereafter it defined the fraternity's activity.

Such privileges were apparently necessary if the confraternities were to pursue and dispose of assets bequeathed to them. In Florence, for example, the communal government in 1329 granted twelve confraternities the right to elect captains and their representatives, who, for the well-being of the poor and the city, could act to gain the possession of properties bequeathed to these confraternities. The right to dipose of these bequeathed properties was also explicitly granted. And in 1331 the communal officials granted the Florentine confraternities the right to serve as fiduciaries and executors of testaments and reaffirmed their authority to compel the payment of bequests from the other heirs.[7]

Largi's profession as a notary and his long experience in the management and recording of the accounts of confraternities ably prepared him for the task that he believed would aid future leaders of the fraternity. In 1437 he went through the books of the fraternity and recorded each bequest of the preceding two centuries. He found 1,033 bequests from 1247 to 1437 and described them in his "Specchio." Together these 1,033 bequests attest to the fraternity's extraordinary ability to attract the benefactions of the citizens of San Sepolcro. For us today, they provide rare serial documentation of the citizens' aspirations for their souls and the imaginative uses that their patrimony could serve. The bequests document the affection and respect that the citizens had for the fraternity.[8]

The transformation of the thirteenth-century pattern to that of the fourteenth century includes qualitative changes, but the change in quantity points to the revolutionary nature of the transformation. In the thirteenth century the overwhelming proportion of the several thousand members contented themselves as death approached with the anticipation of family remembrance, masses in their parish church, and the broad participation of the Fraternity of San Bartolomeo in their death rituals. Of the approximately three thousand members in the thirteenth century, only fifty-eight made testamentary bequests to the fraternity at their deaths[9] (see Table 3.1).

Participation by numerous members in the commemoration of the dead of the fraternity shriveled in the course of the fourteenth century. Likewise payments of dues do not appear in any account book of the fourteenth century.[10] Instead, the charitable activities, which remained considerable, were sustained by large and small bequests from the testaments of the dead. The fraternity continued to be associated with death and charity but failed to inspire large numbers of men and women to become members. It no longer provided mortuary ceremonies that assured the dying individual of memorialization by a large pro-

TABLE 3.1
Bequests to the Fraternity of San Bartolomeo, 1247–1437

	Years	*Number of Bequests*
	1247–1275	8
	1276–1300	50
	1301–1325	530
	1326–1350	324
	1351–1375	52
	1376–1400	52
	1401–1425	16
	1426–1440	1
Total	1247–1440	1,033

Source: Largi, "Specchio," fols. 25r–69v.

portion of the citizenry of San Sepolcro. In the first decades of the fourteenth century the fraternity increasingly functioned as a recipient of citizens' concern for the poor, which expressed itself through bequests by average and wealthy individuals at their death. The 856 bequests of the first half of the fourteenth century, especially the large number of small and "free" bequests, indicate that the fraternity still had wide support in San Sepolcro.

After 1350 the number of bequests dropped precipitously. Only 104 individuals made bequests to the fraternity from 1351 to 1400; this constitutes only 12 percent of that of the previous fifty years. The greatest loss occurred in the categories of "free" gifts and small donors. Nearly one-third of the bequests rendered money, grain, or property to the fraternity only if one or more persons died before adulthood or without heir. The donors of the second half of the fourteenth century often required services of the administrators of the fraternity, forced them to share the bequeathed property with another ecclesiastical corporation, or compelled them to oversee construction of a memorial in the testator's honor. This role of the fraternity as a corporation performing services for a few deceased testators continued through 1437, when Largi recorded the bequests analyzed here. In the first thirty-seven years of the fifteenth century only seventeen individuals made the fraternity an heir of a bequest.

This overview of nearly two hundred years of the history of the Fraternity of San Bartolomeo reveals wide social participation in the remembrance of the dead on the part of the fraternal members in the thirteenth century. In the fourteenth century, administrators rather than members were the constitutive element of the fraternity. The directors served as executors of the testamentary bequests of a large number of individuals. After 1350 fewer individuals made bequests, and they tightly controlled the disbursement of the patrimony for their souls' well-being through testamentary provisions. Despite the wealth of the fraternity in 1437, Largi lamented both the loss of male participation in the weekly services and of wide participation in donations to the poor. By his day the fraternity served as a state institution more adept at seizing the patrimony of a family through a literal reading of a will in court than as brothers appealing to the charitable instincts of a large number of individuals or persuading the citizens of San Sepolcro that the fraternity could provide memorialization in this world and aid salvation in the next.

The 1,033 bequests from 1247 to 1437 abstracted by Largi enable us to view these changes closely and to gain an idea of the esteem with

TABLE 3.2
Bequests (with Years Specified) to the Fraternity of San Bartolomeo, by Decades, 1240–1439

Decade	*Bequests*	*Decade*	*Bequests*
1240–49	2	1340–49	39
1250–59	2	1350–59	10
1260–69	4	1360–69	8
1270–79	6	1370–79	10
1280–89	15	1380–89	21
1290–99	26	1390–99	9
1300–09	24	1400–09	5
1310–19	55	1410–19	2
1320–29	51	1420–29	2
1330–39	34	1430–39	1

Source: Largi, "Specchio," fols. 25r–69v.

which the people of San Sepolcro held the Fraternity of San Bartolomeo over this period of two hundred years. The sudden increase of bequests in the second decade of the fourteenth century (see Table 3.2) reminds the reader that in 1307–8 over 60 percent of those dying within the fraternity endowed it with gifts of money. Just as emphatic is the sudden drop-off of grants in the 1350s, which can partially be traced to the paucity of deaths after the high mortalities of 1348. It is important to note, however, that the decline in gifts to the fraternity had already begun in the 1330s. That decline continued through the end of Largi's life (1447) except for a temporary recovery in the 1380s. The long-term trend is clear; fewer persons endowed the fraternity with benefactions over the final century of the period under study. Table 3.2 is constructed from Largi's notations of gifts for which he gave specific dates; this decade-by-decade examination confirms and makes more precise the quarter-century analysis. The decade-by-decade examination demonstrates that the fraternity stimulated the greatest interest among the residents of San Sepolcro in the twenty-year period from 1310 to 1330 and that the decline began more than ten years before the Black Plague.

In the thirteenth and early fourteenth centuries, when entrance records indicate the size of the fraternity, it is possible to determine the percentage of individuals who made grants of money or property to their corporation. In 1269 and the 1270s, when entrance records show over one thousand members, only four members in the 1260s and six in the 1270s made bequests to the fraternity. On average, only one of the thousand members made a bequest to the fraternity every two years. It is obvious that in this period the fraternity did not exist as a corporation to oversee the patrimony of its members or to serve as a substitute for the family or heirs at the time of death.

The ratio of bequests to entrants rises through the period of documentation of entrance of members (1269 to 1309). Taking the number of bequests per decade that are dated as a fraction of the number of individuals entering in that decade shows a gradual and steady increase of bequests per member (see Table 3.3). Using figures adjusted for lacunae in the documents and for imprecise dating with proportional reconstruction of entrance and bequests reveals even more vividly the rise in the percentage of members making bequests per entrant (see Table 3.4).

There are no entrance records after 1309, but membership diminished in importance because the total value of periodic dues and mortuary dues paid to the fraternity by members would have been a scant percentage of the value of the ever more numerous bequests. In all probability the administrators of the fraternity soon after 1310 discontinued recording those who promised dues at entrance, continued to disregard the question of who paid or did not pay dues, and eventually ceased noting entrants to the fraternity. At the height of its importance in the first third of the fourteenth century, the fraternity found the chief source of its wealth to be the income from bequests; charity and general expenditures were financed from this source. The fraternity passed from a voluntary association of hundreds of men and women of all social origins and statuses who exchanged support at death through corporate memorialization to a self-perpetuating institution of male officers supported by the communal government with fewer but larger testamentary bequests. Citizens of San Sepolcro did not need to enter

TABLE 3.3
Bequests by Decade as a Percentage of Entering Members

Decade	*Bequests*	*Entering Members*	*Percentage*
1270–1279	6	984	0.6
1280–1289	15	979	1.5
1290–1299	26	946	2.7
1300–1309	24	866	2.8

Source: Largi, "Specchio," fols. 25r–69v.

TABLE 3.4
Bequests by Decade as a Percentage of Entering Members Adjusted for Missing Data

Decade	*Bequests*	*Entering Members*	*Percentage*
1270–1279	7*	1667	0.4
1280–1289	16*	978	1.6
1290–1299	27*	946	2.9
1300–1309	193	940	21.0

Source: Largi, "Specchio," fols. 25r–69v.
*Before 1300 there are three bequests that cannot be dated exactly, and I have distributed one in each of the decades of the 1270s, 1280s, and 1290s.

the fraternity because the institution no longer offered assistance at death except to the poor and those who required its aid in the disposal of their patrimony. The Fraternity of San Bartolomeo transformed its services to the people of San Sepolcro from remembrance widely distributed among the deceased's contemporaries to a form of memorialization expressed most fully in bequests for the construction of a physical or perpetual monument.

The Fraternity as Overseer of Privileged Bequests

Remembrance through testamentary bequests for physical or tangible monuments as a means of withstanding the capriciousness of fortune increased steadily in the two hundred years under consideration. Tangible monuments include chapels, sepulchers, houses for the poor, ecclesiastical vestments, anniversary meals, property given in perpetuity for a specific purpose, and similar permanent endowments. The increase in the number of tangible monuments should not be viewed simply as a function of increasing wealth because there were many testators in the early history of the fraternity who donated sufficiently large sums to sponsor the building of such monuments. For example, Nuole d'Anghiari soon after 1300 left four hundred lire to the fraternity, and Cresti de Piero de Mancino in 1318 left two hundred lire ("Specchio," 62v and 28r). These were "free" grants requiring no specific labor by the priors. The absolute number of bequests for tangible monuments dedicated to the honor and well-being of the

TABLE 3.5
Bequests for Tangible Monuments

Period	*Number of Bequests*
1247–1275	0
1276–1300	3
1301–1315	6
1326–1350	5
1351–1375	1
1376–1400	5
1401–1425	2
Total	22

Source: Largi, "Specchio," fols. 25r–69v.

soul of the testator in perpetuity rose from the thirteenth century into the first quarter of the fourteenth century. Thereafter, the demographic disasters and decline in membership made a continued increase in absolute terms difficult (see Table 3.5). The three bequests from 1276 to 1300 were two small grants for ecclesiastical vestments and altar decorations and one for perpetual meals for the poor and the clergy. Moreover, all three bequests occurred within the last five years of the thirteenth century. Thus the practice of a few fraternity members of endowing monuments did not become important until around 1300, but even in these early instances the objects were small or recurring rather than permanent and substantial architectural monuments. The increase in the number of bequests for tangible memorialization is more striking when seen as a percentage of total bequests (see Table 3.6).

An ever-increasing percentage of bequests for the construction of permanent memorials to the donor's memory compelled the executives of the fraternity to maintain supervision of the monuments and land or houses supporting the endowments and marked the fraternity's passage to mere administrative functions. An analogous change occurred in regard to the number and percentage of substantial bequests to the fraternity over the period 1247 to 1437. This category constitutes gifts larger than ten lire, four or more *staia* of grain, grants of land, houses, vineyards, and annual or perpetual gifts of smaller amounts. An analysis of Largi's data demonstrates the displacement of small and medium-sized grants by substantial ones after 1350 (see Table 3.7).

TABLE 3.6
Bequests for Tangible Monuments as a Percentage of Total Bequests per Quarter Century

Period	*Bequests for Tangible Monuments*	*Total Bequests*	*Percentage*
1247–1275	0	8	0
1276–1300	3	50	6
1301–1325	6	530	1
1326–1350	5	324	1.5
1351–1375	1	52	2
1376–1400	5	52	10
1401–1425	2	16	12.5

Source: Largi, "Specchio," fols. 25r–69v.

The fraternity's loss of its singular role among lay institutions in the commemoration of the dead is confirmed by examining another analytical category. In listing the 1,033 bequests to the fraternity, Largi noted when this lay corporation was compelled to share a property or supervision of the donor's patrimony with another lay and or clerical corporation. In the fourteenth century testators apparently believed that the fraternity would comply with their intentions only if a check

TABLE 3.7
Bequests of Substantial Value as a Percentage of Total Bequests per Quarter Century

Period	*Number of Substantial Bequests*	*Total Bequests*	*Percentage*
1247–1275	3	8	38
1276–1300	14	50	28
1301–1325	153	530	29
1326–1350	146	324	45
1351–1375	22	52	42
1376–1400	21	52	40
1401–1425	9	16	56

Source: Largi, "Specchio," fols. 25r–69v.

were placed on its activity. Table 3.8 shows the number of bequests in which testators required the fraternity to share property or supervision jointly with another ecclesiastical institution.

After 1300 an ever-increasing percentage of testators split ownership or responsibility between the fraternity's administrators and one or more other ecclesiastical entities. The testator's choice of granting shared ownership or responsibility did not arise from a simple desire to distribute wealth to several ecclesiastical institutions. Otherwise, he could have made multiple bequests to specific lay and clerical corporations. Many testators had endowed and others continued to endow five, ten, and often twenty or more separate religious entities.[11] The sharing of patrimony and supervision of property by the Fraternity of San Bartolomeo with other lay confraternities, especially the Confraternity of Santa Maria della Notte, witnesses its displacement as the exclusive lay corporation overseeing death and charity in San Sepolcro.

Despite the general decline of the fraternity from the heights of the one-hundred-year period from 1250 to 1350 and the diminished popular participation or membership, the fraternity still retained important townwide obligations for the distribution of charity and supervision of the burial of the dead. It continued to distribute charity, from 1377 shared in social oversight of all deceased individuals of San Sepolcro, and received a mortuary tax or contribution from nearly every deceased citizen.

In summary, Largi's analysis of the 1,033 bequests made to the fra-

TABLE 3.8
Number and Percentage of Bequests Shared with Another Corporation per Quarter Century

Period	*Number of Shared Bequests or Responsibility*	*Percentage*
1247–1275	0	0
1276–1300	6	12
1301–1325	13	2
1326–1350	26	8
1351–1375	8	15
1376–1400	13	25
1410–1425	7	44

Source: Largi, "Specchio," fols. 25r–69v.

ternity during the period 1247 to 1437 yields the following conclusions: (1) the fraternity received only a few bequests in the second half of the thirteenth century, but the number of bequests rose astronomically in the first third of the fourteenth century; (2) from 1250 to 1350 the fraternity transformed itself from an association of men and women with a variety of occupations who exchanged prayers and memorialization and who corporately achieved God's merit through their charity to the poor into a small, largely female institution run by coopting male administrators; (3) the male administrators distributed charity to the poor from property garnered from testamentary bequests; (4) after 1350 the fraternity lost its singular position among lay religious corporations, neglected to recruit members, received ever fewer bequests especially from the broad spectrum of the citizens of San Sepolcro, and devoted itself increasingly to the administration of bequeathed property; and (5) this property was received from a few large benefactors who required the priors to supervise the physical monuments and perpetual prayers for the souls of the few. By Largi's day the Fraternity of San Bartolomeo functioned as an administrative unit in the town of San Sepolcro overseeing charity and burial and serving the few and the wealthy as skilled administrators of large bequests, frequently those with sensitive or conflicting obligations. Despite his notarial training and the spiritual value he ascribed to the administration of bequests and the distribution of charity, Largi nevertheless recognized that by 1437 the fraternity had fallen from its prestigious position of earlier decades to become a mere lay institution with a modicum of devotional activities and a superfluous number of bureaucratic duties. He saw as well that the priors' performance was jeopardized by a decreasing amount of income.

From Memorialization to Administration

The thirteenth-century book of the dead plays an important role in our understanding of the Fraternity of San Bartolomeo in its halcyon days. The books of the dead of San Sepolcro are no longer extant for the period 1309 to 1377; certainly this constitutes a loss of considerable magnitude given the catastrophic events across those years. The fraternity continued to record its deceased brothers and sisters in this period, as is evident from an inventory that Largi made in his "Specchio." In his assessment of the well-being of the fraternity in 1437, Largi noted the existence in the fraternal archives of a book of the dead, in which were recorded deaths from 1317 to 1367.[12] He also inventoried the book into which deaths were recorded beginning in 1416. This and subsequent registers form a continuous extant series until 1727.

The Fraternity of San Bartolomeo had an essential role in death and memorialization, which the citizens acknowledged through their entrance to the brotherhood and through testamentary bequests. By 1377 the importance of membership had waned and few bequests were being made naming the fraternity as beneficiary. No evidence exists that would indicate that the names of the deceased members of the fraternity were called forth in the church of San Bartolomeo, and Largi does not mention such a practice in his own day. In fact, the seat of the fraternity was moved from that church in the southwest corner of the town to a house near Piazza di Berta on the then via Ghiazzari (now via della Fraternità) close to the center of San Sepolcro, whose central feature was its two large granary rooms. From this house the fraternal administrators dispensed the fraternity's charitable grain and sold grain.[13] The precise date of this transferral is impossible to pinpoint, but Largi's penchant to specify the source of his information permits us to estimate the date to be just before 1320 or soon thereafter.[14] His account of the purchase of the house indicates the transformation of the fraternity that occurred around 1320. The priors and men of the fraternity decided they needed "a particular place" or residence, where they could "secretly draw forth the necessary facts."[15] This house of the priors had no chapel or altar and served as a place for debating issues. The relocation separated the administrative from the liturgical activities and the executives from the members. The traditional service in the church of San Bartolomeo ceased being the defining activity of the fraternity.

This change in the focal point of the fraternity's activities was part of several fundamental transformations occurring in the second decade of the fourteenth century. The years from 1311 to 1320 witnessed the sudden increase of bequests, probably more in that decade than any other, which vastly expanded the administrative labors of the executives. Also at this time, the name of the executives was changed from rectors to priors.[16] The implications of the name change are profound. The prior of the fraternity in the thirteenth century had been the priest who officiated at the monthly service at the church of San Bartolomeo, but at some point in the fourteenth century, the prior-priest disappears from documentation. The acquisition of the new name by the executives of the fraternity occurred in the decade of the 1310s and was part of the process by which the lay leaders achieved a sacral quality necessary to carry on their relations with the dead and oversee their property. A final change was that the services in the church of San Bartolomeo were attended primarily by women. Largi recounted that down to his day the "brigata" of the fraternity continued to go to the church of San Bartolomeo but asserts that women alone made up the "brigata." And there is no mention of any memorialization of the dead.[17]

The new administrative activities of the priors are evident in the account books of the decade 1311 to 1320.[18] In the taking of rents, buying and selling of property, haggling over the proper care of agricultural lands, seeking bequests, renting land, and interpreting testaments, the priors acquired great power. In a town where St. Francis had preached and the Franciscans maintained a male priory, a parish church, and three large female convents, the priors' daily involvement with property inevitably detracted from their ability to express a spirituality of rejection of property and worldly involvement. As an alternative to the Franciscan view of property, Largi, in time, elevated these very involvements into a justification for administrative activities in the interest of the poor and the dead.[19]

An idea of the daily routine of the priors can be gained by examining their role as executors of the testament of Donna Nobile, widow of Guido da Vierno.[20] She died sometime before May 19, 1317, when the priors, Angelluccio de Salvucio d'Angelo, Mucio da Cacca, and Cescho de Milionure, sold a house for 108 lire, which Donna Nobile had bequeathed to the fraternity. The priors had already collected the rent on the house before that date and sold some possessions of Donna Nobile for a total of 15 lire. On July 6, they handed over to the Franciscans of San Sepolcro 50 lire willed by the testatrix for the building of a dormitory. The priors also had to pay 5 lire to secure through the Franciscans' procurator an agreement that Donna Nobile's intent had been met. This agreement had to be notarized in a document called a *quietatio*.[21] The next day, following the provisions of Donna Nobile's testament, the priors distributed various sums, including 99 lire to three Franciscan convents, a small sum to two nuns at one convent, one soldo each to 101 nuns at three Franciscan convents, and small amounts to the brothers at the Augustinian convent, to a priest, and to a layman. A notary was present at at least two of these transactions to draft the settlements. After July 26 of that same year the next trio of priors, in conformity with the will of Donna Nobile, gave 2 lire to the Franciscans of San Sepolcro for building and ornamentation of their church, on November 7, 10 lire to a female, on February 15, 1318, 50 lire to the friars of St. Augustine to be converted into a chalice, liturgical books, and other ecclesiastical items, on December 18, 1318, 25 lire to the Camaldolese abbot, on an unspecified date 54 lire to the Franciscans in the diocese of Città di Castello, on an unspecified date 50 lire to the poor to be distributed by the priors, on an unspecified date 25 lire to the fraternity to support a crusade to the Holy Land, and on July 24, 1318, 46 lire to the Franciscan priests at the convent in Assisi, as well as four other smaller sums distributed over that period. In nine of the fifteen distributions, the contract of *quietatio* had to be written. After complying with these twenty-three specific bequests and consulting with the guardian of the Franciscans to determine what to do with the remainder of the value of Donna Nobile's estate, the priors agreed to divide it among the Franciscans of San Sepolcro, who received 15 lire, to an individual in the monastery of Citerna 3 lire, and finally to the poor to be distributed through the fraternity 132 lire. The wearisome chores performed by two sets of priors over two years to meet this will led to twenty-six distributions of a total of 754 lire.

Rents and Charity

The execution of Donna Nobile's testament was relatively extensive but without disputes and contained no bequest for perpetual prayers or distributions. By definition, a bequest with perpetual distributions caused the priors endless administrative duties. Largi recounted the testament of Muccio del Viva, called Muccio the Keymaker, who willed a relatively simple grant of twenty-four *staia* of grain spread over the six years following his death. He made his young son his universal heir, but if this Pietro died without heir, Muccio's substantial agricultural estate in Villa Abocha would pass to four women and the children of a fifth. Little is known about these recipients except that they were not widows. Muccio required that each of the five and their heirs give from their yearly harvests in perpetuity fifteen *staia* of grain (probably wheat) and three *staia* of oats to the fraternity. The priors of the fraternity were in turn obligated by the will to sell the grain and buy clothing that was to be distributed to the poor in the interests of the soul of the testator Muccio.[22]

Largi focused attention on this estate because of its great value. Largi scoured the account books of the preceding 150 years for information on Muccio and his estate. He found that in 1320 the priors noted the death of the son, Pietro de Muccio, which activated the conditional provisions of the testament. Largi tabulated the total amount of grain and oats brought to the residency of the fraternity by the five women and their heirs: 50 *staia* of grain and 24 of oats by 1322 and 550 *staia* of grain and 336 *staia* of oats by 1343. Largi calculated that 1,026 *staia* of wheat and 545 *staia* of oats had been sent through 1360 by the heirs of Muccio's land, thereby overpaying 26 *staia* in wheat and underpaying 55 *staia* in oats. Wheat brought a higher price, and thus the occupants of the land had certainly given the fraternity sufficient value. In the 1360s the army of Città di Castello invaded and occupied San Sepolcro; as a result, ownership of the land at Abocha changed. For whatever reason, the occupants failed to meet their obligations to the fraternity through 1373, and the notaries of the fraternity recorded their deficiencies. By 1374 the priors had successfully encouraged the cultivators of the land to make up these deficiencies; they again surpassed the terms of the testament in grain and fell short for oats.

In the late fourteenth and early fifteenth centuries the possessors of the land created more problems for the priors, and if Largi's account reflects accurately the labor of the notaries, the priors lost interest in these accounts. One hundred years after the death of Muccio the possessors of land had turned over nearly 2,300 *staia* of grain and nearly 1,200 *staia* of oats, a shortfall of approximately 200 and 300 *staia* respectively. After 1420 the priors had difficulty compelling the possessors of the land to pay the yearly assessments. With each of the three possessors, the priors agreed to accept payment of the rents in grain during the 1420s, probably with the priors giving a term of years for the rents. Moreover, they absolved one possessor in 1427 from all delinquent payments and reduced his obligation in the following eight years to three *staia* of wheat annually. The renter apparently had another substantial debt to the fraternity by 1431 because he was released "for the love of God" from all deficiencies except 5 *staia*. Another possessor had his assessment diminished and his past deficiencies forgotten in 1429 because a fire destroyed the *palazzo* and several other buildings on the estate. An equally grievous circumstance faced the third possessor, and the priors lowered his annual payments. Each of the three handed over small amounts of grain in the early 1430s, but there is no record for the years just before 1437, when Largi made this detailed account of Muccio's patrimony.

Largi's account suggests several developments in the history of the fraternity. We may assume that what occurred with this property paralleled that which occurred with other less substantial properties because Largi wrote to inform subsequent priors of the condition of the fraternity and its properties ("Specchio," 4r). Moreover, the account conforms with Largi's concern with rents discussed below. In the decades immediately following the death of the testator, the cultivators of the land paid their assessments and thereby provided the financial basis for the fraternity to dispense cloth and food to the poor even through the demographic disasters of the mid-fourteenth century. By the early fifteenth century the possessors of the land became less able or willing to bring the grains to the fraternity's granaries, and the priors generally accepted the diminution of the claims of Muccio's soul on his former property. A phrase in one of the narrations of the priors' acceptance of the smaller payments suggests a significant shift in the administration of testators' property. The priors released one possessor of Muccio's property from nearly all past and future obligations to the fraternity in 1431 "for the love of God." This phrase is found repeatedly in the documents of the time to represent a charitable impulse or practice performed usually for the poor; here, it is a release from customary obligations because of the renter's unfortunate circumstances. The priors of the fraternity acted as the agent of the deceased and were the procurators for the poor in the original testament; it is evident, however, that they were abrogating the intent of the testator and depriving the poor of their charity. But the priors here performed the central purpose of their office—to mediate between the dead and the living—and would claim that the poor were uppermost in their minds. In this instance the cultivators of the land were themselves the poor; their poverty inspired the influx of the Holy Spirit into the minds of the priors. As Largi stated, the impoverished tenants of land held by the fraternity stirred *misericordia,* that divine quality of merciful love, in the hearts of the priors, who, as a result, lowered the annual rents.[23]

These accounts suggest that the priors had to act as a coercive magistracy in a variety of enforcement procedures as the agents of deceased souls and the protectors of the poor of Christ. The priors often had to compel heirs to report bequests to the fraternity, then to hand over the movable property or entrance to immovable property, to continue payments over decades and centuries after the death of the testator, and often to settle disputes between co-heirs. The communal governors and subsequent rulers of San Sepolcro recognized the priors' need for this coercive authority and granted them privileges and assistance. Largi was aware of the importance of the communal legislation that lent the priors both moral and coercive authority. He extracted from the communal statutes of 1430, which he had copied for the new government of the papacy, all grants of power and assistance to the fraternity.[24] Several examples demonstrate the scope of the priors' authority. Most important, communal laws facilitated the ready transferral of property from the dead to the fraternity. In all testaments in which the fraternity had an interest, the heirs were compelled to pay or hand over bequests within ten days from the time the rectors specified ("Specchio," 7v). Furthermore, if a citizen or noncitizen within the district of San Sepolcro willed any bequest to the poor without specifying the agency to distribute the donation, such as a Franciscan friar or a Camaldolese monk, the Fraternity of San Bartolomeo received and distributed the money to the poor. The *podestà* of the commune and his courts were compelled by statute to aid the rectors in gaining these and other bequests ("Specchio," 7v–8r). Again the *podestà* and his courts were to assist the rectors in maintaining control and ownership of land and other forms of property gained through testament but for which they lacked written proof of ownership. The law forbade any citizen from challenging the fraternity's claim to these properties in the past, present, and future ("Specchio," 9r).

Its involvement with property rights and its coercive power added a great deal to the effective management of the fraternity, but it also lessened the priors' ability, in a society where St. Francis's message remained persuasive, to make claims on the charity of the vast majority of citizens of San Sepolcro. The men and women of the town recognized that the patrimony of the fraternity, supplemented occasionally by a valuable bequest from a member of the elite, was sufficient to maintain the minimum memorialization of the poor at death and charity in life.

Insight may be gained from the accounts of the testament of Muccio because of the size of his original bequest and his requirement that the fraternity sell his property's wheat and oats. This and similar bequests as well as gifts of arable land brought substantial amounts of grain and land to rent. The priors distributed a large proportion of this grain periodically in the thirteenth century; Largi asserted in 1437 that essentially the only remaining charitable practice of the thirteenth century was the distribution of money on Saturday ("Specchio," 6r). But as was reflected in Muccio's case and many others in which grain and other agricultural products supported perpetual prayers or other devotional and charitable acts, the priors had to sell bequeathed grain for money. They thus had to enter the marketplace, and the fraternity was a major merchandiser of grain in San Sepolcro for centuries. The exact year the priors entered the grain market is not clear; in 1316 the fraternity received 154 *staia* of grain per year as rent from the land bequeathed to the corporation. By that date or soon thereafter the fraternity began to sell grain in the market of San Sepolcro. This would also be close to the time when the fraternity bought a residence, essentially a granary, in the center of San Sepolcro. By the 1460s the notary of the fraternity kept a weekly account of the price for grain charged by the priors in the marketplace.[25]

Largi was alarmed in 1437 by the fraternity's deplorable relationship with its tenants and its lack of income. He clearly wished to abandon the older policy of treating the poor tenants with charity. In the fraternity's early history, Largi wrote, it was sufficient for the servants of the priors to go once a year to the tenants to receive the money rents, and the grain rents were brought willingly to the fraternity's granaries. Now, however, he wrote that the fraternity's officials had "to fight all year" to gain the rents from the cultivators of the fraternity's land ("Specchio," 22v). These tenants, who "almost always are poor," succeeded in lowering the rents they ultimately paid by appealing to the *misericordia* of the priors. Largi's remedy for these disastrous practices began with more efficient administration on the part of the priors, including more careful scrutinizing of prospective tenants to eliminate any who might be impoverished. One means of achieving this was to require the tenants to post security. To attract safe tenants, he admitted, it might be necessary to lower the rents on land.[26]

Largi's discussion of the fraternity's problems with efficient management of its landed property and his remedy for these problems illustrates the dilemma that faced the administrators of the confraternities as they sought to maintain their income. In the demographic surpluses and subsequent high mortalities of the fourteenth century a large number of benefactors provided sufficient land and income to meet that age's conception of the charitable needs of the poor. If Largi's analysis of the problems of administration of the fraternity's property was accurate, the large endowment of land led the fraternal administrators to regard the renting of land as an opportunity to exercise charity. By 1437 the management of property inspired by charitable concern for the agricultural tenants no longer permitted the priors to perform the customary charity to the poor. Perhaps the less than rigorous enforcement of the provisions of the older testaments and the loose supervision of the older property discouraged a large number of new benefactors. The decline of property bequests lessened the amount of income available to the priors to maintain their annual obligations to the poor. In hindsight, the decline of the fraternity can also be traced to the failure of the priors to inspire "the love of God" in the dying; the average citizens of the town no longer conceived of the fraternity as the institution most adept at realizing their souls' eternal bliss.

The Fraternity's Death Tax

Despite the changes around 1320 and the increased administrative labor required of the priors, the association of the fraternity with death remained intimately linked in the minds of the citizens of San Sepolcro. No longer accepting pledges of variable "charity" as dues for membership, the fraternity at some point did begin to collect a mortuary tax from nearly everyone buried in the town. An analysis of the book of the dead that begins in 1377 demonstrates that the fraternity was involved in nearly every burial. Each entry in this book of the dead contains the given or Christian name of the deceased in addition to his or her father's and at times grandfather's name, the place of origin if not residing in San Sepolcro, whether the individual was a child, widow, poor, titled, cleric, or nun, and whether death occurred at a hospital. The entry always included the date of burial. For example, in 1400 "Biagio de Mateo de Pichi died on the aforementioned day [September 13, 1400]. He was buried at San Francesco." The given names of females and children are frequently omitted, as in the following examples from 1388: "The wife of Simone de Mangia died on day 28 of June, and she was buried at San Francesco"; "The son of Vanni de Paulo de Maestro died on day 28 of June, and he was buried at San Francesco."[27] The notary occasionally made additional comments concerning the deceased if peculiar circumstances surrounded the death or if the individual had made a bequest to the fraternity. The phrase "We have the wax" is often recorded.[28] After a burial in San Sepolcro one of the four servants of the fraternity went to the burial church and took the remains of one candle.

These candle remnants (*moccholi*) were brought to the residency of the fraternity and placed in a cupboard reserved for that purpose.[29] The notary of the book of the dead at times writes instead "for the love of God" or "We lent them the candles," symbolizing grants by the fraternity to the poor of the community and others who for some reason could not pay for their bodies' illumination. For example, on October 2, 1389, the fraternity lent a nonresident soldier candles for his burial mass at the priory of San Niccolò, presumably performed by the Camaldolese monks there as charity. Moreover, Largi noted that in an earlier book of the dead, "It appears that the priors lent to the dead the *palio* [sepulchral pall] and candles and received from the deceased individual from ten soldi up to forty soldi."[30] The extant books of the dead confirm Largi's observation that in one year—1400—the fraternity's notary did enter these sums. Two lire (forty soldi) would certainly be greater than the value of a candle end; therefore, in addition to taking the remains of one candle for each dead person of the town, the fraternity may have sold one or more candles to each of the dead in 1400. Largi's apparent surprise at the large sums of money recorded next to the names of the dead in that year indicates that by his day the fraternity probably no longer sold candles for the dead or lent the pall. The fraternity gained a high percentage of its annual income for a time from candle sales and reselling candle remains. The burials of nearly all the men and women of San Sepolcro yielded a small amount of wax that the fraternity sent to a *ceraiuolo* (vendor of candles), who melted the *moccholi* and then sold candles to the fraternity. The priors distributed these candles to the poor as charity or sold them for profit.

An inventory of the fraternity's possessions in 1405 includes all the practical and ceremonial objects necessary for the burial of the dead: two funeral palls, a "vermilion pall for the dead with a well-finished crozier" and a "green pall for the dead with a crozier," as well as two "coffins for the dead" and four large double candles on poles.[31] One may imagine a dead person being carried from his home to the burial church on the fraternal bier, covered with the fraternal pall with decorated bars, and accompanied by the four priors, each carrying double candles raised on poles. But for whom was this service performed? It is clear that the fraternity furnished the poor with candles and the pall, but did it provide this honor for all those inscribed on its books of the dead? If so, the priors accompanied each citizen of San Sepolcro to his or her burial because by 1380 the fraternity's notary was recording all the dead, young and old, of the town. The presence of the priors in the funeral procession would explain why the fraternity gained the right to one candle from every deceased person in San Sepolcro. Largi, however, did not mention the priors accompanying every deceased person to his or her burial. Moreover, the services of the fraternity, as discussed in Chapter 2, supplemented the family and parish funeral services. The tax of one candle or wax remains derived either from the fraternity providing one candle at the burial or from the custom, already evident in 1307–8, of many deceased members giving the fraternity a gift at their deaths. This voluntary gift of the early fourteenth century had become a mortuary tax by the 1380s and was required of everyone to gain passage from this world. The only exceptions were the poor, who received candles as charity from the fraternity. And the remnants of these borrowed candles were taken by the fraternal servants as the customary tax on death.

The repeated attempts of the ecclesiastical authorities in San Sepolcro to exempt the candles of their subordinates from the claims of the fraternity attest to the value of the *moccholi*. The example of Don Ottaviano well illustrates the authority of the fraternity over this aspect of death. Ottaviano had been the abbot of the Camaldolese monastery at Diciano and died on March 21, 1414, while a resident of San Sepolcro. "As it was according to custom," a lengthy note in the account books of the fraternity reads, "that his body was carried into the church of the abbey of Borgo, and there the solemn office of the dead having been completed, he was buried. And [the fraternity] waited until Saturday to have the candle as it has from the other dead; the abbot [of San Sepolcro] refused to give it." The priors first sent their servant to beseech the abbot, the spiritual authority of San Sepolcro, to permit the fraternity to take the candle. The abbot refused. Then the priors, including Francesco de Largi, plead their case to the abbot with pliant words, "begging him not to take from us the ancient accounts and given to the fraternity by statute and by custom. And he replied that he did not want to give it to us . . . because it was not reasonable." The priors then called a meeting of the notables of San Sepolcro to seek their counsel on how to deal with the abbot's assertion that the statute granting the fraternity the candle lacked validity because it conflicted with clerical immunities. A certain Mastino responded that it countered "custom" for the abbot to take this approach with the commune, considering that "the wax is distributed for the love of God to the poor." The citizens recommended that the priors return to the abbot and report the counsel of the citizens and ask again for the candle. More was at stake here than the candle of Don Ottaviano; the priors feared losing both prestige and a customary right to an important source of income. The abbot finally heeded the priors' renewed plea, and, following an apology for his earlier behavior, he "gladly" gave the candle. The fraternity received the candle of Don Ottaviano, but the writer noted that subsequent priors faced similar situations, which, he said, have brought "evil to the House, to God, and to the world."[32]

The financial accounts of the fraternity yield an idea of the income derived from the *moccholi*. In 1443, an average year, apothecaries purchased from the fraternity on six different dates nearly four hundred pounds of old wax for 192 lire. The *moccholi* returned a regular and assured income that underlay the administration of the several responsibilities of the fraternity. The communal authorities recognized its need for an assured income. As Largi hinted when he noted that every dead resident of San Sepolcro paid a small death tax and as the priors claimed in their dispute over Don Ottaviano's candle, the commune by statute guaranteed a portion of the wax of those dying in San Sepolcro to the fraternity. A priest who said mass in the fraternity's chapel was given authority over the wax. He stated that he oversaw the wax "that pertains to my hands from the bodies which are buried in the church of Borgo; these churches, according to the statutes of Borgo, ought to give to the fraternity one candle from every body which is buried in these churches."[33]

A portion of the accumulated candles was refashioned by the candlemakers of San Sepolcro for the officials of the fraternity. For example, on May 28, 1442, the priest who kept the wax handed over thirty pounds to the candlemakers for four double candles and five tapers for the priors and rector, one taper for the notary, and three tapers for the servants of the fraternity. The officials of the fraternity were endowed with candles for their honor in funerals and processions generally. The overseer of the wax periodically dispensed portions for liturgical purposes, including forty-seven pounds for the Corpus Christi festival of 1443 and the wax that was part of his salary as officiating priest in the Chapel of Sant'Antonio in Santa Maria della Pieve.[34] This chapel came to the fraternity in a bequest that gave the priors the right to choose its priest; the chapel became the central focus of the priors' liturgical activity. By 1407 this chapel housed, and the fraternity had authority over, the extraordinary Volto Santo (wooden sculpture of Christ) that has been the focal point of disputes and worship in San Sepolcro for five centuries.[35] The fraternity's rights over this chapel and the Volto Santo in the church of Santa Maria della Pieve adds another element to the fraternity's move from the early center of its activities in the church of San Bartolomeo. Administrative activities had been moved to the center of the town in the early fourteenth century, and the liturgical services for the priors were moved to the chapel of the Volto Santo in the early fifteenth century.

Though the priest of this chapel in his accounts of the fraternity's wax does not mention extracting *moccholi* for the poor, the books of the dead show definitely that the fraternity lent the candles to the poor as a charitable act. The remainder of the candles from the office of the dead went to the clergy of the burial church. Thus the one candle taken by the fraternity was a mortuary tax imposed on the dead in San Sepolcro, so it could continue its labor for the poor and infirm of the community. When exactly the tax was imposed is less clear, but it probably occurred in the middle of the fourteenth century and was based on the early voluntary gift of a candle or money at death by members to the fraternity. This tax, together with the lending of the fraternal pall and the participation of the priors in the funeral processions, represents a means of socializing the burial expenses of the poor. But the imposition of the tax bespeaks the vast distance the fraternity had traveled from the thirteenth century, when, as a voluntaristic society, it welcomed all living and dead, poor and rich, and gave memorialization to all at death.

The rectors of the fraternity in the thirteenth century recorded the names of the members of the corporation as part of the process of memorializing the dead. In the course of the fourteenth century communal statute confirmed the ancient practice of giving the fraternity candle remains from each person's burial mass. Thus in both instances the purpose of recording the names of the dead was religious. The recording of all the dead of a community was in 1377 just beginning to become a practice in a few Italian towns and cities. Arezzo has a book of the dead from the fourteenth century, but, like the Fraternity of San Bartolomeo, the Arezzo Confraternity of Santa Maria dei Laici noted initially the deaths of its members, not all the citizens of the town.[36] The book of the dead in the communes of the fourteenth and fifteenth centuries have served various purposes, and attempts to find one explanation of their purpose have proved fruitless thus far.[37] In San Sepolcro the purposes changed radically over the course of the fourteenth century from memorialization of the deceased of one lay corporation to a method of accounting for the tax of one candle for all the dead of the town. Certainly by 1400, the fraternity's recording of the dead led to a third purpose. The communal government by statute required the priors to inform the authorities of the approach of the bubonic plague and to remind the communal officials to initiate the extraordinary measures found in this legislation.[38] The recording of the dead of San Sepolcro endowed the priors with the lugubrious knowledge of an increase in the number of deaths. For example, in 1400 the first six months had witnessed an average of 10 deaths per month, but in July the notary of the fraternity recorded 64 deaths, followed by 178 in August, 193 in September, and 100 in October.[39] Deaths totaled 660 that year, including more than 300 children. The pattern of a sudden increase in the number of deaths with the onset of summer was repeated in 1417.[40] As required by the legislation, the fraternity's notary recorded the specific laws for the crisis and the standard mortuary laws that remained in effect. On receiving this terrifying information, the vicar of San Sepolcro was to instruct the town criers to traverse the town's territory shouting the crisis legislation and, at least by inference, the presence of the plague.[41]

The Fraternity's Distribution of Cloth

Largi intended his criticism of the priors' practices and his dirge of the fraternity's decline to stir a renewal of interest in the fraternity. He may have overstated the fraternity's decline, but his pessimistic view is confirmed by the decrease in the distribution of cloth to the poor. The statutes of 1269 provided for distribution of wool in early November and linen in the spring (lines 51–53). There is no estimate of the quantity of cloth distributed until the end of the fourteenth century, when the fraternity purchased and distributed substantial amounts. Largi noted the existence of four books of vestments of the poor, in which the officials of the fraternity recorded the distribution of clothing to the poor from 1315 to 1437. The last book of this series, which begins in 1411, is extant; it and several random entries in the account books permit us to draw the dimensions of the fraternity's charity in cloth.

The priors made prodigious purchases of cloth for distribution around 1400. In the priory year of 1397–98 the priors purchased more than 600 lire worth of cloth.[42] In 1407–8 the priors paid the cloth merchants 365 lire and the following year 469 lire. Purchases continued to decline at least through 1416–17, when 447 lire worth of cloth were acquired.[43]

The mechanisms for distributing the cloth are never explicitly discussed. Each of the priors of the fraternity distributed cloth to individuals judged needy.[44] The priors purchased large pieces of cloth from the wool merchants; for example, in 1407–8 they paid 10.5 lire for 6 *braccia* (a *braccio* equals approximately twenty-five inches) of cloth.[45] Most of the dated distributions occurred in December, thus signaling that the cloth was wool. There is no explicit notice of distribution of linen in the spring as the 1269 statutes had provided. The purchase of the large pieces of wool implies that the priors handed out new or least refashioned cloth, not simply secondhand clothing. By 1417 there were four priors, one for each quarter, and probably each distributed in his own quarter. Each distributed an equal amount of cloth, a hundred *braccia* in that year.[46] The 400 *braccia* distributed in 1417 were bought by the fraternity for approximately 267 lire. This decline from the nearly 600 lire worth of cloth (approximately 400 *braccia*) purchased in 1397–98 to the early years of the 1400s, when purchases averaged around 400 lire, is indicative of a continuing downward trend. This decline is difficult to chart in detail because the register of cloth distributed to the poor has several lacunae. From 1434 to 1449, the notaries recorded distributions in only a few years, and even these are seldom complete. The two priors whose distributions are recorded in 1437 averaged 74 *braccia,* so we may assume that at most 300 *braccia* were given to the poor in that year. In 1440 again two priors made distributions with an average of 60 *braccia* each, which resulted in a total of 240 *braccia*. In 1450 the total cloth distribution was 241 *braccia*. The extant evidence confirms that the decline in cloth purchases continued at least through the middle of the fifteenth century. Largi's computations point to the same conclusion. In calculating the yearly expenses of the fraternity in 1437 he included an entry of 350 lire for "clothing for the poor every year commonly according to custom." This sum would have purchased approximately 233 *braccia* of common wool cloth.[47] The 233 *braccia* are consistent with the totals for 1440 and 1450 discussed above.

The Wealth of the Fraternity

Bequests of property and the mortuary tax brought the fraternity vast wealth. Largi's lament on its decline should not lead one to conclude that the fraternity had lost all its authority and wealth by the fifteenth century. The testators of San Sepolcro had endowed the fraternity with agricultural land in the course of the fourteenth century, which led the priors to assume a permanent presence in the weekly grain market of the town. A census of the land held by religious corporations of San Sepolcro from the 1440s reveals three great landholders: the Fraternity of San Bartolomeo, the abbot of the Camaldolese abbey, and the Confraternity of Santa Maria della Notte[48] (see Table 3.9).

Each of these corporations held more land than any other known landowner of San Sepolcro.[49] Much of the fraternity's land, as well as that of the other religious corporations, derived from bequests and

TABLE 3.9

Land Held by Religious Corporations of San Sepolcro in the 1440s (amounts in tavole; *values rounded off to nearest lira)*

Corporation	*Number of Pieces of Land*	Tavole *of Land*	*Assessed Value*
Camaldolese Abbey of San Giovanni	96	25,562	33,435
Confraternity of Santa Maria della Notte	101	17,437	32,998
Fraternity of San Bartolomeo	108	22,287	24,217
Mendicant Church of Santa Maria dei Servi	22	5,847	–
Church of Santa Maria della Pieve (secular clergy)	13	4,172	–
Santa Maria Novella	16	3,927	–
Church of San Bartolomeo del Fondaccio, including its fabric's wealth (secular clergy)	19	2,289	–
Confraternity of Santa Maria della Misericordia	13	2,094	5,877

Source: AC, SS, 32, reg. 173, fol. 77r–82v, 107r–114r, 89r–96v, 146r–147v, 104r–105r, 167r–v, 152r–153v, 174r–175r.

Note: I have included figures only for the richer corporations. The *tavola* is equal to 144 square feet.

carried obligations to support perpetual prayers, to maintain and administer chapels, hospitals, and the land itself, and to dispense specific amounts of charity to the poor. Thus the land required efficient administration to assure a continuing income. Striking evidence of this need is the number of registers devoted exclusively to recording the rents of the fraternity—five such large books from 1322 to 1437 ("Specchio," 23v). Largi summarized the rents due to the fraternity in 1316. In that year thirty-two individuals paid rents totaling 222 lire and 154 *staia* of grain. Accepting Fanfani's estimate of the value of a *staio* at one and one-half lire would mean the fraternity's yearly income from agricultural land totaled approximately 450 lire.[50] The number of rents climbed for at least two decades thereafter so that the amount calculated here is in no sense the maximum received after 1316. Though there is no explicit evidence on annual income from rents, it is clear from the numerous bequests thereafter that the money and grain rents continued to grow into the 1340s. At some point in the second half of the fourteenth century, income began to deteriorate as the number of bequests declined drastically, as several of the fixed-term grants of rents or grain expired, and as the fraternity sold land that had no specific prohibition against any form of alienation. Moreover, rents on land declined considerably with the drop of population resulting from the Black Death of 1348.[51]

Given Largi's penchant for data and his concern for the well-being of the fraternity, it is not surprising that he attempted to calculate the corporation's solvency by comparing income with expenses. He had already enumerated the bequests, rents, possessions, and even the forgotten sums kept in the account books for the next crusade to the Holy Land. His calculations demonstrate that the fraternity's fourteenth-century bequests provided nearly enough income for the priors to meet their payments to the poor, whose numbers may have been diminished by the great mortalities.

In 1437 the fraternity had three sources of income, according to Largi's summary. Before examining the actual income, it is instructive to note possible sources omitted by Largi, such as dues from members or donations from the citizens of San Sepolcro. The lack of information on income from dues or donations confirms my earlier comments on the decline of their importance. Fundamental was the loss of the fraternity's ability to spark the charitable impulse in the vast majority of individuals of the town. The first two sources of income were from bequests; the fraternity received 253 lire and 239.5 *staia* of grain ("Specchio," 133r). Using again Fanfani's estimate of the value of one *staio* of grain at 1.5 lire, the income from these sources totaled 613 lire. Two of the fourteen money bequests and nine of the twenty-nine grain bequests indicate no income. Thus in approximately 25 percent of the bequests from which the fraternity should have been receiving value, Largi could not find any income. The failure of the priors to maintain these incomes and their records appalled Largi and led him to write his "Specchio." But even Largi's monumental accounting energies were not sufficient to incorporate all of the fraternity's income. He noted a third source, the sale of candles taken at burials, but failed to calculate its worth. As we have seen above from financial records for 1443, the fraternity received 192 lire from the sale of candle ends. Combining Largi's estimates of the income from money and grain rents with the wax account yields a total of 800 lire annual income, a modest sum for the fraternity's numerous charitable responsibilities around 1437.

The annual expenses of the fraternity totaled 890 lire.[52] Largi, however, did not give totals for either income or expenses, probably because he regarded both as general estimates rather than exact amounts. The deficit of 90 lire expresses in numerical form Largi's concern for the poor financial state of the fraternity in his day. And his opinion that charity to the poor was the expenditure to suffer from the fraternity's feeble financial state was doubtless accurate. This expense, in fact, constituted the largest outflow of money and could be diminished, whereas the other expenditures were set by specific bequests. An analysis of the expenses of the fraternity in 1437 reveals that the priors spent relatively small amounts on the administration of charity and on wealth given to the clergy, approximately 25 percent of the annual expenses.[53] The bulk of the expenses of the fraternity, nearly 75 percent, constituted direct alms to the poor. The largest single expenditure was the 350 lire for cloth; the second largest expense was the 5 lire given every Saturday for "the small plate for the poor according to custom" and was 260 lire annually.[54] These distributions of cloth and money constituted the priors' most visible and continuous eleemosynary activity. The cloth was distributed once or twice a year and the few soldi for each poor person on Saturday; the remainder of the gifts to the poor were integrated into the annual liturgical festivals. At Christmas and Easter the priors purchased 30 lire worth of meat and gave it to the poor. On the festivals of San Bartolomeo in August and San Jacomo and San Christopher in July, the priors also gave out meat, wine, fruit, money, and sugar to both the poor and the clergy. This expenditure amounted to 49 lire.

These accounts of 1437–38 show the priors of the Fraternity of San Bartolomeo, despite Largi's gloomy portrait, maintaining an active presence in San Sepolcro. Ignoring the rents and possible income not collected by the priors, we may judge that the monies collected were administered efficiently, but the fraternity had been surpassed by Largi's day in the quantity of charity given to the poor by the Confraternity of Santa Maria della Notte. Largi did not lament this subordination to the *laudesi* brotherhood, though he was in a position to make such a comparison. Rather, he contrasted the Fraternity of San Bartolomeo of his day with the fraternity in earlier times, when it garnered contributions from masses of individuals in the Upper Tiber

Valley and distributed incalculable amounts of charity to the poor of San Sepolcro.

The Social Composition of the Fraternity's Priory

We have seen that the rectors of the thirteenth-century fraternity represented the broad spectrum of the membership of the fraternity, which itself represented all but the poorest urban and rural social groups. When membership fell dramatically in the course of the fourteenth century, the priors virtually became the fraternity. An analysis of the social composition of the members is neither possible nor meaningful. It is possible, however, to gain a clear idea of which social groups in San Sepolcro sent their representatives to the priorate of the Fraternity of San Bartolomeo. The insignificance of membership and the recruitment of priors from the most prestigious social groups of the town casts in stark light the alienation from the fraternity of the vast majority of the residents of San Sepolcro. A list of names drawn from the dominant legislative body of the communal government of San Sepolcro enables us to establish the political class of the town in the 1390s. The lord of San Sepolcro, Carlo Malatesta, ordered in 1390 that a New Council (Nuovo Conseglio) be established composed of 300 men, who were divided into fifteen groups; each group was led by a "head of the list" (*capolista*), who was drawn from one of the great families of the town. Each group had 10 men from the east side of the town and 10 men from the west side. San Sepolcro was at the low point of its demographic history in the 1390s and contained from 900 to 1,000 households within its walls. Thus the New Council directly represented approximately one out of three of the town's households. It was the chief legislative body and, in the absence of Carlo Malatesta, nominated the governing executive. A member remained in or eligible for the New Council until death. On January 1, 1391, the chancellor of San Sepolcro recorded the names of the 300 men of the New Council and through 1398 inscribed 53 others, who entered on the occasion of the deaths of several of the original 300. These 353 men constituted at the widest level the participants in the political life of the town in the 1390s.[55]

The 353 men of the New Council of San Sepolcro were drawn from the greater families of the town with a few craftsmen, whose names frequently appeared toward the bottom of the lists. The traditionally influential families sent several members to the New Council and occupied the places of honor as the *capoliste*. Led by the Pichi and Graziani families, who had eight and seven members on the New Council, the fourteen leading families garnered 50 of the 353 places on the New Council and 12 of the 15 *capoliste*.[56] Most of these same families—the Pichi, Dotti, Bifolco, Bercordati, and Ugucci—were represented as priors for the fraternity in the late fourteenth century. To form a more precise idea of the degree to which the families and the political men of San Sepolcro participated in directing the fraternity, a sample has been constructed of the priors of the fraternity from July 1388 to July 1400.[57] In this twelve-year period, 45 different men served in the priory. Of these, 24 sat on the New Council. Many of the remaining 21 possessed some other distinguishing mark or membership. Three of the 21 who failed to receive nomination to the New Council were either judges or notaries, and another was the son of a judge or notary. A second group of 4 priors had fathers, brothers, and, in one case, a grandfather on the New Council. Finally, a third group of 4 priors was drawn from the inner group of the most prestigious families. Two Dotti, a Pichi, and a Carsidoni were priors but not councilmen. Indeed, these three families placed 9 members in the priory of the fraternity in this twelve-year period. Thus 36 of the 45 priors had some mark of political or social distinction. Only 9 priors lacked any such sign.

The prestige and power of those who held the office of prior in the late fourteenth century may be better grasped by comparing them with the general population. As stated above, approximately one-third of the households of San Sepolcro were represented in the New Council, and over 50 percent of the priors sat in the communal legislative council; if the four with a close family member on the New Council are added, the percentage rises to 62. The highest honor for those on the New Council was to be chosen as a *capolista*. Three fraternal priors served as *capoliste,* again members of the Bifolco, Dotti, and Bercordati families. The high percentage of priors serving as political advisers to the communal government in the New Council, and at the top of its lists, demonstrates the nexus between the exercise of political power and the holding of the executive office in the Fraternity of San Bartolomeo.

The social elite of San Sepolcro continued to place its members in the highest offices of the commune and of the fraternity through and beyond the middle of the fifteenth century, despite changes in the supreme authority of the commune. In 1441 Florence acquired San Sepolcro and abolished the office of the Twenty-Four, which had served as the chief executive in the two centuries under study here. Thereafter the Florentines yearly sent a captain as a representative of their sovereignty over San Sepolcro.[58] In this reorganization of government, the New Council was renamed the Conseglio dei Popoli (Council of the People) but retained its legislative preeminence and its 300 members with the *capoliste* as heads of the lists. Again the members were drawn from the greater families of the town with the honor of the title *capolista* reserved for the most prestigious. An extant list of members of this council for 1442 contains 300 names with 42 men added in the following years to replace deceased members. Comparing these politically active men of the town with the 44 priors who directed the fraternity from 1440 to 1450 yields percentages similar to those of the 1390s.[59] Of the 44 who served as priors in the 1440s, a total of 29 (66 percent) sat on the Council of the People. Two other priors belonged to the Pichi and Bercordati families, and two more had brothers on the communal council. The linkage of the two groups is perhaps most fully revealed in the fact that 6 of the 15 *capoliste* also served as priors in the decade under consideration. The 11 priors who neither sat on the communal council nor had close family members in it may have been guildsmen of more or less wealth and social esteem. Perhaps a *calzolaio* or *fabro* was selected to serve as prior. There is no precise evidence from existing documentation, although both of these *arti* sent several of their members to the fraternity's priorate in the thirteenth century. Even if an occasional craftsman or tenant of agricultural land was selected to the priory, he and his views would be ignored or overwhelmed by the large majority of priors drawn from the great families.

It is instructive to place these figures in a historical framework. The fraternal executives, who in the thirteenth century represented the various social groups of the fraternity's membership and the town including its countryside, by the 1390s were drawn from the governing social and political elite of San Sepolcro. By 1390 the fraternity was indistinguishable from the communal government. This linkage of the priors with the social elite and the fraternity with the commune assured the continuing importance of the fraternity in the distribution of charity and the supervision of aspects of death in San Sepolcro, but at the same time it eroded the fraternity's ability to inspire the piety of large segments of the population of San Sepolcro.

The changes in the Fraternity of San Bartolomeo from the thirteenth to the fifteenth centuries should not be viewed as the atomization of the thirteenth-century community in the fourteenth century. Rather, it is as though the thirteenth-century aspirations, manifest in the fraternity, shifted to a more fundamental level that required no formal or overt organization, no signing up as a member or paying dues to belong. Doubtless linked to changes in communal governance, the new sense of community gave grounds for the assumption that each person of the town would receive at least minimal aid and memorialization at death by virtue of birth within the town's walls. Thus it is no accident that San Sepolcro, which so early in European history recorded its dead, was one of the earliest of the Italian communes to register all its births. By the fifteenth century bequests from the wealthy and heirless supported an institution that in some broad sense belonged to all the citizenry as much as the thirteenth-century fraternity had with its memorialization by name of nearly all the men and women of the town. Membership in the fraternity after 1350 no longer served the same purposes, but the priors did provide occasional services to nearly everyone in the town. Each resident could appeal to the fraternity for food and clothing if poor, candles and pall at death if impoverished, supervision of the building of a memorial chapel and perpetual prayers if wealthy, guardianship of children if early deceased, and the honor of holding the office of prior if among the elite. Granted the fraternity no longer voiced memorialization for the vast majority of the dead of San Sepolcro, and granted the rich and well-born received the most tangible benefits, but each adult of the town knew he could turn to the fraternity at a time of need. An active community of practically all the households had become an administrative bureau with a residual community basis. The Fraternity of San Bartolomeo assured each resident of the town that a basic human need would be met. At burial the deceased—no matter how poor, or far from home, or infirm waiting to die in a hospice—would receive at least some minimal honor and remembrance at burial. This assurance liberated each resident from a basic fear. Those who desired greater honor and memorialization than the fraternity afforded could seek more adventuresome forms now that the fraternity had secured a minimal honor for all. Membership in the fraternity was not needed because it belonged to the community. This radical change in the possession of the fraternity from the many members to the community of citizens occurred in the early years of the fourteenth century when the laity was taking political responsibility for the town.

Whether we accept as accurate Largi's interpretation that the Fraternity of San Bartolomeo developed because the laymen of San Sepolcro formed a corporation to hold property bequeathed for charitable purposes to the Franciscans, by the fifteenth century the fraternity did function as the administrator of property of the dead. We should not be surprised that such a powerful corporation belonging to the community was tapped for other purposes as well. It supervised several of the hospitals of San Sepolcro and named their administrators. Throughout the 1420s and 1430s, the various governments of the town placed forced loans (*prestanze*) on the fraternity. And when San Sepolcro went to war in the 1420s and 1430s, the fraternity supplied food and other goods to the soldiers who fought the wars.[60] The involvement of the fraternity in the world took its most exquisite form in 1418, when the town's ruler Carlo Malatesta bestowed upon the fraternity the property seized from those families of San Sepolcro that he declared rebels to his rule.[61]

Largi gloried in the knowledge that he had been chosen on three occasions as a prior of the Fraternity of San Bartolomeo and was immensely proud of the fraternity's achievements in his town of San Sepolcro. He was aware of the fraternity's failure to perform the spiritual and charitable functions it had in the thirteenth and early fourteenth centuries. For Largi, reform was a relatively simple matter of efficient management. He saw no contradiction between the needs of the administration of the fraternity's property and involvement with communal government on one hand and the administration of the pious bequests of dead souls on the other. Largi rested secure in the belief that efficient and honest management of either communal exactions or pious bequests would gain him honor in San Sepolcro and Paradise.

CHAPTER FOUR

The Confraternity of Santa Maria della Notte: From Processional Chanting to Administrative Devotion

In the years during which the Fraternity of San Bartolomeo evolved from a body of brothers and sisters, who donated and distributed large quantities of food and money, to an administrative entity of a few leaders overseeing testamentary bequests, two diverse types of confraternities with radically different means of acquiring merit and preparing for death were founded in San Sepolcro. In the first half of the fourteenth century the town sponsored the birth of fourteen new confraternities. These new organizations shattered the town's previously unified lay system of memorialization and charity. The most important of these new confraternities appeared in 1301, at the time lay leaders gained control of the government of San Sepolcro from the abbot of the Camaldolese monastery. Abbot Giovanni II conveyed his feudal rights over the territory of San Sepolcro to the magistracy of the Twenty-Four. The communal government required the rectors of the Fraternity of San Bartolomeo to compensate the Camaldolese abbey with fourteen pieces of land totaling over 2,500 *tavole* (260,000 square feet).[1]

The circumstances under which the fraternity gained these properties illustrate its mediating role between the individual's desire for salvation and the town's earthly concerns. In 1276, Giovanni de Cristofano bequeathed most of his property to the poor and named the Fraternity of San Bartolomeo as his *fideicommissarius,* if his son Latino died without a wife. Giovanni had acquired at least part of these possessions through usurious practices; in making his own testament in 1300, Latino instituted the fraternity as his heir and required it to return the usurious profits of his father.[2] These properties passed via the fraternity to the Camaldolese abbey; in exchange the laity of San Sepolcro acquired self-rule. The Fraternity of San Bartolomeo received only a sum of money and the poor lost a valuable source of annual income for their food and clothing. Needless to say, the Fraternity of San Bartolomeo had become more deeply involved in politics than intended in its charge of overseeing the rights of the poor of the town. This political involvement did not immediately discourage bequests; their numbers increased in the decades immediately after these events of 1301. The transferral of this land from the fraternity as the agent of the commune to the abbey underlines the fraternity's role as a corporate expression of the townspeople of San Sepolcro, even though the enhancement of political independence came at the expense of its special charges, the poor.

Precisely when the three predominant institutions of the town were making this transaction, a novel form of confraternity was born in San Sepolcro. Largi later asserted that the lay seizure of political power from the clergy paralleled a bid by the laity to control dispensation of charity to the poor.[3] This new brotherhood, one of the many *laudesi* confraternities that was founded in Italy before and after 1300, initially gathered to sing praises to Mary and Christ. Several other *laudesi* brotherhoods appeared in the first decades of the fourteenth century; and if tradition is accurate, a second novel form of confraternity, the *disciplinati,* found institutional expression in San Sepolcro in the year or years immediately following the abbot's sale of his political power. The *laudesi* and the *disciplinati* flourished in San Sepolcro as the Fraternity of San Bartolomeo became progressively less concerned with recruiting members and increasingly involved in the administration of testamentary bequests.[4]

The members of the *laudesi* and *disciplinati* confraternities exercised their piety in patterns different from those of the members of the Fraternity of San Bartolomeo. The *laudesi* sang praises to Christ and Mary in their oratories and in public processions, and the *disciplinati* flagellated themselves in their private oratories and in public processions. Both demanded of their members an intensely pious life, an active participation in charity to the poor and infirm, a closely scrutinized form of social behavior, and an intense participation in the liturgical life of the church. In many other Italian towns and cities the appearance of the *laudesi* and *disciplinati* coincided with the grasping of power by regimes of the *popolo.*[5] In Florence, for example, at least one *laudesi* confraternity (the Bigallo) was formed by Peter Martyr to aid in defeating the Ghibellines in the 1240s. And if a fourteenth-century account is accurate, a second confraternity, Santa Maria della Misericordia, was founded in the 1240s as part of the Guelf popular movement to defeat the Ghibellines.[6] Both flourished in the 1250s with the appearance of Il Primo Popolo and played a vital role in the religious and charitable life of the Florentine laity for centuries thereafter. Florentine lay piety was strengthened by the appearance of several other *laudesi* confraternities in the 1270s and 1280s, contemporaneous with the seizure of political control of Florence by the major guilds. At approximately this time (the exact years are not certain) several confraternities of discipline appeared in northern and central Italy, for example, in Padua following the expulsion of Ezzelino da Romano and in Perugia following the victory of the *popolo*. The first Bolognese confraternity of discipline coincided with the participation of the modest tradesmen in government and with a sustained attack on serfdom and the nobility.[7]

In San Sepolcro the *laudesi* confraternity, founded at the time the laity of the town purchased its independence from the Camaldolese abbot, superseded all other *laudesi* confraternities to become by the late fourteenth century a rival of the Fraternity of San Bartolomeo. In the fifteenth century Largi referred to this brotherhood as the "Compagnia dele Laude de Sancte Maria dela Nocte del Borgo San Sepolcro."[8] The history of this confraternity in the fourteenth century remains obscure but can be illuminated by notarial authentications of elections of confraternal officers and testaments, including Largi's analysis of more than six hundred bequests from 1316 to the 1440s. Information on this confraternity, together with a general knowledge of *laudesi* confraternities in northern and central Italy, furthers our understanding of the religious life of the laity of San Sepolcro.

The one feature that the notaries of the town employed to differentiate this confraternity from other *laudesi* brotherhoods of San Sepolcro was its processional character. The notaries repeatedly identified this confraternity by its processions on the festival days and vigils of Christ and Mary. In the evenings the members marched through the streets of San Sepolcro and sang praises to their God and His mother.[9] The principal devotions of this confraternity in the fourteenth century revolved around processional singing of praises. The 1441 statutes of the *laudesi* describe fourteenth-century practices when the brothers were required to visit the churches of the town every Sunday and principal festival with the *mayestade* (a processional banner of the enthroned Mary and child) (XII). These same statutes held that the pious activity of chanting praises gained merit in the eyes of God: "To the praise of omnipotent God and health of the soul, the brothers are held the customary festival days with the *mayestade* processionally to go visiting the churches of Borgo singing the chants of praise and other things in the usual way; and other days, if they will not be constrained by necessity, all should visit the church and recommend themselves to God and to the Virgin Mary, our advocate" (XVI). The church mentioned here was probably the Oratory of Santa Maria Novella; its location remains a mystery, but it may have been on the site of the fifteenth-century confraternal chapel and meeting place, which was on the central piazza of San Sepolcro between the Camaldolese abbey and palazzo of the commune. By 1334 the *laudesi* had their own house, which presumably adjoined the Oratory of Santa Maria Novella.[10]

Devotion to Mary and invocation of her intercessory powers were not limited to the Confraternity of Santa Maria della Notte. Six other confraternities of praise germinated from the rich lay piety of this time. The Franciscans were the first to establish a lay confraternity with Mary as advocate in San Sepolcro, probably before the creation of the Confraternity of Santa Maria della Notte. Largi recorded a bequest in 1300 of a candle to the Confraternity "della Laude di Sancte Maria della Chiesa di San Francesco" ("Specchio," 26r). A subsequent bequest to the "Laudesi fratrum minorum Sancti Francisci virginis Marie de ecclesia fratrum minorum Sancti Francisci" reveals the continued existence of this confraternity through 1348.[11] Soon thereafter it passed out of existence, and its members joined the Confraternity of Santa Maria della Notte or the Misericordia Confraternity or the plague decimated its members.

A second sedentary *laudesi* confraternity with Mary as its advocate and intercessor received a testamentary bequest around 1320, though it may have existed for some time earlier.[12] This group of chanters worshiped a few yards away from the *laudesi* of Santa Maria della Notte in a chapel in the Camaldolese abbey. The formation of this "societas laudum qui cantantur in Abbatia dicti Burgi" may have been encouraged by the Camaldolese abbot soon after 1300, in conjunction with a building project in the church of the abbey and as a means of sharing in the Marian piety that moved the citizenry to support construction of the church. By 1361 the *laudesi* of the abbey had an image or sculpture of the Virgin Mary that testators associated with the confraternity. The confraternity received several bequests through 1364, but devotion waned in the last third of the fourteenth century.[13] In the following century the Confraternity of the Virgin Mary in the abbey again flourished, when its painting of Mary became one of the town's most important devotional images and the chapel of the confraternity received numerous bequests in exchange for burial.

Three other *laudesi* confraternities were founded at approximately the same time as that of the *laudesi* of the abbey. By 1317 the *laudesi* Confraternity of Sant'Agostino gathered near the Augustinian convent and oratory on the present-day Piazza Chiara in the southwest corner of San Sepolcro. This group continued to chant praises at least through 1348, the year of the last known bequest to the lay corporation.[14] In this same area and at approximately the same time, the *laudesi* confraternity associated with the church of San Bartolomeo received a bequest. Never possessing the size or the importance of the Fraternity of San Bartolomeo with which for a time it shared this church, the *laudesi* Confraternity of San Bartolomeo nevertheless provided an expression for lay devotion from at least 1319 to 1348.[15] Another *laudesi* brotherhood received a bequest in 1318; this group gathered near the Camaldolese priory of San Niccolò in the northeast corner of the town and adopted that saint as its protector.[16] An additional confraternity of *laudesi* gathered in the center of the city near the dominant tower of San Sepolcro. Named the *laudesi* of Venerable Mary, this brotherhood came into existence sometime before 1348 and doubtless dissolved in that year or soon thereafter.[17]

In the first half of the fourteenth century the laymen of San Sepolcro founded seven brotherhoods to chant praises to God and to Mary (see map in Chapter 1). The confraternities of the Virgin Mary in the abbey, Sant'Agostino, San Bartolomeo, and San Niccolò followed the pattern set by the Confraternity of Santa Maria della Notte. They were founded soon after 1300 and received testamentary bequests a half generation later in the period 1316–20. These five brotherhoods joined the Confraternity of San Francesco, already in existence in 1300, in providing choirs to chant praises to Christ and Mary as well as to distribute charity to the poor. The *laudesi* confraternities divided the town with three in the center (including the *laudesi* of Venerable Mary, in existence for a shorter period) and two each in the southwest and northeast corners. Affiliation with clerical corporations was also varied. Two brotherhoods associated with mendicant confessors, two with Camaldolese confessors, and one with the secular clergy; two had no clerical ties. Only two survived the Black Plague, and one of these, the *laudesi* of the abbey, appears to have been severely weakened by a second series of demographic and political disasters in the mid-1360s. Their survival was not based on large membership. The more important of the two was the Confraternity of Santa Maria della Notte, and it will be the focus of attention in this chapter. In addition to its processional chanting of praises, this confraternity was distinctive in its recruitment throughout the town. Not linked to any particular church or area of the town, this confraternity survived because it received a large number of bequests in 1348 and because it was the sole *laudesi* corporation with townwide affiliation. Its substantial financial endowment and townwide processions attracted the bequests of the dying through the demographic and political disasters of the middle of the fourteenth century.

An analysis of the membership of the Confraternity of Santa Maria della Notte at various points in the period from its founding around 1300 to 1450 indicates the size and social affiliations of the sodality. In writing the statutes of the confraternity in 1441, Francesco de Largi asserted that the founders of the brotherhood were "simple, just, and pious" men (I) and that new members should be "good and simple" (XX). Does an analysis of the membership bear out Largi's description of the members as "simple"? And how many men made up the membership of the brotherhood?

Only in 1345, after nearly half a century of confraternal existence, are we able to gain knowledge of the size of the brotherhood. The confraternity was headed by two priors who served for six-month terms, beginning on March 1 and September 1. On August 28, 1345, thirty-four men attended a meeting to elect the new priors. In the next election in February 1346, twenty-two men attended. In each instance they represented at least two-thirds of the male membership.[18] We may safely conclude that the number of members did not surpass thirty-five. Following the plague of 1348, not surprisingly, the number of electors, and presumably members, dropped considerably; seventeen men voted in February 1349.[19] The number of electors at six meetings from 1365 to 1380 ranged from twenty to twenty-six, implying a membership of thirty to forty laymen.[20] After 1348 twenty to thirty men attended the important gatherings, when the highest officers of the brotherhood were elected, and total membership probably remained under forty men.

Documentation of membership is lacking from 1381 to 1441. Largi listed the two priors elected semiannually from 1415 to 1441. These lists recount the same names every two or three years, suggesting a limited number of members. This theory is confirmed in the 1441 statutes, which list the names of fourteen members, nearly all of whom served as prior in the years before 1441. The Confraternity of Santa Maria della Notte, at least from the 1340s, was composed of a small nucleus of men whose number diminished in the mid-fourteenth century followed by a limited recovery after midcentury. The membership declined in the fifteenth century and remained relatively constant at around twelve to fourteen until the eighteenth century. During this time, the members served as administrators.[21]

By 1445, and doubtless earlier as well, a member of the confraternity could anticipate leading his confreres as prior soon after entering and several times thereafter. Madalo de Bartolomeo, for example, became prior in 1430 and was elected to that office four more times through 1440.[22] Members could expect to hold one of the several offices every year or at least once every two years. In the 1440s the members chose by lot two priors, a provost to oversee the priors, two councillors to advise the priors, two visitors to visit sick members, and two laborers to do the manual work of the confraternity.[23] Of the fourteen members in 1441 all but two held an office that year. A typical member, Checcho de Feo de ser Fino, who belonged to the confraternity from 1415 to 1450, was seldom without office over that thirty-five-year period. Checcho held the following offices:

1417	prior-treasurer
1420–21	prior
1422–23	prior
1424–25	prior
1426	prior-treasurer
1427–28	prior
1428	prior (from May 15 following the death of his cousin while in office)
1432	prior
1434–35	prior
1437	prior-treasurer
1442	visitor
1442–43	councillor
1443–44	provost
1446	laborer
1446–47	provost
1447–48	prior
1449	laborer
1449–50	councillor

Checcho may have been extraordinarily favored by the electors and later in the selection by lot, but it is accurate to say that by the fifteenth century each member of the confraternity held some office nearly continually and could expect to hold the executive office at least once every two or three years.[24]

Social Composition and Political Participation of the Laudesi

The membership of the confraternity that Largi described as "simple" men cannot be precisely defined by occupation, but a reliable fixing of the social composition of the brotherhood can be discovered by a process of elimination of many of the chief social categories of the town. First, the members of the Confraternity of Santa Maria della Notte did not belong to the group of great merchants or the local nobility that had provided leadership in San Sepolcro from the thirteenth century until Florence gained control of the town in 1441. The possession of a family name differentiated the merchant-noble elite from the remainder of society in northern and central Italy in the Late Middle Ages. Only individuals with an exalted social status had the honor of a family name.[25] The notary who authenticated the elections of the priors of the confraternity from 1345 to 1380 listed the names of those members present and voting. Among the thirty-four men voting on August 28, 1345, only one possessed a family name, one of the most eminent of San Sepolcro, Graziani. In February 1346 twenty-two men voted, and one member, in addition to this Graziani, carried a family name, Benedatis.[26] A comparison with the fifteenth century shows remarkable consistency. Between 1415 and 1443, of thirty-five men who served as prior for at least one term, only one had a family name, Cipolli.[27] And among the fourteen men listed as members in the statutes of 1441, not one possessed a family name or was a member of one of the families of the local social elite.[28]

From 1366 to 1380 approximately forty-two men were voting members of the confraternity.[29] The names of these men do not appear on the membership lists of several guilds of the period, thereby demonstrating that the confraternal members were not in craft or merchant occupations. Fanfani has asserted, and my research bears out, that the guilds of San Sepolcro developed late; the craftsmen and merchants were organized into corporations after 1300. In December of 1375 the members of the wool guild ("Homines artis lane terre Burgi") elected their seven consuls and counselors, and not one of them belonged to the Confraternity of Santa Maria della Notte.[30] This group may have been wool workers or local dealers in wool because there was another guild named the "Merchatores pannorum camsores retalliatorum merciariorum et banbaciorum," none of whose members in 1380 belonged to the Confraternity of Santa Maria della Notte.[31] This group of cloth merchants included several members of the greatest families of the town: four Pichi and two Carsidoni. Nor did any members of the confraternity belong to the tower society that gathered in the piazza just south of the great Camaldolese abbey in the center of San Sepolcro. Here the oldest families congregated, including five Graziani, two Dotti, a Befulcis, and an Acerbis.[32] None of the three consuls of the *Arte spetiarorum* (apothecaries) in 1376 or the nineteen members of the *Arte sartorie* (tailors) in 1366 or the twenty-one notaries listed on the matricola of the *Arte notatorium* (guild of notaries) in 1363–64 appears among the forty-two members of the confraternity from 1366 to 1380.[33] The confraternity did not recruit from these incorporated craft and merchant guilds, and, in all likelihood, there were no other guilds in San Sepolcro at this time.

Political participation of the members of the confraternity can be established by analyzing the dominant legislative body and the tax records of the communal government of San Sepolcro. Following a procedure similar to that applied to the priors of the Fraternity of San Bartolomeo in Chapter 3, the members of the Confraternity of Santa Maria della Notte will be compared to the members of the New Council in the 1390s and the Council of the People in the 1440s.[34]

Were the men of the Confraternity of Santa Maria della Notte among the 353 men who advised the government of Carlo Malatesta in the 1390s? Unfortunately, the documents do not permit an exact comparison of the men of the New Council and those of the confraternity. We only have a list of thirty-two confraternal members from an electoral meeting in 1380 and the names of ten other men from 1366 to 1380 to compare with the 353 men of the New Council. To compensate for the eleven years between 1380 and 1391, the names of the New Council members have been examined to determine whether the sons or fathers of the men of the confraternity sat in this the most important legislative body of San Sepolcro.[35] Of these forty-two men of the confraternity, only one, Mucius Bartoli, belonged to the political class of the town. And only three sons of members were selected to the legislative council: Mucius Casucii's son Paulus, Andreas Cissci Bonansegne's son Iohannes, and Iohannes de Cipolli's son Meus. Approximately one out of ten of the confraternity members was represented in the legislature, whereas in the town as a whole at least one out every three households was represented by a male. Not one member was among the fifteen *capoliste* who headed the legislative council. The conclusion that the members of the confraternity did not belong to the political class of the town is also substantiated by comparing the names of 242 men in 1393 who were creditors to the communal government, most as a result of forced loans, with these same forty-two men of the confraternity.[36] Again only one man (Stephanus Dini) and the sons of three men of the confraternity (Meus, son of Iohannes Cipolli, Finucius, son of Feus Riche, and Iohannes, son of Andreas Cissci Bonansegne) were listed as creditors of the commune. Other members of the confraternity may have been assessed a forced loan and had not yet paid it in 1393, but the conclusion is unassailable that the vast majority of members of the Confraternity of Santa Maria della Notte escaped taxation and were excluded from political participation in the 1390s.[37]

By 1442 the New Council had been renamed the Council of the People but was still composed of 300 men, again divided into groups of 20, each headed by members of the great families of San Sepolcro. Again, as individuals died, they were replaced; membership in the 1440s totaled 342.[38] Twenty-six men who served in offices of the confraternity in the 1440s have been taken as a sample to compare with the names of the men on the legislative council.[39] Of these 26 men, only 3 (Madalo de Bartolomeo, Niccolò de Cristofano de Condei, and Checcho de Feo de ser Fino) sat on the communal legislature. As in the 1390s, the 11 percent of men of the *laudesi* confraternity participating in politics was substantially lower than the percentage of households of the town represented on the broadest-based political institution of San Sepolcro.

The social composition of the Confraternity of Santa Maria della Notte from the 1340s through the 1440s has been defined negatively to exclude noble families, the great merchant families, the political class, and, at least at certain points in the fourteenth century, several of the urban guilds, including tailors and notaries. The evidence is remarkably consistent. This process of exclusion leaves us with two principal social groups that might have constituted the areas of recruitment, the urban underclass—the poor and unclassified laborers—and agrarian tenants residing in the town. The urban underclass can be eliminated because of the presence of a smattering of the socially prestigious—the De Cipolli, a Graziani—and the fact that each member reciprocally led the sodality; it is doubtful that a Graziani would accept the leadership of a porter. Finally, notarial acts occasionally yield contracts of substantially large transfers of money or property of members of the confraternity. This view is substantiated by a provision in the statutes of 1441 that expressly forbids the recruitment of the poor.[40]

Agricultural Labor and the Laudesi

The central importance of the cultivation of land for the members of the confraternity and the close relationship of the town to the fertile Upper Tiber Valley answer the question of the social basis of the Confraternity of Santa Maria della Notte. An analysis of the brotherhood's financial records from the fifteenth century makes clear its agricultural orientation. An examination of these activities is possible again because of the administrative labor of Francesco de Largi, whose accounts survive for the period 1415 through 1440. In addition, they give substance to a tradition first claimed by an eighteenth-century historian of San Sepolcro, Francesco Pignani, that the dominant means of tilling the rich agricultural land of the Tiber Valley near San Sepolcro was with a spade rather than with ox-drawn plows. Agricultural laborers with their spades left San Sepolcro early each morning to trudge to the valley below. To awaken the late sleepers, their companions sang praises to Mary, and, once gathered, they exited in procession singing their chants. So many were their number, he said, that it took almost a half-hour for them to clear the gates of the town.[41] The historian did not specify when these practices began but noted that they had continued until his day. Others have conjectured that Pignani related events that first occurred in the thirteenth century.[42] Pignani wrote that a century after the confraternity's founding, the *gonfaloniere* of San Sepolcro, Cristoforo Corsidoni, made a bequest to the Confraternity of Santa Maria della Notte, whereby the Camaldolese abbot celebrated a mass at dawn for the congregated agricultural workers before they left for their daily work. Pignani gave no source for this information, but this Cristoforo served as *gonfaloniere* in 1441. His explanation would place the origins of the practice of singing *laude* back in the 1340s.[43] It is possible that agricultural laborers sang *laude* as they went to their labor, but the fourteenth-century documents reiterate two fundamental elements concerning the confraternity under consideration in this chapter: first, the *laude* were sung in conjunction with the festival days of Christ and Mary, which, in all likelihood, were not work days, and second, the *laude* were sung in the evening, as was the practice in most confraternities of the Late Middle Ages. It is more probable that the practice of singing *laude* while walking to work developed only in the course of the fifteenth century.

Pignani is correct, however, that the membership of the Confraternity of Santa Maria della Notte was drawn from residents of San

Sepolcro who labored in the agricultural fields of the Upper Tiber Valley. By the beginning of the fifteenth century, the members, as well as the confraternity itself, had substantial links to the countryside. A recurring expense in the financial records of the confraternity is a small daily wage paid to individuals, many of whom were members of the confraternity or of their families. Among the monies paid out by the treasurer of the confraternity from 1415 through 1450 were small payments "per aconchiare le vigne," "per portare le litanie," "per andare alla vendemmia," and for performing other agricultural tasks. The treasurer of the confraternity served as a hiring officer of day laborers who maintained the group's land and vineyards. That the tasks of pruning the vines, carrying the manure, and harvesting the grapes were done by groups of laborers, including many members of the confraternity, points to a social organization of labor. The laborers received varying sums, from one lira to thirteen soldi, apparently for a day's work, though there were some larger expenditures for these agricultural tasks. In these instances the confraternity probably empowered one of its members to act as foreman, and he paid laborers for their work in the fields.[44]

Among the several bonds of the confraternity with the countryside was the corporation's ownership of substantial quantities of agricultural land, some of which was rented to tenants. Members also received land as agricultural tenants, but it is not clear whether they actually worked the land or hired subtenants. A discussion of the renting of confraternal land by members is found in a provision of the 1441 statutes, which attempted to end abuses that resulted from members' rental of confraternal lands. To end all suspicion, the provision forbade any brother from leasing or renting any property of the confraternity unless three-fourths of the members approved in a secret vote. Moreover, should the brother lease confraternal land, he had to work the land "in the manner of a good laborer"; failing this, he would be forced to give up his lease (XXX). As will be discussed below, the Confraternity of Santa Maria della Notte owned a large amount of land in the Upper Tiber Valley and acted as landlord for the deceased, who had bequeathed the land tracts to the brotherhood. In the interests of the deceased, who were to receive the benefits of their land, the priors supervised laborers and tenants, whose work supported the poor, the clergy, and the administration of the confraternity. The mediating role of the priors over decades and centuries sustained a vast network of earthly and religious relationships.

Largi's description of the *palazzo* of the *laudesi* confraternity provides a sense of the scale of the brotherhood's role as mediator between countryside and town as well as its services to the poor of the town. The principal residence of the fifteenth-century confraternity was adjacent to the Camaldolese abbey. The present-day Palazzo dei Laudi is a sixteenth-century remodeling of that earlier building, which Largi described in the statutes. Sitting in the central piazza of San Sepolcro between the Camaldolese abbey and the palace of the communal government, the *laudesi palazzo* was well situated to serve the people of the town. In an entranceway near the abbey, the members of the confraternity built a fireplace that served in winter to warm the poor; overhead on the ceiling were paintings of God the Father and the Virgin Mary. The ground floor was divided into two principal rooms, the meeting hall, in which the members congregated to discuss the needs of the corporation, and a granary, from which they sold or gave the grains of the storehouse. Under the granary were two rooms for the preparation of the grain brought at the time of harvest. In a second story there were three more granaries, one each above the entranceway, the meeting hall, and the ground-floor granary. The *palazzo* also housed a wine cellar, which, in a manner identical to the granaries, was carefully guarded by keys and by harsh punishments for unauthorized entrance. Finally, there was a room to store the possessions of the confraternity, doubtless including those from the patrimonies of testators (XXI–XXIV).

The priors and the members decided which of the poor of the town were deserving of dowries, burial assistance, aid at the time of pregnancies, and medicines from the confraternal pharmacy (XXV). From the *palazzo* they sent out cloth to the poor and meat to the needy and to the clergy at Easter and All Saints Vigil (XV). The financial records fully describe the relationship of the town *palazzo* and the countryside. The confraternity was obligated to maintain a bridge in the center of the Tiber Valley after 1415.[45] From the agricultural lands of the confraternity, the lay laborers and tenants brought grain, wine, legumes, animals for slaughter, and the woad plant to the confraternal storehouses. The statutes reminded the members that the priors were required every Saturday and Sunday and on major feast days to give bread to the poor at the entrance of the *palazzo*. Weekly and on festival days the priors distributed grain to the poor, who with others gathered in the large piazza in front of the confraternal palace. From its lands and from bequests, the confraternity drew substantial quantities of grain. The priors sold more grain in late winter and spring than in other seasons, which suggests that their stores of grain were placed on sale when other stores were drying up or as a means of keeping grain sales and prices stable. In the priory from March through August 1417, on eighteen occasions the officers of the confraternity sold grain at a cost of 26 to 28 bolognini per *staio*. They sold 88 *staia* to the men of the town. In the following six months only 7.5 *staia* were sold on two occasions in addition to one sale of 10 *staia* of spelt. Less numerous sales of large quantities of wine totaled in value for the six months in 1417 over 100 lire. And in the period March 1417 through February 1418, at least twenty payments of rent on land and vineyards were deposited with the treasurer of the confraternity.[46]

The accumulation of loans, rents, and sales and the distribution and administration of agricultural produce and property occupied the priors of the confraternity in the fifteenth century. In addition to the distribution of meat to the poor at Easter and All Saints Vigil and the weekly sales and distribution of grain and bread in the central piazza, the priors bought large quantities of cloth to be handed out to the poor in December (XV). The confraternity bought beige cloth for 328 lire in 1415 and 456 lire in 1432, to mention only two of many purchases in the first half of the fifteenth century.[47] The *laudesi* corporation acquired these substantial quantities of cloth from the merchants of San Sepolcro. Another register kept by Largi recorded all the cloth purchased "to dress the poor of God" and dispersed per year by the priors. In a six-month period in 1417 under the priory of Niccolò de Bartolo de Cola and Cristofano de Nieri dal Casalino, the confraternity purchased approximately 168 yards of beige cloth from four merchants for a total of 313 lire.[48]

Largi also recorded the distribution of cloth to the needy of the town. Examining the recipients of one prior, Cristofano de Nieri dal Casolino in 1417, we find that on thirty-one separate occasions in his six-month priory he or his representative carried cloth to an individual or groups of the needy. Cristofano gave cloth to thirteen shame-faced poor, ten children, a friar, several immigrants, and the "cristiani infecte" in the leprosarium of San Lazzaro outside San Sepolcro.[49]

The confraternity also lent money to various institutions of San Sepolcro, including substantial forced loans to the communal government. For example, in February 1436 Francesco de Largi handed over one hundred lire to the town government in the form of a loan.[50] Of interest in the present context are the numerous small loans made by the priors to the agricultural cultivators of the Tiber Valley, presumably the tenants of confraternal lands.[51] The confraternity acted in a manner similar to other landlords of the time, lending money to its tenants for seed and other necessities before harvest. To loan under five lire, a prior needed the approval of the other prior and three advisers. A loan over five lire required the affirmative vote of the brothers (XI and XXVI). When the town government founded a communal loan office, the *Monte della Pietà,* in 1466, it required the Confraternity of Santa Maria della Notte and the Fraternity of San Bartolomeo to endow this public loan office with eight hundred florins. The *laudesi* confraternity also provided the rooms for administrators of this communal pawn office.[52] Thus before the constituting of the *Monte della* Pietà, the confraternity played an important role in financing agricultural labor, and after 1466 its financial endowment underlay the success of the charitable loan institution.

The confraternity's links to the countryside can be seen most clearly through an examination of bequests of agricultural properties to the lay corporation. From 1320 to 1450, seventy-six individuals bequeathed land, mostly agricultural, to the confraternity (see Table 4.5). Twenty-one vineyards were bequeathed to the corporation in this same period. Many of these properties were to remain in the hands of the confraternity in perpetuity, but an examination of the financial accounts of the corporation demonstrates that the sale of agricultural lands and other properties provided much of the liquid capital required to continue the charitable and administrative activities of the *laudesi* brotherhood. For example, in the semester September 1415 through February 1416, more than one-third of the confraternity's income derived from the sale of one piece of land—294 lire out of the semiannual income of 839 lire; and in the period March through August 1420, 200 out of the total income of 480 lire came to the confraternity through the sale of one parcel of land. On other occasions the priors sold property to buy other land; for example, in March through August 1416, they sold a parcel of land for 500 lire—72 percent of the total income of the semester—and then proceeded to buy a house for 307 lire. And in the period September 1422 through February 1423, of an income of 614 lire, 544 lire (89 percent) derived from two land sales. In 1426 the priors sold three parcels of land worth 522 lire so as to hand over 513 lire in a forced loan to the communal government.[53] Such substantial sales of land and vineyards continued throughout the period under scrutiny here.

These periodic sales of land should not be taken to mean that the priors stripped the confraternity of its landed wealth. In fact, it remained one of the two largest possessors of land in San Sepolcro in the 1440s. As discussed above in regard to the Fraternity of San Bartolomeo, all the landed property of ecclesiastical corporations of San Sepolcro was listed in the 1440s. Again Francesco de Largi served by drawing up the list of land possessed by the brotherhood. He recorded 17,045 *tavole* of land in the possession of the confraternity.[54] This figure agrees with a second manuscript that records a land tax in which the confraternity is shown to possess 17,437 *tavole* of land, vineyards, and other pieces of real estate in 101 separate properties. This register assesses the value of ninety-three of these parcels of land at 32,998 lire. These figures acquire significance when compared with the other ecclesiastical institutions of San Sepolcro (see Table 3.9). For example, Santa Maria della Pieve was the most important church in San Sepolcro staffed by secular priests and representing the bishop of Città di Castello. This baptismal church was supported by only 4,172 *tavole,* approximately one-quarter of the land held by the *laudesi* confraternity. The value of the land possessed by the Confraternity of Santa Maria della Notte was greater than that of any other ecclesiastical institution in San Sepolcro except the abbey of the Camaldolese, which possessed 25,562 *tavole* valued at 33,435 lire. Thus it is evident that, though the abbey possessed approximately 8,000 additional *tavole,* the value of the confraternity's land was higher per *tavola* and in total value nearly equal that of the Camaldolese of San Sepolcro.[55] Despite the periodic sale of real property, the Confraternity of Santa Maria della Notte retained a large store of tangible capital in the form of land, vineyards, and houses. This property provided the material basis that assured the dying citizens of San Sepolcro of the sempiternal existence of the confraternity. Only such longevity could comfort the dying and sustain the hope that their material wealth would serve spiritual purposes in subsequent decades and centuries.

The Administration of Charity

The transformation of the wealth of the deceased to spiritual purposes ranged from distribution of food and clothing to the poor to the administration of properties for perpetual masses. We can better understand the confraternity by looking at the acts of the priory of the one semester from March through August 1417. Checcho de Feo de ser Fino as prior-treasurer and Checcho d'Agnilo del Nuto as prior first donned the full-length ceremonial black robes that were decorated at the neck with a white collar and accepted one florin from the outgoing priors.[56] The income to the confraternity totaled 644 lire; and as has already been discussed, the three principal sources of income were the sale of grain, real property, and wine. Other substantial sources of income included over 25 lire from rents of a furnace, land, vineyard, and house and over 10 *lire* each from the repayment of loans and the sale of cloth. A large number of land rents came to the confraternal coffers in the second semester of the confraternal year.[57]

The expenses of the confraternity during the priory of the two Checchos were more varied and totaled 597 lire. A weighty proportion of this money went to the lord of the town, Pandolfo Malatesta, for a "cut" (*taglia*). This tax constituted an extraordinary impost for the purpose of raising money to pay a ransom for their lord, and it made up nearly 17 percent of the expenses of the semester. The remainder went to pay for a variety of purchases and services. In the months of March and April alone, expenses of 54 and 79 lire respectively are noted. Expenditures for the poor included 28 lire for food, which was primarily the weekly distributions of grain in the Saturday market, 16 lire for clothing, and 5 lire to dower the daughter of Agnuluccio de Giovanni del Brancho, who presumably was impoverished. Thus 40 of the 133 lire, or 37 percent of these two months' expenses, went directly to the poor. Approximately one-third or 45 lire paid for the production of agricultural goods, mainly for day laborers. The remainder of the expenses was made up of a variety of small expenditures, including 10 lire to pay the salary of the confraternity's officials and 5 lire to priests.[58] From this sample of the expenses of the confraternity, it is clear that nearly two-thirds of its expenses constituted charity to the poor and maintenance of the agricultural lands. The remaining third paid for the salaries and materials that underlay the sacred and charitable acts of the priors.

Testamentary Bequests to the Laudesi

Over the years from 1415 to 1440 the confraternity maintained its ability to attract the support of the people of San Sepolcro, or at least to garner large bequests from a relatively small number of individuals. Table 4.1 shows the total amount of income and expenses over these years with an average income of 995 lire and average expenses of 992 lire per year. Several important conclusions may be drawn from the data. First, the last five years witnessed a substantially higher level of income and expenses, averaging 1,317 and 1,318 lire respectively. After 1440, Largi changed the methods of accounting so any continued analysis is impossible.[59] Through the end of the period under study here, the confraternity remained financially solvent and was capable of gaining large sums of money and distributing a significant proportion to the poor and needy of the town. Second, the administration by the priors of this money did not require close methods of accounting, despite Largi's recommendation that the confraternity use the accounting methods of the merchants. Frequently, the sum of money on hand when the outgoing priors left office was less than that recorded by the new priors when they began their office. The financial records demonstrate that the priors had great latitude in the amount they spent and could, if necessary, sell parcels of land or houses to expand their income and balance their accounts (see Table 4.1).

An analysis of wills and bequests to the Confraternity of Santa Maria della Notte demonstrates that this corporation, in the same fashion as the Fraternity of San Bartolomeo, mediated between the dead and the living. To do so, its priors had to become administrators of various forms of property and vicars of the deceased souls' well-being. The members as administrators of the confraternity oversaw the harvesting of vast amounts of liquid and physical capital from the bequests of the dead for both pious and secular purposes. Its transmission of this capital from one generation to the next took complex forms, including redistribution from the wealthy to the poor and holding property for decades with the requirement of managing it in the interests of the dead, their families, the poor, and the confraternity itself. The priors also had to manage a spiritual economy through the administration of the fruit of the bequests and property. They labored to aid the poor of Christ and to assure the performance of pious rites, so that the souls of the deceased did not lose the benefit of their bequests. The labor of the Confraternity of Santa Maria della Notte, as with the Fraternity of San Bartolomeo, depended upon its priors addressing the relationship between the living and the dead as well as the material and spiritual spheres. Needless to say, this mediation required the priors to have a certain charisma and occasionally led to conflict with the traditional order of mediation, the clergy, who also dealt with these social groups and abstract spheres.

The confraternity received a large number of bequests in the fourteenth and fifteenth centuries for various reasons; the two most important were the increased popularity of the testament for nearly all segments of society by the middle of the fourteenth century and the increasing complexities of a literate-legal society. Both led individuals to rely on a sempiternal institution such as the Confraternity of Santa

TABLE 4.1

Income and Expenses of the Confraternity of Santa Maria della Notte, 1415–1440 (all figures in lire)*

Period	*Expenses*	*Income*	*Surplus*	*Deficit*	*To Next Priors*
Sept.–Feb. 1415–16	607	839	232	–	362
March–Feb.	485	485	–	–	358
1416–17	832	486	–	346	–
	1,317	971			
March–Feb.	597	644	47	–	47
1417–18	423	410	13	–	33
	1,020	1,054			
March–Feb.	314	857	442	–	0
1418–19	405	444	39	–	0
	719	1,301			
March–Feb.	148	165	17	–	17
1419–20	236	231	–	5	12
	384	396			
March–Feb.	484	480	–	4	9
1420–21	508	500	–	8	0
	992	980			
March–Feb.	638	638	–	–	0
1421–22	327	330	3	–	22
	965	968			
March–Feb.	430	98	–	332	0
1422–23	576	614	38	–	30
	1,006	712			
March–Feb.	216	207	–	9	16
1423–24	443	523	80	–	96
	659	730			
March–Feb.	111	34	–	77	16
1424–25	946	1,023	77	–	93
	1,057	1,057			
March–Feb.	363	260	–	103	0
1425–26	245	273	28	–	28
	608	533			
March–Feb.	797	824	27	–	56
1426–27	338	310	–	28	27
	1,135	1,134			
March–Feb.	282	286	4	–	26
1427–28	359	348	–	11	4
	641	634			
March–Feb.	315	342	27	–	2
1428–29	231	249	28	–	18
	546	591			
March–Feb.	397	381	–	16	3
1429–30	463	465	2	–	5
	860	846			

(continued)

TABLE 4.1 (*Continued*)

Period	*Expenses*	*Income*	*Surplus*	*Deficit*	*To Next Priors*
March–Feb.	418	476	58	–	52
1430–31	441	600	159	–	207
	859	1,076			
March–Feb.	545	565	20	–	226
1431–32	734	521	–	213	12
	1,279	1,086			
March–Feb.	775	718	–	57	0
1432–33	713	679	–	34	6
	1,488	1,397			
March–Feb.	496	516	20		15
1433–34	300	300	–	–	15
	796	816			
March–Feb.	474	462	–	12	89
1434–35	282	190	–	92	2
	756	652			
March–Feb.	246	269	23	–	25
1435–36	943	1,002	59	–	78
	1,189	1,271			
March–Feb.	854	782	–	72	33
1436–37	978	1,083	105	–	103
	1,832	1,865			
March–Feb.	347	257	–	90	18
1437–38	888	849	–	39	0
	1,235	1,106			
March–Feb.	390	391	1	–	0
1438–39	727	748	21	–	16
	1,117	1,139			
March–Feb.	643	634	–	9	5
1439–40	574	568	–	6	0
	1,217	1,202			

Source: ASF, *CRS*, SS, L.XX.27, 2v–307r.

Note: All these figures should be regarded as approximate; they were evidently thought to be that by Largi because his totals often do not correspond with his preliminary computations found on scraps of paper inserted into the account book. Frequently his totals for a semester show a deficit, and yet he recounts sums of money being passed to the next priors; often a semester showing a surplus fails to yield any or an equal amount of money being passed to the new priors. Largi also adds later expenses or income after his totals are computed; loans as well as payments of loans are often written as addenda. Problems are multiplied when a prior dies in office and when priors borrow money or are charged with loans. All this slippage in Largi's accounts indicates that there was a good deal of loose change around and at times he adds the small change at the end of his semester's computation to balance his books.

*I have rounded off soldi and denari to the nearest whole lira. I have computed all ducats and florins at a flat rate of 1 ducat or florin to 5 lire. The last category, "to next priors," is the amount Largi records the outgoing priors passed to their successors. Thus when these accounts begin in September 1415, the new priors had about 140 lire in hand. The accounts begin in 1415, and in 1440 Largi changed the procedures, making it impossible to continue comparable accounts.

Maria della Notte, whose leaders were experienced in dealing with testaments and their disposition. The Confraternity of Santa Maria della Notte received bequests in at least 63 of 238 wills redacted by the notary Paolo di Ciuccio from 1347 to 1373. In 18 others, the corporation was made either a substitute or universal heir.[60] Thus in over one-third of this sample, the dying of San Sepolcro regarded the confraternity as an appropriate institution for receiving or overseeing their property and for overseeing the interests of their souls and families.

Thanks to the labor of Francesco de Largi, it is possible to know the total number of bequests to the corporation in the fourteenth and first half of the fifteenth centuries. Largi recorded the bequests in favor of the Confraternity of Santa Maria della Notte sometime between the writing of the "Specchio" for the Fraternity of San Bartolomeo in 1437 and his death in 1447. In four series he abstracted 621 wills and noted benefits to the confraternity from testators shown in the manuscripts at that time in the possession of the confraternity (see Table 4.2).

These figures establish that a substantial proportion of citizens of San Sepolcro and its vicinity endowed the confraternity with bequests and their trust. The table is divided at 1380 because in the preceding seven decades numerous citizens made bequests to the Confraternity of Santa Maria della Notte, but after that date ever fewer citizens did so.

The activities of the priors required by the testators varied a great deal from guardianship of children through overseeing perpetual bequests. A large number of individuals simply granted a sum of money or amount of grain to the confraternity without any reciprocal obligation on the part of the brotherhood or the priors. Such pious bequests were intended to support the administration of the corporation and constituted charity to the poor. It certainly was regarded as a pious bequest (*pro anima*), and in the testaments of the time, these simple or "free" bequests immediately followed the disposition of the body and accompanied the pious bequests to other religious corporations—churches, hospitals, convents, and the like.

A proportion of these simple bequests was for substantial amounts of money, especially for a small agricultural and market community. For example, in 1327 one testator granted the confraternity 100 lire and another in 1348 bequeathed 250 lire.[61] Clearly, as was true in the free bequests to the Fraternity of San Bartolomeo, these grants of money or produce without specific reciprocal acts on the part of the confraternity indicate the assumption that the brotherhood administered efficaciously the sums of money and goods in the interests of the soul of the donor and the poor of God. These benefactors apparently felt no need to bind the priors to specific pious purposes; rather, they be-

TABLE 4.2

*Bequests to the Confraternity of Santa Maria della Notte, 1311–1450**

Decade	*Men*	*Women*	*Total*
1311–20	1	1	2
1321–30	12	3	15
1331–40	56	13	69
1341–50	172	82	254
1351–60	11	2	13
1361–70	40	30	70
1371–80	40	22	62
Total, 1311–80	332	153	485
1381–90	19	18	37
1391–1400	7	5	12
1401–10	11	9	20
1411–20	14	6	20
1421–30	7	7	14
1431–40	13	6	19
1441–50	7	7	14
Total, 1381–1450	78	58	136
Total, 1311–1450	410	211	621

Source: ASF, *CRS,* San Sepolcro, L.XX.8, fols. 13r–85r.

*The vast majority of these abstracts were written in the hand of Francesco de Largi. Occasionally he placed the same bequest in more than one series; consequently, these figures may be slightly inflated. Also, some of the bequests do not have dates, but when dates are lacking, they are usually in chronological sequence. Moreover, Largi noted the folio number of the register from which he took his information, again in sequence, so that we may assume the dates of bequests from those that precede and follow. For the fourteenth century the dates are almost always in chronological sequence, but in the fifteenth century 29 percent of the bequests are entered out of sequence. For this table, I have, for the fourteenth century, judged which decade is correct, when necessary, from the sequence of years and a proportional estimate from the folio sequence. For the fifteenth century I have placed the bequests for which I have a definite date in their decades and have distributed those lacking a date over the first five decades based on the proportions from the dated bequests.

lieved that merit would accrue to their souls through the corporate labor of the pious entity. This form of free benefaction found its fullest expression in the fifty-year period from 1330 to 1380. Despite the occasional large sums, the vast majority of outright gifts in this period were for relatively small amounts.

Seldom does one see the small unconditional bequests of a *staio* of grain, or ten soldi, or a lira to the confraternity in the fifteenth century (see Table 4.3). A large proportion of the children of the original contributors ignored the confraternity when they wrote wills after 1380. It continued to receive bequests from the more wealthy and demanding but could not sustain the interest of the small contributors, who had constituted the overwhelming percentage of benefactors in the middle of the fourteenth century.

Many of the larger bequests, especially of real property, carried heavy obligations or were of a conditional nature. Moreover, over the fourteenth century and into the fifteenth century, the testators or their notaries became more adept at securing value or labor from the confraternity for their bequests. The citizens of San Sepolcro often required the priors to hold a certain sum of money or take the "fruit" from a piece of land and distribute a percentage for a set number of years and occasionally in perpetuity. In 1345, for example, Cambio de Rigo Brescholanio granted the confraternity forty lire to be paid over eight years. Cescho de Lenciole in 1348 bestowed upon the corporation a landed estate with its large house and required the priors to pay several bequests to his family and pious corporations. In addition, the confraternity received an "honfrantoio di guado," a mill to grind the woad plant. It received these properties with the understanding that ownership would remain in the brotherhood's hands in perpetuity, yet a century later Largi noted, without explanation, that nothing remained of this substantial bequest. The complex testament of Ser Bartolomeo de Messer Ranieri in 1350 made the confraternity universal heir and required the priors to restore all ill-gotten gains to his victims. The testator did not specify the amount, so that we do not know whether this provision consumed all or most of the estate. The priors were obligated to pay one hundred lire to Ser Bartolomeo's daughter when she married or entered a convent. In the meantime, they were to invest the one hundred lire with a merchant. If the young girl died before marriage or entering a convent, the confraternity as substituted heir would receive the one hundred lire and other property.[62]

Often the priors of the confraternity simply served as holders of money or property for a term of years or in perpetuity, spending the income for the poor or for prayers for the soul of the testator. In 1362 Cescha, the widow of Cescho from the nearby village of Latignano, bequeathed to the confraternity a vineyard and land that the priors were to hold in perpetuity for the poor. The confraternity served the people of San Sepolcro as an institution to receive property after life use by the testator or his heir. More often the confraternity served as ultimate heir if the family heir died without issue, frequently through a number of substitute heirs. If the family heir lived, the confraternity often received a token bequest to assure its supervision of the will's provisions. In these conditional or substitute bequests, the confraternity served as the heir of last resort that guaranteed the dying individual a recipient for his patrimony and a form of remembrance of his soul.[63] The confraternity and its priors carried on a varied series of administrative acts in the interest of the souls of the benefactors, including distributing grain, money, or clothing to the poor over a period of years or in perpetuity, dispatching pilgrims to Rome and Sant'Antonio's church in Padua, paying dowries of young girls, overseeing houses for "poor women," supervising the building of chapels and sepulchers, purchasing oil to burn before an altar, providing for anniversary masses, and paying for annual meals for the clergy.[64]

The position of the priors of the confraternity between the dead testator and the living is more fully revealed in several explanatory notes that Largi added to several of the 621 testaments. These notes demonstrate that, despite the contemporary commonplace that the will of the individual reigned supreme, the priors of the confraternity often circumvented the provisions of the testament or conversely attempted to protect the will of the deceased when his bequests and provisions were challenged by others, particularly by superior authorities. For example, in 1384 Landino de Bartolo d'Avidelone made the Confraternity of Santa Maria della Notte his heir and passed on unspecified patrimony to the corporation. The priors, however, for "the love of God" gave the full inheritance to Landino's niece.[65] In all likelihood, this niece was destitute, and the priors circumvented the testator's will on the basis of the superior impulse of the "love of God." Ignoring the testator's intention in other cases may not have been motivated by charitable impulses. The ironworker Simone de Jacomuccio gave 305 *tavole* of land and asked the confraternity to build a stone tomb for him in 1378, for which the priors were to spend twenty-five lire. Largi, writing around 1440, asserted that the confraternity had failed to construct this monument. Perhaps because the benefactor was a long-term member and former prior of the confraternity, his confreres felt liberated from the moral imperative of fulfilling his will.[66] The priors were seldom so assertive in superseding the will of the testator, and into the fifteenth century testament writers continued to entrust the confraternity with their property, though on a vastly diminished scale after 1380.

Despite the decline of the number of individuals granting bequests to the confraternity, the *laudesi* corporation continued to receive many substantial bequests in part because of its zealous defense of the rights of the deceased against those who would usurp his will. For example, in 1362 Vanni de Bonavere instituted the confraternity as his heir and granted it a house, which was to be dedicated to the benefit of the poor in perpetuity. In 1367, however, German troops under the pay of the government of Città di Castello occupied this house after the army of that city had seized San Sepolcro. Largi wrote that, in occupying the house, the troops had "defrauded the will" of Vanni, who had declared the rents of the house to be employed to maintain the poor. In that same year the priors of the confraternity brought suit before the bishop of Città di Castello. Bishop Sucao allowed the priors to abrogate Vanni's testament by selling the bequeathed house, but the priors were to reserve two pieces of land in perpetuity in his name "for service to the poor."[67] By the fifteenth century the task of guarding the will and the patrimony of the dead and, when necessary, readjusting its provisions, evolved into the essential services of this confraternity, as they had for the Fraternity of San Bartolomeo.

The temporal pattern of making bequests to the confraternity is clear from an examination of Table 4.2. Soon after its founding around 1300, the confraternity received a few bequests. The 1330s marked the beginning of a half-century of growth. The 1340s and particularly 1348 marked the moment of greatest confidence in the confraternity. The number of bequests dropped off in the 1350s, probably reflecting the reduction in mortality as a consequence of the plague of 1348. The number of bequests in the 1360s and 1370s matched those of the 1330s and completes the fifty years in which the confraternity drew the largest number of bequests. In the decade of the 1380s bequests dropped off by 40 percent from the preceding decade and a radical decline began. In the period from 1381 to 1450 the number of bequests averaged sixty-nine per decade.

A closer analysis shows that the proportion of large and small bequests changed radically in the 140 years under scrutiny (see Tables 4.3 and 4.4). In the 1340s bequests of less than one lire made up 10 percent of all bequests. From 1311 to 1380, bequests of ten lire or less totaled

TABLE 4.3

Bequests of Money to the Confraternity of Santa Maria della Notte, 1311–1450 (all sums in lire)

Decade	Number of Bequests	Less Than One Lire	Percent	1–2 Lire	Percent	2+–10 Lire	Percent	11–50 Lire	Percent	50+ Lire	Percent	Number of Money Bequests	Percent of Total Bequests
1311–20	2	2	100									2	100
1321–30	15	1	7	0	0	5	33	2	13	2	13	10	67
1331–40	69	7	10	9	13	12	17	6	9	1	1	35	51
1341–50	254	26	10	43	17	48	19	12	5	14	6	143	56
1351–60	13	0	0	0	0	1	7	0	0	3	21	4	31
1361–70	70	3	4	7	10	16	23	7	10	6	9	39	56
1371–80	62	4	6	8	13	11	18	4	6	2	3	29	47
Totals, 1311–80	485	43	9	67	14	93	19	31	6	28	6	262	54
1381–90	37	0	0	0	0	3	8	4	11	1	3	8	22
1391–1400	12	0	0	0	0	0	0	1	8	1	8	2	17
1401–10	14	0	0	0	0	1	7	0	0	0	0	1	7
1411–20	14	0	0	0	0	0	0	0	0	2	14	2	14
1421–30	10	0	0	0	0	0	0	0	0	1	10	1	10
1431–40	14	0	0	0	0	0	0	1	7	0	0	1	7
1441–50	10	0	0	0	0	0	0	0	0	0	0	0	0
1401–50 (Without date)	25	0	0	0	0	2	8	4	16	3	12	9	36
Totals, 1381–1450	136	0	0	0	0	6	4	10	7	8	6	24	18

Source: ASF, *CRS,* San Sepolcro, L.XX.8, fols. 13r–85r.

Note: Any money an individual bequested is eliminated from this table if he or she also made a bequest of land, house, or other property. Perpetual grants capitalized at fifty years.

TABLE 4.4

Bequests of Grain to the Confraternity of Santa Maria della Notte, 1311–1450

Decade	*Total Bequests*	1/2 Staio	*Percent*	1–2 Staia	*Percent*	2+–10 Staia	*Percent*	10+ Staia	*Percent*	*Total Grain Bequests*	*Percent of All Bequests*
1311–20	2	0	0	0	0	0	0	0	0	0	0
1321–30	15	1	7	0	0	0	0	1	7	2	13
1331–40	69	3	4	6	9	9	13	4	6	22	32
1341–50	254	1	0	7	3	26	10	11	4	45	18
1351–60	13	0	0	0	0	0	0	1	7	1	7
1361–70	70	0	0	1	1	4	6	1	1	6	9
1371–80	62	0	0	1	2	3	5	1	2	5	8
Total, 1311–80	485	5	1	15	3	42	9	19	4	81	17
1381–90	37	0	0	0	0	2	5	5	14	7	19
1391–1400	12	0	0	0	0	1	8	0	0	1	8
1401–10	14	0	0	0	0	0	0	1	7	1	7
1411–20	14	0	0	0	0	0	0	0	0	0	0
1421–30	10	0	0	0	0	0	0	0	0	0	0
1431–40	14	0	0	0	0	2	14	0	0	2	14
1441–50	10	0	0	0	0	0	0	0	0	0	0
1401–50 (without date)	25	0	0	1	4	3	12	2	8	6	20
Total, 1381–1450	136	0	0	1	1	8	6	8	6	17	13

Source: ASF, *CRS,* SS, L.XX.8, fols. 13r–85r.

Note: Two bequests of beans are included. As with the money bequests, in the grain bequests, bequests of houses, land, and other property supersede a grain bequest by the same benefactor. Thus some bequests are not tabulated here.

203 and accounted for 42 percent of all bequests. From 1381 to 1450, however, there were only six of these small money bequests, and they accounted for 4 percent of the total.[68] The absolute number of bequests over ten lire also declined after 1380, though the proportion of total bequests increased slightly from 12 percent through 1380 to 13 percent from 1380 to 1450. Of great significance here is the radical shift in the importance of all money grants. Before 1380, these made up over 50 percent of all bequests to the confraternity; after 1380 money grants constituted only 18 percent of the bequests through 1450. Simple sums of money were not adequate to achieve the testators' intentions and particularly to extend the labor of their bequests long after their deaths. Gifts of property provided long-term profits for the soul's benefit.

An examination of gifts of grain reveals approximately the same pattern (Table 4.4). The number of bequests of grain was substantial; eighty-one individuals bequeathed grain to the confraternity before 1380, to make up 17 percent of all bequests. Between 1381 and 1450, only sixteen testators or 12 percent donated grain. Thus after 1381 the confraternity seldom received small quantities of grain; the vast percentage was donations of ten *staia* or more. The earlier pattern of a large number of bequests with a substantial proportion of small grants of money or grain, totaling 46 percent, contrasts with the post-1380 period, when only a few citizens of San Sepolcro made the corporation their heir and only 5 percent of the diminished number of testators bequeathed paltry gifts to the confraternity.[69] But the other half of the pattern remains to be described. The proportion of testators making substantial bequests of real property increased dramatically after 1380. The change is masked because in absolute figures no decade surpasses the 1340s, when twenty-two grants of real property came to the confraternity, and the 1350s had a large percentage of grants of property. Despite the anomalies of 1348 and the 1350s, the division at 1380 remains valid. Before that time, only 16 percent of testators made bequests of real property. From 1381 to 1450 nearly half—43 percent—of the testators made at least one grant of land, vineyard, house, a landed estate with a house, or other property (Table 4.5).

The near elimination of small bequests and the emphasis on large money grants or of property is complemented by a decisive increase in the bequests requiring some labor or administration by the priors of the confraternity (see Table 4.6). These administrative services of the priors, similar to the services provided by the priors of the Fraternity of San Bartolomeo, included paying the testator's debts or ill-gotten

TABLE 4.5

Bequests of Real Property to the Confraternity of Santa Maria della Notte, 1311–1450

Decade	*Total Bequests*	*Land*	*Percent*	*Vineyard*	*Percent*	*House*	*Percent*	*Other Property*	*Percent*	*Total Property Bequests*	*Percent*
1311–20	2	0	0	0	0	0	0	0	0	0	0
1321–30	15	1	7	0	0	0	0	1	7	2	13
1331–40	69	5	7	2	3	3	4	1	1	11	16
1341–50	254	14	6	2	1	5	2	1	0	22	9
1351–60	13	5	38	2	15	2	15	0	0	9	69
1361–70	70	7	10	2	3	7	10	0	0	16	23
1371–80	62	9	15	2	3	4	6	1	2	16	26
Total, 1311–80	485	41	8	10	2	21	4	4	1	76	16
1381–90	37	11	30	2	5	2	5	0	0	15	41
1391–1400	12	2	17	2	17	1	8	0	0	5	42
1401–10	14	8	57	3	21	5	36	0	0	16	114
1411–20	14	6	43	2	14	2	14	0	0	10	71
1421–30	10	0	0	1	10	1	10	0	0	2	20
1431–40	14	5	36	1	7	0	0	0	0	6	43
1441–50	10	2	20	0	0	0	0	0	0	2	20
1401–50 (without date)	25	1	4	0	0	1	4	0	0	2	8
Total, 1381–1450	136	35	26	11	8	12	9	0	0	58	43

Source: ASF, *CRS,* SS, L.XX.8, fols. 13r–85r.

Note: Bequests of real property superseded money and grain bequests from the same benefactor. Also, if one testator made several bequests of real property to the confraternity, all are computed. Thus, these numbers and percentages are inflated.

profits, supervising the building of a tomb or chapel, distributing money, grain, or rents over a determinate number of years or in perpetuity, standing in as a substitute heir, and receiving property after the life use by the testator or his immediate recipient's death. Again 1380 is the dividing line between two radically different periods. From 1310 to 1380, only 32 percent of the testament writers required services from the confraternity in exchange for their donations. After 1380 72 percent endowed the confraternity with money or other forms of property with the legally valid requirement that the priors perform some labor. The donor frequently made this requirement explicit by stating in the testament that, should the priors refuse to carry out his wishes, the property bequeathed to the confraternity would instead go to a substitute heir.

As in the case of the Fraternity of San Bartolomeo, the Confraternity of Santa Maria della Notte went through a transformation in the century and a half under consideration. Organized originally for the pious purpose of charity and singing praises to Mary and Christ, the confraternity convinced citizens of San Sepolcro to view it as a virtuous recipient of their pious bequests. To maintain their devotional purposes, the *laudesi* required only a modest income. The citizens of the town shared in the meritorious labor of the confraternity through their gifts. Early in the corporation's history these went into a general fund for unspecified purposes, were freed from compensatory services, and carried the obligation of being performed in the name of a specific person or his soul. The citizens had so much confidence in the devotion of the corporation that they blithely endowed the *laudesi* with a significant share of their property. This confidence diminished in the course of the fourteenth century. It was no longer possible simply to donate a sum of money or grain and expect some merit to trickle back to the donor. Gratuitous charity gave way to a quid pro quo charity in which the testator required some tangible return for his material donation. The interests of his family or his soul in eternity were apparently best served through legally obligating the priors of the confraternity to perform a precise service in the donor's or his soul's name. The greatest percentage increase of confraternal labor is in the category of conditional bequests, grants to the confraternity only if some fortuitous event occurred such as the testator or his son dying without heir. Before the 1380s only 5 percent of the testators added this conditional provision, but in the period from 1381 to 1450 27 percent granted the confraternity money or property only if some disastrous event were to befall the donor or his family. By the fifteenth century the confrater-

TABLE 4.6

Bequests to the Confraternity of Santa Maria della Notte Requiring Administrative Labor of the Priors, 1311–1450

Decade	*Total Bequests*	*Service by Priors*	*Percent*	*In Perpetuity*	*Percent*	*Over Period of Years*	*Percent*	*Conditional Grants*	*Percent*	*Life Use*	*Percent*	*Institute Heir*	*Percent*	*Total*	*Percent*
1311–20	2	0	0	0	0	0	0	0	0	0	0	0	0	0	0
1321–30	15	0	0	0	0	0	0	0	0	0	0	2	13	2	13
1331–40	69	0	0	1	1	6	9	4	6	0	0	2	3	13	17
1341–50	254	7	3	9	4	18	7	7	3	4	2	32	13	77	30
1351–60	13	2	15	2	15	0	0	2	15	3	23	3	23	12	92
1361–70	70	9	13	5	7	2	3	4	6	1	1	5	7	26	37
1371–80	62	10	16	3	5	0	0	7	11	1	2	3	5	24	39
Total, 1311–80	485	28	6	20	4	26	5	24	5	9	2	47	10	154	32
1381–90	37	8	22	4	11	1	3	9	24	0	0	7	19	29	78
1391–1400	12	3	25	0	0	0	0	2	17	1	8	0	0	6	50
1401–10	14	4	29	1	7	1	7	3	21	0	0	1	7	10	71
1411–20	14	3	21	3	21	0	0	5	36	0	0	2	14	13	93
1421–30	10	0	0	1	10	1	10	4	40	0	0	4	40	10	100

1431–40	14	1	7	3	21	0	0	3	21	1	7	1	7	9	64
1441–50	10	0	0	1	10	0	0	4	40	0	0	5	50	10	100
1401–50 (without date)	25	0	0	0	0	1	4	7	28	0	0	3	12	11	44
Total, 1381–1450	136	19	14	13	10	4	3	37	27	2	1	23	17	98	72

Source: ASF, *CRS,* SS, L.XX.8 fols. 13r–85r.

Note: Several bequests have more than one provision and thus could be tabulated more than once in this computation. To understand the percentage of testators requiring administrative labor by the priors, I have counted only one provision per testator. Priority is given to bequests to service by priors (first column) over bequests in perpetuity (second column) and the remaining categories, then priority is given to bequests in perpetuity over bequests to be distributed over a period of years (third column) and the remaining categories, and so forth, moving from left to right.

The categories are defined as follows: *Service by priors:* As a condition of receiving the bequest and property or money the priors were required to perform some service such as paying debts, building a chapel, repaying illicitly received value, and the like.

In perpetuity: The testator granted property in perpetuity to the confraternity, which the priors administered and also in perpetuity would oversee distribution of the fruits of the property for prayers for the testator's soul, for the poor, and so on.

Over period of years: The same as "in perpetuity" except over a determinate number of years rather than in perpetuity.

Conditional grant: The testator made the confraternity the heir or granted the corporation a bequest in the event of the death of an heir or heirs; usually the confraternity was the substitute heir should a family member die without an heir.

Life use: The testator made the confraternity the heir after the testator or other individual had possession and use of a property; at his or her death the property would pass to the confraternity.

Institute heir: Largi often simply noted that the testator had instituted the confraternity his or her heir, and those wills are tabulated here. If Largi then went on and noted the provisions of the wills, I calculated them in one of the above categories.

Total: A sum of the above categories that yields an idea of how many testators required the priors of the confraternity to perform some labor in exchange for the bequests followed by the proportion of total testators making grants to the confraternity that required such services.

nity had become an administrative agent, serving San Sepolcro as a holding company for those citizens who did not have a secure line of heirs, required special administrative skills to accomplish a project, needed protection for their patrimony from the attack of individuals or other corporate entities, or desired service to the poor for long periods after their death.

Administrative Piety

These radical changes in the activities of the confraternity transformed the members' view of their tasks and by inference their devotion. Although some of the fifteenth-century documents retain the name *Laude* in the title of the confraternity, there is no evidence in the confraternal financial records of any outlays of money for instruction in music or purchase of manuscripts of music. The act of singing was not professionalized in San Sepolcro, as it was in several *laudesi* confraternities in northern and central Italy at this time. By the fifteenth century the piety of the members of the Confraternity of Santa Maria della Notte had become primarily administrative in nature. From their origins as a group of men who processed from sacred place to sacred place on feast days, the confreres had become administrators of bequests and disposers of goods for the poor of San Sepolcro. By the fifteenth century, the diminution in the number of members allowed each member to participate in the administration of the charitable love of the deceased and to perform the testators' demands for administration of their property for ten or fifty years or in perpetuity. Each member could anticipate holding an office every year and doubtless knew he would, within a year or two, serve as prior.

The responsibilities of administrating the bequests of hundreds of individuals diminished the importance of processional chanting and redirected the pious corporation into an administrative-charitable entity. The securing of merit through the processional chanting of *laude* had conferred on the corporation a sacred quality that empowered it to receive the bequests of the deceased, to hold these goods and take rents, and in time to dispose of them (unless they were to be held in perpetuity) in the interests of the deceased, the poor, and the corporation. Just as in the "Specchio," written to reform the administrative practices of the Fraternity of San Bartolomeo, so too in his writings as secretary for the Confraternity of Santa Maria della Notte for four decades, Francesco de Largi attempted to elevate this administrative labor to a moral-spiritual plane. He related the priors' labor as administrators and his labor as secretary of the confraternity to the interests of the poor and the desire of the dying for remembrance and formulated what may be termed a bureaucratic or administrative piety. This piety has at its core the idea that the supervision of charity to the poor and control of pious bequests for the well-being of departed souls constituted religious activity.

The unparalleled expansion of the number of individuals making wills in the course of the fourteenth century necessitated a large corps of notaries and confraternal officers to record and administer pious bequests. This is not to say that confraternities came into existence to administer the properties of the deceased, but the early confraternities with their pious activity of caring for the poor and burying the dead with memorialization permitted the priors to garner a sacral quality, which came to the minds of the dying as they made their testaments. In a century of recurring plagues and truncated families, the confraternities appeared as sempiternal institutions with a tradition of dealing with property and death. To many, these institutions constituted the surest trump against the vagaries of fortune, the surest means of using one's patrimony to secure the well-being of one's children and one's own soul. This does not answer the question of why the traditional repository of disinterested administration of property for the dead, the church, did not reap the benefits of the prosperity and high death rates of the early fourteenth century.

The lay notaries and lay confraternal officers gained authority over a large proportion of bequests for the well-being of deceased souls and over bequests for those whose family, for whatever reason, could not adequately or equitably supervise the administration of the testators' property. By the fifteenth century Francesco de Largi justified the activities and the rewards of the officers of the administrative confraternities. He perceived that the confraternity's paramount responsibility was to the dead and the provisions of the testaments that provided wealth to the brotherhood. These activities required the brothers' careful and sustained attention. When he wrote the confraternal statutes in 1441, he had spent twenty-eight years as the notary of the confraternity and was to spend six more before his death, and he had not failed to notice the primary place of testamentary income and resulting priory labor.

In these statutes that he formulated and copied, Largi stated the central tenet of the administrative piety of the fifteenth century in his discussion of the charitable activities of the confraternity, which he entitled "On the charity that ought to be done through bequests" (XV). After recounting the various charities the legacies were to support, Largi exhorted future priors that "above everything the priors are held quickly to satisfy the particular bequests and the annual bequests. And upon this they are admonished and pressed by the provost in every way, and if the said priors in this will be negligent and will not pay the legacies, they will be written into the Book of Debtors and [their names] will not be placed in the sacks" for the next selection for the office of the priory (XV). The notary should maintain all the accounts of income, expenses, grain given and sold, and cloth bought and given in charity, along with several other registers according to the "customs of the good merchants." This record keeping would preclude all doubts and suspicions about the work of the confraternity. Indeed the books and accounts should be able to withstand the continuous inspection of all men and God (XV). He termed "pious works" the accumulation and distribution of charity to the poor and administration of the property of the dead for their souls. In 1439 Largi began one of the administrative books of the Confraternity of Santa Maria della Notte by asserting that he would record the "pious works" (*pietose opere*) of the officers, who, we should remember, constituted the membership. Largi wrote that "we shall begin by writing all the works, salaries, and offices that will be done in the future and all the commissions for the pardons of the souls of these good people, who have their hope and faith in this blessed and devout confraternity and in the excellent fathers of it."[70]

At the end of the statutes Largi reminded his "companions and brothers" of the confraternity that he had conceived and written the statutes for his love of them and without any temporal reward; he then requested that while his brothers kneeled before the painting of God and the Virgin Mary, they would pray for him: "And, my sweetest brothers, always for you and your salvation I want to pray so that one for the other praying we merit to acquire the grace of God in this way and in the other glory, and thus mutual love has been from the one to the other promised in perpetuity to observe" (XXXIV). In the end, then, Largi declares the basic idea of the confraternities—men equal in quality reciprocally praying for the salvation of one another. These prayers also acquired merit because the beseechers of God's mercy performed a myriad of administrative tasks in supervising the "sacred" possessions bequeathed to the confraternity and in distributing charity to the poor of the community.[71]

CHAPTER FIVE

Flagellant Confraternities: Purged Social Behaviors and Sacred Communities

In the thirteenth century the mendicants along with the confreres of the Fraternity of San Bartolomeo had been in the forefront of religious activity in San Sepolcro. The response of the people of the town to the ministry of the mendicants has come down to us in the form of several ecclesiastical edifices and in documents recording the presence of a few men and many women in Franciscan convents. The few clerical building projects of the early fourteenth century were at previously existing sites or structures and do not constitute an expansion of the clerical presence in San Sepolcro. In the first half of that century, however, the number of religious corporations initiated and directed by the laity expanded rapidly. Then for more than a century after 1348 not one clerical or lay religious corporation was founded. The religious corporations already in existence in 1348 seem to have met the religious aspirations of the townspeople. Only in the second half of the fifteenth century were new religious corporations, lay or clerical, founded.[1] The halt in new foundations in the century after the Black Death should not be surprising; the population of the town declined after that demographic disaster and the earthquake of 1352. Though the dead were rapidly replaced by the children of the surviving adults, who married and procreated at a younger age than before 1348, and by migrants from the countryside, the number of residents in San Sepolcro stabilized around the 4,397 computed in the survey of the 1440s.[2] The failure to construct traditional or new additional religious corporations between 1350 and 1450 bespeaks the adequacy of implanted forms.

As Chapters 3 and 4 demonstrate, this is not to say that the religious life of the townspeople remained static. Within the traditional corporations and practices, fundamental changes transformed the character of religious life. The vast majority of adults of San Sepolcro rarely participated, other than through bequests, in the two important confraternities of San Bartolomeo and Santa Maria della Notte that garnered and dispensed the greatest amount of charity and performed a large number of social services. Excepting this latter confraternity and the *laudesi* confraternity in the abbey, the five other *laudesi* brotherhoods in existence before 1348 failed to survive beyond midcentury. The question thus arises whether lay participation exhausted itself in bequests to various lay and clerical corporations and in the yearly round of feasts and sacramental occasions in the monastic and parish churches. This question must be answered with a resounding no. The laymen—but not laywomen—of San Sepolcro participated most widely and most intensely from 1350 to 1450 in the flagellant confraternities that were founded in the half-century before the Black Death. In San Sepolcro the confraternities of flagellation were well established several decades before the visitations of death of 1348 and the earthquake of 1352.[3]

Lay Flagellant Movements in Northern and Central Italy

The exemplary expression of lay penitence in Italy was that of Fra Ranieri Fasani, who in 1260 persuaded the communal magistrates of Perugia to proclaim a season of penitence. Fra Ranieri led adults and children, men and women, shopkeepers and noblemen in self-flagellating processions in Perugia. These groups thereafter appeared in many of the towns and cities of northern and central Italy. These devout men and women cannot be considered members of confraternities because they did not establish permanent oratories or regular rounds of devotional activities. Moreover, the confraternities of flagellation did not permit women to enter as members or to participate in their processions of self-wounding. The processions of 1260, however, spawned the first confraternities of discipline in Perugia and Bologna; several others followed with the Bolognese confraternity as model.[4] In San Sepolcro the traditional date for the founding of the first confraternities of discipline is given as the first decade of the fourteenth century, and my research has yielded evidence that tends to confirm that dating.[5]

Raffaello Morghen, the most recent historian to examine critically the texts of the 1260 processions, finds the ideational kernel of the penitential marching in the desire to bring social peace to Italy after the decades of war associated with the Emperor Frederick II and his sons. In their processions through the streets of Perugia, Fra Ranieri's laymen and women took upon themselves the burden of conflict in their society. They believed that through self-flagellation, the aggressive nature of man could be beaten into submission, leading to an end of hostilities.[6] Meersseman also insists that the *disciplinati* acted in a manner similar to Christ. The flagellants scourged themselves to redeem others and society generally. Another interpretation is put forward by De la Roncière, who views the disciplining of the body as an act of individual motivation, albeit in organized groups, with each person striving to identify with the passion of Christ.[7] The flagellants submitted their bodies to the pain of the whip or branches as Christ submitted himself to the violence of flagellation at the post and crucifixion. In both instances the submission of the self constitutes a mortification of the body as recompense for sin.

Many confraternities of discipline, however, sentenced their members to the punishment of flagellation for their failure to carry out the provisions of the statutes or the will of the confraternal executive. This penitential flagellation did not result from ignoring or countering God's or the church's commands but from the voluntary acceptance by the individual of the confraternal statutes. Thus flagellation was not punishment or penance for sin; rather, it was prescribed by the officers of the brotherhood for the member's failure to comply with the confraternal statutes. The compliance with the statutes represents an important expression of the member's willing enlargement of his sphere of ethical behavior.

The statutes of the Confraternity of Sant'Antonio of Città di Castello illustrate the disciplinary nature of flagellation. Ignoring for the moment the identification with the passion of Christ, we note that these statutes, written in the middle of the fourteenth century, required the executive of the confraternity—a prior—to sentence members to discipline as punishment for twenty-five categories of noncompliance. In addition, there were eight acts or failures to act that the writers of the statutes judged to be so reprehensible that they should result in expulsion from the brotherhood. For laxity in applying these punishments to the members, the prior himself could be sent on processional flagellation by subordinate officials in eight instances and cashiered from the confraternity in six others.[8]

The context of the discussion of flagellation in the statutes of the confraternities of discipline suggests that the passion of Christ served as a means of social control. The statutes frequently linked the suffering at the post and on the cross, and by inference the flagellation by members, with a set of social norms. Members were encouraged to repress certain social behaviors by recalling the events in the last hours before Christ's death. Again the statutes of the Confraternity of Sant'Antonio of Città di Castello illustrate this linkage. The brothers were prohibited from lending money at usurious rates under any circumstances; they were also forbidden "to hold" the wife of another man or any female and to indulge in an act of "sodomy, that is, not to practice or use in an evil way any boy, not recalling to themselves the passion of our Lord Jesus Christ." Again the authors of the statutes warned their confreres to avoid being "misled by the enemy of human nature, not recalling to one's self and to one's mind how [Christ] died on the cross for us sinners; but if for any cause it happens that he blasphemes God or Holy Mary or Saint Anthony or any other male or female saint in any way," the prior might immediately expel that brother without intermediate penitence.[9] In each case remembering the passion of Christ functioned to repress specific social behaviors. Though it is not possible to distinguish social from religious purposes, nevertheless it is clear that this goes beyond an identification with or a sharing in the passion of God.

Penitents and Flagellants in San Sepolcro

In San Sepolcro men and women of penitence were organized in the thirteenth century and thus were in existence in the half-century before the confraternities of discipline. Male and female penitents occupied the middle ground between the laity and the clergy. Our knowledge of these penitents of San Sepolcro is severely limited; their size and particular qualities cannot be known. A 1292 testament contains a small bequest to them, and within the Franciscan order the tradition that male penitents served the Franciscan hermitage of Monte Casale to the southeast of the town remains alive to this day.[10] One assumes that the penitents in San Sepolcro held to the values of the rule of the Brothers and Sisters of the Order of Penitence as proclaimed in the bull *Supra montem* of Pope Nicholas IV in 1289. This rule was translated into the *volgare* soon thereafter in the diocese of the bishop of Città di Castello.[11]

The rule of the Franciscan penitents required a chaste life of fasting, frequent confession, limited consumption of meat, peace with fellow penitents and nonpenitents, restitution for wrongs and debts, solicitous care for the sick, and prayers for brothers and sisters at death. The rule was written to achieve a life of behavior purged of excesses and jeweled with prayers several times a day. Whatever the strength of the penitents in San Sepolcro in the second half of the thirteenth century, there is no evidence of their activity in the fourteenth century. Had the penitents continued in existence after 1300, at least one of the four hundred testaments examined from the fourteenth century would have contained a few soldi for the necessities of penitents, as did the one extant testament from San Sepolcro of the thirteenth century.

When the option of joining the Brothers and Sisters of the Order of Penitence disappeared in San Sepolcro in the fourteenth century, those who wished to withdraw from intimate involvement with lay society joined the mendicant convents or one of the several hermitages. If men preferred to remain in the world and yet to participate in the higher spiritual form of flagellation, they entered the confraternities of discipline. That they were limited to men may explain the discrepancy in size between the female Franciscan convents, with slightly over one hundred females, and the relatively small number of men in the Franciscan or other male houses in San Sepolcro. In the thirteenth century females did participate actively in the penitential movement, but in the fourteenth century they were not permitted to join confraternal organizations of flagellation.

Several profound changes transformed the lay devotion of males in the first decades of the fourteenth century. Women were excluded from the new confraternities, and they played a passive and inconsequential role in the Fraternity of San Bartolomeo. Females were shunted into the more private spheres of convents and *carcere*. Public singing and flagellating became reserved for those males who joined the *laudesi* and discipline confraternities. As males participated more actively in the morally ambiguous activities of merchandising the labor of others, borrowing or lending money, calculating the political profit of going to war, and debating what behavior should result in death, they also actively sought to expiate their participation in these marginal acts. Women, sheltered from the new questionable social practices, could not help directly in the expiation through public acts. Nor were women permitted the positive results of membership, which were the achieving of social behavior purged of the worst aspects of the new social life.[12]

The flagellant confraternities appeared in San Sepolcro soon after 1300. Agnoletti cites tradition when he asserts that the Camaldolese

Abbot Giovanni II, soon after giving up his claim to temporal authority in San Sepolcro and during the rebuilding of his abbey, in some way encouraged the founding of two companies of discipline.[13] Actually, neither confraternity had manifest links to the Camaldolese abbey or Abbot Giovanni II. It is clear, however, that sometime after 1300 the first discipline confraternity, the Compagnia di Santa Maria della Misericordia, supervised the hospital of the same name and its members practiced flagellation. The founding of the hospital may have preceded the founding of the confraternity or vice versa; the origins of both are unclear. The first extant reference to the Confraternity of Santa Maria della Misericordia is from a bequest of 1338.[14] Agnoletti recognizes the dearth of evidence before 1500 and attempts to fill this historical lacuna by attributing to this and other fourteenth-century confraternities functions known from the sixteenth century. He ascribes to the flagellants of the Misericordia the charitable task of consoling the condemned to death.[15] The documents of the fourteenth century neither confirm nor deny this assertion, but it is clear from the testaments that by 1338 the *disciplinati* of Santa Maria della Misericordia possessed a hospital of that name.[16]

This hospital of the Misericordia stirred the charitable impulse of the citizens during the plague of 1348. In ninety-seven extant testaments redacted in the year of the Black Death in San Sepolcro, at least forty-six testators bequeathed money or property to the brotherhood.[17] Doubtless the flagellants served the dead and dying generally through that terrible year. Some individuals on their deathbeds sought entrance to the brotherhood and its benefits. Writing his will in August, when the plague raged in San Sepolcro, Cola di Jacopo, a saddler or harnessmaker, bequeathed a piece of land to the Confraternity of Santa Maria della Misericordia, whose members were to honor him by carrying his remains to his burial church, being present at his burial, and bestowing upon him every other honor given to the brothers.[18] Most benefactors bequeathed the confraternity money or land, but others gave their beds to the confraternal hospital.[19] In 1360 Francesco of the local noble family of the Mazetti bequeathed a substantial sum and his bed to the hospital of the Misericordia in exchange for burial in the brothers' black cloak.[20] Finally, probably in 1348 but at least by 1362, the brotherhood had its own sepulcher (*avellum*) on the side of the Camaldolese abbey.[21]

Tradition also holds that the abbot initiated the Confraternity of Santa Croce in the first decade of the fourteenth century. The 1364 statutes of this corporation are extant, but bequests demonstrate the existence of this group only as early as 1339.[22] The flagellants of this company constructed an oratory on Via Santa Croce in the southwest corner of the town.

A third discipline confraternity, which took Santa Maria Maddalena as patroness, was active in the first decade of the fourteenth century. In 1302 Abbot Giovanni II conceded the flagellants of this confraternity rights to certain property. Already by that date they possessed their own house.[23] A document of the 1330s indicates that their residence was a large building near the monastery of the nuns of Santa Maria Maddalena, who were successors to those Santuccie who had moved to the monastery of San Lorenzo in 1271. The document mentions a "new church of the new monastery of the sisters of Santa Maria Maddalena in Borghetto."[24] The abbot of San Giovanni assisted members of the Confraternity of Santa Maria Maddalena in building the new church outside the western Porta Pieve. In 1345 Abbot Francesco conceded an indulgence to encourage contributions for the construction of the church. Notaries viewed the church as under the patronage of the laymen of the confraternity; it is referred to as the "ecclesia disciplinatorum Sancte Marie Magdalene."[25] Thereafter, many bequests were given to this male company of flagellants as well as to the monastery of nuns of Santa Maria Maddalena. The members of the confraternity are said to have gathered in their building, and in August of 1349 twenty-seven members met there to conduct their business meeting.[26]

In the course of the fourteenth century the flagellant companies expressed the new intensive devotion of an ever larger number of males. In addition to the confraternities of discipline of Santa Maria della Misericordia, Santa Croce, and Santa Maria della Maddalena, extant testaments of 1318–19 contain bequests to two new companies. Wills of 1318 and 1319 mention the "Societas frustatorum Sancti Bartolomei" that presumably gathered at the church of San Bartolomeo in the southeast corner of the town and may have been associated with the older and larger Fraternity of San Bartolomeo, but the testaments make explicit that they were separate corporations.[27] The fifth discipline confraternity was associated with the Camaldolese priory and hospital of San Niccolò, where its members gathered for flagellation.[28] By the date of the only existing bequests to this confraternity, 1318, the priory and hospital of San Niccolò were located near the eastern Porta. The available documentation does not indicate the size or the duration of these two confraternities of discipline.

By the 1330s two additional confraternities of discipline were established. According to an eighteenth-century historian of San Sepolcro, Farulli, several pious citizens of the town founded the Confraternity of Sant'Antonio. This group of laymen practiced public and private flagellation as well as assisting travelers and the sick poor.[29] To carry out this mission to the sick and the pilgrims, the Confraternity of Sant'Antonio built a hospital and a church. The Camaldolese abbot in 1345 gave the flagellants a concession to build a church. There are references to this church before 1348, during the Black Plague, and to the flagellants' hospital soon thereafter. Indeed, in the church of Sant'Antonio today, there is an inscription that reads: "Questo è l'ospedale di carità di Borgo" with the year 1350. This church of Sant'Antonio in the notarial documents is called the "ecclesia disciplinatorum Sancti Antonii," which emphasizes the role of laymen in the supervision and patronage of the church.[30] The patron of the confraternity was Sant'Antonio Abate, which suggests association with the Camaldolese, though it is possible the members chose this monastic exemplar solely because of his ascetic qualities. The church and hospital were located on the east side of San Sepolcro near the Porta di San Niccolò. A miller in his testament informs us of one of the charitable activities of this brotherhood; in August 1348, while the plague was taking its greatest toll, this miller gave twenty-five lire to the *disciplinati* of Sant'Antonio for "a box to carry the cadavers or bodies of the dead."[31]

The Confraternity of Discipline of Santa Caterina was associated with the female Camaldolese monastery of Santa Caterina. Agnoletti holds that the Camaldolese Abbot Angelo II sponsored the founding of this confraternity in the northwest corner of San Sepolcro as a means of collecting and dispensing contributions for female orphans and later for dowries of orphans and poor girls of the town.[32] By 1331 there had been an "ecclesia" of the *Disciplinati* of Santa Caterina, and in 1339 the Camaldolese abbot conceded to these flagellants the right to build another church.[33] These *disciplinati* also honored their members at death, and nonmembers could contribute to the confraternal treasury at their last moments and enter the brotherhood. In August 1348, a priest, Giovanni di Cescho, bequeathed twenty-five lire to the *disciplinati* of Santa Caterina who, in exchange, were to carry his body to the church of the Augustinian friars, where they were to bestow honors identical to those owed to one of their members.[34]

The men of San Sepolcro had substantially expanded their associations for cultic purposes in the century before the plague of 1348. For general charitable aid to the poor and memorialization at death, men and women of the town joined the large Fraternity of San Bartolomeo, though by that date it had lost a great deal of the affection of the men as it increasingly became an institution in the communal government. For organized choirs and chanting praises of Mary and Christ, the men of the town joined one of the seven *laudesi* brotherhoods. Among these groups the Confraternity of Santa Maria della Notte assumed greater and greater importance. It received an ever larger number of bequests, even though it had relatively few members, and eventually assumed possession of an oratory in the center of San Sepolcro. For private and public flagellation, care for the indigent and dying, and an honorable burial, the men of the town joined one of the seven confraternities of discipline spread around the perimeter of the town: the confraternities of Santa Croce, Sant'Antonio, Santa Maria della Misericordia, Santa Maria Maddalena, Santa Caterina, and, if still in existence, San Niccolò and San Bartolomeo. Robert Davidsohn's judgment that each church had its own confraternity in this period in Florence is borne out in San Sepolcro, where nearly every clerical corporation—churches, nunneries, and monasteries—had a confraternity, and several had more than one, associated with them.[35] It is also clear that all the confraternities were founded before the disasters of the Black Plague in 1348 and the great earthquake of 1352.

The Sacred Community of the Flagellants

The existence of these seven confraternities of flagellation demonstrates that a significant proportion of males in San Sepolcro sought a more intense devotion organized specifically for the laymen. The men of the town borrowed from monastic customs, perhaps mediated by the penitents, the practice of flagellation that had for centuries represented a higher form of religious life.[36] Within the secular world of labor, family, and politics, these laymen attempted to construct a sacred community. To achieve that community, they had to purge from their social behavior all those acts that detracted from their purity, including those that the church forbade but others as well carrying no danger to the eternal well-being of their souls, and to supplement this repressive process with a positive molding of their spiritual lives. To achieve a state beyond that necessary for salvation, the members of the confraternities of discipline chose flagellation as the monastic practice that set them apart from other laymen. In adopting flagellation, these laymen of San Sepolcro participated with thousands of others in northern and central Italy.[37]

The nature of one flagellant confraternity in San Sepolcro can be known in detail after 1348. Seldom did the testators of San Sepolcro grant bequests to this confraternity, named the Flagellants of the Holy Cross; among a sample of 351 wills from 1318 to 1373 only seven individuals bestowed their patrimony on the *disciplinati* of Santa Croce. And not one of these seven gave more than ten lire.[38] Therefore, this confraternity was probably one of the smaller and less wealthy of the flagellant groups. The principal source on this brotherhood is a manuscript that contains its statutes written in 1364 but with additions through 1451. The statutes of 1364 enable us to understand the purposes of the members and the additions permit us to trace some changes in the confraternity through 1451.[39]

The statutes of this confraternity of flagellation in 1364 show a narrowing of concern for nonmembers compared to the charitable vision of the Fraternity of San Bartolomeo and the Confraternity of Santa Maria della Notte. There were also lowered expectations about the effects of flagellation compared to the first confraternities of discipline in Perugia, Bologna, and Vicenza, which emphasized the far-ranging results of their devotion. Fra Raniero Fasani and the flagellants in Perugia in 1260 had hoped their processional self-whipping would halt the wars between the Guelf and Ghibelline factions and pacify personal conflicts that plagued the Italian communes. The citizens of Bologna, who in 1260–61 founded one of the first lay confraternities of flagellation, anticipated that their whippings would bring social peace. So too the members of these groups possessed a vision of a greater world that their flagellation and prayers could serve. Their concerns led outward from their brotherhood to their city, to concern for all Christendom, and finally to the infidels from whom the members wanted to take Jerusalem. Their statutes projected the possibility of remaking Christian society by excluding anyone who had conflicts with any individual in or out of the brotherhood as well as anyone who participated in the armed conflicts of the city and by praying for the Roman church, the popes, all the faithful, Bologna, and all the cities of Italy.[40]

In San Sepolcro the members of the Confraternity of Santa Croce gave tacit recognition of their inability to reform Christendom and to end its conflicts.[41] These *disciplinati* of the fourteenth century satisfied themselves with the project of constructing a micro-society that was sacred in itself. In their invocation the statute writers anticipated that their acts would work for the honor of the Church of Rome and for peace in San Sepolcro, but neither was to be achieved by addressing the conflicts between members and nonmembers or among nonmembers. The well-being of their town, not to mention Christendom, would not be elevated or honored by their charity to the poor because on only one day a year—the day of the festival of Santa Croce—did the members give anything to the poor (1 and 40). The members of this confraternity believed that they served the honor of the Roman church and best achieved a peaceful San Sepolcro by eliminating their own profane behavior. But the primary purpose of the reformulation of the statutes, and by inference the purpose of the confraternity itself, was a religious concern for the fate of their souls. It was their "great desire that the aforementioned confraternity become enlarged for the health of the souls of the members" (1).

The construction of a sacred community required the recruitment of men who possessed exemplary character; if a prospective member lacked such character, the confraternity provided a series of rituals to gain it. The first precaution in bringing new members to the brotherhood consisted in sponsorship by a current member. A brother recommending a candidate for membership would screen out any individual whose values and behaviors differed radically from those of the members. The prospective member had to be willing to bring as an entrance fee a large linen cloth that would serve as a cowllike full cloak—or three lire, presumably to buy such a cloth—and twenty-five soldi. The process of determining the quality of the candidate continued when the executive of the confraternity, a prior, read his full name in chapter, after which eight days had to elapse before the brothers voted whether to accept the candidate. In the interim the members reported and discussed any moral or character deficiencies of the candidate. The statutes addressed two particular problems, both of which were accentuated in the urban milieu. Entrance to the sacred community was denied to men who had taken usurious profits on loans or in any way fraudulently dispossessed others of their property. To gain entrance such an unworthy candidate had to pay the prior a restitution determined by the responsible clerical authority. Also, if the candidate had a conflict with an existing member of the confraternity, his candidacy was rejected, and this determination preceded the vote. Presuming that no one had raised questions regarding the candidate in the eight-day period, the prior again read the name to the assembled brothers and asked if anyone "wished evil for him" or if any brother not in attendance had "evil" with the candidate. The prior directed the members' awareness onto themselves and their possible conflicts with the candidate, rather than their possible conflicts in San Sepolcro with any other citizen. The logic of attempting to pacify all the town would have been more in the mental universe of the earlier *disciplinati* of the thirteenth century. The statute-writers in the Confraternity of Santa Croce took every precaution to avoid introducing already existing animosities into their sacred circle. If an existing member and a candidate had conflicts, the two were to address the differences and make peace; however, no one was to resolve conflict by undue pressure. Lacking an amicable solution, the members were to reject the applying individual (36).

Following a positive vote of admission to the confraternity, the incoming member had to purge his being of all contamination to avoid introducing profane matter to the brotherhood. This was achieved by confessing his sins immediately before entering and attesting to the prior that he had done so (36). Confession served as a means of cleansing members in other ways as well. Incoming officers of the confraternity were compelled to confess (9). And to maintain the purity of the brotherhood, each member had to confess his sins monthly, although in this period generally the church required the lay person to confess once a year (10). So important was this provision that if a member confessed elsewhere than in the church of Santa Croce, he had to bring proof from the officiating priest to the officers, who entered it in the confraternal records (5). Again, each member confessed on Holy Thursday before going to the chapter room in the church of Santa Croce for the reenacting of the Last Supper, in which the prior washed the feet of the assembled members. After the confessions and the holy meal, they all took "charity together." The statutes required the prior to ask each member if he had received confession before this significant rite of confraternal integration. If members failed to prove they had taken confession, "they were thrown out of the church and given a harsh punishment" (23).

The preservation of the sacredness of the brotherhood required more than the minimum of thirteen yearly confessions. Within the confraternity a parallel monthly ritual of confession of the members widened the arc of examined behavior. The prior had full authority over members, who had to obey his every demand (14, 21). This did not exhaust the statute-writers' intent to purge members of their profane character. The overprior, an official of the confraternity who oversaw the acts of the prior and searched for his failures (17), examined "the men of the Confraternity once a month, under penalty of being cashiered, to determine if any defect had not been punished by the prior" (23). Besides the rigorous examination of the behavior of members by officers and officers by officers, each brother reported on the behavior of every other member, if the statute cautioning against false accusation has any meaning at all (22).

The sanctity of the confraternity and its members removed the brothers from several vitally important aspects of contemporary life. Perhaps they were not to appear in court; in any event members were not permitted to represent the corporation in the courts of San Sepolcro (50). The defilement of the confraternity's sanctity threatened from every direction. As we have seen in the Confraternity of Sant'Antonio in Città di Castello, sodomy and extramarital intercourse threatened the well-being of the sacred communities. The statute-writers of the Confraternity of Santa Croce believed that sodomy was an act contrary to nature and highly despicable to God. Therefore it had to be rigorously prohibited and an erring brother removed from the confraternity (44). The sodomite could appeal for readmittance after three years, but if he persevered in his vice during this period, his nature had been so befouled, the statute-writers believed, that he could never again enter the brotherhood (44). Likewise, no member should have "carnal practice" with anyone's wife and thereby destroy the couple's "one life." The officials were to oust the offending member from the confraternity (24). Nor should a married member possess a young girl or consort with a certain woman who lived in the parish of San Bartolomeo (39). Members should refrain from visiting bordellos; offenders were either to be punished or removed from the confraternity. Members were also to guarantee that their minds were clear when in attendance at confraternal meetings by avoiding taverns on the mornings of gatherings of the brothers (38). The statute-writers forbade playing with dice; the offenders were thrown out of the brotherhood (46), and those who played any game of chance that resulted in gain or loss of money received a punishment determined by the prior (47).

The purging of the social behavior of members of the Confraternity of Santa Croce cleansed their souls and held them secure from the lacerations of the social evils of the town. In its prohibitions against civil suits and some activities of merchants, the Confraternity of Santa Croce attempted to protect its members from newer forms of social conflict, which in San Sepolcro had become prevalent only in the late thirteenth century. The flagellants attempted to reconstruct for the members many of the values and the memorialization that the Fraternity of San Bartolomeo had provided for the entire town in the thirteenth century.

The corporation itself likewise had to be isolated from as many of the vices of the urban world as possible. Protection of the brotherhood's sanctity was placed in the hands of the prior, assisted and checked by the overprior, who in turn was examined after his term of office by a syndic (16). Members who failed to conform to the prior's will or responded to his demands in any way that injured his dignity or shouted in chapter meetings were to be punished by the prior and his council (14). The peace of the brotherhood blocked off any appeal to outside authorities. Therefore, a member could not take the prior or the corporation to the courts of San Sepolcro; if he did, he was expelled from the confraternity (45).

The "Honest Life"

The construction of a sacred community required more than purging the members and the corporation of uncleanliness. Through what other confraternities called the "honest life," positive acts demonstrating the fullness of the spirit in the individual's life, a member endowed himself with a substantive character. Supplementing the cleansing effects of confession and the examinations of the officers and brothers of the confraternity were specific acts of devotion and worship. On rising from bed and before sleeping, the member recited one Our Father and one Hail Mary, which he repeated at meals (35). Every Friday the member was to say five Our Fathers and five Hail Marys in honor of the passion of Christ (35). This practice was borrowed from the monastic hours, although it was vastly weakened and had been adopted by the penitents.[42]

The honest life required frequent attendance at the meetings of the confraternity. The brothers congregated every Sunday in their oratory off the church of Santa Croce in the southwest corner of the town. They went there as well on the festival days of Christ, All Saints, St. Catherine, and St. Mary Magdalene (34, 35). On these occasions the brothers were first to kneel before their venerable cross and to say five Our Fathers and a like number of Hail Marys, to bless themselves with holy water, and to kiss the altar. Then they said, "Praise and blessed is Christ," to which the others were to respond, "Always is he praised." The member took his assigned seat repeating Our Fathers and Hail

Marys until all the brothers had gathered. As one body, they then passed from their oratory to the church of Santa Croce, where they heard mass and witnessed the elevation of the Host. Together with their devotion to the cross, this ritual illustrates the Christocentric nature of their worship.[43] The statutes indicate that this mass was in addition to the masses for the nonmembers in the church (34).

Flagellation is not described in the statutes, though such devotion would customarily be carried out before the members left their chapel for the church of Santa Croce. The testaments of the fourteenth century employed the term "*disciplinati* of the church of Santa Croce" to define the recipients of their bequests, thereby indicating that flagellation was crucial to the brotherhood.[44] But in nearly every case the statutes employed terms such as "penitence" to denote discipline in the modern sense of the word, that is, punishment. Other confraternities of flagellation may have emphasized voluntary whipping as an identification with the passion of Christ. But here among the partisans of Santa Croce, as among the flagellants of Sant'Antonio in Città di Castello, the voluntary element involved accepting the punishments handed down by the prior for failure to maintain the level of behavior required by the statutes.[45] The individual could refuse to perform self-whipping, but that would result in banishment from the brotherhood. The repetitious punishments and constant watchfulness weigh oppressively on the reader today and must have required constant vigilance on the part of the fourteenth-century brother. Punishment of the members for acts of commission and omission overshadows the members' flagellating as an identification with the passion of Christ.

Acts punished by discipline appear in nearly each of the 1364 statutes. The prior could send a member to flagellation for failure to confess before coming to a chapter meeting on Holy Thursday and its holy meal. The delinquent member was banished from the presence of the confraternity and given "strong discipline" (23). The same punishment was laid upon any member who failed to resolve conflicts with a brother (26). Also, anyone who lent a gown of the confraternity was sent to discipline (27). These 1364 statutes stipulated that after a brother committed five wrongful acts the prior had to send him to flagellation (61). For eight breaches of the statutes, the prior was obligated to punish members at his discretion. Among these eight were failure to confess before taking office, failure to attend the confraternal feast of Santa Croce or mass for a dead brother, and bringing nonmembers to the chapter meetings. One assumes that the prior could chastise the member verbally, but more often he assigned the culprit to discipline within the confraternal chapel or to the public humiliation of processional flagellation to churches in and around San Sepolcro. And for sixteen additional errors of commission or omission the prior had to cashier the member from the brotherhood.[46] And there were many more occasions for banishment in the statutes passed after 1364. Several of the expulsions related to failure to pay financial assessments, others to maintaining the purity of the member or the corporation, and many to the efficient running of the confraternity. The character of this organization, as known through the statutes, is most fully revealed in the provision that defines the authority of the prior to supervise the members through appealing to the passion of the cross. Members should obey the prior "for reverence for our Lord Jesus Christ and for the venerable Holy Cross" (14).

Reciprocity

The prior's power to control members' behavior and the members' right to report the illicit acts of fellow members conjure up the image of a reciprocal disciplinary society (61). The reciprocity of this confraternity, as with most *disciplinati* confraternities of this period, derives from the nature of the organization in which all offices were distributed widely and were largely determined by lot. Every three years the chief executive chose three men who nominated the men for the four principal offices: prior, overprior, vicar, and treasurer. The three nominators placed names for these four offices on six ballots of wax, which were placed in a box to be withdrawn by lot every six months for the subsequent three years. Each group remained in office for six months; over the three-year period all those nominated served in turn (3). A council of four men to aid the prior was elected by lot from all the men of the brotherhood (4). In addition, two officials of the sick, chosen by each incoming prior, and a syndic, chosen by the prior and his council, served for the identical six months (6, 7). Thus a total of eleven men held office every six months. One may assume that the councillors chosen by lot and the appointed officials of the sick and syndic changed in step with the other officers so that some fifty or sixty men held confraternal office over the three-year period. The number of members can be estimated for 1407, when a quorum of sixty men was required to change a statute regarding the celebration of the festival of Santa Croce (82). From this, we may assert with confidence that these sixty men constituted at least two-thirds of the total membership. Therefore, in the early fifteenth century the Confraternity of Santa Croce had a membership of up to ninety men. In a three-year cycle at least sixty men or approximately 70 percent of the membership participated in governing the lay corporation.

Reciprocity was also expressed in the fundamental service provided to members, care in sickness and at death. This concern included financial and psychological support. The officials of the sick administered this charity for members suffering illness. These two officers were to watch the health of members and solicitously care for ill brothers. The prior and the overprior were informed of any illnesses so they could determine whether the condition of their stricken brother necessitated the allocation of up to ten soldi from the treasury of the confraternity. If the illness continued, the officers could call out the brothers to provide the infirm with constant care (33). By the 1380s the officials of the sick had authority to give thirty additional soldi to the sick of the brotherhood (65).

Death of a member aroused the brothers to a series of acts that brought them to the center of the mortuary rituals in San Sepolcro and thereby supplemented or replaced a portion of the family's responsibilities. Upon the death of a member the prior sent six men dressed in the confraternal white mantle (*vesta*) with its insignia of a green cross.[47] They took with them the deceased's *vesta* and his whip of reeds or rope *disciplina*. The six brothers dressed the corpse and then carried the deceased in the procession to the burial church (33). The confraternity also sent two candles, which flanked the body in the procession; if the deceased was an officer of the confraternity, he was entitled to four candles for the procession and the mass (55). In addition, the cross of the confraternity could be sent to head the procession (80). These provisions for the deceased brother were recognized by communal statutes that limited the honor at funerals accorded the citizens of San Sepolcro. These communal laws allowed the deceased to have the confraternal *gonfalone* or banner in the processions. The mortuary laws treat the flagellants, here called *frustati,* as a special case, though the two candles were the limit for most processions. In times of high mortality, although the average individual was limited to one candle, the priors of the confraternities of the town could have their customary four candles. These laws for moments of high mortality also denied individuals the right to buy candles for the flagellants. Apparently some nonmembers attempted to add to their honor at death by purchasing the participation of the flagellants in their funeral procession.[48] An addition to the statutes of the Confraternity of Santa

Croce in 1408 may have been enacted to forestall any attempt to make the flagellants professional mourners (80).

The sacred community at these moments of death fulfilled its reason for being. Individual and corporate voices came to the assistance of the deceased to aid in the passage to the next world. And since men in San Sepolcro as well as in the rest of western Europe anticipated that the period of purgation was becoming more lengthy, the confraternal members had to provide prayers to aid their deceased brother through the purging fires. The prior informed each man of the death of a fellow member to assure that he would meet his obligation of attending the funeral. This exchange of presence by members at burial constituted the fundamental honor one member could give to another. The statutes also obligated each member to say one hundred Our Fathers and one hundred Hail Marys for the deceased's soul within fifteen days; within the same period the prior and the members made a procession to the deceased member's burial church, where an office for the dead was said for his soul. Within a month of the death, the prior paid for candles and one hundred more masses at churches of his choice in the town (33). Finally, in the week after All Saints Day, the prior arranged for a memorial mass attended by the entire brotherhood at which they offered some contribution in honor of all their deceased brothers (42). In constructing the sacred community, the brothers accumulated material wealth sufficient to honor and memorialize their deceased brothers. More important, the sacredness of the individuals and the corporation claimed a merit that endowed their prayers for their brother's soul with a substantive authority.

The Confraternity of Santa Croce attempted to achieve a practice analogous to the Aristotelian perfection of ruling and being ruled. Each member served as an officer requiring discipline of every other member and in turn was required to receive discipline. Members chose to burden themselves with an enlarged sphere of watched behavior for the honor of God and reverence to Christ's cross as well as for the salvation of their souls (1). The intense discipline replete with punishments and expulsions was not projected outward for the well-being of the poor of San Sepolcro. The members worked for the "peaceful state" of San Sepolcro, but the only benefit for the citizenry would be the presence in the town of a group of men who obeyed the laws. The only charity the *disciplinati* of Santa Croce performed in the fourteenth century was to give an undefined gift to the poor of the town on the festival of Santa Croce celebrated in early May (40). But the additional statutes of 1393 do not mention this charity to the poor and explicitly prohibit any payments other than to the officiating priest, unless voted by the members (73). By 1407, however, the brothers administered a hospital, though the communal authorities had given the confraternity this responsibility (90). In fact, the hospital had been under the authority of the Fraternity of San Bartolomeo, and its administration involved the flagellants of Santa Croce in a series of troublesome disputes. By the early fifteenth century most of the confraternities of flagellation possessed hospitals.

Except for the administration of this hospital, members of the confraternity gave charity only to fellow members. If a nonmember wanted the substantial death benefits but had neglected to join the confraternity, he could, analogous to a monastic "knocker at the door," pay ten lire and join the brotherhood (58). More illustrative of this involuted charity is the practice initiated in 1392 of giving death benefits "for the love of God" to members who were in arrears on payment of dues or other obligations (74). This charitable impulse had meaning only within the brotherhood. Discounting the administration of its hospital, the Confraternity of Santa Croce by 1440 had given up its charity for nonmembers and contented itself with the round of illness payments and death benefits to members. Such payments required close accounting procedures that were akin to actuarial thinking to assure sufficient income to cover the costs of these services.

Social and Political Participation of the Flagellants

This examination of death and confraternities in San Sepolcro has demonstrated that the monastic practices of charity and memorialization profoundly influenced lay devotion. Monasticism rejected the values and practices of the laity, especially urban society, though the monks served the laity through their penitential acts and prayers. Such a monastic sacred community could persuasively appeal to the divine for the souls of the dead. The virtue of the few religious men and women served to redeem the laity. The Fraternity of San Bartolomeo gained a similar sacred character through its charity so that, as a corporate entity, it could beseech God in the interest of the dead. When the Fraternity of San Bartolomeo and the Confraternity of Santa Maria della Notte lost their membership and the vast majority of the laity had no effective way of gaining merit or memorialization in these two corporations, the individual laymen sought an alternative means of gaining merit from the divine and remembrance at death. For many, the confraternities of flagellation served this purpose. But how is membership in the flagellant movement to be perceived? Should the flagellants of San Sepolcro be viewed as the few who withdrew from society and thereby redeemed the many, analogous to monks who for centuries had practiced self-whipping and analogous to the flagellants of 1260? Did a few men reject and hope to redeem urban society and its values by constructing a purged personal character and a sacred community? Or, despite their rejection of the more flagrant exploitive practices of urban society, did the flagellants represent the even more radical religious idea that laymen could construct a sacred community with sufficient merit to promise memorialization after death for laypersons? Could this be accomplished while still maintaining intimate contact and participation in the paramount pursuits of urban society—gaining wealth through the manufacture or sale of goods, supervision of one's family, and sitting on the councils of the town deciding public policy?

The evidence from San Sepolcro emphatically demonstrates that the flagellants participated in politics, represented the middle social groups that participated most fully in the market activities of this market town, and constituted a substantial proportion of the male adults of the town. In discussing the Confraternity of Santa Croce, we have seen that charity and memorialization focused inward on members rather than out toward the broader community. Nonmembers could gain burial with the honors of the flagellants but were required to pay a relatively large amount of money, five to ten lire.[49] And seldom did the *disciplinati* of Santa Croce express concern for the remainder of the citizenry of San Sepolcro in the form of charity or for the salvation of their souls. Distribution of food and clothing or a charitable burial occurred mainly under the auspices of the Fraternity of San Bartolomeo and the Confraternity of Santa Maria della Notte. The *disciplinati* of Santa Croce occasionally permitted an individual to enter their sodality without paying the heavy entrance fees, though often enough another member paid the impost for the impoverished entrant.[50] After 1350 the *disciplinati* rejected the aspirations of monks and penitents who had striven to redeem all of Christendom; the *disciplinati* of San Sepolcro ignored the example of the early flagellant confraternities and rejected any attempt to redeem their town as a corporate entity. Other than the hospitals that they administered, their concern focused upon dues-paying members. This exclusive concern with members precluded a communitywide charity and points to a corporation that had narrowly focused intent and means of reaching nonmembers and thus little basis for redeeming the wider society.

An examination of the membership of the flagellants of Santa Croce and of Sant'Antonio demonstrates their participation in the chief legislative bodies of the town. For the Confraternity of Santa Croce there are no extant lists of members, but the manuscript of the statutes here discussed contains the names of some officers and those charged with the task of reforming the statutes. This source from the 1380s, 1392, 1401, 1407, and 1408, yields the names of twenty-two brothers that can be compared with the 353 names of men who constituted the political class of San Sepolcro in the 1390s. As was done for the Fraternity of San Bartolomeo and the Confraternity of Santa Maria della Notte, the 353 men who made up the New Council of the Commune of Borgo from 1391 to 1398 have been compared to the twenty-two men of the Confraternity of Santa Croce.[51] Thirteen of these men in the confraternity from 1381 to 1408 participated in the political debates of the New Council. In San Sepolcro as a whole, the men on the New Council represented approximately one out of three hearths; the ratio of politically active members of the confraternity to the total members was nearly six of ten. The men of the Confraternity of Santa Croce were twice as likely to be on the New Council as other adult males of San Sepolcro.[52]

Their participation in the chief legislative council of the commune should dispel any notion that the *disciplinati* represented the underclass or the powerless. It is true that of the wealthiest and most prestigious families only one, the Dotti, appears among the members of the flagellant brotherhood. Two other family names, Del Doro and Del Cisschio, are among the twenty-two names, but neither was of great social or political importance in San Sepolcro. It is also true that not one of the confraternal members held the position of head of the lists of the council. The Confraternity of Santa Croce represented neither the political-social elite of San Sepolcro nor the poor and powerless. Rather, it recruited from the middle ranges of society.

The conclusion that a substantial proportion of the flagellants participated in the politics of San Sepolcro indicated by evidence from the Confraternity of Santa Croce can be tested by examining the more extensive membership lists of the Confraternity of Sant'Antonio. This flagellant corporation on the east side of the town had been in existence since at least the 1330s. The members administered a church and a hospital. No statutes from this period are extant, but financial accounts provide the basis for an analysis of the confraternity's activities and character. First, as in the case of the flagellants of Santa Croce, the entrance fee was substantial, twenty-five soldi in addition to a *vesta,* which the confraternity valued at three lire.[53] Because of the initial investment, the *vesta* or cloak carried an immense importance in the Confraternity of Sant'Antonio and in other flagellant groups. Administration of the *veste* and payments for them generated two registers that are extant for the confreres of Sant'Antonio for the period 1354 to 1450. These registers recount the attempts of the confraternal officers to secure payment by members of entrance fees and subsequent assessments for the needs of the brotherhood. Of utmost importance was to assure that members paid or brought cloth for the *veste,* which then remained in the confraternal meeting hall. If an incoming individual failed to complete payment of the twenty-five soldi and the *vesta* at the moment of entrance, someone—often a member, parent, or prior—had to guarantee eventual payment.[54] If the entrant failed to meet these financial obligations, including assessments for occasional expenses such as repair or improvement of the confraternal oratory, he could be cashiered from the brotherhood. From the perspective of the financial registers, however, it appears that the confraternal officers were solicitous toward their members. The critical question was control of and payment for the *vesta.* With the assurance that someone would complete payments for the *vesta,* a member would be kept in the confraternal registers for decades. At his death the confraternal cloak would be sent to his home if a family member promised to return it after burial or complete payment; in either case the deceased could be buried in the confraternal cloak.[55] For example, Nieri di Marcho joined the confraternity in 1429 but failed to complete payment for his entrance. Nevertheless, when he died on October 7, 1448, the confraternal officials sent his *vesta* to his home, so Nieri could be buried with the honors of the brotherhood. The body was buried with the *vesta,* and the family bought another to replace it, for in June 1449 the family "sent the *vesta*" to the confraternity.[56] That the members of the confraternity customarily continued to wear their *veste* after burial is confirmed by the statement of the prior on November 23, 1449, that the confraternity's supply of *veste* had been depleted because of the great mortality of that year. In the "greatest of need" the members voted to have new *veste* made.[57]

The heavy entrance fee should not lead one to infer that the confraternity had great expenses and income. Its paucity of wealth emphasizes the singular place of the entrance fee and the confraternal cloak.

The refusal of the flagellants to accumulate property and wealth is evident from the bequests they received. The overwhelming proportion of gifts were bequests of small amounts of money with no specific or conditional obligations. For example, among 351 testators in San Sepolcro from 1317 to 1373, only nine individuals endowed the Confraternity of Sant'Antonio with a gift. Moreover, only one of these surpassed the modest sum of ten lire, and no property was bequeathed to the flagellant confraternity.[58] The one larger sum (twenty-five lire) from Mucius olim Comandi was to be consumed immediately in the construction of a funeral bier on which the brothers carried their dead to burial.[59]

The flagellant Confraternity of Santa Maria della Misericordia, on the other hand, received a large number of gifts. In a survey of bequests to this brotherhood, the confraternal notary writing about 1400 recorded 185 bequests from around 1348 to 1400. Of these 185 individuals, 105 gave one lira or less to the brotherhood. Of the 75 testators who gave money gifts of more than one lira, only 10 exceeded ten lire, including several who gave their beds. And only 3 individuals bequeathed land to the brothers of the Misericordia.[60] Likewise the Confraternity of Santa Croce received only a few bequests and of paltry amounts. Seven testators remembered the brothers of Santa Croce, and not one of the gifts exceeded ten lire.

The financial records of the brotherhoods of Sant'Antonio and Santa Maria della Misericordia and the statutes of Santa Croce lack any reference to dues.[61] There were occasional assessments for specific projects as mentioned above. In the Confraternity of Sant'Antonio the two recurring sources of income were the sale of candles and gifts placed on the "altar of Sant'Antonio." The gifts were modest and included clothing, sheets, roosters, and other animals. In the semester from May 1 to October 30, 1392, the income of the brotherhood totaled only thirteen lire, excluding the extraordinary sale of a horse for seventeen florins. Expenses for the period were seventy-one lire with a substantial proportion going for maintaining the horse and paying a dowry. Ordinary expenses included payments for cloth for a poor woman (ten soldi), a loan to the Franciscan hospital at Monte Casale, candles and masses, and outlays for the festival of Corpus Christi. In the following semester the festival for Sant'Antonio accounted for a substantial proportion of the expenses, which were higher because the prior bought a house from his sister and in turn purchased a less expensive house for her.[62]

The Confraternity of Sant'Antonio derived most of its income from the entrance fees of twenty-five soldi and three lire for the *vesta*. The importance placed on the confraternal cloak for processions and burial divided the confraternity. The emphasis on the cloak places in stark light the significance of the flagellants in San Sepolcro and is necessary for understanding the proportion of flagellants in the communal legislature and in the male population of the town. The registers of the Confraternity of Sant'Antonio reveal a membership of approximately 200 men in the 1390s, although 30 to 40 men regularly attended the meetings and voted on issues, especially on who to accept into the brotherhood.[63] The larger list included all those men who initiated entrance into the confraternity; some simply promised to pay the entrance fee and buy or bring a *vesta* to the confraternal house, whereas others met the initial expenses completely or in part. Even if the negligent members were given a term of years to complete their obligations to the confraternity or their family paid after burial, all were considered members. Only a portion of the membership regularly attended the business meetings, though for important decisions more than one hundred men were in attendance. For example, in April 1429, when three confessed but penitent murderers sought to be reinstated in the brotherhood, 120 members voted—116 affirmatively. Usually, however, from the 1390s through the end of the fifteenth century, no more than 40 men regularly voted on confraternal proposals.[64] Thus there were two levels of membership: a large body of partly committed men, many of whom seldom attended business meetings and who may have been present at the monthly masses and festivals, and a smaller body of 15 to 25 percent of the larger group that attended business meetings. Whether the same men regularly attended the business meetings and what percentage of the membership flagellated themselves in public processions or in the confraternal house are questions for which there is no evidence.

The proportion of the larger membership of the Confraternity of Sant'Antonio that participated in politics in the 1390s was not large compared to the percentage of politically active men of the Confraternity of Santa Croce. In the 1390s the notary of the brothers of Sant'Antonio recorded the names of 198 men who had affiliated themselves with the brotherhood. Again comparing the 353 men of the New Council of San Sepolcro with the men of a confraternity enables us to see the degree of political participation. Of the broad membership of 198 men of the Confraternity of Sant'Antonio, 39 sat on the legislative council of the commune. Thus only 20 percent of the members of the confraternity participated in the politics of the town, though three of the fifteen *capoliste* of the New Council were members of the Confraternity of Sant'Antonio. Among the 198 men of the confraternity, four were members of the great families: a Carsidoni, a Pichi, and two Graziani. The notary seldom specified the status or occupation of members. Among the twelve men so noted, there were an archpriest, two friars, a painter, dyer, ironworker, wall-maker, and two tailors.[65] The evidence is thin for the Confraternity of Sant'Antonio in the 1390s, but a large proportion of the membership was not politically active, a few members of the great families joined the brotherhood, and of those with occupations noted most were in the middle group of the craft guilds.

Although the political participation of the members of the confraternity was slight compared to that of the leadership of the Fraternity of San Bartolomeo or the members of the Confraternity of Santa Croce in the 1390s, an examination of the more active group who attended the confraternal business meetings shows this group to be politically active. A comparison for the 1390s is not possible, but we can determine which active confraternal members sat on the legislative council of the commune in the 1440s. A list of members attending a business meeting in the 1440s yields 28 names to compare with the 342 names of the Council of the People in 1442.[66] Of the 28 members of the confraternity, 14 voted in the chief legislative council of San Sepolcro. This 50 percent of the membership of the confraternity should be contrasted with approximately 33 percent of the men of the town who sat on the council. Not one of the 28 brothers was a *capolista,* and only one member of a great family voted in the business meeting. In conclusion, the membership of the confraternity included a few from the great and, because of the stiff entrance payments, probably none or few of the poor. A high percentage of the active members of the confraternity participated in politics. Such guild affiliation as is indicated is overwhelmingly representative of the craft guilds.

Participation of the Men of San Sepolcro in the Confraternities of Discipline

Extraordinary numbers of the men of San Sepolcro affiliated themselves with the confraternities of discipline. The most complete information for calculating the number and percentage of men joining the *disciplinati* brotherhoods exists for the period just after the Black Death. Only the flagellant brotherhoods of San Niccolò and San Bartolomeo did not survive beyond the Black Death; therefore, San Sepolcro supported the five discipline corporations of Santa Croce, Sant'Antonio, Santa Caterina, Santa Maria Maddalena, and Santa Maria della Misericordia. There are extant records for the years from 1349 to 1374 on membership for four of these five flagellant confraternities. The exact number of members is never stated. In three cases the documents recorded the number of members attending confraternal meetings. As has been the practice in earlier chapters, the number of members attending is taken as the minimum membership, and a maximum is calculated by assuming that the number of members attending is the two-thirds of the membership necessary for a quorum. From the discussion of the Confraternity of Sant'Antonio, however, we know that this is a measurement of the active portion of the membership and that there probably existed a large number of inactive members.[67] In a 1349 meeting of the Confraternity of Santa Maria Maddalena, 29 members attended so we may assume a membership of 29 to 45. In 1357 the Confraternity of Santa Maria della Misericordia had 20 members in attendance at a business meeting, which implies a maximum of 30 members. In 1359, 25 men attended a meeting of the *disciplinati* of Santa Caterina, from which we may assume a maximum of 38 members.[68] For the fourth group of flagellants, that of Sant'Antonio, more evidence is available. In the period 1354 to 1374, the Confraternity of Sant'Antonio had at least 45 members.[69] Taking the middle number between those attending and those implied by a quorum for the three confraternities yields the average of 31 active members. This number is used as an estimate for the Confraternity of Santa Croce because no membership data on this brotherhood exist for this period, even though in 1407 a confraternal statute required a quorum of 60 members to change a particular provision (82). Adding the 45 members of the Confraternity of Sant'Antonio to the four others with an average of 31 members brings a total of 169 flagellants in San Sepolcro in the third quarter of the fourteenth century.

There was little likelihood of an individual joining more than one confraternity of discipline because the Confraternity of Santa Croce and most other contemporary flagellant groups prohibited members from joining another one. Nor had the practice of permitting members to enroll their children become widespread in the fourteenth century.[70] After the Black Death approximately 169 men participated in the flagellant confraternities out of an estimated population of San Sepolcro in 1350 of 3,000 with perhaps 900 households. Thus the flagellants were less than 1 percent of the total population. But because all of these 169 males were adults, the heads of approximately 20 percent of the families of the town were in one of the flagellant confraternities.

The knowledge that the Confraternity of Sant'Antonio had a secondary and larger membership in the 1390s complicates this picture. That the 1390s were not unusual is apparent from the number of members who joined in the subsequent fifty years. In 1426–27 the prior of the confraternity, Marcolino of the Pichi family, ordered the notary to scan the confraternal registers to gain a list of living men who had at any time participated in the brotherhood.[71] The notary recorded all those living men who had at least initiated membership in the confraternity, and his records demonstrate great interest in the confraternity on the part of the laymen of San Sepolcro. He found the names of 219 men, and 102 men were added in the subsequent four years[72] (see Table 5.1). Removing those who died in the interim and children placed in the confraternity by their parents yields a membership in 1430 of 252 men. Though the late 1420s witnessed the greatest recruitment, large numbers of the men of San Sepolcro continued to enter the confraternity through the end of the fifteenth century. Not all the inscribed men maintained their initial impulse to join the brotherhood of flagellants or completed their payments of the entrance fee and subsequent assessments. Nevertheless, as of 1426–27, the notary regarded the men as in some way among the brothers. The act of recording the names may have been part of an extensive recruitment campaign or the result of overwhelming interest, because the late 1420s witnessed the highest number of entrants over the fifteenth century. Or it was the result of the great plague of 1425.[73]

The 252 flagellants of Sant'Antonio constituted an extraordinary percentage of the adult males of the town. The number of people in San Sepolcro in about 1440 was estimated by a contemporary to be 4,397, and we may assume that approximately a thousand households existed, as in 1606 when the town had a similar population. The 252 men affiliated with the confraternity represented fully 25 percent of the households of the town.

But was each of the other four flagellant confraternities as successful in recruiting members? This question cannot be answered as securely as one would want, and it should be recalled that the 252 affiliates did not all maintain active membership in every year, nor did they all attend business meetings. The issue of permitting three confessed murderers to reenter the brotherhood brought 120 members to vote in 1429, but usually the number of voters at meetings in the fifteenth century ranged

TABLE 5.1

Entrants to the Confraternity of Sant'Antonio 1380–1450

Years	*Entrants*	*Years*	*Entrants*
1380–84	4	1415–19	28
1385–89	1	1420–24	43
1390–94	4	1425–29	109
1395–99	23	1430–34	55
1400–1404	42	1435–39	56
1405–9	25	1440–44	61
1410–14	20	1445–50	60
Total			531

Source: ASF, *CRS*, A.CCCXLIII, 35, fols. 1r–77v.

from 30 to around 50. Except for the Confraternity of Santa Maria della Misericordia in the late 1420s, when 34 of the brothers gathered for a meeting, no membership lists for the fifteenth century are known.[74] Thus there can be no final reckoning of the total number of males in the five confraternities. It is not important that three of the four confraternities had relatively small memberships in the middle of the fourteenth century because the Confraternity of Sant'Antonio had relatively the same number of members at that time. In the absence of all the entrance records heretofore discussed, there would be no reason to assume that the Confraternity of Sant'Antonio was extraordinarily large. It never gained the fame of the Confraternity of Santa Maria della Misericordia.

TABLE 5.2

*Total Bequests to Confraternities of Discipline in San Sepolcro in a Sample of 351 Testaments, 1317–1373**

Confraternity	*Number of Bequests*
Santa Maria della Misericordia	62
Santa Maria Maddalena	20
Santa Caterina	18
Sant'Antonio	9
Santa Croce	7

Source: See Appendix IV.

*The total number for each confraternity has not been tabulated because only the five largest bequests are tallied.

Moreover, the income and expenses of the two lay corporations were roughly the same.[75] The only comparative evidence for all five confraternities of discipline is from the fourteenth century and does not directly address the problem of the total number of members. The number of citizens who endowed the flagellants with bequests can be discerned from an examination of 351 testaments from 1317 to 1373. Table 5.2 presents the evidence of the testators' respect for and interest in the flagellant corporations on a comparative basis. We can assume as well that members, their friends, and families would tend to endow the member's brotherhood with a gift rather than a corporation with which they had no social ties.[76] The striking fact derived from Table 5.2 is the miniscule interest on the part of the dying of San Sepolcro in the flagellants of Sant'Antonio, particularly in comparison to the Confraternities of Santa Maria della Misericordia, Santa Caterina, and Santa Maria Maddalena. One would assume that the confraternity with the greater number of members would have the most bequests from the members themselves, relatives, and friends.

Though there is no overwhelming evidence, the four other flagellant confraternities may well have had memberships equal in number to that of the Confraternity of Sant'Antonio. If the five confraternities of discipline of San Sepolcro each had relatively the same number of members, every adult male in the town would have had some form of membership in the flagellant confraternities in the first half of the fifteenth century. The male head of each household would have belonged to a flagellant confraternity. All the evidence suggests that a large proportion of male adults, particularly those in the middle of the social-economic range, affiliated with confraternities of discipline. Minimally, it is clear that the flagellants of San Sepolcro in the fourteenth and the fifteenth centuries constituted more than a separated remnant of society, who withdrew with guilt from urban and commercial life. In this period membership in the flagellant brotherhoods was a necessary component of social and religious life for a high percentage of males in the micro-urban society of San Sepolcro.

Conclusion

This study has viewed death as crucial to the lay confraternities because, despite the many services provided by the brotherhoods, the association of individuals for joint remembrance and assistance at burial best explains the widest range of evidence on the confraternities. The sacred communities of monks who exchanged prayers among themselves and for their associates served as the model for the laity. The monks employed the term *confraternitas* to designate those with a right to prayers at death and other forms of intensive commemoration; that term provides the most cogent evidence of the intimate link between death and confraternities. The laity retained the linkage of the name and the practice in their construction of sacred communities and gained enhanced status by borrowing other functions of the monastic communities, including gifts of food, money, cloth, and hospital care as charity to the poor. From the monastic communities the men of the confraternities also borrowed the practice of burying the indigent, one of the seven acts of charity today largely forgotten. The exchange of services among the members of the confraternities assured honor in this world at burial and salvation in the afterlife. These services could be carried out at minimal expense, within the secular world of family and economic activity, and without a denial of the value of their members' lives at death. In the course of the thirteenth century the laity of San Sepolcro, together with laypersons throughout western Europe, constructed confraternities in which they integrated these elements from the monastic model. The exponential increase in the number of confraternities in that century cannot be linked simply to urban growth and mendicant activity because the lay brotherhoods germinated in every social ground and had the support of every clerical corporation. Rural confraternities arose synchronically with city manifestations of lay brotherhood.[1] A town of five thousand persons, San Sepolcro for example, and a city approaching one hundred thousand persons, Florence for example, each supported the founding of confraternities at precisely the same time, the middle of the thirteenth century. And in the course of the late thirteenth and fourteenth centuries, the *laudesi* and *disciplinati* variants followed in step in the cities, towns, and villages of northern and central Italy.

The founding of the thousands of confraternities cannot be seen as a lay appropriation of an earlier means of achieving "tamed death." The confraternities did borrow several monastic practices of death and remembrance, but the notion of a tamed death within or without the monasteries is misleading because it fails to incorporate the vast social investment of human labor to contain and express medieval man's fear of death. Monastic institutions required extensive socialization of the preparation for death and elaborate forms of memorialization. From a twentieth-century perspective, that may appear to be a tamed death, but on close examination fear of death and concern for personal immortality, which Ariès claimed were of no consequence through approximately 1200, must be seen as an integral part of the psychology of the individual throughout the Middle Ages. The achievement of monastic culture in regard to death was to enable the individual to live in and contribute to a community in which fear of death was dissipated in ritualized behavior. Prayers for the departed brothers, networks of monasteries with obligatory prayers for the dead of each of the associated monasteries, the presence of chanting and praying brothers at the deathbed and the vigil thereafter, prayers for the safe passage of the soul to the afterlife, and annual or perpetual prayers and masses served to distribute apprehension of death within the community. But the evident elaborateness of the rituals surrounding death attests to individual concern and widespread involvement with death. In this sense, death in the Middle Ages through 1200, the period of Ariès's tamed death for all members of society, was corporate, but this socialization of death cannot be conceived as defining the psychological state of the individual.

The characterizing of death as "tamed" in this period has utterly no meaning when associated with lay society. Though lay practices are more difficult to discern than monastic practices, the mortuary laws of the High and Late Middle Ages reveal anything but calm acceptance of death on the part of lay men and women. The occasion of an individual death in the family and neighborhood activated social mechanisms of great emotional intensity. The ripping of clothing, the scratching of cheeks and tearing of hair by surviving females, the displaying of costly trappings, the exposing of the face of the deceased in the procession to the burial church often prolonged by circuitous routes, the destroying of wealth, and the mourning demonstrate the extensive involvement of the community. These forms cannot be evidence for a casual psychological response on the part of the medieval individual, whether in the state of dying or as a mourner. The costliness and wide social involvement suggest, rather, that death triggered an elaborate social project that served to contain and express the individual's fear and the community's loss. In the early as well as the Late Middle Ages the rituals surrounding death expressed simultaneously the individual's fear and society's loss. Ariès's interpretation fails to give sufficient weight to the great social investment in achieving tamed death in the period before 1200 and fails to acknowledge the social involvement in the period thereafter necessary to achieve what he termed "one's own death." The concept of one's own death also has little meaning in the history of the confraternities. The death of the individual necessitates some social or transpersonal mechanism in every age to assure commemoration, faithful handing down of the deceased's property to the next generation, and aid in gaining a beatific afterlife. The form of social involvement with death may change, but it is always present.

The lay confraternities arose from the longing of laypeople for a new form of memorialization that transcended family and neighborhood and avoided monkish denial of the value of achievements in the secular world. The confraternities grafted the superior forms of spiritual life of the monks to the laypeople's desire to gain eternal life and recognition for their quotidian social acts. The monopoly of the regular and secular clergy over eternal memorialization was broken in San Sepolcro in the thirteenth century when the Fraternity of San Bartolomeo acquired merit by channeling members' charitable gifts to the poor. Episcopal indulgences and recognition served to aid the fraternity in acquiring merit, but the fraternity's existence preceded the assistance of the bishops of Città di Castello. It was the fraternity's functional acts of aiding the poor of Christ, and not the bishop's indulgences, that gained for the lay organization sufficient merit to honor its dead at its monthly meetings. The fraternity was then able to confer a townwide remembrance and to guarantee a corporate claim on divine mercy. Through a voluntary gift of charity stimulated by the "love of God," the individual participated in corporate distributions of clothing, food, and money to the "poor of Christ" and in return could expect remembrance before the community and the divine. Confraternal administration of charity and memorialization were part of laypeople's growing desire to play a part in their own remembrance and salvation. The church reacted to the laity's more intense desire for formal means of influencing the afterlife by changing church doctrine and practice. The proliferation of indulgences and the solidification of the idea of purgatory most fully express the laity's new concern and the church's response.[2] The new definition of purgatory as a place where the soul endures a period of cleansing served to undergird the church's various indulgences principally in university and clerical settings. Among the people of San Sepolcro and of the well-researched Avignon, despite the presence of the papal court, the concept of purgatory failed to become a part of the laypeople's conception of the afterlife in the fourteenth century. This ignorance of, or reluctance to use, the term *purgatory* is excellent linguistic evidence to prove that church doctrine and theological terms followed from or expressed already existing attitudes of the laity.[3] The people of San Sepolcro responded to the indulgences offered by the clergy of the town long before they knew of the term *purgatory* because the indulgences captured their longing for an assured afterlife for themselves and their deceased family members.

The interest of the laypeople in confraternities goes far beyond a concern for the specific reduction of punishments for sins. The diminution of penalties in the afterlife could have been easily achieved by enlarging monasteries and mendicant institutions, which frequently served to convey indulgences to the laity. The large number of females in convents, more than one hundred Franciscan nuns alone in San Sepolcro in 1317, suggests that male monastic houses could have been expanded to serve the lay concern for the afterlife. To answer the question of why lay confraternities proliferated, it is necessary to hypothesize the existence of an enlarged sense of a sacred community within the laity. Several authors, Marvin Becker and Lauro Martines, among others, have attempted to define the nature of this solidified sense of a sacred community among the laity in the thirteenth century. Bernd Moeller for German cities and Donald Weinstein for Florence have discussed the belief of citizens in the Late Middle Ages that their cities possessed sacred qualities.[4] The joining of the sacred to the civic could not have been accomplished without the laity performing acts that traditionally had been viewed as sacred. The acquisition of control over death and memorialization, the administration of the property of the dead, and the supervision of charity by the Fraternity of San Bartolomeo and the Confraternity of Santa Maria della Notte, not to mention the more intense forms of devotion of the flagellants, conferred a sacred identity upon the laity. In those confraternities in which only the executives performed the sacred acts, the identity secured in the ceremonial labor was widely distributed by assuring that the offices were frequently rotated among the members. In the documents of the confraternities the divine appears frequently; the laypeople were motivated by the "love of God" to hand out the "bread of God" to the "poor of Christ." In an extension of the divine economy, the confraternities elevated lay communities by serving as mediators between the dead and the living and by memorializing their members.

In San Sepolcro the Fraternity of San Bartolomeo gained authority as the laymen of the town took political power from the Camaldolese abbot in the course of the thirteenth century. The existence of the sacred lay community explains several phenomena that evade conventional interpretations. The fraternity's responsibility for the poor of God is compelling evidence for the existence of a sacred community of the laity. Previously in the hands of the clergy, charity to the poor was shifted to the laity when the communal government empowered the fraternity to act as the legal representative of the poor. The fraternity served as the chief distributor of charity to the poor as well as to several clerical corporations. In the decades thereafter, the lay confraternities constructed and administered the new hospitals and took control of the older hospitals formerly under the clergy. In the course of the fourteenth century, the commune placed all the hospitals of the town under the general authority of the fraternity and required its priors to visit them as a means of guaranteeing proper care for the poor and infirm.[5] When the communal government established a public lending office, the Monte della Pietà, the lay corporations of San Bartolomeo and Santa Maria della Notte provided, as directed by the political authority of the town, the initial endowment of this public charity.[6] By the mid-fifteenth century two of the three pious corporations, lay or clerical, with the greatest wealth were the lay confraternities of San Bartolomeo and Santa Maria della Notte. This wealth derived from the confidence of the dying in the rectitude and permanence of the lay confraternities and is the best quantitative evidence of lay preeminence in the charity of San Sepolcro.

The confraternities' wealth is also evidence of their mediating role between the living and the dead because most of the recorded wealth came to the confraternal coffers from the last testaments and contributions of the dead. The authority of the laymen of the confraternities to administer the property of the dead testifies to the shifting of sacred responsibilities from the clergy to the laymen. The charisma of the executives of the confraternities derived originally from the instrumental acts discussed above and was heightened by the ceremonial robes worn by confraternal leaders. Through the acts of charity and memorialization, priestly vestments, and care for the property of the dead, the leadership of the confraternities, and in particular the priors of the Fraternity of San Bartolomeo, gained a priestlike character. Perhaps this explains why the executives of the fraternity in the decade of the 1310s appropriated the title "prior," formerly held by the priest who recommended the deceased members of the fraternity to God.

To serve the sacral purposes surrounding death as executives of the fraternity, the laity required an analogous assumption of spiritual qualities. This was particularly problematic in the thirteenth century because the executors of the fraternity were drawn from a wide range of social groups, including shoemakers, blacksmiths, and other craftsmen lacking social status. Consequently, these men required another means of establishing their claim to the elevated position of memorializing the dead, in addition to their labor in seeking and distributing charity. Inseparable from this instrumental cause is a change in the names of the laymen themselves.

The rise of the Fraternity of San Bartolomeo and the laity's assumption of the administration and memorialization of the dead occurred contemporaneously with an onomastic revolution. From the second half of the thirteenth century to the second half of the fourteenth century, the practice of naming newborns changed radically in San Sepolcro. The fundament of names that parents drew from in naming their babies at baptism enlarged significantly, and a portion of the available names, those of Germanic origin, fell into disuse. Names drawn from Scripture, the Church Fathers, and the saints were by the second half of the fourteenth century seen as appropriate or expressing the capacities inherent within the newborn. A comparison of the names of the male entrants to the Fraternity of San Bartolomeo in the 1280s with the males in the Confraternity of Sant'Antonio in 1393 demonstrates this revolution in the naming of children. The names of the male entrants in 1285 to 1289 were drawn almost exclusively from Germanic sources. Examples would include Hondeus, Mutius, Rosellus, Brunatius, Torengellus, Ramaldus, Ugolinus, and Ghigus. These and similar Germanic names made up 85 percent of the 185 male entrants to the fraternity in the sample years. Infrequently does one find a Jacobus, Matheus, Johannes, or Martinus.[7]

The revolution in naming children implies a change in the character parents wanted to impart to their offspring. By the end of the fourteenth century the majority of males in San Sepolcro carried the names of the heroes of Christian history. Taken as a whole, this transformation denotes a radical change in the way a society conceives of itself. Of the 198 men of the Confraternity of Sant'Antonio in 1393, 123, or 62 percent, went by Christian names. This represents a 400 percent increase over the sample taken from the Fraternity of San Bartolomeo a century earlier. The number of Christian names in the 1280s, 28, was equaled in 1393 by men who possessed the name of the confraternal patron saint, Antonio.[8] The possession of Christian names integrated these men into participation in the divine economy. In later centuries, when Christian names were customarily employed, their use lost a great deal of its significance. But in these generations of transition from one system of naming to another, the men with Christian names were at birth veritable Christian reincarnations, carrying their parents' hopes that the children would be replications of their namesakes. The importance of this imitation of historical forebears cannot easily be measured for the individual, but the quantitative change and the timing with the confraternal assumption of sacred tasks suggests an appropriation of a sacred character for the laymen.[9]

The familiarity of the priors of the fraternity with the dead further substantiates the idea of the sacred community of the laity. The consolidation of the priors' responsibility over death is evident in their administration of a large proportion of the deceased souls' property. Supervising the property and implementing the intentions of the dead in the interests of the deceased's family and his soul, assuring that a portion of the patrimony went to the poor and other recipients, and judging which of the dead were so destitute as to warrant socialized burial, the priors of the fraternity were burdened with most of the town's mortuary responsibilities. The masses for the dead remained the sole preserve of the clergy. But the designating of priests to give the masses for the dead, the administering of the deceased's property, and the securing of the well-being of the soul fell to the prior of the fraternity by the first quarter of the fourteenth century.

The Fraternity of San Bartolomeo and its priors had been elevated to a negotiating position between the dead and the living with the support of the majority of the adult inhabitants of San Sepolcro, who bestowed free and unencumbered dues and bequests on the fraternity. But from the middle of the fourteenth century onward, ever fewer of the dying gave free gifts to the fraternity, and those who granted bequests required burdensome administrative acts from the priors and the application of the profits of the property to specific ends for the soul's benefit. In an analogous process, though delayed thirty years, the Confraternity of Santa Maria della Notte attracted a large number of free and unburdened gifts in the same years when the fraternity lost these bequests. Despite the lack of social status of the *laudesi* priors and the day labor on the agricultural land of the confraternity by some of its members, this pious corporation acquired a great deal of prestige and valuable real property. After 1380, however, the citizens of San Sepolcro seldom made free gifts to the confraternity at death, and the few bequests that were bestowed were laden with entangling obligations and heavy burdens on their worth. In this process the priors of the Confraternity of Santa Maria della Notte, exactly as the executives of the Fraternity of San Bartolomeo, were compelled to act as the agents of the dead and to oversee the deceased's property, frequently laboring in the interests of the departed soul and the poor against the living.

Charles de la Roncière has found from his study of confraternities in the Val d'Elsa in the Tuscan countryside that these pious groups were founded and flourished at times when the towns and villages suffered economic, demographic, and political crises. The confraternities, he asserts, expressed a sense of spiritual community after social cohesion fractured from the strain of the simultaneous crises in the sociopolitical world.[10] In San Sepolcro the Fraternity of San Bartolomeo and, to a lesser extent, the Confraternity of Santa Maria della Notte flourished while the commune gained political authority and retained its economic vitality. In its initial stage the fraternity expressed and contributed to the social cohesion of the town. The decline in membership and wide-based citizen support of the fraternity was contemporaneous with the demographic disasters and political crises of the mid-fourteenth century. Acting ever more often in the interests of the souls of those who died with substantial property and of the poor, the priors of the fraternity served as mediators between the few propertied souls and the living poor. These services continued through the end of the eighteenth century. The fraternity's possession of the property of the dead and obligations to perform services for the testators endowed it with the appearance of sempiternal existence, which in the crises appealed especially to those who approached death with no family or with entangling claims on their patrimony. In and after the crises, the fraternity retained its importance in the life of the town, though its relationship to the majority of the citizens radically changed. From the mid-fourteenth century, an individual in San Sepolcro knew that, if he became destitute, the fraternity would provide a modicum of honor and burial at death; this knowledge released him from an elementary fear. And the fraternity provided the wealthy with the assurance that their property could be used for the benefit of their souls if their families failed to give them that assurance.

The Fraternity of San Bartolomeo continued to express an aspect of the cohesion of the town, though it may have been driven to a subterranean level in the minds of the citizens. The conjecture of De la Roncière that the confraternities of Val d'Elsa reestablished a social cohesion fractured by social crises has some validity in understanding the flagellant groups of San Sepolcro, though not their founding. The flagellants as well as the *laudesi* came into existence in the early decades of the fourteenth century. The following contemporaneous social transformations suggest that the flagellant confraternities initially were founded as a result of positive factors in the society of San Sepolcro in the early fourteenth century. The town flourished economically; the males of San Sepolcro gained political authority from the Camaldolese abbot; the males adopted flagellation, which for centuries had been associated with a higher form of spirituality; confraternities of praise were founded; and the priors of the fraternity gained vast amounts of wealth from the dying. The exclusion of females from the new confraternities of praise and discipline occurred at precisely this moment. This exclusion was based on the brotherhoods' practice of requiring members to undergo a rigorous process of self-examination and self-discipline that was deemed inappropriate for females. These disparate social transformations are best explained as the male laity, in full confidence of their abilities, grasping control over areas of their lives formerly regarded as outside their responsibility. But control over political decision making, charity to the poor, commemoration of the dead, and the property of the dead was not simply a matter of grasping power or primarily a matter of supplanting the clergy. The laymen had to gain some quality of character or spirituality that would make them fit for these responsibilities. Evidence for later in the fourteenth century demonstrates that exactly the middling group of society, those who had not previously been politically influential when the abbot held political authority in the thirteenth century, joined the flagellant confraternities and exercised political power. Conversely, the local nobility, whose members did have political influence under the abbot, are seldom found in the lists of the flagellants. Participation in the confraternities of discipline appears, therefore, to be a necessary preparation or a correlative activity for political participation of new groups of men. The precise nature of flagellation's relationship to politics is problematic; the act of flagellating could have purged the new men in preparation for their political participation or have been a purgation for grasping power away from the traditional authorities and for deciding questions of political calculation.

The bubonic plague in 1348 and the earthquake of 1352 were social dislocations of great importance and brought on other social crises, which in San Sepolcro were heightened by political uncertainty. In the mid-fourteenth century the town suffered recurring invasion and occupation by aggressive lords of the region and by nearby cities, Città di Castello and Arezzo in particular. These dislocations fractured the social cohesion of the late thirteenth and early fourteenth centuries, which the Fraternity of San Bartolomeo has so eloquently conveyed to us. After the crises of midcentury, the flagellants of San Sepolcro, having rejected the universal goals of the thirteenth-century flagellants and even the aim of uniting all of the town under one confraternity, attempted to reestablish social cohesion within their own membership. The *disciplinati* confraternities seldom, if ever, acted in concert, preferring to construct microcommunities organized around their chapels and services to members alone. Within their sacred communities, the flagellants sought to renew the concern for others by exchanging the services between themselves, which in the thirteenth century the Fraternity of San Bartolomeo had liberally bestowed upon all members of the town. The flagellants exchanged psychological and material support at moments of crisis in an individual's life: food and presence at the sickbed, hospital beds, sick pay, the honor of attendance at burial with *vesta,* pall, and candles, as well as individual and corporate prayers at the moment of and long after burial.

Most confraternities of discipline in the fourteenth century refused to accept property or, if they did so, compelled their officers to sell it immediately. An examination of 351 testaments in fourteenth-century San Sepolcro reveals that the vast majority of testators decided not to bequeath property to the flagellant confraternities. Even the comparatively wealthy hospital of the Confraternity of Santa Maria della Misericordia received few grants of property; of the 62 individuals in the sample who made a bequest to the confraternity, only 6 percent gave the flagellants property.[11] Rather, the vast majority of testators gave small free bequests to the flagellant confraternities, similar to those given to the Fraternity of San Bartolomeo and the Confraternity of Santa Maria della Notte in the first phase of their histories. Moreover, the sum of twenty-five soldi, required by the flagellant confraternities of Santa Croce and Sant'Antonio as an entrance fee, recalls the most repeated of pious bequests in the earliest extant testaments of San Sepolcro in the 1310s, 1320s, and 1330s.[12] Many of these testators gave only one bequest of twenty-five soldi for the health of their souls without naming a recipient. Others specified a pious corporation as recipient and stated that this amount should be placed on its altar. The notary of the Confraternity of Sant'Antonio, in recording the gifts to the brotherhood, stated that such gifts, including food, animals, and money, were brought to the "altar of Sant'Antonio."

The flagellants' possession of the privilege of mourning in forms denied to most other groups of society also suggests that they labored to renew a lost or threatened memorialization. The exempting of the flagellant confraternities from mourning restrictions enhances the view that these brotherhoods served as substitutes for the family and neighborhood, whose representatives were frequently denied the activities practiced by the flagellants. Though the flagellants tended to deemphasize large dispositions of money or food for the poor, they practiced a face-to-face charity of giving small sums of money to individuals and of serving in hospitals. At times, they permitted the poor to join their brotherhoods without paying the substantial entrance fees. These acts of charity by individuals or the corporation were animated by "the love of God."

The renewing or reestablishing at the spiritual level of an older sense of community, hypothesized by De la Roncière for confraternities generally, can best be applied to the flagellants, though not to the entire town. The laity of the town split along social, economic, and political lines. Only the confraternities of San Bartolomeo and Santa Maria della Notte with their large endowments of property possessed townwide functions of substantial and periodic charity to the poor; by the fifteenth century both were located in the center of the town and essentially performed government functions. The flagellant confraternities, however, were located around the periphery of the town and after 1348 split the town into five sacred communities. They divided the town on a gender basis; males alone were permitted to enter as members. Though the flagellant confraternities may have made processions together during the great festivals of the church, they contributed to the fissures of the town by focusing inward upon themselves. The exclusivity of each flagellant group is probably best expressed in the prohibition against a member joining another flagellant confraternity.

These fissures in the town of San Sepolcro may have been partially sealed over by the common practices of the five flagellant confraternities. If the number of members in the Confraternity of Sant'Antonio can be assumed to be roughly equal to the number of men in the four other flagellant brotherhoods, we can assert that nearly all adult males of the town participated in some fashion in the lay devotion of flagellation in the fifteenth century. Even if we assume relatively modest estimates based on actual lists of memberships and voters, the males of the *disciplinati* constitute a large proportion of the men of San Sepolcro. Using either assumption, it is clear that this devotional form was not limited to a small circle of men. Neither did it serve as a novitiate for those who planned to enter monasteries. Nor were the flagellants of San Sepolcro a small group who withdrew from urban society as a means of redeeming the large majority of sinful men. The founding of these confraternities of discipline before the crises of the mid-fourteenth century and the large percentage of men who joined the groups should also destroy any notion that confraternal flagellation was a mass neurotic or psychotic response to unfathomable events.

The flagellant movement constituted a determined effort of laymen to construct sacred communities in which they aided one another to live a social-devotional life beyond that required by the laws of the church. The men of the confraternities of discipline made the distinction between upholding the teachings of Scripture and the Holy Catholic church on one hand and following the statutes of one's confraternity on the other. Failure to fulfill the laws of the church constituted sin and required confession to a priest and requisite penitence here and possibly in the hereafter. Failure to comply with the statutes of the confraternity was not sin and required no confession to a priest. Noncompliance, however, did bring the flagellant under the confraternity's scrutiny and punishments, which were recounted in Chapter 5 for the Confraternity of Santa Croce. Within the confraternities, members were instructed not to swear to uphold the statutes of the confraternity because failure to comply with the statutes after swearing would constitute mortal sin and place the sinner back into the church's penitential system. The flagellant's committing of himself to follow and enact his confraternity's statutes involved him in a rigorous disciplinary system outside that of the church. Within and beyond the medieval church, the confraternities of discipline constituted a voluntary church in which members permitted their social and devotional lives to be judged by peers and their bodies punished for their transgression of confraternal standards.[13] The restraints from certain practices and the requirement of additional devotions linked to the passion of Christ enlarged the sphere of voluntary ethical behavior, although it remained voluntary because the member could always withdraw from the brotherhood; for those within the brotherhood, social and devotional life came under the watchful eye of brothers and officials. Failure to comply subjected members to judgment and punishment within the forum of the brotherhood.

This voluntary enlargement of the sphere of behavior under a disciplinary system had a profound cause. The confraternities served many purposes and satisfied several mundane aspirations. But their early association with death, commemoration of laymen active in politics and trade, and administration of hospitals, primarily for the dying, has compelled this writer to interpret the confraternities as institutions whose paramount concern was with death. The enlarged ethical sense of the flagellants can best be understood as arising from the necessity of acquiring merit of sufficient worth in their minds and before the divine. This became necessary when the older confraternities of San Bartolomeo and Santa Maria della Notte lost the inclination or ability to confer sufficient merit on the majority of citizens. Unable to acquire merit for participation in the older associations, the average citizen sought merit through flagellation and his purged social behavior.

At the center of the history of confraternities from 1250 to 1450 is a lay community that endeavored to provide means of assurance to the individual that his memory would not be obliterated as his body decayed. Rather, memory of the deceased would be fixed at the time of burial and retained in the memory of his brotherhood. The confraternities enhanced the laymen's ability to gain merit in the eyes of the divine with minimal clerical assistance by serving as mediators between the dead and the living. Members of the confraternities were animated by the anticipation of divine reward as well as by a compassion for the poor and the unfortunate that they attributed to the influx of "the love of God."

Appendixes

Appendixes I, II, and III consist of transcriptions of the statutes of the confraternities of San Bartolomeo, Santa Maria della Notte, and Santa Croce. The statutes provide a substantial portion of the evidence for the arguments of the respective chapters and are intended for this purpose. The texts have value as examples of the organization of confraternal piety and of linguistic usage in San Sepolcro in the thirteenth through the fifteenth centuries. Therefore, I have retained the spellings of the text even when they differ from line to line, the grammar, and paragraphs despite different modern usages. I have extended the abbreviations, employed the z, and provided punctuation and accent marks.

Appendix IV contains information on the notaries whose protocols of testaments provide evidence for this study. The information includes the names of the notaries, the number of testaments consulted, the years of the notary's testaments consulted, and the archival notation.

APPENDIX I

The 1269 Statutes of the Fraternity of San Bartolomeo

Ordo Fraternitatis Sancti Bartholomei de Burgo Sancti Sepulcri

Predicta Fraternitas habet tres Rectores qui sunt de hominibus dicte fraternitatis qui debent esse spirituales et solliciti et sagaces in dicto offitio exercendo, quorum offitium durat spatio unius anni, et anno completo eliguntur alii per eosdem Rectores in ecclesia Sancti Bartholomei die festivitatis beatorum [5] sanctorum Iacobi et Cristofani presentibus aliquibus bonis hominibus de Fraternitate et de electione conficitur publicum instrumentum. Quorum Rectorum offitium est helemosinas legata et relicta et omnes proventus Fraternitatis exigere et recolligere et distribuere presertim pauperibus verecundis et aliis et locis religiosis et piis ut infra dicetur. Item quicumque [10] vult esse de Fraternitate recipitur per dictos Rectores et scribitur in libro Fraternitatis, mares in una parte libri et femine in alia parte, et ponuntur anni domini et temporis cuius rectorie intrant. Et quando intrant promittunt se daturos helemosinas, aliqui enim promittunt se daturos quolibet anno x solidos, aliqui v, aliqui unum librum gratiam et aliqui plus et aliqui minus, [15] et aliqui promittunt pro quolibet die sabati I denarium et pro quolibet mortuo de Fraternitate I alium denarium et in festo omnium sanctorum 2 denarios et hic est helemosina ordinata quam maior persona servata. Perceptio et exactio helemosinarum fit per dictos Rectores hoc modo: Ipsi omni quolibet die sabati post tertiam vadunt per terram specialiter per stratas et vicos [20] ubi morantur artifices et boni homines et illi qui sunt de Fraternitate petendo denarios dei et unus eorum portat thefamam, et tunc omnis qui promiserunt se daturos denarios quolibet die sabati offerunt denarios in thefama, et etiam multi alii qui non sunt de Fraternitate. Item die do-

Source: AC, SS, 32, reg. 159, 1r. The numbers in brackets with the text of these statutes refer to lines cited in the body of the book.

minica prima cuiuslibet mensis omnes de Fraternitate et multi alii qui non sunt de Fraternitate [25] congregantur apud ecclesiam Sancti Bartholomei voce preconia et sonitu campane post tertiam sumpto prandio, et interim dum gens in ipsa ecclesia congregat predicti Rectores quilibet cum sua thefama vadunt per ecclesiam dicendo tot sunt mortium precedentis mensis et tunc illi qui promiserunt pro quolibet mortuo 1 denarium offerunt tot denarios quot sunt mortui illius precendentis mensis, et [30] aliqui offerunt secundum promissionem eorum et aliqui secundum eorum voluntatem, et etiam mulieres offerunt panem ova et denarios. Et congregata gente in ipsa ecclesia antequam surgat predicator qui debet predicare surgit quidam presbyter qui est Prior Fraternitatis qui eligitur quando eliguntur dicti Rectores per eos de Rectoribus precedentes et permanet in offitio priorati similiter uno anno [35] et hic Prior in ipsa congregatione adnuntiat et dicit mortuos Fraternitatis et alios qui non sunt de Fraternitate qui Fraternitati aliquid relinquerunt dicendo talis erat de Fraternitate et obiit et reliquit Fraternitati tamen rogate deum pro ipsius anima et sic de ceteris. Postea talis non erat de Fraternitate tamen reliquid Fraternitati tamen rogate deum pro ipsius anima. [40] Et hic Prior non habet aliud offitium exercere; de inde surgit predicator et adnuntiat verbum dei. Item dicti Rectores simul et separatim et die qualibet recipiunt helemosinas ab offerentibus et exigunt legata et relicta et omnes proventus Fraternitatis. Distributio helemosinarum et proventuum Fraternitatis fit per dictos Rectores hoc modo: Ipsi omnes habent quolibet die iovis certam [45] quantitatem primis[?] cocti paratum et carnes, porcinas, fruttanti[?], meisas, et quilibet Rectorum cum sua maletta cum pane et quidam puer cum eis cum cista carnium simul vadant per omnos vicos terre exibendo pauperibus et locis religiosis et incarceratis helemosinam panis et carnium tribuendo cuilibet ut inspiciunt convenire, et aliquibus pauperibus exibent helemosinam per interpositam [50] personarum, et ipso die a multis dominabis panem et ova recipiunt quem et quae distribuunt simul cum pane quem portant. Item dant pauperibus vestimenta lanea et linea, lanea videlicet in inceptione iemis circa festum omnium sanctorum et linea tempore estatis. Item predicti Rectores per edogmadam et qualibet die separatim tribuunt helemosinas hoc modo videlicet [55] quod considerantur in terra tres contratae et cuilibet Rectori commitatur cura pauperum sue contrate, et quilibet ipsorum Rectorum habet marsumpium in quo portat semper de denariis Fraternitatis ex quibus per edogmadam providet pauperibus sue contrate presertim verecundis et infirmis dando denarios, panem, carnes, pullos et volatilia et alia quibus infirmi et pauperes indigent et [60] quilibet ipsorum Rectorum potest solus providere pauperi et familiae usque ad quantitatem XII denarium si autem expedit ut in maiori quantitati provideat debet vocare sotios vel unum ex eis. Item panem et ova quem et quae habent apud ecclesiam in congregationi die dominica prima cuiuslibet mensis distribuunt tamen locis religiosis et incarceratis et pauperibus verecundis ipsa die dominica. Item predicti Rectores nomine Fraternitatis a multis instituuntur herede ut hereditatem distribuunt pro anima testatoris. Item a multis constituuntur fideicommissarii ad legata et relicta testamentorum solvenda et distribuenda. Item dicti Rectores ex lege municipali dicuntur generales administrationes pauperis et possunt et debent eos defendere et iuvare in curia et extra et iura eorum manutenere. Item ex lege municipali commune Burgi debet ipsam Fraternitatem et Rectores manutenere et defendere. Item omnes qui intrant Fraternitatem et in ea manus porrigunt adiutores coniectuntur a diocesano specialem indulgentiam peccatoris, et Rectores qui portant malettam habent illam indulgentiam quam haberent si beati Iacobi limina visitarent. Item omnes qui moriuntur de Fraternitate scribuntur in libro Fraternitatis et quo anno et mense et tempore cuius Rectorie decerunt.

APPENDIX II

The 1441 Statutes of the Confraternity of Santa Maria della Notte

Ordinamenti dela Compania dele Laude de
Sancta Maria dela Nocte del Borgo San Sepolcro

[2r] Prohemio: Le pietose congregationi sopra il fondamento della Cristiana fede edificate et con la speranza della retributione eterna a pocho a poco dirizando il capo, tucto il dì più ardentemente se rescaldano nella carità de Dio et del proximo et de virtù in virtù favente Dio grandissime richezze temporali et spirituali sono accumulate. E questo certamente ai nostri tempi per experientia havem veduto in questo pietoso collegio dela Compania, già dicta "dela Karità dela Laude de Sancta Maria ai povari" anche dicta "Compania dele Laude de Sancta Maria dela Nocte." Narrarò a noi i padri nostri et scripto alcuna volta nei nostri codici havem trovato: Nel mille trecento como per li apostoli homini materiali et rudi la nostra sacratissima fede cusì questa devota e pietosa Compania dali homini semplici sumpse principio perche a quel tempo certi idoti et seculari homini dericti e timenti Dio havendo la fame valida assalita la patria usati gran seperanza in quello che administrà al semenatore il seme et il pane al comendente dei loro proprii granari pochi semi d'orzo adunati, pochi pani d'orzo aparechiaro. Aciochè la fame licha turba perente per fame con messer Iesu largamente satiassero. Et ecco como quel pan d'orzo nelle mani del benedetto Iesu e nelle mani apostollice [illeg.] multiplico et creve[?], così questo tra le mani de questi semplici et giusti et pietoso homini multiplicato. E facto pane cotidiano de buon grano, cibo di famelia, di sitienti vino, salute deli infirmanti, redemptione di pregioni, vestimenti di nudi, dele donzelle povere dota, e di tucti li oppressi poveri è facto refugio, benedetto Dio nei suoi doni et sancto in tucte le sue opere. E perche, "Se doi o tre congregati siranno nel

Source: ASF, CRS, SS, L.XX. 2, 2r–13r.

mio nome, io so in mezzo de loro" disse Ihesu. Havendo quella sancta semplici et devota congregatione messer Ihesu in mezzo stante lui inspirante certe ordinationi secondo il loro modo o spirituale de vivere agionsaro, peroche [2v] ove non è ordine, sempiterno horrore ci abbita, per le quali con devotione e fede se exercitassero nelle laude de Dio et dela beata vergine e in piccholine elimosine ma perche hora maximamente per la conversatione e costumi et exemplo loro, essa congregatione per le oblatione di fideli è augmentata de molte richezze e per gratia de Dio tucto il dì se augmenta per la experientia maestra è cognoscuto che nella conservation d'esse et in modo del distribuire e per accrescere la dovotion di fideli bisogna certe cose agiognere. E per ciò l'infrascripte buoni, semplici e dericti homini le antique ordinationi reformando in meglio et sopragiognendo le nove, le infrascripte constitutioni et ordinationi da observare per li futuri tempi hanno soprainducto, constitiuto et ordinato, comandando e exortando per lo advenire observare doverse per li homini d'essa congregatione a laude delo omnipotente Dio e della beatissima vergine Maria, sua madre, e sotto cui devotione et vocabulo questa Compania è congregata e de messer Sancto Giovanni Evangelista e del seraphyco messer Sancto Francesco e di tucti i sancti de Dio, a reverentia et exaltatione dela sacrosancto Romana et universale ecclesia, e del sommo pontifice messer Eugenio Papa quarto, a stato e universale pace del comune et popolo del Borgo Sansepolcro, ad honore et conservatione et augmento d'essa Compania, a pace e salute eterna di fratelli, e perpetua consolatione e refugio di povari de Ihesu Cristo, sotto li anno suoi mille quatrocento quarantuno in kalende marzo.

I nomi di questi devoti homini sono questi, cioè:

Priori
Gerolimo de Nicolò de Mirabuccio
Checcho d'Anthoniô del Cescho

Checcho de Feo de ser Fino
Nicolò de Cristofano de Condeo
Goro de Prochaccia
[3r]Checcho de Nicolo de Checcho
Semone de Checcho de Bartolo
Iacomo d'Agniluccio de Bartolo
Iacomo de Checcho da Carsugha

Meo de Giovanni de Sancti
Ambrogio de Massa da Monte

Marino de Borghese
Cristofano de Gianni de Cescho
Agostino de Giovanni Casuccio

I. Dela Carità de Dio e de proximo.

Perche la Karità de Dio copre la multitudine di peccati, sopra omni cosa se servi fratelli carissimi quanto la humana fragilità servare permette quello divino Comandamento: "Ama il signor Dio tuo con tucto il tuo core, con tucta l'anima tua, con tucta la tua mente et il proximo tuo como te medesimo", acciochè per la dilection de Dio e del proximo mertando la divina gratia ai gaudi eterni pervenire podiamo.

II. Dela electione di Priori et officiali dela Compania.

Benchè secondo le usanze antique Priori et officiali de questa Compania si costumasse creare a voci, a tollere dissensione alcuna volta nata tra i fratelli sopra ciò, è statiuto che ciaschun di fratelli nel suo brevicello se scriva e ponganse quelli che siranno di quartieri de San Nicolò in una brosa e quelli che sirono di quartieri dela Porta dela Pieve in un'altra borsa, e nel tempo usato dela electione di Priori doi tempi del anno, cioè, il dì dela festività de Sancto Mathia apostolo a dì XXIII de febraio e il dì de Santo Bartholomeo, XXIIII d'agosto, audita prima la messa delo spiritu sancto ala Capella dela Compania in l'Abbadia del Borgo, e poi adunati i fratelli nella audentia se extria de ciaschuna dele dette borse un brevicello per uno mamoletto e quelli doi che siranno in essi scripti sieno Priori dela Compania per sei mesi che comencarono in kalende marzo e in kalende septembre. E fornita la tracta di tucti, de nuovo se inborsino como de sopra. [3v] E così se faccia la electione d'un Preposto dela dicta Compania che tucti i fratelli se insacchino in doi altre borse et a suo tempo s'etria fuore uno d'una dele dette borse e l'altra volta uno de l'altra. Et quel medesimo si observi de doi savi Consiglieri et di doi Revisori e di doi Manuali anchora in ciascuna borsa de per sè como di Priori è ordinato, le qual borse se chuidino sotto doi chiavi nel cofino dele insaccationi dele quali l'una servi il Preposto e l'altra il Notaro Scrivano dela detta Compania el qual cofino così chiuso se riponga e conservase nel scrigno dele pecunie per lo Priore.

III. Del officio di Priori dela Compania et auctorità loro.

Sia l'officio di detti Priori tucte le facende dela dicta Compania portare et administrare in giudicio e fore domandando e defendendo, contrahere, vendere, alienare, locare, e dislocare et omni generation de'contracti in nome dela decta Compania fare, domandare, exigere tucto quello si dovesse dare ala decta Compania. Anchora per vigore di guarentigia, absolvere et getare i paganti et omni altra cosa a modo usato secondo la forma di statuti del Comune del Borgo e di presenti ordini et commo al loro sirà commesso per lo collegio e spetialemente uno de loro habbia il deposito, conversatione et administratione dele pecunie e l'altro far fare distribuire il pane. E sia tenuto il Priore dele pecune far redure in scripto per lo Notaio Scrivano dela Compania nei libri d'essa, le intrate dele pecunie e le expese, e la prima domenica di nuovi Priori sia tenuto rendere ragione dela sua administratione ala Compania e sempre tucto administrare a bona fede e il resto consignare al nuovo Priore. E più in scripto faccia redure per lo detto Scrivano tucti i debitore e quelli fare manifesti ai nuovi Priori et ala Compania. Habbino ancho i detti Priori auctorità remectere tucti i delecti di fratelli humilianti che havessero peccato contra i presenti ordinamenti quando non concerne- [4r] rse il dampno o victuperio dela Compania. Dechiarando che niuno di Priori solo possa per alcuna modo contrahere e presumendo il contracto non vaglia e tal Priore ipso facto sia dela decta Compania casso. Agiognendo che 'l Priore che nel rendere dela ragione remarrà debitore da vinti livere de'denari in su e la dicta quantità infra il mese proximo non restituira ala Compania, sia casso ipso facto del consortio et per tucti i modi sia conscrecto a pagare.

IV. Del officio del Preposto dela Compania.

L'officio del Preposto sia supplire le negligentie defecti di Priori, deli altri officiali, e de tucti i fratelli e quelli admonire, confortare e sollicitare ale facende dela Compania et ala observantia deli ordenamenti, ceremonie et bone consuetudini et al continuo canto dele laude. E se quando alcuno di Priori infermasse o absente fosse dal Boro et suo destrecto, debba tenere il luoco delo absente o infirmante, sichè esso Preposto con l'altro Priore possa contrahere et in tucto administrare como de sopra dei doi Priori è detto. El cui officio duri sei mesi.

V. Delo officio di Savi dela Compania.

I Savi Consiglieri habbino l'officio del consigliare i Priori et homini dela dicta Compania fidelmente et a bona fede secondo Dio et bona conscientia sopra le facende dela Compania e insiem sempre coi Priori adunarse nella audentia tucto il tempo del loro officio, il qual duri sei mesi.

VI. Del officio di Visitatori.

Sia l'officio di Visitatori personalmente transferirse et andare a vedere le casi, il molino nel fiume del'Afra, i forni, poderi, et tucte le possessioni et beni dela Compania, almeno una volta il mese, e considerare le necessità et manchamenti nei lavorii, animali, et de tucte le cose, e quello che a ciaschuna cosa secondo i tempi mancha et bisogna, sollicitare i lavoratori et conductori nella cultura et studio dela cose. Et tucto reportino al officio et scrivere [4v] faccino al Scrivano nel libro di reporti aciochè optima provision se faccia circha al tucto. Habbino anchora il studio del colombaio della torre che fo de Madonna Lucia de Guidobaldo, e andare coi tavlatoni far tavlare le possessioni et altre simili cose fare como sirà opportuno. Et per tucti questi exercitii habbiano per parte de remuneratione dele fatiche et andamenti loro, soldi cinquanta de'denari per ciaschuno dela pecunia dela Compania.

VII. Del officio di doi Manuali.

Habbia anchora la detta Compania doi Manuali dei proprii fratelli i quali sieno tenuti fare l'imbasciate, adunare i fratelli, accendere i lumi, portare le elimosine, et procesionalmente la mayestade, tenere il canestro al braccio quando se fa elimosina del pane ala porta dela casa et onni altra cosa fare al comandmento di Priori tucti i sei mesi. E chi sirà stato Priore o Preposto non debba essere tracto manuale de lì a uno anno. E non se vergorgranno i padri antiqui essere manuali quando se recordaranno che Yhesu non venne per essere servito, ma per ministrare et servire, et per dare exemplo d'umilità lavò i polverosi piedi di suoi discipuli.

VIII. Del officio del Capellano.

Ancho habbia la detta Compania uno devoto et honesto sacerdote seculare in Capellano dela capella novamente edificata in la chiesa dela Pieve del Borgo per l'anima de Don Rigo de Iacomo de Vanni del Dino, devotissimo dela detta Compania, il quale se elegga omni volta morisse quello che hora officia per la magior parte di fratelli a voci o a partito secreto dele fave. El quale Capellano porti i fratelli nelle vistere dela sua carità. E rechesto dai Priori debbase presentare in tucte le opportunità et bisogni dela Compania. E sia tenuto secondo la forma del testamento del detto Don Rigo tucti i suoi dì officiare la detta capella tre dì onni septimana, [5r] cioè, il lunedì, mercorledì et sabbato dire la messa per l'anima del detto Don Rigo e omni anno il dì de San Barnabo apostolo a dì XI de giugno cantar la messa ala detta capella coi sacerdoti chiamati per lui, i Priori et i fratelli dela Compania i quali sieno tenuti processionalmente andare con la mayestade et devotamente ala detta messa pregar Dio per l'anima de questo devoto benefactor nostro, e qualche pietosa elimosina fare a quelli sacerdoti. Et habbia il detto Capellano omni anno per suo salario livere trentasei dei denari dela Compania.

IX. Delo Advocato dela Compania.

Habbia la detta Compania uno Advocato dela terra del Borgo il quale vederanno intra li altri più devoto ala Compania col quale si tengha amicità, et habbia se recorso in le necessità et in qualunche questioni et casi, con salario condecente qualunche volta, pero l'officio suo operarà per la Compania denanze ai guidici. E onni anno in lui qualche pietoso donarello confereschino et largitione in conservation dela benivolentia con la Compania e aciochè sempre in favore ad essa et a tucti i fratelli sia.

X. Del Procuratore dela Compania.

Uno Procuratore experto, fidele et devoto dela detta Compania s'abbia continuo, possidente di beni de questo mondo; in tucte le questioni et controversie dela decta Compania a domandare et defendere, il quale sollicitamente administri denaze ai guidici tucto qullo al suo officio s'aparteve in guidicio et for de guidicio lealmente et a bona fede. Et habbia per suo salario un fiorino da ciaschun priorato, benchè nel tempo alcuna lite per la Compania non agitasse.

XI. Del Notario Scrivano dela Compania.

Perche li homini dela detta Compania sono ignari de lettere, habbia la detta Compania continuo uno dei [5v] notari dela terra del Borgo fidele e devoto e dela substantia de questo mondo possidente buono scriptore sufficiente abochista che sappia ponere i calculi dela ragione, il quale sia scrivano, reveditore e calculatore dele intrate et expese de ciascuno Priore, come per fine ad hora è consueto in la detta Compania. Apresso rogato se faccia deli instrumenti e testamenti, e quelli publici scriva nel libro di testamenti a modo usato. Et per suo salario per tucto habbia da ciaschun priorato doi fiorini e per ciaschun testamento così fornito uno fiorino et i venti più habbia per alcuna cagione, il quale manutengha il stilo rito et ordine novamente comenzato nelle scripture dele ragione ai libri dela detta Compania, cioè: al libro initulato "Intrate et expese", le intrate et expese et calculo nel fine a ciascun priorato. Item nel "Libro delle vendite", le vendite et alienationi dele cose et beni coi confini et tavlati et ragioni chiare, i pagamenti di pregi con le quantità et dì et nomi del Priore che riceve et di pagatori. Et che le ragioni a costume de'buoni mercatanti se chiamino insieme nel libro dele intrate ponendo i fogli per abocho de ciaschun libro in ciascun libro. Et nel "Libro di pescioni et affícti", le ragion dele possesioni a locate coi nomi di conductori, quantità di pecunie o de grano o biado, et le rendite dai lavoratori, il qual libro quanto ai denari chiami il "Libro dele intrate" e quanto al grano et biadi chiami il "Libro del grano", et nel detto libro del grano scriva et reduca in esso del detto "Libro deli affciti" li annuati recolti coi nomi di pagatori et conductori così de grano como de'biadi et altri fructi et i fogli del libro a tucte le poste, aciochè a un luoco veder se possa chiaramente li recolti di ciascuno anno de grano da per sè et di biadi et fructi ancho da per sè, et in un altro foglio le prestanze ai lavoratori, et poi le particulari elimosine. Et poi il grano che se macina de dì in dì coi pesi, e le ragioni dele pani facole et forni, sichè di ciaschun priorato veder se possa chiaramente le ragion del recolto, il logro [6r] et il residuo del granaio. E nel altro "Libro di vestimenti" notare le compare di panni colle mesure et pregi et da poi i pagamenti coi dì et quantità li quali chiamino i fogli del "Libro dele intrate et expese" et l'uno l'altro, e nel sequente foglio i vestimenti di ciaschun Priore da per sè dati ai povari coi nomi de chi receve et del manuale che'l porta et quantità del panno. E nel "Libro dei debitori" scriva i debitori dela Compania per qualunche cagione coi dì et quantità et i fogli dequel libro onde descendano, et ancho i defecti di Priori, deli officiali et di fratelli secondo la forma di presenti ordenamenti. Et nel "Libro grande nero", le note di testamenti et ultime voluntà scriva como perfine ad hora. Et nel "Libro di reporti", tucto quello che i Reveditori trovaranno di manchamento secondo il loro officio. E sia presente et rogato se facci a dela tracta di Priori e deli offici a suoi tempi. E tucto distinctamente et chiaro et fidelmente scriva aciochè niun suspecto o dubbio nascha nelle ragioni et aciochè che essi libri se possino continuamente presentare nel cospecto de Dio et deli homini. E apparire possa la deritta simplicità et devota administratione di beni dela detta Compania nei fratelli. Et che tucto precede senza dolo o spetie de male. Sia in pero tenuto esso per bono consuetudine quando la ragion del Priore doi volte l'anno se reduce in calculo chiamare et caritativamente recevere a casa sua tucti i fratelli et con le scaciatole gialle et fructi et vino et tal cose quelli benignamente et devotemente recreare.

XII. Dela congregatione et concilio dela Compania et dele sedie.

Segghino i doi Priori nella audientia in luoco designato et più honorato et il Preposto in mezzo a loro e doi Savi dala mano deritta et sinistra di Priori, et nell'altro luocho designato segghino d'aprese doi Reveditori, et i doi Manuali apresso da omni mano uno, et li altri fratelli nelli altri sedili d'apresa. E in questo luocho s'adunino i fra [6v] telli insiemi al comandamento di Priori omni volta che sirano rechiesti per i Manuali predetti, e nominamente sieno tenuti i Priori adunare il concilio la seconda domenica del mese de marzo et la seconda domenica del mese de septembre e denaze ai fratelli proponere delo honore et buono stato dela Compania ascrescere et conservare et quello si debba fare sopra de ciò. E ciaschuno di fratelli levandose in [illeg.] possa consegliare i Priori et la Compania quello che utile cognosceranno et opportuno; e tucto quello che consegliato et obtenuto sirà per la magiure parte intra i fratelli a fave in secreto o a voce se observi et refereschase et reducase in nota per lo Scrivano nel libro raporti et dele reformagioni dela Compania. Ancho s'adunino tucti i fratelli onni domenica e festività principali de tutto l'anno nelle quali la Compania è consueta processionalmente andar colla mayestade visitare le chiese del Borgo, ancho quando si fa la tracta deli offici e quando si rende ragione per li Priori, e quando si publicano e leggono i presenti ordinamenti e le facende dela Compania doi volte l'anno; e qualunche di fratelli senza urgente cagione et senza licentia di Priori non s'adunarà nei detti tempi coi fratelli, cioè, chi starà tre domeniche continuamente non comparendo sia tolto dela Compania, e chi nelli altri tempi non comparirà senza manifesta cagione sia scripto per debitore nel Libro di debitori dela Compania. E se i Priori le predette cose non servaranno le predette cose non scrivaranno contra i fratelli che non comparissaro, sieno sottoposti et puniti ale medesime pene de privatione et inscriptione, et sieno private et scripti nel detto Libro de debitori per lo Preposto loro, aciochè a meno per timore di pena s'avezzino i fratelli frequentare la Compania.

XIII. Dela pace et unione di fratelli.

Perche scripto è nel libro di Psalmi, "Ectho quanto è buono et quanto è giochondo i fratelli habitare in unione," per ciò sieno tenuti i fratelli insiemi tractarse pacificamente et con carità in parole et in facti, como si convene ai buoni huomini et fratelli dele pietose congregatione (et ove situano insiemi honorase et mostrarse in tucto benivolia) [7r] et se alcuno per qualunque cagione s'adirarà col suo fratello dela Compania, sia tenuto al comandamento di Priori ponere giù la ira et ranchore, et l'uno verso l'altro humiliarese et rendere pace. Altramente il fratello che tre volte admonito per li Priori così non farà al tucto sia casso dela Compania, aciochè'l superbo fratello non habbia sorte con il humili.

XIV. Dela obedientia et honore si debba ai Priori.

Tenuti sieno i fratelli fermamente obedire ai Priori in ciaschune cose licite et honeste apartenenti ala Compania e che non sieno contra Dio li instituti dela chiesa e contrarie al, anima sua e a quello che non obedirà possino in iungere penitentia salutare, overo andare a visitare la chiesa del luocho del Vepre o del Melello o le chiese del Borgo overo orationi o altre opere de pietà como a essi Priori parrà. E quelli che siranno contumaci non obediendo et non exequendo la penitentia ingionta come superbi et rebelli sieno tolti dela Compania. Apresso sieno tenuti i fratelli venendo de nuovo in l'audentia sedenti i Priori et l'officio essi Priori et l'officio assidente col capo inclinato honorare, et questo per bona consuetudine se observi, così quando de nuovo s'entrà como quando si leva a consegliare. Ma recordinse i fratelli quando alo intrare in l'audentia tucti prima se in ginochino denanze ala mayesta de Dio et dela sua madre, salutino i fratelli contranunptiado loro la pace. E da poi si ponghino a sedere nel luocho debito et con modestia et mansuetudine sempre parlino como si convene ai probi et sapienti homini. E uno parlante tucti gli altri con silentio ascoltino, guardinse inpero i Priori che non credino nè voglino essere signori deli altri fratelli, ma onni cosa con benignità et carità faccino.

XV. Dele elimosine si debanno fare per legati.

Sino tenuti i Priori nel tempo del loro officio, havendo sempre denanze agli occhi Dio, e largire i beni dela Compania ai povari de Yhesu Cristo con devotione et modestia et reverentia, come che a esso Cristo che disse, "quello che a uno di miei minimi farete, a me farate." E recordinse che [7v] tali beni non sono loro, ma dei fideli devoti che questi tali beni per l'anime loro per donagioni et ultime voluntà hanno lasciati in questi pietosi usi. Et pero come fideli ministri omni cosa fidelmente mandino ad executione e ale grinse essere per gratia di Dio esser stati chiamati dispensatori di tali beni e per tal fatige et exercitii reportare li eterni premii. Et pero il Priore o qualunche di fratelli che arrogantia o inpatientia usarà in parole o in facti elargiendo cotali elimosine sia admonito per lo Preposto e se tre volte correpto non se emendarà sia privato del officio et de tucte preheminentie così del Comune como dela Compania. E il suo Preposto fornescha l'officio tucto il tempo et goda i suoi beneficii. Et nominatamente sieno tenuti per reverentia dela beata vergine Maria omni sabato a sera et omni dì de domenica, de pasque, de beata Maria, deli apostoli et feste principali dare del pane ai povari al uscio dela casa, e il Manuale tengha il canestro al braccio col pane ben cotto et ben studiato. Anco nel dì dele vigilie dela natività del nostro Signore, resurrexione et dela festività de'tucti i sancti omni anno dare sieno tenuti ai povari de buona carne et grano. Ancho del mese de dicembre de ciaschuno anno sieno tenuti comperare quattro et perfine i sei pezze di panno bigello et secondo la Compania poderà più largamente. Et quello distribuire in vestimenti di povari secondo la loro discreptione et de tutta la Compania. Et per le mani di Manuali discretamente mandare secondo se coniurrà ala honesta del vergognoso povero recipiente. E più dare debbino dele pecunie a menuti, e per maritar zitole perfine in lire cinque per una, per recompare prigione, per sepellire i morti, et per li peregrini et viandanti, et per l'infermanti povari et donne in parto. Et per liquali anchora tolghino dal spetiale dela Compania dela confectioni et medecine necessarie. Ancho tucto l'anno dieno ai povari et infermi del vino che sirà nel cellaio dela Compania e altre pietose opere per loro se exeratino a modo usato et larga- [8r] mente secondo che la Compania a suoi tempi habondarà nei beni, et nel core habbino la parolla de Yhesu Cristo che disse: "Date et sirà dato a vuoi." E sopra omni cosa sieno tenuti i Priori subito satisfare i legati particulari e così i legati annuali. E sopra ciò dal Preposto sieno per tucti i modi amoniti et sollicitta et se i detti Priori in ciò negligenti sirano et non pagaranno i detti legati sieno scripti nel Libro di debitori et non possino essere in saccati in l'officio del priorato in la proxima futura inborsationi. Anco habbino a memoria più largamente distribuire ai povari religiosi et maxiamente ai predicatori et a quelli che attendono alle confessioni.

XVI. Dela observatione di fratelli nelle orationi.

A laude de l'omnipotente Dio e salute de l'anime sieno tenuti i fratelli le festività usate con le mayestude procesionalmente andare visitando le chiese del Borgo cantare le laude et altre cose a modo usato, e li altri dì se per necessità non siranno constrecti tucti visitino la chiesa et recomandise a Dio et ala vergine Maria nostra advocata, et altramente non presumino andar fuori ale opere et exercitii loro. Ancho al ora prima, terza, sexta, nona, vespero, compieta et matutinale sieno tenuti i fratelli dire in genochioni cinque paternostri et cinque avemarie per ciaschuna dele dette hore canoniche, e non se verghognino i fratelli anchora lavorando nel campo ponar giù i ferramenti et pieghare genocchia per amore de Messer Cristo che per noi in croce fo tanto stirato che tucti gli ossa suoi se secieno annomerati. Questo anchor faccino, che vedendo li altri homini le devotioni di fratelli, sieno ancho provocati a bene et glorifichino il padre nostro il quale è in cielo. E così tucto il dì s'accrescha la devotione et il buono odore dela Compania appo i buoni et gravi, et così bene faciendo faciamo star mute le lengue deli huomini che sono senza pietà. Et qualunche questo tal muodo de orare non observarà, sia admonito per li Priori, et a lui sia imposta penitentia salutare, visitation, cioè, dele chiese del Vepre o del Melello o altro como ai Priori parrà.

[8v] XVII. Dela observantia di comandamenti dela chiesa.

Tenuti sieno i fratelli al meno una volta l'anno confessare i suoi peccati al sacerdote e il dì dela pasqua dela resurrexione de Dio tucti insiemi comunicare in la chiesa del'Abbadia del Borgo se licentia haveranno dai proprii sacerdoti altramente ciaschuno ale chiese loro, ma quelli che meglio disposti sirono omni mese se confessino et ancho nella natività de Dio et nella festa dela assumptione dela nostra donna del mese d'agosto con la benedictione de Dio se comunichino et generalmente tucti li altri comandamenti dela chiesa a pieno adempino. E chi almeno una volta l'anno non se confessarà et comunicarà al tucto dela Compania sia cancellato. Et i Priori sopra ciò inquerino e chi questo non haverà adempito cassino. Altramente essi per lo Proposto sieno scripti nel Libro di debitori et nella proxima imborsatione non sieno posti per Priori. Sieno tenuti ancho i Priori almeno una volta il mese far fare la confessione generale ai fratelli sopra omni cosa contramessa overo obmessa contra la forma di presenti ordinamenti et altri peccati per lo Capellano dela Compania o per altro sacerdote et a loro imponare penitentia salutare.

XVIII. Dela sancta conversatione di fratelli tra li altri huomini.

Perche quelli che sono posti in alcuno ordine o in alcuno grado d'officio non solo se medesimi peccando offendono et ala loro fama nocciano ma a tucti li altri de quel medesimo ordine et officio et a quel luoco pietoso ove sono conversi; pero tucti i fratelli nella loro conversatione rendino bona oppinione, fama et exemplo de loro: non sieno biastimiatori, non giochatori, non usurari, et inlicitamente aquestanti, non bugiardi, non rixosi, non iracundi, non superbi et altri non maldicenti, non susurroni, non ebrii, non gran favellatori, ma mansueti, benigni, pacifici, benedicenti, humili, bene amonenti, le chiese et bone opere seguitanti, odore de sè in omni parte de bono nome portanti et in casa et de fore tucti composti. Et nominata- [9r] mente i Priori ai quali convene essere specchio de tucta la Compania tucto il tempo del loro officio non vadino a taverne, nè il Proposto il quale ha a correggere i loro defecti pero che male corregge altri de quel peccato che lui medesimo ad opera, nè ancho i savi Conseglieri pero che chi è macero de vino, perde il consiglio. E se alcuno de loro in ciò contrafacesse i Reveditori li facci scrivere al Libro di debitori, e nella sequente proxima imborsatione non sieno remessi a quelli officii. Ancho niuno di fratelli tucto il tempo dela Quaresime maguire non vada a taverna. Altramente chi contrafarà una volta amonito per li Priori et non remanendose de ciò, sia per omni volta a lui imposto per penitentia andare a visitare la chiesa del Vepre o del Melello o altro simile. E se al tucto fosse incorrigibile dela Compania sia tolto.

XIX. Dela observatione quando i fratelli infermano o moyano.

Scripto è: "Chi ama il fratello suo, ha adimpito la legge." Et pero infirmantese i fratelli in alcuna adversità constituti, sieno tenuti i Priori, l'officio et i fratelli personalmente visitare tal fratello et lui ad patientia indure, et ala salute del'anima sua amonire. E se sirà in alcuna necessità, caritativamente subvenire a lui per amor de Dio secondo il suo bisogno. E quando alcuno di fratelli morisse, sia tentuta la Compania processionalmente andare colla mayestade ala sepultura del corpo suo, portarlo ala chiesa, cantare le laude, e ciaschuno di fratelli dica per l'anima sua vintacinque paternostri et XXV avemaria con requiem eternam per l'anima sua devotamente. E la matina sequente in quella chiesa, ove sirà il suo corpo sepellito, faccino i Priori cantare le messa di morti per lui et quelle elimosine faccino ai sacredoti et religiosi che ai Priori parerà. E i fratelli con la mayestade processionalmente vadino et con devotione preghino per l'anima sua et dichino quelle orationi sirà a loro imposto per li Priori.

[9v] XX. De introdure buoni huomini intrare questa congregatione.

Debbano i Priori et l'officio coi fratelli persuadere i buoni et semplici huomini intrare in questa devota congregatione, sì per salute del'anima loro como per augmento et buono stato dela Compania. E tali a ciò recerchino et induchino et seco acompagnino che conoscerono essere fideli, devoti et de sè bona opinione et fama de sè in omni luochi portanti, e quali de sopra è scripto debbano essere, e maximamente quelli che utilmente et honoratamente tractano i facti de casa loro. Perochè chi fa male i suoi facti, rade volte farà bene li altrui. E ancho non sieno notati di povertà, con questo che sempre a partito si mettino tra i fratelli et il partito se vencha per le tre parti dele quattro di tucti i fratelli o a fave secreto o a voci como parrà ai Priori. E questi così recevuti si possino inborsare ali officii, ma non sieno tracti al officio del priorato et prepostorato se non finito l'anno dal dì dela sua receptione.

XXI. Dele mansioni dele case dela Compania.

La prima mansione dele case dela Compania è l'intrata e la sua porta resguarda la porta septemtrionale dela chiesa dela Abbadia del Borgo et in quella mansone è il camino dal fuocho al tempo freddo per li povari et per li fratelli. E nella parete è depenta la figura de Dio padre et la nostra advocata et la lampana del vetro. Le chiavi de questa mansione sono due: dele quali ciaschuno Priore tene la sua. E più oltra ce è uno repositorio con uno luocho ai secreti dela natura. A mano sinistra è l'audientia in la quale si fa il collegio di fratelli, et ove se tractano le facende dela Compania. A mano dextra è il granaio terreno, et ha la intrata per la via publica con doi chiavi ale mani di doi Priori. Nel quale se ripone al tempo di recolti il grano et biadi; perochè è a pie piano senza gradi et amannito, el qual ricolto poi si porta nei granari de sopra. Et c'è l'altra mansione denanze che guarda l'occidente a lato la piazza sotto la volta di matoni con [10r] doi usci la quale saloga a pescione. E intra mezzo a queste è una porta nova che resguarda la parte australe et in pede a quella dentro sono le scale de petra per la intrata di granari de sopra con doi chiave per ciaschuno Priore. De sotto ale scale et de sopra sono doi stantiole che stanno palese; questa solia essere via del comuno donata ala Compania per la gloriosa memoria Signor, Karlo di Malatesti. Nella summita dele dette scale a mano sinistra è il granaio dela piazza con l'uscio chiuso et dala dextra, l'altro uscio chiuso et il granaio del'audentia. Questa chiave serva il Preposto. E più oltra ala detta mano dextra è l'altro granaio dela intrata. E da poi apresso seguita la camera dele masave dela Compania con l'uscio chiuso. La chiave appose retene et serva il Priore dal pane, et questa camera resguarda l'oriente.

XXII. Dela guardia dei granari.

Per la guardia del grano et biadi dela detta Compania et a tollere onni suspictione de male, habbianse et continuamente se tenghino le dette chiavi ai dette granari, et se alcuno di detti Priori o Preposto la sua chiave in alcuno luocho palese spontaneamente lasciarà sichè senza lui si possa intrare i detti granari, sia ipso facto casso dela Compania. Possa pero ciascun de loro per cagione de absentia, infirmità, o de eminente necessità, ad alcuno di fratelli la sua chiave consignare, sichè sempre tre sieno presenti quando grano o biando per alcuna bona cagione se cava di granari. Agiognendo che quando il grano si porta del granaio de sotto in quelli de sopra, si debba mesurare con la mesura giusta del communo. Et il numero deli staia si ponga in nota nel Libro del grano.

XXIII. Dela guardia del vino dela Compania.

Per la guardia del vino, si facciano et continua se tenghino ale celle dal vino doi chiavi appo ciascuno di Priori. Et senza loro consentimento aperire non si possino per alcuno modo. E guardinse i fratelli quanto amano Dio che elli non s'adunino nelle dette celle senza evidente neces- [10v] sità, overo de elimosina o per cagione di vendere il vino, e se i Priori contrafaranno in questo, sieno correpto per lo Preposto. Et se emendaranno, sieno scripti nel Libro di debitori per la prima imborsatine. E se il Preposto in questo sirà negilgente, per li Savi et per li Visitatori nel detto modo sia scripto al detto Libro. Et questo medesimo dele doi chiavi et non praticare, se observi inqualunche casa o luocho la Compania per alcuna aquistata hereditá havesse vino, grano o beni mobili, sotto le dette pene.

XXIV. Dela guarda dele massarie.

In la camera dela massarie se ce ponghino tucte le massarie et mobile dela Compania, che in quella comodamente se porrà reponere, sotto la chiave et guardia del Priore dal pane. E nella intrata de ciascuno priorato si faccia l'inventario dele dette masaritie et nel fine se ne faccia la rassegna, et se alcuna mancharà, sia tenuto il Priore quella emendare in questo modo, cioè, che i nuovi Priori e il Proposto infra octo dì proximi sieno tenuti tal massaria se trovare non, se poderà extimare lealmente et a bona fede, la quale extima il detto Priore infrà dieci dì al'ora proximi, sia tenuto pagare al nuovo Priore, et se quella non pagarà, passato il detto termine sia scripto per debitore nel Libro di debitore et se i nuovi Priori nol faranno scrivere, il loro Preposto faccia quelli scrivere al detta pena.

XXV. Dele observantie nel dare le elimosine.

Niuna elimosina fare si possa anchor piccola senza licentia di ammen'doi i Priori nè anchor de pane nè de vino, e de grano et biadi senza licentia dei Priori, Preposto et di doi Savi. Et da vinti soldi in su senza consentimento dela magiur parte di fratelli. Et questo medesimo nei contracti se observi, et s'el Priore in questo contrafarà quello non sia admesso a sua ragione, salvo la occurrentia dela necessità per sepulture di morti poveri, per adiutare infirmi et [11r] donne poverelle inparto et simili, nei quali casi solo il Priore dale pecunie, se'l compagno non poderà comodamente havere, possa questo per se medesimo fare, con questo che quanto più presto poderà havere i compagni, faccia a loro noto, così havere facto.

XXVI. Dele credenze et prestanze dela Compania.

Niuno Priore debba fare credenza o fare prestanza d'alcuna quantità o cosa perfine a lire cinque senza licentia del suo compagno e del Preposto et di doi Savi. E da cinque lire in su di denari senza licentia et consentimento dela magiur parte di fratelli altramente sia a lui a scripto a debito. E chi farà tal credenze o prestanze con voluntà di predetti, sia obligato quelle reschotere nel temine dato a tale dibitore, et da poi a quattro mesi al'ora proximi secuturi. Altramente a lui sia scripto a debito et como sua scegurta, et così scripto stia perfine rescoterà o pagarà il quale debba essere rescosso dia Priori futuri. Altramente essi non rescotendo sieno a scripti per debitori al detto Libro, dechiarando che colui che farà la credenza o prestanza continuamente et sempre sia exactore et non altri. E chi pagarà niente per altrui habbia le ragioni dela Compania contra tale debitore, per cui havesse pagato. Et se'l debitore sirà di fratelli, aprova de tal pagamento per lui facto ala Compania basti la scriptura del Libro dei debitore denanze ai guidici de Messer lo Podestà, contra il quale niente se possa opponere, se non solo la exceptione del pagamento. Et se'l fratello così exacto altro opponesse, ipso facto sia casso dela compania.

XXVII. Dela admonitione et correptione di fratelli.

I Priori sieno tenuti almeno una volta il mese amonire i fratelli ala observantia di comandamenti dela chiesa et di presenti ordinamenti, et che honestamente conversino intra i fratelli et l'altre persone, et che de sè faccino bona opinione et nome tra'l popolo. E chi contrafacesse secondo la via evangelica tre volte amoneschino. E al contra fa [11v] ciente et in obediente imponghino penitentie per quali che cagioni como a essi Priori parrà. E chi sirà incorrigible facta le terza admonitione sia al tucto privato dela Compania acciochè non corrompa i buon costumi deli altri fratelli di quali è la fede pura et l'opere bone. E se i detti Priori tal monitione non faranno almeno onni mese, sieno mandati per lo Preposto et per li Savi visitare la chiesa del luocho del Vepre o del Melello o altro per penitentia. E questo per bona consuetudine se observi.

XXVIII. De non publicare i secreti et de non fraudare la Compania.

Niuno di fratello per alcuno modo per parolle o per segno faccia palese alcuno parlamento che si farà nella congregatione di fratelli per le facende della Compania, che possa essere dampno o infamia dela detta Compania, et chi contrafarà, sia scripto per debitore nel Libro di debitori dela Compania. Et chi revelarà alcuna facenda sopra la quale fosse imposto et comandato il silentio per li Priori dela detta Compania al tucto sia chacciato. Ancho se alcuno Priore, officiale o fratello fraude che Dio tolgha dela mente de tucte commenttarà contra la

Compania, de facto sia dela congregatione privato e in perpetuo remettere non se possa.

XXIX. Che niuno metta la falce nella metitura altrui.

Niuno di fratelli habbia ardire o presuma a domandare, rescotere o recevere da alcuno debitore dela Compania alcuna quantità de pecunia o grano o altra cosa debita ala Compania, ma queste cose et simili fare et administrare lascino ai Priori, et obligati o deputati o chi havesse mandato dai Priori, e chi contrafarà dela Compania sia casso e generalmente niuno di fratelli se intermetta dele facende dela Compania a sè non pertinente, et sopra le quali non havessero in mandato et in commissione, anchora d'uno solo pane ala detta pena. E se alcuno di fratelli torrà alcuna cosa apartenente ala Compania et porta- [12r] ta via d'alcuna casa, luocho o mansione o anchora in prestanze senza licentia di Priori et del Preposto o anchora piccola cosa senza licentia al meno d'uno di Priori ipso facto sia casso dela Compania et mai possa remesso ma como sacrilego sia tenuto et reputato.

XXX. Che i beni dela Compania non saloghino ai fratelli.

Acciochè dai fratelli si tolla onni suspitione sopra le rendite di beni dela Compania, è ordinato che niuno di fratelli da hora inanze possa condure a lavorio e a fitto o pescione alcuna cosa dela Compania se tre parti dei fratelli non siranno d'acordo al partito dele fave secreto; et se i Priori altramente alocassero et contra la forma del presente capitulo, sieno cassi dela Compania. Et se alcuno di fratelli non lavoraranno le possesioni condocte dala Compania a modo de buon lavoratore, sia tenuto relapsare subito. Poi che per li Reviditori sirà reportato del male lavorio de tal cosa. Et questo non facendo sia casso dela Compania et niente de meno la possessione allocata lasci. Altramente contra de lui si proceda denanze al giudici secondo la forma del statuto del comuno del Borgo.

XXXI. Del libro di debitori.

Habbiase continuamente un Libro in la Compania intitulato di debitori nel quale se reduchino in nota per le mani del Scrivano dela Compania tucti i debitori per qualunche cagione deli altri libri. E nominamente i fratelli che sirono debitori dela Compania in alcuna quantità overo per alcuno excesso notati per haver contrafacto ai presenti ordinamenti. Et qualunche sirà descripto in quello per alcuna dele dette cagioni, se sirà tracto ad alcuno officio, sia remesso nelle borse perfine che satisfarà il debito o sopra quello haverà concordia con la Compania overamente non si metta nelle borse al tempo dela insaccatione como nei presenti ordini è proveduto. Et questo non s'entenda per li Manuali.

[12v] XXXII. De publicare li ordini et facende dela Compania doi volte l'anno.

Tenuti et obigati sieno i Priori che per lo tempo sirano, la prima domenica del mese de maggio et la prima domenica del mese de novembre onni anno in perpetuo adunare i fratelli nella audientia per li loro Manuali, e in quella congregatione faccino leggere et publicare questi ordini novamente compillati. E le poste di libri dele vendite, deli afficti et debitori accese, e le poste del libro delo Specchio quando sirà fornito e l'altre cose parrà ai Priori acciochè i fratelli che non sanno lettere dieno et reduchino ala memoria tucto quello è salute del'anime et stato, honore et augmento dela Compania et di fratelli et tali cose non sieno ignoranti. Pena ai Priori che questo non faranno almeno una volta in tucto il loro officio, che nella futura insacchatione non sieno ad alcuno officio in borsati, salvo che per Manuali. Et il loro Preposto l'ultimo dì del loro officio faccia quelli scrivere, altramente i nuovi Priori quel tal Preposto instruiere faccino nel detto libro, et questo capitulo per bona consuetudine se observi in perpetuo.

XXXIII. Dela utilità di presenti ordinamenti.

Ma acciochè de questa congregatione et de queste ordinamenti, fructo senza periculo dele anime se reporti, proveduto è che se i fratelli presenti et futuri non observassero questi ordini, non sia pero nè possa essere appo die ascripto a loro per alcun modo a peccato. E così como scripto è universalmente è piaciuto a tucti i fratelli.

XXXIV. Che i fratelli pregino Dio per la salute de Ser Francescho.

Et io Francescho de Cristofano del Cescho Largi, compagno et figliuolo vostro, et servo di tucti i fratelli el quale tucti questi ordini secondo la nostra pietosa volontà, Dio inspirante, a vostri prieghi ho forniti [13r] compillati et scripti, per karità la quale a questa devota Compania et a tucti i fratelli molti anni ho portato et porto con molta instantia ve pregho che questi vostre ordinamenti con gran letitia receviate et con grande reverentia et devotione come cosa divina observiate per salute vostra et conservatione et augmento de questo congregatione. Et perche questa fatiche senza alcun premio temporale ho presa per voi et per questa pietosa Compania, tucti voi fratelli miei presenti et che per il tempo futuri sirono in questa pietosa casa humilmente prego che in premio de ciò lecti questi ordini secondo l'usanza tucti parimente denanze ala mayesta de Dio et dela beata vergine Maria, preghati iginocchi in terra per la salute mia, me vivo et anchor morto vi piaccia devotamente dire tre paternostri et tre ave Maria. E io, fratelli miei dulcissimi, sempre per voi et per la salute vostra, pregar voglio aciochè l'uno per l'altre pregando meritiamo aguistare la gratia de Dio in questo mondo et nel altro la gloria et così per mutua carità e stato dal uno altro promesso in perpetuo observare. A laude de Dio onnipotente il quale sia per tucti i seculi benedeto. Amen.

Finiti sono li ordini dela pietosa Compania dele Laude de Sancta Maria dela Nocte del Borgo San Sepolcro felicemente.

APPENDIX III

The 1364 Statutes of the Confraternity of Santa Croce

Quelli sono gl'ordini della Chompania della Verace Sancta Croce.

[1r]1. Il nostro principio, el mezzo, e'l fine en tutte le cose quante e quali che per noi se diranno e faranno sì sieno a nome e a reverentia del padre, del filglio, e delo spirito sancte e dela pretiosa vergine intercedente beatissima madona sancta Maria, madre del nostro salvatore Yesu Cristo e de'tutti i sancti e sancte del regno del cielo e a honore e reverentia dela sanctissima beata vera croce la quale è capo e guida e mantenimento dela compagnia d'essa santa croce hedificata ello Borgo San Sepolcro e a honore e reverenza dela santa ghiesa de Roma, a buono e pacifico stato del Comune e del popolo dela terra del Borgo predecto e a mantenimento e a crescimento degl'uomeni dela decta Compagnia de Sancta Croce la quale Cristo crucifisso per la sua sanctissima passione sempre la cresta e mandienanze al suo servisato. Considerando gli omeni dela predecta Compagnia de Sancta Croce avendo desidare con grande volontà che la Compagnia predecta abbia acresamento aciò che sia salute del'anime degli omini dela decta Compania deliberate fo intra loro de comuna concordia e voluntà de volere renovare loro ordenamenti e statuti e commo de sotto sono scripti e i quali ordinamenti infrascripti fuoro facti, composti e ordenati per li savi [1v] homeni infrascripti posti et electi concordeloelmente per essa compagnia a fare correggiare, ordenare e comporere essi ordinamenti comme appare scripto per mano delo scriptore d'essa Compagnia socto gli anni del nostro Signore Giesu Cristo Mille trecento sexantaquatro, indictione seconda, el tempo del sanctissimo padre e signore messer Urbano papa quinto del mese de febraio. E i nomi d'essi savi homeni i quali essi ordinamenti de sotto scripti fecero, ordenaro e composero sono questi, cioè:

Source: AC, SS, 32, reg. 152, 1r–27r.

Maffeo del Doro Priore del decta Compania
Pace de Iacomo de Vanni de Castellano
Giovanni del Cescho del Preito
Padanale de Ceschino
Giovadio del Ceschono
Matteo de Nese

[2r]2. Questi sono gli ordenamenti e capitolo della Compagnia dela verasgie Sancto Croce e de coloro che sono e per inanze sirano d'essa Compania facti, composti e ordenati anno e mese de sopra scripti al tempo del distrecto homo Maffeo del Doro, Priore dela decta Compagnia de Sancta Croce.

3. Della'letione del Priore, Vichario, Soprapriore e Chamarlenggo chommo se dei fare.

Il prima stantiaro e ordenaro che la electione del Priore, Sopriore, Vicario e Camarlongo dela Compagnia de Sancte Croce predecta se facia damo inanzi en questo modo, cioè, che'l Priore, Sopriore e Vicaro che al presente sono in offitio debbiano e sieno tenuti eleggere e nominare tre buoni homini d'essa Compagnia. E i quali tre così electi debbiano e sieno tenuti eleggare e nominare e i Priore, Sopriore, Vicari e Camarlenghi d'essa Compagnia per tre anni proximi che viranno e scrivarsi overo farli scrivare in VI brevi di carta, cioè, in ciasuno breve e i nomi del Priore, Sopriore, Vicaro, e Camarlengo, e essi brevi così scripti in volgare in sei palocte di cera, e poi esse palocte dobbia el Priore d'essa Compagnia fare mectare ello ceppo el quale è a lato l'altare dela ghiessa dela dicta Compagnia [2v] el quale ceppo abbia doe chiavi, l'una dele quali tenere debbia el Priore e l'altra el Sopriore d'essa Compagnia. E poi sia tenuto e debbia ciascuno Priore che per lo tempo sirà, quindici die inanzi la fine del suo offitio fare trare del decto ceppo una dele decte palocte, e coloro che sirano scripti ello breve che sirà in essa palocta sieno Priore, Sopriore, Vicaro e Camarlengo per li sei mesi che seguitarono comme in esso breve scripto fosse. E così poi el quinto Priore, Sopriore e Vicaro de'predecti debbiano doi mesi inanze la fine del loro offitio eleggere tre buoni homeni d'essa Compagnia e i quali abbiano a elleggere e refare i decti offitiali per li altri tre anni che seguitarono, e essi scrivare e in lo decto ceppo mettere al modo sopradecto sichè sempre l'offitio del Priore, Sopriore, Vicaro e Camarlengo duri sei mesi e non più. E debbia ciascuno Priore la prima domenica del suo offitio elleggere gl'Infermieri e gli altri offitiali d'essa Compagnia de quali non fosse loro electione dechiarata. E duri e vallia questo ordine e capitolo nove anni proximi che veranno, e sieno tenuti i decti electori tenere rifecceto i nomi degli ofitiali sopradecti per loro electi fieni che sirano tracti a pena d'essere cassi.

4. Dela electione degli offitiali.

Ancho ordenaro che'l Priore, Vicaro, Sopriore e Camarlengo che siranno electi ai sopradecti offitii non possano tornare d'essere in quello offitio spirato el loro offitio a tre anni proximi veneti e così s'entenda [3r] per coloro che sono passati, e non possa essere Priore se lli non è stato uno anno ella decta Compania.

5. Dela electione dei Consellieri.

Ordenamo che i Consellieri se facciano en quessto modo che la decta matina che'l Priore nuovo sirà electo sieno scritti tucti gli huomini dela Compania en i polize e quali siranno stati ella Compania sei mesi, e sieno messi a gulupati e a mesti en uno sachetto omni uno per sè; e puoi el Priore vecchio sia tenuto de fare trare del decto sachetto quattro polize e leggha li nomina en capitulo e quali sieno Consellieri del Priore nuovo. E se avenisse che alchuno dei quattro tratti fosse casso dela Compania overo che avesse oltre offitio non possa essere Consellieri, nè remesso ello saccho'nanze encontinente, nè sia tratto per omni uno un'altro e quello sia en suo luogho e le fosse casso staendo en offitio che'l Priore encontenente casso esse, nè debbia trare uno altro del dette saccho. E'l Priore possa chiamare quando non avesse tucto el suo Conselglio per ciaschuno che fosse meino un'altro del Compania e valglia per quella volta comme ei fosse Priore. E sempre el saccetto dei decti Consellieri stia sogellato del segello del Priore ala guardia del Camarlengho.

[3v] 6. Dela electione del Sindico che dia sindicare el Priore vecchio.

Ancho ordenamo che'l Priore nuovo collo suo Consellio la prima domennicha che'ntrara en offitio debbiano eleggere uno dela detta Compania el quale sia Sindico a sindicare el Soprapriore. E debbialo avere sindicato enfra octo dì e se avesse fallato, da lli la penetenza secondo l'ofesa commessa presente la Compania sotto pena d'essere casso dela Compania.

7. Che la Compania abbia uno Priore, uno Vicaro, uno Soprapriore e uno Camarlengo.

Ordenamo che la Compania predetta abbia uno Priore, e uno Vicaro, e uno Soprapriore e uno Sindico che sindichi el Soprapriore e uno Camarlengo, e quattro Consellieri e doi Enfermieri; e duri el loro officio sei mesi e non più.

8. Come el Priore vecchio ene tenuto dechiamare el Priore nuovo a sè.

Anco ordenamo che'l Priore vecchio debbia chiamare a sè el Priore nuovo presente tucta la Compania e preghilo umilemente che le piaccia de recevare el suo officio e così faccia a ciascuno altro offitiale, e chi el suo officio non volesse recevare sia al tucto casso dela Compania.

[4r] 9. Ciascuno che sirà chiamato ad alcuno ofitio se debbia confessare.

Se alcuno dela predetta Compania sirà chiamato ad alcuno dei sopradetti ofici se debbia confessare de tucto el suo pecato enanzi che comenizi el suo offitio, e chi non fosse confesso sia ponito per lo Priore gravissimamente.

10. Ciascuno dela Compania se confessi una volta el mese.

Ciascheduno dela detta Compania sia tenuto de confesarse una volta per ciascuno mese e che'l Priore sia tenuto de farli confessare e fare scrivare ciascheduno che se confessa el quando e da chi per ubedienza.

11. El Priore nuovo debbia sindicare el Priore vecchio.

Ordenamo che'l Priore nuovo debbia sindicare el Priore vecchio e d'esaminarlo del bene e del male e dela vita ch'esso à portata ello suo officio e se avesse fallato, òno asciorliarlo o legarlo e fra octo dì.

12. Tutte le cose dela Compania stieno appo el Camarlengo.

Ancho ordenamo che tucte le cose dela Compania pervengnano ale mani del Camarlengo salvo le cose dela cassa grande, e sia tenuto de recevare omni [4v] cosa per scritto e per scritto rasegnare e rendere raisgone omni capo de doi meisi agli huomini dela Compania.

13. Possa spendare el Priore de quello dela Compania fini a vinti soldi.

Ancho ordenamo che'l Priore non possa spendare da vinti soldi en su senza la volontà dele doe parti dela Compania e che'l Carmarlengho non possa spendire da deci soldi en su senza la volontà del Priore.

14. Ciascuno sia tenuto d'obedire el Priore della Compania.

Per reverenza del nostro signore Ihesu Cristo e dela verasgie Sancta Croce ordenamo che ciascheduno dela detta Compania sia tenuto d'obedire reverentemente el Priore nostro en tucte cose che s'apartenessero a Compania e chi noll'obedisse o respondesse engiuriosamente, facesse grido o remore en Compania ad alta voce overo che revelasse alcuno secreto dela Compania ad alcuna persona che non fosse dela Compania predetta o giurasse ella Compania sarà nienti[?] troppo desonessti, o dicesse engiuria dela Compania o facesse meschie overo cancasse a bordelli che'l Priore collo suo Consellio el possa [5r] ponire e cassare ala sua vollia guardando al'ofesa commessa.[1]

15. Ciascuno sia tenuto de pagare doi denari per oferta.

Ordenamo che ciascheduno dela decta Compania sia tenuto de pagare omni domenicha doi denari per oferta e chi stesse più domeniche che non pagasse sia tenuto de pagare omni cosa ensieme; e sia tenuto el Priore de rescotare e fare pagare omni persona ch'avesse a pagare oferte XV dì enanze che se fenescha el suo officio e chi non pagasse ala fine del suo officio l'oferte del detto Priore che'l Priore el debbia cassare dela Compania. E s'esso non rescotesse nè casasse chi non avesse pagate le sue oferte, che'l Priore nuovo sia tenuto de cassare el Priore vecchio.

16. Che'l Priore sia tenuto dare per scritto al Soprapriore omni comandamento.

Ancho ordenamo che'l Priore debbia encontenente dare per scritto al Soprapriore omni comandmento e omni penetenza ch'esso desse a ciaschuno dela Compania; e entendase per li comandamenti che se scrivono ello libro per le mani del Camarlengo. E si esso nolli desse per scritti che'l Soprapriore sia tenuto e possa dare al Priore quella penetenza che'l Priore avesse empossta a colui che fallato [5v] avesse. E s'el Soprapriore questo non facesse che'l Sindico el quale facto e ordenato secondamente che se contene ello capitulo el possa sindicare ala fine del suo officio e dalli penetenza chome a lui piacesse guardando al defetto commesso.

17. Del ofitio del Soprapriore.

Ordenamo ancora che'l Soprapriore abbia quessto officio che s'el Priore fallasse en alcuna cosa contra gli ordenamenti ch'esso el possa ponire come a lui parrà guardando ai defecti commessi per lui. E se neuno dela Compania se sentisse gravato per lo Priore o per lo suo Vicario per neuna cosa d'essere casso, o d'altro gravamento debbia recorrere al Soprapriore e al Soprapriore dire el suo gravamente. El Soprapriore deliberandose con quelli che parrà a lui sufficienti dela detta Compania debbia cognoscere e vedere s'esso fosse agravato e o dire quello che dice; e se fosse agravato sgravarlo fra quindici dì doppo el die dela mentagione facta per lo detto gravato.

18. Dela esaminatione che de fare el Soprapriore.
Ancho ordenamo che'l Soprapriore sia tenuto de esaminare tucti gli huomini dela Compania una volta el mese sotto pena d'essere casso e guardare se [6r] alcuno defetto ei fosse non ponito el Priore perche nolla ponito.

19. El Priore sia tenuto de dare a ciascuno el suo luogo.
Ancho ordenamo ch'l Priore sia tenuto de dare a ciaschuno dela Compania el suo luogho ella ghiesa predetta de Sancta Croce.

20. El Priore sia tenuto de fare leggere gl'ordenamenti.
El Priore collo suo Consellio sia tenuto de fare leggiare omni capo de doi mesi gli ordenamenti almeno uno volta fra la Compania e fare proposte generali fra la Compania e ciò che se farà per loro se vencha per le tre parti dele doe dela Compania.

21. Ciascuno sia tenuto d'obedire el Priore.
Ordenamo che ciaschuno debbia obedire el Priore d'ongni comandamento che esso li comandarà che s'apartenesse a Compania e chi non obedisse a tre comandamenti sia al tucto casso e debbiano se fare ei tre comandamenti en tre domeniche, cioè, omni domenicha uno comandamento; e debbiali el Priore fare scrivare al Camarlengo ello suo libro. E chi stesse [6v] tre domeniche che non venisse a capitulo sia al tucto casso salvo s'esso non fosse ella terra overo che non fosse sano de sua persona o che avesse altra legiptima scusa remangha ello Priore de saperne el vero.[2]

22. Neuno debbia acusare l'altro de cosa non facta.
Neuno dei detti fratelli possa nè debbia acusare alcuno altro dei detti fratelli de Compania al Priore d'alcuno cosa la quale esso non avesse facta si esso nol vedesse o sapesse per certo; e se alcuno acusasse e non provasse, el Priore sia tenuto de fare de quello come de colui che l'avesse fatta e remangha ello Priore sapere el vero.

23. De venire al luogo nostro el giovedì sancto.
Tutti e fratelli dela detta Compania seino tenuti e debbiano bene essere el giovedì sancto al luogo nostro ordenato. El Priore sia tenuto

de lavare ei piei a tucti quelli dela detta Compania e fare carità ensieme. E che neuno debbia venire ala detta Compania se prima non ene confesso de tucto el suo peccato. El Priore sia tenuto de domandarne ciascuno per sè per obedientia e chi contra facesse el cacci fore dela ghiesa e dieli forte penetenza.

[7r] 24. Ancho ordenaro che niuno del decta Compania debbiano avere carnale usanza com niune persona matrimonale overo mollie altrui che sieno ensieme a una vita come fare debbono. E chi contrafacesse sia al tutto casso dela Compania e non ce possa rentrare al tempo de quello Priore che'l cassarà a uno anno. E se per lo decto tempo perseverasse ello decto vitio, non ce possa rentrare en vita sua e se fosse persona matrimoniale si corrocta che fosse generale per omni persona el Priore collo suo Conselgilio avuta deliberatione con doi buoni homeni dela Compagnia chiamati per lo Priore el possano punice alla loro voluntà, e remanga ello Priore de saperne el vero.[3]

25. Ordenaro che'l Priore che sirà per lo tempo non possa vestire, nè fare vestire neuno che non sia dela Compagnia predecta, nè prestare vesta. E che non sia neuna persona che ala morte se possa sepellire colla vesta dela detta Compania si esso non fosse prima della Compagnia predecta.

26. Ciaschuno dela decta Compania sia tenuto d'amarse e honorarse ensieme sì come buoni fratelli e se alcuno venisse en discordia l'uno coll'altro el Priore sia [7v] tenuto de pacificarli ensieme fra'l terzo die e chi non se volesse redure a concordia sia tenuto el Priore de darli forte penetenza, e chi per penetenza non se concordasse colui per chui remanesse la concordia sia al tutto casso dela Compagnia e si essi se reducessero a concordia senza correctione del Priore, el Priore sia tenuto de recevarli benignamente e darli legiera penetenza.

27. Ordenaro che neuno dela decta Compagnia debbia prestare vesta ad alcuna persona che non sia de questa Compagnia e chi contrafacesse sia punito per lo Priore e per lo suo Consellio la quale penetenza li sia inposta presente tutta la Compagnia quando ene radunata e che neuno debbia tolglere altrui o desciplina senza licentia del Priore se nolla perdesse per necessità e al'ora la debbia reponere in e onde esso la leva. E chi contrafacesse sia tenuto el Priore de darli forte penetenza come a lui parrà.

28. Anco ordenaro che onni partito che se mettarà fra la Compagnia non se possa permettare se prima non se mette fra'l Priore e'l suo

Consellio e onni partito che [8r] se mecterà fra'l Priore el suo Consellio se vencha per quatro de loro e altramente non se vencha. E si se perdesse, non se debbia mectare fra la Compagnia. E se avenisse che alcuno dei Consellieri non fosse al'ora a capitolo, el Priore con quelli Consellieri che siranno al'ora a capitolo en Compagnia possano chiamare per onni uno un'altro, entandase per lo die decto e vallia e tenga como se fosse presente.

29. Non se possa mettere alcuno partito fra la Compania senza volontà del Priore o del suo Vicario o del suo Consellio. E onni partito che se mettarà fra la Compania se debbia venciare per lo doe parti de quelli dela Compania; e non se possa mettare palotta palese e chi contrafacesse sia ponito per lo Priore gravissimamente e onni persona l'accusi en capitolo al Priore.

30. Se acadesse acadente o caso che bisognasse de sospendere alcuno capitolo fra la Compania el Priore collo suo Comselglio el possano sospendare e venchase per le tre parti le doe de loro.

[8v] 31. Ordenaro che se'l Priore che sirà per lo tempo tenesse si facta vita che non paresse agli omeni dela decta Compagnia che fosse degnio d'avere quello honore d'essere Priore chi i decti homeni el possano de sponare del suo offitio. E si esso commectesse cola da essere casso che avuta deliberatione colle quatro parti dela Compagnia s'il possano de sponare e cassare dela Compagnia e non se ne passa mettere partito se nonne racolta la Compagnia, e sieno en concordia e venchase per le tre parti de loro.

32. El Vicario del Priore dela decta Compania possa comandare e dare penetenze e cassare e fare tutte quelle cose che podesse fare el decto Priore quando non fosse el Priore a capitolo.

33. L'offitio del'infermieri sia questo che se alcuno dela Compagnia enfermasse, solicitamente sieno tenuti d'andare a quello cotale enfermo s'ei bisognasse alcuno cosa debbialo dire al Priore e al Sopriore e vigitarlo solicitamente. E se quello cotale enfermo fosse bisognose, passano a lui sovenire fini en deci soldi de quello dela Compania. E Camarlengo sia tenuto de darli e si à bisognasse [9r] veghiare possano comandare a ciaschuno dela Compania ch'à loro parrà ch'ei debbia veghiare e chi non obedisse sia ponito per lo Priore gravissimamente. E se avenisse che neuno dela Compania pasasse de questa vita e giudicassese colla vesta sepelirse sieno tenuti defarle sapere a quelli dela

Compania e d'essere ala sua sepoltura a farli l'onore che se converra e farlo portare a quelli dela Compania e fra octo dì deppo la sua morte ciascuno dela Compania sia tenuto de dire 100 paternoster e 100 ave maria per l'anima sua. E sì come el Priore sentirà la morte dequello cotale enfermo sia tenuto demandarli la vesta e la desciplina ala casa sua per sei buoni huomini dela Compagnia vestiti dele veste e colle quali cose esso se debbia sepelire. Fra quindici die deppo la sua morte sia tenuto el Priore con quelli dela Compania andare a processione ala sepoltura del detto morto e fare l'oficio che a ciò se convene e che'l Priore sia tenuto de fare dire cento messe per l'anima del detto morto a uno meise deppo la sua morte; l'una messa faccia dire ala ghiesa là ova elli sirà sepelito el detto morto, e dare faccia per la detta messa sei denari e tre candele, e l'altre faccia dire là ova parrà al Priore che sirà per [9v] lo tempo e facciase ala spese dela detta Compania.

34. Ciascuno sia tenuto de venire a capitulo.

Sieno tenuti quelli dela Compania e debbiano racolgliarse al luogo dela ghiesa predetta omni domenicha matina e dì de pasque e feste de postoli e de Santa Maria e'l dì de Santa Caterina e de Santa Maria Madalena la matina ala campana dela porta e quando entraranno ella ghiesa debbianse engenocchiare denanze al crocefisso e dire cinque paternoster e cinque avemaria a poi gettarse l'acqua sancta ello viso e basci l'altare e dica, "Laudato e benedetto sia Cristo". E li altri respondano, "Per sempre sia laudato e benedetto". E ponase a sedere e dica ave maria e paternoster fine ch'esso stane ella ghiesa e poi debbia andare a odire la santa messa e a vedere el corpo de Cristo. E questo s'entenda quando ella ghiesa de Santa Croce predetta non fosse detta ella detta matina messa, o non fosse stato ad odire la messa e a vedere el corpo de Cristo. E non sia neuno dela detta Compania che fosse chiamato en capitulo che debbia respondere se non "laudato e benedetto sia Cristo" e andare a fare quello che sirà comandato.

[10r] 35. Del paternoster e ave maria dire.

Ordenamo che ciaschuno dela Compania predetta sia tenuto de dire per dei VII paternoster e VII ave maria e omni venardì ne giongha V a detti sette ad onore e reverenza dela passione de Cristo. E quando se colcha o leva de letto, dica uno paternostro e una ave maria e quando se pone o leva da mensa el se megliate.

36. De chi volessere essere de'nostri fratelli.

Se alcuno volesse entrare e d'essere de'nostri fratelli dela Compania predetta ordenamo ch'esso sia tenuto de fare dare al Priore una poliza ella quale sia scritto el nome de chi ce vole entrare el'l sopranome e chi la recha, e non ce possa entrare se non mette tre luire overo una vesta de panno de lino nuovo e soldi XXV de denari. E non ce possa entrare neuna persona che sia usurale overo ch'avesse maltoletto se prima non saldasse el Priore recevendo per mesere l'Abade overo per alcun'altra persona che'l possa ragionevelemente a sciolgliare de restituire a quello termene che sirà dechiarato. E non se ne possa mettere nè fare de ciò partito, se non la domenica matina e la sera de giovedì sancto. [10v] E non ce possa entrare neuno se fra la Compania fosse alcuno ch'ei volesse male se prima non s'aconcia pacifica ensieme e non de possa essere forzato. El Priore sia tenuto de fare la demanda s'ella Compania fosse alchuno che stesse male col lui e s'ei sapesse che neuno che non fosse a capitulo chon chui esso stesse male. E non debbia venire a capitulo se prima non se confessa del suo pecato e de ciò faccia fede al Priore. E omni poliza che sirà data al Priore se debbia leggere en capitulo octo dì anzi che se metta a partito a ciò che ciascheduno possa sapere chi ene quelli che vole entrare anzi che se metta a partito.

37. De chi fosse casso dela Compania.

Ordenamo che se alcuno fosse stato casso dela detta Compania per alcuna caigone e volesse tornare a misericordia esendo correpto del suo pecato debbia fare dare una poliza al Priore collo nome e collo sopranome suo como en quello modo ch'entrasse de nuovo e quello ordine soservi, e sia tenuto de pagare deci soldi e le spese passate e omni altra spese ch'ei fosse toccata de pagare esendo stato ella Compania. E non se possa mettere a partito se prima non deposita la sopradetta [11r] offerta e l'altre spese al Camarlengo. E si se vencie se debbia mettare encontenente ello ceppo. E se così non facesse, non se possa nè debbia mettere a partito.

38. De non bere taverna certi die.

Ancho ordenamo che neuno dela detta Compania debbia bere en taverna el venerdì nela domemnica matina overo altro die che se racolgha la Compania la matina anzi che vengha a capitulo. E si tenuto ciascuno dela Compania de degiunare el venardì overo un altro die dela stomana. El Priore ne possa a sciolgliare ala fine del suo offitio che falasse.

39. De chi tenesse fancella.

Neuno dela detta Compania ch'abbia molglie debbia tenere fancella e chi contrafacesse sia casso dela Compania. E se megliantemente sia casso ciaschuno che tenesse fancella overo che usasse desonestamente con femmena che habitasse de Sancto Bartolomeo ella paroffia[?].

40. El Priore sia tenuto anuntiare la festa de Sancta Croce.

El dì dela fessta dela verasgie Sancta Croce la quale se cellebra a die XIIII de setenbre el Priore sia tenuto [11v] anuntiare e predire XV die enanzi la detta fessta aciò che tucte ei fratelli sieno ala detta festa se non avessero legiptima scusa. E de ciò faccia el Priore diligente inquistione e ponirlo gravassimamente e fare l'emosina a'povari e fare celebrare divino offitio dal primo vespero fine al secondo e dire messa ordenata e fare predicare a fare offitio doppio fini al'ottava ad onore e reverenza dela beata Sancta Croce.

41. Neuno dela Compania debbia in tutte altri fore de Compania.

Ancho ordenamo che neuno dela Compania non debbia menare fra la Compania neuna persona che non sia dela detta Compania quando ella fosse racolta senza licenza del Priore o del suo Vicario. E chi contrafacesse el Priore el possa ponire ala sua volglia.

42. De fare dire una messa per l'anima de'morti.

Sia tenuto el Priore en fra otto die deppo la festa de tucti e santi de fare dire una messa per l'anima de tucti quelli dela Compania venire e essere ala detta messa e andare o d'ofrire honestamente. E chi ala detta messa non fosse sia ponito per lo Priore gravissimamente.

[12r] 43. Che neuno dei fratelli debbia entrare en altra compania.

Ordenamo che neuno dela detta Compania debbia entrare en altra compania fini ch'elli ene de questa e chi contrafacesse sia al tucto casso. E non ce possa entrare neuno che sia d'altra compania; e se fosse messo quello partitio, non valglia.

44. Che neuno sodomito possa essere de'nostri fratelli.

Perciò che'l vitio dela sodomia ene vitio contra natura e de spiacevole molto a Deo, ordenamo che neuno dela detta Compania debbia en esso vitio accadere. E chi contrafacesse sia al tucto casso e non ce possa rentrare dal tempo del Priore che'l cassarà a tre anni; e se per lo tempo de'tre anni perseverasse ello detto vitio non possa rentrare ella detta Compania en vita sua.

45. De chi facesse requela o la mentanaza.

Ancho ordenamo che non sia neuno dela Compania predetta che

debbia fare requela overo la mentanza en corte per neuna caisgione che fosse facta per lo Priore e per la Compania, e chi contrafacesse sia al tutto casso dela Compania en vita sua. E così sia de ciascuno ch'ei fosse recorso infini amo[?]. E così sia de ciascuno de ch'ei desse aiuto o favore; e non s'entenda per chi dovesse avere [12v] dela Compania o fosse obrigato per essa Compania. E questo capitulo non se possa sospendare e se sospendesse non vallia.

46. Del giuoco de'dadi.

Neuno de'fratelli dela Compania predetta debbia giocare, nè fare giocare, nè retenere giucho de'dadi; e chi contrafacesse sia al tucto casso dela Compania e non ce possa rentrare se prima non pagha vinti soldi e le spese che fossaro corse fra'l tempo che stesse casso.

47. De non giocare a neuno giocho.

Ordenamo che non sia neuno dei detti frattelli che debbia giocare a neuno giucho là ova se vencha o perda denaio, e chi contrafacesse el Priore el possa ponire colli parrà.

48. Che Cescho de Torello sia scrittore dela Compania.

Ancho ordenamo che Cescho de Torello sia scrittore dela Compania perfine a tanto che parrà ala Compania.

49. Che la Compania abbia uno libro.

La Compania predetta abbia uno libro ello quale se debbiano scrivare tutte le raisgioni dela Compania e tutti coloro che dovessero dare per quanlunche cosa ala detta Compania. El Camarlengo sia tenuto d'asengnarli enfra octo die deppo lo spirare del suo offitio a colui che sirà scrittore de sopra a questo libro. E s'esso noll'asegnasse che'l Priore el possa ponire gravissimamente al sua volglia. [13r] E debbiase scrivare ello detto libro chi avesse ad avere per neuna caisgione dala Compania. E non s'entenda per olio nè per candeli menuti questo remangha a scrivare al Camarlengo ello suo libro. E debbiase scrivare ello detto libro la somma del'entrate e dele spese del Camarlengo al fine del suo tempo. E scrivase ancora ello sopradetto el residuo del ceppo. E tucto quello debbia asengnare el Camarlengho vecchio al detto scrittore, e debbia avere una casetta la ostengha el detto libro.

50. Degli scotitori dela Compania.

Ordenamo che la detta Compania abbia doi rescotitori che rescotano en corte e fore de corte per omni modo che la Compania avesse ad avere. E non s'entenda per li huomini che sono dentro ella predetta

Compania de Sancta Croce. E faccialli coloro che fanno gli altri officiali e quali campano ello bosselo la matina quando ene tratto el Priore.

51. La Compania abbia uno libro.

Ancho ordenamo che la Compania abbia uno libro ello quale omni capo de sei mesi, cioè, al fine del ofitio del Priore si debbia el Priore ello detto libro fare scrivare ciascheduno dela Compania ch'averà ne [13v] presa penetanza ella predetta ghiesa de Sancta Croce e chi se confessasse fore dela detta ghiesa sia tenuto de darne prove e fare fede al Priore là ova esso se confessa e da chui. E altramente ello detto libro non se scriva. E nientemeno se debbia confessare ciascheduno una volta el mese al muodo usato; e questo libro stia ala guardia del Camarlengo sogellato del sogello delo scritore che sirà del detto libro.

52. De non sedere ella banca del Priore.

Ella bancha là ova sede el Priore la domemnicha a matina quando ene racolta la Compania a capitulo overo altra matina quando la Compania serà cogliesso neuno en essa bancha debbia sedere salvo che i suoi consellieri e 'l suo Camarlengo. E'l detto Camarlengo debbia sedere dal mezzo dela bancha en giù, e chi contrafacesse el Priore el debbia ponire come a lui parrà.

53. Del libro dela provedenza.

La Compania predetta ordenamo ch'essa abbia e avere debbia uno libro el quale se chiami el libro horiginale dela provedenza; ello quale libro sieno e debbiano essere scritti tucti gli huomini dela Compania predetta en questo modo che degli huomini dela Compania [14r] predetta se facciano sei cerne, cioè, comenciando al'una e seguiti de grado en grado fine al fine dei sei. E ciascheduno sia cernuto e posto ello detto libro a quella cerna e in quello grado che possa portare la sua posibilità, entendase che ciascheduno dela Compania come ene cernuto e scritto ello detto libro dela provedenza ch'esso a quella cerna si se debbia stare e in quello grado che posto ene. E quando entrarà alcuna persona per volete essere de' nostri fratelli, che dal die ch'el gli entra, a octo die poi el debbia avere cernuto e posto ello detto libro horiginale dela provedenza el Priore collo suo consellio. E quando pervenisse che alcuno dela detta Compania fosse casso, el Priore en quello die ch'esso el casarà el debbia retrovare ello detto libro horiginale si se debbia aprire quando bisognasse de fare alcuna colta en utilita dela predetta Compania de Santa Croce. E debbia se ne gire secondamento ch'ene ordenato, e dal die che questo predetto libro s'aprirà per fare alcuna colta [14v] a uno mese si debbia avere pagato ciascuno dela Compania quello che diràne la sua cerna. E se pagato non avesse al detto termine che'l Priore el debbia cassare, e si esso nol casasse che'l Soprapriore debia cassare lui. E questo libro debbia stare ala guardia del Camarlengo sogellato del sogello dela scritore del detto libro.

54. Del valore dei presenti ordinamenti.

Ancho ordenamo che i detti ordenamenti non se debbiano nè possano mutare e valgliano nove anni e più fini a tanto che la Compania nolli refacesse de niuno o facesse altra novità, e non se possa fare ala detta fine del tempo se non de fossero en concordia le doe parti dela Compania predetta.[4]

55. Che non se mandi più che doi ceri al morto.

Ordenaro che ada conpagniare alcuno morto d'essa Compagnia non se possano mandare nè fare mandare più che doi ceri dela Compania salvo che quando morisse alcuno che fosse Priore, Vicario, o Soprapriore o Camarlengo d'essa Compagnia se possano mandare ada compagniare quello morto che in alcuno de detti offitii fosse quatro ceri dela Compagnia e non piu. E chi contrafacesse sia al tutto casso de'essa Compagnia.

[15r] 56. Quando se facesse domanda intra gli omeni della Compagnia per alcuno che volesse entrare in essa, e alcuno dela Compagnia dicesse che stesse male con quello cotale che volesse intrare in essa Compagnia, sia tenuto el Priore e'l Vicario tenerlo secreto e non manifestarlo nè in lla Compagnia fore dela Compagnia per niuno modo; e chi contrafacesse sia casso della Compagnia.

57. Per reverenza dela beata Sancta Croce fo ordenato che qualunche persona volesse in la decta Compagnia entrare e mandasse la poliza nella quale fosse scripto el suo nome e sopranome al muodo usato el die che se fa la festa di Santa Croce e die tre di maggio e a die XIIII di septenbre ce possa entrare come la sera de giovedie sancto remanendo gli ordenamenti e capitoli en l'altre cose fermi.

58. Ancho ordinaro che se alcuno essendo in caso de morte volesse entrare ella decta Compagnia, debbia in prima pagare al Camarlengo dela Compagnia dieci liure; e non se possa questo capitolo sospendere, nè contra de ciò fare per lo Priore nè per lo Vicario nè per altri se non ne fossaro en concordia le quarto parti delo cinqua d'essa Compagnia;

e chi contrafacesse sia al tutto casso salvo che questo non s'intenda per niuno che prima fosse stato d'essa Compagnia ma per lui se possa questo capitolo per lo Priore e per lo suo Consellio sospendere e quello che prima ne fosse stato recevere.

[15v] 59. Ciascuno dela Compagnia predecta el quale maneggiarà per qualunche modo del avere overo pecunia d'essa Compania o che portarà alcuno offitio sia tenuto e debbia infra uno mese dal dì che finisse el suo offitio rassegnare omni sua ragione e omni peccunia e avere che appo lui fosse ai ragionieri che dati li fossero per lo Priore elquale sia tenuto de darli essi ragionieri; e chi cose non asegnasse sia in perpetuo casso dela decta Compagnia e mai rentrare non ce possa in caso de morte. E questo capitolo sospendare non se possa per lo Priore ne per suo vicaro, e se contrafacessero sieno al tutto cassi d'essa Compania.

60. Ordenaro che la decta Compagnia abbia uno tesaurieri al quale pervengano tutti i denari d'essa Compania e che el Camarlengo d'essa Compania li debbia dare ciascuno mese omni denaio che li fosse entrato e'l Priore li faccia dare; e quando se lavorasse ala ghiesa d'essa Compania debbia dare esso tesaurieri agli operieri d'esso lavorio i denari ch'avesse. E sia tenuto de scrive l'entrate e le spese tutte e ciascuno mese en capitolo fare leggiere tutti debitori d'essa Compania che li siranno dati scripti per coloro che sono a retrovare le ragione dela Compagnia. E chi contrafacesse o a queste cose contradicesse sia al tutto casso.

61. Niuno dela decta Compagnia debbia giocare a veruno gioco de dado sotto pena d'essare casso dela Compania, e non ce possa rentrare se prima non pagasse XXV soldi e le [16r] spese passate sieni che fosse stato casso, salvo che chi giochasse en pasqua de natale debbia reportarse al Priore infra tre domeniche deppo la decta pasqua e a domandarli misericordia e pagare cinque soldi e fare la penitenza che per lo Priore li fosse inposta la quale inponere li debbia secondo l'offesa commessa. E chi stesse deppo tre domeniche che non venisse ala Compagnia non avando legiptima scusa caggia a quello pena che colui ch'avesse giocato en pasque de natale. E debbia el Priore per obedienza domandare chi avesse giochato o veduto giochare en pasqua, e se nuino el quale non se fosse reportato al Priore fosse da altri reportato ch'avesse giochato sia casso e non possa rentrarce se non per novitio. Ancho se alcuno giochasse a tempo che guerra fosse al Borgo per niuna casgione stia a quella pena come se giochato avesse en pasqua de natale.

62. Se alcuno dela Compagnia s'apellasse per veruna casgione al Soprapriore e perdesse l'apellagione non possa ella Compagnia tornare en vita sua se non n'e in caso de morte e se niuno Priore lo recevesse stia a quella pena che colui ch'avesse perduta l'apellasgione.[5]

[18r] 63. Queste sono additioni, constitutioni et ordinanmenti facte, constitute, et ordinate per li infra scripti sei buoni savi discreti homini della Compagnia a corregiare, agiognare, et scemare agl'ordinamenti d'essa Compagnia secondo che a loro pare che se convengha. Facte del anno, mese et die infra scripti. E i nomi dei quali buoni homini sono questi, cioè:

Giovanni del Cescho dela Guiduccia
Nicholò de Zacharia
Matteo del Cescho d'Orlando
Angnilo de Muccio de Guiduccino
Muccio de Bartolo de Morrali
Andrea de Donato

64. Ordenaro li soprascripti electi chi facesse contra quello che se contene ello LVIIII capitulo rimanga la pena in l'albitrio del Priore la punitione di quello contra le contrafaciente como a lui parrà.

65. Anco ordenaro che l'infermieri della detta Compagnia possano senza loro preiudicio et dampno spendere de quello dela Compagnia a ciascuno infermo detta Compagnia bisognoso oltra quello che se contene elli ordenamenti XXX solidi e che'l Camarlengo della Compagnia dare li debbia a loro per essa senza cagione suo dampno.

[18v] 66. Anco ordenaro che como se contene ello LX captiulo deli ordini d'essa Compagnia che la Compagnia abbia uno tesorieri al quale pervenga tucta la pecunia d'essa Compagnia deposto et finito el suo offitio infra VIII dì puoi che sirà sindicato per li sindichi della Compagnia debbia dare a esso Tesorieri omni quantite de'fiori e de pecunia che appo lui fosse de quello della Compagnia sotto pena d'essere casso et niente meno a restitutione de quello ch'elli avesse della Compagnia sia tenuto. E s'el Priore non le cassasse che'l Priore nuovo cassare debbia esso Priore vecchio, et damo li detti buoni homini per vigore de loro arbitrio elessero et nominaro Angnilo de Muccio de Guiduccino per lo primo Tesorieri, el cui offitio duri per tempo de nove anni proximi che vengono e tanto più sfini che per la Compagnia

d'uno altro sirà proveduto. Et se infra'l decto tempo el decto Angnilo, perche semo tucti mortali e a petitione del nostro creatore, morisse che'l Priore collo suo Conseglio possa eleggere uno altro en suo luogo; et non possa esso Tesorieri spendere de quello della Compagnia se quello che spendesso non fosse vento per le doue parti dele tre delli homini della Compagnia.

67. Anco ordenaro che scriptore della detta Compagnia sia Smiraldo de Lazzaro per tempo de nove anni prosimi che vengono e tanto piu sfini che per la Compagnia non fosse du'uno altro veduto; e scrivare debbia et [19r] fare memoria de'facti dela Compagnia a mantenimento dele raigioni della Compagnia e l'entrate e quantità di che per verano ale mani del decto Tesorieri e de'pagamenti ch'esso Tesorieri farà e altre cose che s'apartengono a utile d'essa Compagnia.

68. Ancho per lo tempo decto de VIIII anni a raggionare e vedere le ragioni del Camarlengo elessero Angnilo de Muccio de Guiduccino e Smiraldo predecto.

69. Ancho ch'el Chamarlengo presente debbai fare fare uno libro de tre quarderni de carta o più [per] le spese dela Compagnia. Nel quale libro tucti i Camarlenghi che sirano de qui a nove anni debbiano scrivare tucte le sue entrate per sè et le spese per sè sichè in esso libro ordenatamente se trovi l'entrate e le spese d'essi Camarlenchi in uno volume de libro, e che smarire non si possa in uno libro del uno Camarlengo che in fine al decto tempo fosse state Camarlengo e aciò che le ragioni d'essa Compagnia meglo si mantengano et che Francesscho de Gilio Camarlengo che presente debbia in esso primamente scrivare le sue entrate et le sue spese.

70. Anco ordenaro che qualunche de'nostri fratelli che fosse stato in la Compagnia tre anni possa mectere [19v] el figlolo ella decta Compagnia daendo la vesta e facta prima per lo Priore la domanda secondo l'ordine.

[20r] 71. Queste sono additioni, constitutioni et ordinamenti fatte et costitute et ordinate infra gl'omini dela Compania de Sanca Croci del Borgo San Sepolcro et confermate per li savi e descretti homini infra scritti et eletti dala decta Compania a revedere e confemare secondo che a loro parrà sotto gli anni del nostro Signore Ieshu Cristo, mille

trecento novantotto del mese de maggio et nomina de quelli buoni homini sono questti, cioè:

Matteo del Cesscho d'Orlando
Andrea de Donato
Giovanni de Casuccio
Giovanni de Simone
Lucha de Fratre Pietro del Doro

72. Ordinaro li soprascritti eletti che'l Priore d'essa Compania che al presente et tutti gli altri che per l'avenire sirano non possano nè debbiano recevare niuno che volgla entrare dela decta Compania se prima non paga soldi vintacinque per entrata et una vessta de panno de lino la quale vessta sia sì grande che sia bona a omni homo et altramente non la receva, et s'elli la recevesse el Soprapriore sia tenuto a farne pagare al Priore un altra vessta che sia grande comme de sopra se contene. Et quessto che detto non s'entenda per gli omini che sono stati dela Compania tre anni [20v] che ciaschuno di loro possa mettare el suo figluolo dela decta Compania pagando solamente la vessta comme dinanze ne'presenti ordini se contene e intendase che la vessta sia grande comme de sopra se contene.

73. Ancho ordenaro che la fessta dela beata Santa Croci, la quale se celebra a dì IIII de maggio che per utile dela decta Compania se faccia, damo innanze a quessto muodo, cioè, che'l dì dela detta fessta se faccia dire messe legendo quelle che parà al Priore et non se dicha messa cantando et non se preddichi nè dicha vesspri ma facciase l'uffitio per gli omini dela Compania, la vigilia et la fessta doppo vesstro. Et non se faccia altra spesa se non quella de'preiti che dirano le decta messe, et s'el Priore o Camarlengo facessaro o facessaro fare per quessta caigione altra spesa che Raigionieri non lai[?] debbiano amettare et s'elli lai amettessaro sieno al tutto cassi dela Compania.

74. Ancho ordenaro che quando caso acadesse che Dio chiamasse a sè niuno dela decta Compania, et esso non avesse pagate le sue offerte che'l Priore che sirà al'ora non li debbia mandare la vessta se prima per quessto cotale non se paga l'ufferte ch'esso dovesse pagare ala decta Compania overo che per l'amore di Dio fossaro domandate overo se domandassaro per parte de decto [21r] morto. Et s'el Priore li desse o mandasse la decta vessta et non se pagassaro prima le decte offerte overo domandassaro al muodo sopradecto che'l Priore sia tenuto de

pagare quella quantità che dovessa pagare quello cotale a chui esso Priore avesse mandata la vessta.

[21v] 75. Queste sono aditioni, constitutioni et ordinamenti fatte, constitute et ordinate per l'infrascritti cinque buoni et descreti homini dela Compania de Santa Croci del Borgo eletti per essa Compania a correggiare, agiongnare et a sciemare agli ordini d'essa Compania secondo che a loro parrà che se convenga fatte sotto gli anni del nostro Signore Ihesu Cristo mille quatrocento uno, dì XXVIII del mese de dicembre. Et i nomi de decti homini sono questi, cioè:

Signorello d'Agnilo de Feo, Priore
Arigo de Giovanse
Andrea de Donato
Antonio de Santi de Gnuolo
Lucha de Ser Pietro del Doro

76. Ordenaro a reverentia de Dio et dela beata Santa Croci che se caso avenisse che niuno dela decta Compania facesse humicidio, cioè, che hucidesse alcuna persona che'lli sia al tutto casso dela Compania predecta et inn esso non possa mai rentrare nè ala vita nè ala morte. Et questo che decto non se intenda quando compagna venisse in lo destretto del Borgo overo che'l Comune del Borgo avesse guerra che se niuno facesse humicidio contra quelli dela compagna overo anemici del Comune per questo niuno sia casso dela Compania.

[22r] 77. Ancho providdaro et ordenaro per hutile et per devotione d'essa Compania che niuno che sia overo sirà chiamato a ffare la fessta dela beata Santa Croci non debbia ponare nè fare ponare in la ghiesa de Santa Croci del Borgo nè a essa appicare bandiere al'aremi overo ansegne de niuna persona salvo s'elle non fossaro propie dela Compania et chi lei ponesse o facesse ponare sia al tutto casso dela Compania predecta.

78. Queste sono aditioni, constitutioni, ordenamenti fatte et constitute et ordenate per lo Priore et Consilglio et homeni dela Compania di Santa Croci predetto adunati a capitolo la sera giovedì santo sotto gli anni del nostro signore Ihesu Cristo mille quattrocento otto, dì XII del mese d'aprile se cominciaro et fornierse domenicha de passqua dela resuressione a dì XV del presente mese al tempo de Giovanni de Paci de Iacomo, Priore dela detta Compania.

79. In prima ordenaro el decto Priore, el suo Consilglio et capitolo a onere et reverenza del omnipotente Dio et dela gliorosa vergine Maria, sua madre e dela [22v] beata Santa Croci et de tutti e santi et sante de vita eterna che se per niuno tenpo avenisse che niuno dela detta Compania in niuno muodo overo in niuno luogo et niuno tenpo biastimasse o spregiasse Dio o la vergine Maria overo Santa Croci overo niuno sante o santa de paradiso che sia al tucto casso dela decta Compania nè inn essa possa rentrare se prima non vene corretto et confesso del suo pecato et paghi vinti soldi et la spesa passate. Et Priore sia tenuto de fare la domanda fra la Compania et oservare tutto quello muodo chomme se quello cotale volesse entrare de nuovo; et s'el Priore non observasse el muodo sopradecto remanga al tutto casso dela Compania.

80. Ancho ordenaro el decto Priore et suo Consilglio in capitolo domennicha de passqua anno et mese infrascritto come denanze se contene per tolgliare via li scandali che niuno dela decta Compania non ardessca nè presumi pilgliare la croce per portarla quando la Compania adasse a processione overo a sepelire alcuno morto overo in qualunche altro luogo andassero vestiti fore dela decta Compania senza la licenze del Priore overo del Vicaro quando non ce fosse el Priore et così faccia el Soprapriore overo Conseglieri non essendo et nè el Priore o Vicario o Soprapriore, Priore inanza che s'uscisse dela ghiesa dela Compania.

[23r] 81. Queste sono additioni, constitutioni et ordenamenti fatte, constitute et ordinate per l'infrascritti nove buoni savi discreti homini dela Compania de Sancta Croci infra scritta eletti per essa Compania a correggiare et agiongnare e sciemare agli ordini d'essa Compania secondo che a loro pare che se convenga fatte et costitute sotto gli anni del nostro signore mille quattrocento sette, a dì XXIIII d'aprile.

Et nomi del'infrascritti nove buoni homini sono questi, cioè:

Massciolino de Giovanni de Bocognani
Vicho d'Uguccio de Dotto
Franceschо de Giovanni de maestro Berardino
Matteo del Cesscho d'Orlando
Vane de Muccio de Casuccio al ora Priore
Arigo de Giovanse
Meo de Iacomo de Fuccio
Giovanni de Simone de Vannii
Giovanni de Donato da Carciano

82. Ordenaro e soprascritti che la fessta de Santa Croci che se cellebra a dì III de maggio se faccia in quella forma che se faciva quella de setenbre honorevelimente quanto sempre. Et quella de setenbre se faccia dire cinque messe legento overo quattro legendo et una cantando et non se preddichi et non se dicha vessparo nela vegigha nela fessta. Et quessta delibaratione volgliono se oservi et non se possa anullare se non se racolgono LX homini dela Compania et vencase per le doi parti de loro.

[23v] 83. Ancho ordenaro e sopradecti che niuna persona dela Compania debbia ballare dentro nella ghiesa de Sancta Croci et che'l Priore li debbia fare o far fare comandamento a quelli dela Compania che inn essa ghiesa ballassaro ch'essi più non ballino in la decta ghiesa et se non hobedisse el Priore al primo comandamento sia tenuto el Priore de cassarlo et s'elli non casasse che'l Soprapriore debbia dare penetenza al Priore et mandarelo fore del contado del Borgo et s'el Priore non facesse la penetenza a lui data per lo Soprapriore remanga al tutto casso.

84. Ancho ordenaro che'l primo Priore che uscirà doppo quessto che al presente non duri el suo offitio, se non cinque mesi cominiciando a calenne de guigno et duri fine a calenne de novembre, et che'l Priore che sirà al tenpo che vene la fessta de Santa Croci de maggio sia tenuto chiamare quelli che a lui parrà che sieno sopra a fare la decta fessta XV dì innanze a essa.

85. Ancho ordenaro che ciò che fo fatto da dì XXIIII de marzo fine a dì XXIIII d'aprile, cioè, contra degli ordini o per di subidenza o per altro muodo fallito per lo Priore o per niun'altra persona dela decta Compania non se possa nè debbia cognosciare per niuno muode et da quessto el Priore et gli otto del albittro da omni cosa gli asciolgono et libarano.

86. Qualunche persona contradicesse agli ordini fatti per lo Priore et per quelli otto del albitro o renotassele per muodo che scandalo nè venisse in la casa dela Compania o in niuno altro luogo che'l Priore li dia per penetenza ch'esso vada a Castello al Priore de Sancta Croci [24r] de Castello con la lettara dela Compania sogellata del sugello dela Compania, et faccia quella penetenza che'l Priore dela Compania de Santa Croce de Castello li darà et arechi la respossta dal decto Priore. Et chi non obedisse el Priore del Borgo et quello de Castello remanga al tutto casso.

87. Ancho ordenaro che ciaschuno Camarlengo sia tenuto et d'ubedire et scrivare omni cosa che comandesse el Priore che s'apartenga ala Compania et s'el Camarlengo non l'ubedisse al primo comandamento el Priore li possa dare assprissima penetenza comme parrà a lui.

88. Ancho ordenaro che Nanni del Cisschio el quale una volta fo casso dela Compania et faccie remesso a dì XXIIII de marzo se debbia scrivare in lo libro due sono scritti gli altri homeni dela Compania, et volgliono che quella remesio ne valglia per loro albitro et per qualunche muodo po valere.

89. Ancho ordenaro che'l Priore e li Spedalieri che siano per li tempo non possino afitta e cinque posesione della Compania overo dello Spedale se prima non si mette alla trebba e li fermallo con soficienti e boni schienta dil pagamento, e s'el detto Priore e Spedelieri ell'eno senza trenba che'l Priore e lli Spedalieri che vengono doppo loro possino di nuovo reafitta a utile della Compania.

[24v] 90. Queste sono adictioni, constituctioni et ordinamenti facte et constiute et ordenite per l'infrascripti buoni homini dela Compania de Sancta Croce del Borgo eletti per essa Compania a correggiare, agiognare et a sciemare agli ordini d'essa Compania secondo che a loro parrà che se convenga fatte sotto gli anni del nostro signore MCCCCXXXII, a dì XV del mese de guigno. E nomi de'decti buoni homini sono questi, cioè:

Arizzo de Giovanse de Mazetti
Bevenuto de Matheo de Veci
Romano de Martino
Nicholò de Giovanni d'Andrea
Giovanni de Lazaro de Tofanello

91. Ordenaro sopra i facti del oferte che ciaschuno che à a pagare oferta niuna le debbia avere pagato per tutto ottobre prossimo che vene quello che esso vole de quella quantità che esso avesse a pagare et sirà asciolto le tutta la quantità che esso avesse a pagare et sirà asciolto de tutta la quantità che avesse a pagare per quella quantità che pagasse infra el decto tempo. Et quale non pagasse infra el decto, tempo como è decte sia tenuto a pagare tutta la quantità.

92. Ancho ordenaro che per lo tempo che virrà incomenzando a kalende novenbre se paghi omni sei mesi per sue offetta ciaschuno cinque

quantrini cassando et ravocando omni altro capitulo che perlasse de magiure quantità. Et non sia tenuto a pagare le decte offerte niuno menore d'età de X anni.

[25r] 93. Ancho ordenaro che li Spedalieri che siranno delo Spedale de Sancta Maria del Fondaccio el quale fo dato per lo comune del Borgo ala Compania de Sancta Croce predecta non possino spendare de quello delo Spedale a loro albitrio per del decta Spedale più che la quantità de XL soldi. Et se accadesse fare in lo decto Spedale per utile d'esso magiure spesi nol possino fare senza la licenza aperendo per puliza del Priore che sirà in quello tempo. Et chi contrafacesse non gli sia amessa la spesa che essi faciessaro de loro albitrio più che infine ala quantità predecta. Questo non si tenda per Luchino de ser Meo e i compangni i quali sono al presente intendase per l'avenire.

Ancho ordenaro che'l Priore col suo Conseglio essendo in concordia insiemi possino trare lo Spedalieri, cioè, la guardia alo Spedale como parrà a loro.

95. Ancho ordenaro che la Compania avia doi Raigionieri che avino arrucdere et recorcare tutti i libri dela Compania et delo Spedale et retrare tutti de'vitizi et creditori e rescotare tutta la quantità che fosse a rescotare in quali resacotitori sieno salariati ale spese dela Compania, et abbino per loro salario de tutta la quantità che essi rescotarano senza questione soldi doi per liura. Item che i Raigionieri rescolitori possino fare procuradore et avocato ale spese dela decta Compania.

96. Ancho ordenaro che qualunche persona volesse intrare dei nostri ala morte debbia pagare liure tre et la vesta.

[25v] 97. Anco ordenaro che se alcuno volesse intrare de'nostri fratelli et non avesse in quella ora d'a pagare quello che dovesse et volesse termene, nol possa rectuare la Compania senza la promessa del Camarlengo. El quale Camarlengo per tutte el tempo del suo offictio sia tenuto a rescotare da quello tale o tagli che intrassaro de'nostri fratelli al suo tempo tutta quella quantità che dovesse o dovessero pagare. In case che non rescotesse sia al tutto casso et niente de meno remanga debitore dela Compania de tutta la quantità che avesse a rescotare, cioè, che avesse promesso per lui overo per loro.

98. Anco ordenaro che non se possa insaccare in la saccactione niuno Chamarlengo che sia menore de XX anni et chi fosse non se possa

mettare in l'altra. Et che Raigionieri che sirano a vedere le raigioni de niuno Chamarlengo, non possino nè debbino a mettare nè aconciare le ragioni de quello Chamarlengo se prima el decto Camarlengo non à satesfatto omni pecunia o robba che esso avesso de quello dela Compania, et chi contrafacesse sia al tutto casso.

99. Anco ordenaro che non se possa dare niuna possessione delo Spedale nè dela Compania a niuno homo dela Compania a lavorio et questo non s'intenda a mettare per opera.

100. Anco ordenaro che li Spedalieri non possino dare niuno lavorio de magistero delo Spedale nè dela Compania da uno fiorino in su se non se manda ala tromba.

[26r] 101. Anco ordenaro che'l Priore dela Compania sia tenuto et debbia visitare lo Spedale et i povari omni domenicha matina quando se parte dela Compania.

102. Anco ordenaro che qualunche sirà dela Compania predecta el quale maneggiare per qualunche muodo del avere, olio, pecunia d'essa Compania o che portarà alcuno offictio sia tenuto et debbia infra otto dì fenito el suo offictio et asegnare omni sua raigione ai Raigionieri i quali li siranno dati per lo Priore et dare et numerare omni pecunia et avere et omni altra cosa che appo lui fosse al suo precessore overo precessori; et chi cusì non facesse sia perpetuo casso dela decta Compania et mai rentrare non ci possa se non in caso de morte. Et questo capitulo sospendare non se possa per lo Priore nè per suo Vicaro, e se contrafacessaro sieno al tutto cassi dela decta Compania.

103. Al nome de Dio amen, a dì 3 de maggio 1433.

Ancho hordenaro el Priore e'l suo Chonseglio e'l chorpo dela Chonpania che sia nesuna persona a chapitolo dela detta Chonpania dega parlare parole ingiurione nè in detti nè in fatti chontra nisuno dela detta Chonpania nè ragionare se non dele chose le quali s'apartengano dela detta Chonpania. E se nesuno chontrafacesse che el Priore sia tenuto de chassarlo de la detta Chonpania; e non ce possa essare rimesso se non chome nuvizo e in chaxo che Priore el quale al'ora fosse non chassare el detto non hobediente che Priore che vina de poi dega chasare el detto Priore che non avesse hoservatore fatto o servare el detto ordine.

[26v] 104. Al nome de Dio amen, a dì III de maggio 1435.

Ordeno la Compania de Sancta Croce che per reverenza d'essa che'l dì dela festa de Sancta Croce la quale se celebra a dì tre de maggio che'l Priore sirà in qual tempo sia tenuto radunare gli omini dela Compania predecta in la Abadia del Borgo et venire ad insieme con li decti homini a offerire ala decta Compania con quella offitia che particularemente volessero et in caso che quello Priore che sirà a quello tempo non oservasse le predete cose che'l Priore che seguirà doppo lui el debbia cassare, et non ci possa mai rentrare infine ala morte.

105. Anco ordenaro che'l dì de Sancta Chatarina che se celebra a dì XXV de novembre che'l Priore che sirà in quello tempo sia tenuto radunare gli omini dela decta Compania et andare co la vesta in dosso a offrire ala Compania de Sancta Chatarina predecta et sia licito a ciascheduno lancando le veste possino andare ad insiemi con loro senza vesta con vintuna liura de cera, cioè, doi doppieri de peso de liura VI et le facole de liura XV si che sieno in tutto liura XXI. E in caso che'l Priore che sirà in quello tempo non oservasse le predecte cose che'l Priore che sirà doppo lui cassarlo lo debbia, e mai ci possa rentrare se non per novizio.

[27r] 106. Al nome de Dio amen, a dì primo de novembre 1451.
Anco ordinaro el Priore e'l suo Consiglio con tucto il corpo della Compania che nel dì della festa de'tucti i sancti che se celebra a dì primo de novembre che'l Priore che serà in quel tempo debba et sia tenuto farfare uno officio in l'Abadia del Borgo a reverenza de Dio et de'tucti i sancti e per l'animo de tucte quelle persone le quali sonno passate di questa vita che sonno state della benedecta casa et Compania de Sancta Croce acciochè Dio abbia misericordia di loro, e che esso Priore del predecto tempo abbia licentia et auctorità possere spendere dei beni et della intrata della decta casa per fare el decto officio fine in la quantità d'uno fiorino. E più s'el decto Priore serà negligente et non farà fare il decto officio sia et per omni muodo se intenda essere al tucto casso d'essa benedecta Compagnia.

APPENDIX IV

Notaries and Their Protocols Found in the Notarile Antecosimiano of the Archivio di Stato of Florence

1. Fedele de Ruzzalo, 40 testaments from 1317 to 1320; ASF, NA, F. 123, unfol.

2. Christoforo de Fedele, 73 testaments from 1329 to 1341; ASF, NA, C. 714, unfol.

3. Paolo de Ciuccio, 238 testaments from 1347 to 1373; ASF, NA, P. 121, fols. 1v–189r.

Notes

Introduction

1. Robert Brentano, *Rome before Avignon: A Social History of Thirteenth-Century Rome* (New York: Basic Books, 1974), pp. 263–64.

2. Jacques Le Goff, *The Birth of Purgatory,* trans. Arthur Goldhammer (Chicago: University of Chicago Press, 1984).

3. The bibliography on monastic practices surrounding death is extensive; we are now fortunate to have the introduction to it of N. Huyghebaert in his *Les documents necrologiques,* in *Typologie des sources du moyen âge occidental,* 4 (Turnhout: Brepols, 1972). The most valuable commentaries on this tradition include the following: Leopold Delisle, "Monuments paleographiques concernant l'usage de prier pour les defunts," *Bibliotheque de l'Ecole des Chartres* 8 (1946): 361–411; Auguste Molinier, *Les obituaires français du moyen âge* (Paris: Imprimerie nationale, 1890); Jean Le Clercq, "Documents sur la mort des moines," *Revue Mabillon* 65 (1955): 165–80, and 66 (1956): 65–81; Giles Constable, "The *Liber Memorialis* of Remiremont," *Speculum* 47 (1972): 261–77; Louis Gougaud, "La mort du moine," *Revue Mabillon* 19 (1929): 281–302.

4. I shall discuss here only the more recent and significant interpretations of death, confraternities, and lay spirituality. Among the many important contributions that I have omitted are those of Alberto Tenenti, *Il senso della morte e l'amore della vità nel rinascimento (Francia e Italia)* (Turin: Giulio Einaudi, 1957), and Michel Vovelle, *La mort et l'occident de 1300 à nos jours* (Paris: Gallimard, 1983).

5. Arsenio Frugoni, "I temi della morte nell'affresco della chiesa dei disciplinati a Clusone," *Bullettino dell'Istituto storico italiano per il medioevo* 69 (1957): 175–212.

6. See, for example, one of the many works of Raffaello Morghen, *Il passaggio dal Medioevo al Rinascimento nelle aspettative escatologiche del secolo XIV* (Rome: N.p., n.d.), pp. 20, 32–35, 81–84, 154.

7. Among the many works on death by Philippe Ariès, see *Western Attitudes toward Death,* trans. Patricia M. Ranum (Baltimore: Johns Hopkins University Press, 1974), and published with additional materials as *Essais sur l'histoire de la mort* (Paris: Editions du Seuil, 1975); Ariès, *L'homme devant la mort* (Paris, 1977),

trans. Helen Weaver as *The Hour of Our Death* (New York: Knopf, 1981). See the reviews of John McManners, "The History of Death," *Times Literary Supplement,* December 14, 1979, pp. 111–13; Lawrence Stone, "Death and Its History," *New York Review of Books,* October 12, 1978, pp. 22–32; and the comments of A. J. Gurevich, "Medieval Culture and Mentality according to the New French Historiography," *Archives Européennes de Sociologie* 24 (1983): 167–95.

8. Georges Duby, *The Early Growth of the European Economy: Warriors and Peasants from the Seventh to the Twelfth Century,* trans. Howard B. Clarke (Ithaca: Cornell University Press, 1974); Lester Little, *Religious Poverty and the Profit Economy in Medieval Europe* (Ithaca: Cornell University Press, 1978); Marvin B. Becker, *Medieval Italy: Constraints and Creativity* (Bloomington: Indiana University Press, 1981).

9. Le Goff, *Birth of Purgatory,* esp. pp. 135–76, 229–30.

10. Jacques Chiffoleau, "Pratiques funéraires et images de la mort à Marseille, en Avignon et dans le comtat Venaissin (vers 1280–vers 1350)," *Cahiers de Fanjeaux* 11 (1976): 271–303; Chiffoleau, *La comptabilité de l'au-delà: Les hommes, la mort et la religion dans la région d'Avignon à la fin du moyen âge* (vers 1320–vers 1480) (Rome: Ecole française de Rome, 1980); Chiffoleau, "Perché cambia la morte nella regione di Avignone alla fine del medioevo," *Quaderni storici* 50 (1982): 449–65.

11. Robert Hertz, "Contribution a une étude sur la representation collective de la mort," *Année sociologique* 10 (1907): 48–137; Arnold van Gennep, *The Rites of Passage,* trans. Monika B. Vizedom and Gabrielle L. Caffee (Chicago: University of Chicago Press, 1960), pp. 146–65.

12. This introduction was written before I had the opportunity to see John Van Engen's "The Christian Middle Ages as an Historiographical Problem," *American Historical Review* 91 (1986): 519–52. He has brilliantly organized and commented upon both older and more recent historiographical treatments and tendencies. He has advocated incorporating the best of the anthropological orientations with an attentiveness to the religious practices of all social groups without prejudice for or against any of them. At the same time, he is critical of those who simply assert the existence of a popular religion separate from Christian tradition. For an excellent discussion of the relationship of religion and culture, see Clifford Geertz, "Religion as a Cultural System," in Michael Banton, ed., *Anthropological Approaches to the Study of Religion* (London: Tavistock, 1966), pp. 1–46, and see the essays in Kaspar von Greyerz, ed., *Religion and Society in Early Modern Europe, 1500–1800* (London: George Allen & Unwin, 1984), esp. the editor's introduction, pp. 1–14.

13. Thomas Tentler, "Seventeen Authors in Search of Two Religious Cultures," *Catholic Historical Review* 71 (1985): 248–57.

14. Gilles G. Meersseman, with Gian P. Pacini, *Ordo fraternitatis: Confraternite e pietà dei laici nel medioevo,* 3 vols., in *Italia Sacra: Studi e documenti di storia ecclesiastica,* 24–26 (Rome: Herder editrice e liberia, 1977).

15. Ronald Weissman, *Ritual Brotherhood in Renaissance Florence* (New York: Academic Press, 1982).

16. For the village of Linari, see the excellent study by Charles de la Roncière, "La place des confréries dans encadrement religieux du contado Florentin au XIVe siècle: L'exemple de la Val d'Elsa," *Mélanges de l'Ecole française de Rome: Moyen âge—Temps modernes* 85 (1973): 31–77, 633–71; for Florence, see Massimo Papi, "Per un censimento delle fonti relative alle confraternite laiche fiorentine: Primi risultati," in Domenico Maselli, ed., *Da Dante a Cosimo I: Ricerche di storia religiosa e culturale toscana nei secoli XIV–XVI* (Pistoia: Liberia Editrice Tellini, 1976), pp. 112–21, and John Henderson, "Society and Religion in Renaissance Florence," *Historical Journal* 29 (1986): 213–25. De la Roncière has asserted that rural areas tended to have fewer confraternities; see his comments in an important article that attempts to integrate recent research into a general explanation of how confraternities developed in Florence, "Les confréries en Toscane XIV et XV siècles d'après les travaux recents," in Luigi Fiorani, ed., *Le confraternite romane: Esperienza religiosa, società, committenza artistica,* in *Ricerche per la storia religiosa di Roma* 5 (1984): 51.

17. Gennaro M. Monti, *Le confraternite medievali dell'alta e media Italia,* 2 vols. (Venice: La Nuova Italia, 1927), 1:50–53, 2:8; Meersseman, *Ordo fraternitatis,* 1:10–11; for the comments of De Sandre Gasparini, see her edition of *Statuti di confraternite religiose di Padova nel medio evo* (Padua: Istituto per la storia ecclesiastica padovana, 1974), p. cxi.

18. Jack Goody, *Death, Property, and the Ancestors: A Study of the Mortuary Customs of the LoDagaa of West Africa* (Stanford: Stanford University Press, 1962).

19. Michel Vovelle, *Piété baroque et déchristianisation en Provence au XVIIIe siècle: Les attitudes devant la mort d'après les clauses des testaments* (Paris: Librairie Plon, 1973).

CHAPTER ONE
The Topography of Worship: Religious Corporations and the Paucity of Clerics in San Sepolcro

1. Georges Duby, *Medieval Marriage: Two Models from Twelfth-Century France,* trans. Edborg Forster (Baltimore: Johns Hopkins University Press, 1978), pp. 1–22; Christiane Klapisch-Zuber, "Zacharias, or the Ousted Father: Nuptial Rites in Tuscany between Giotto and the Council of Trent," in her *Women, Family and Ritual in Renaissance Italy,* trans. Lydia C. Cochrane (Chicago: University of Chicago Press, 1985), pp. 178–212; Ariès, *Hour of Our Death,* pp. 13–19, 140–46.

2. See Coste, "L'institution paroissiale à la fin du moyen âge: Approche bibliographique en vue d'enquêtes possibles," *Mélanges de l'Ecole française de Rome: Moyen âge—Temps modernes* 96 (1984): 296–326, a bibliographical essay. See also the essay of Cinzio Violante, "Sistemi organizzativi della cura d'anime in Italia tra Medioevo e Rinascimento: Discorso introduttivo," in *Pievi e parrochie in Italia nel Basso Medio Evo (secc. XIII–XIV),* Atti del VI convegno di storia della

chiesa in Italia (Firenze, 21–25 settembre 1981), in *Italia sacra,* 35–36 (Rome: Herder editrice e libreria, 1984), 1:1–19.

3. Coste, "L'institution paroissiale," 306–8.

4. Ercole Agnoletti, *Sansepolcro nel periodo degli abati (1012–1521)* (Sansepolcro: N. p., 1976), pp. 31–32. Violante notes that *pievi* often were located a distance from the greatest concentrations of population in the eleventh and twelfth centuries. He suggests that the location of the baptismal churches *(pievi)* was usually determined by the proximity of roads and rivers and thus convenience for the people and clerics ("Sistemi organizzativi della cura d'anime," I: 19).

5. The basic sources for the history of San Sepolcro begin with two fifteenth-century works on the first four hundred years of the town's existence. In the first half of the fifteenth century an unknown Camaldolese monk wrote an untitled work on San Sepolcro that attempted to establish through documents the Camaldolese abbot's claim to full spiritual jurisdiction in the town. This manuscript is in Florence, Biblioteca Mediceo-Laurenziana, Plut. 66, cod. 25. The second work is Francesco de Largi's "Lo Specchio dela Pietosa Fraternità de San Bartolomeo del San Sepolcro" (1437), in which he discussed the founding and early history of the town and the fraternity. The manuscript containing the "Specchio" (hereafter cited in the text as "Specchio" with folio number) is in San Sepolcro, Archivio Comunale (hereafter SS, AC), cl. 32, reg. 182. Giustiniano Degli Azzi cataloged the communal archive of San Sepolcro and published excerpts from various documents, including Largi's "Specchio," in his "Inventario degli archivi di San Sepolcro," *Archivi della storia d'Italia,* 2d ser., 4 (1914): 77–194, esp. 143–50. Amintore Fanfani has also published portions of the "Specchio" in his excellent study "La beneficenza in un comune toscano dal XIII al XV secolo," in his *Saggi di storia economica italiana* (Milan: Società editrice "Vita e pensiero," 1936), pp. 37–82. There are numerous documents and notices relevant to the history of San Sepolcro in the nine volumes of Giovanni Mittarelli and Anselmo Costadoni, eds., *Annales Camadulenses Ordinis S. Benedicti* (Venice: Prostant apud Jo. Baptistam Pasquali, 1755–73). In the eighteenth century several histories of San Sepolcro were written, though only the first of the following has been published: Pietro Farulli, *Annali e memorie dell'antica e nobile città di S. Sepolcro* (Foligno: N. Canpitelli, 1713); Francesco G. Pignani, "Compendio istorico di memorie della città di Sansepolcro"; and S. Lancisi, "Storia di Borgo Sansepolcro." These three authors borrowed heavily from a seventeenth-century work, "Cronaca di Borgo S. Sepolcro," by Francesco Bercordati, which is on permanent display in SS, AC. Giovanni Muzi has written several volumes on the history of Città di Castello that contain numerous references and documents on San Sepolcro: *Memorie ecclesiastiche di Città di Castello,* 5 vols. (Città di Castello: F. Donati, 1843). The most authoritative modern study of San Sepolcro is that of Lorenzo Coleschi, whose *Storia della città di Sansepolcro* (Città di Castello, 1886), has been recently republished as *La storia di Sansepolcro* (San Sepolcro: C.L.E.A.T., 1966), with an excellent chapter on the town's history in the twentieth century by Franco Polcri. I am deeply indebted to the re-

search of Ercole Agnoletti, who has published several studies of San Sepolcro. I have borrowed extensively from the following of his works: *Memorie religiose inedite di Sansepolcro* (Sansepolcro: Tipografia Boncompagni, 1970); *I vescovi di Sansepolcro,* vol. 1 (Sansepolcro: Tipografia Boncompagni, 1972); and *Sansepolcro degli abati.*

6. Agnoletti, *Sansepolcro degli abati,* pp. 34–35, 42–43, 58.

7. The present-day Porta del Ponte was formerly named Porta San Cristofano from which I assume that the church of the same name was nearby (Agnoletti, *Memorie religiose,* p. 27). In the thirteenth century the Camaldolese abbots gave this church to the nuns of Santa Catherina and in the fourteenth century to a group of nuns called the Santuccie.

8. Coleschi, *Storia di San Sepolcro,* p. 101.

9. Muzi, *Memorie ecclesiastiche,* 5:49–50; Agnoletti, *Sansepolcro degli abati,* pp. 42–43; St. Bonaventure, "Major Lives of St. Francis," trans. B. K. Fahy in *St. Francis of Assisi: Writings and Early Biographies,* ed. M. A. Habig, 3d rev. ed. (Chicago: Franciscan Herald Press, 1973), pp. 706–7.

10. There are only a few documents with evidence on the nature of government in San Sepolcro through the middle of the fifteenth century. My summary is taken from Muzi, *Memorie ecclesiastiche,* 4:63–70; Coleschi, *Storia di Sansepolcro,* pp. 33–35; Agnoletti, *Sansepolcro degli abati,* pp. 33–35.

11. Agnoletti, *Sansepolcro degli abati,* pp. 45–48, and *Memorie religiose,* pp. 24–26. The secular clergy also gained control of the church of San Giovanni Battista d'Afra some time before 1348; this small church had been outside the walls and was located in the southeast corner of the town on the present-day via Giovanni Buitoni, once via San Giovanni. See the testament of the rector of the church in 1348, Archivio di stato di Firenze (hereafter ASF), Notarile Antecosimiano (hereafter NA), P. 121, fols. 17r–18r. On the church of San Giovanni d'Afra, see Ercole Agnoletti, *La Madonna della Misericordia e il Battesimo di Cristo di Piero della Francesca* (Sansepolcro: N.p., 1977). In addition, the small oratories of San Pietro and Santa Maria Nuova may have been in the jurisdiction of the archpriest; see Muzi, *Memorie ecclesiastiche,* 3:22–26 and 4:82–83.

12. Muzi, *Memorie ecclesiastiche,* 4:70–72; Agnoletti, *Memorie religiose,* pp. 24–27; Agnoletti, *Sansepolcro degli abati,* pp. 45–47. This movement of the *pieve* from the rural setting of Melello to the urban concentration appears to have occurred earlier in San Sepolcro than elsewhere. Violante finds such moves generally occurring in the late thirteenth and early fourteenth centuries; see his "Sistemi organizzativi della cura d'anime," I: 26.

13. See the list of churches under the authority of the archpriest of Santa Maria della Pieve in 1349 in Pietro Sella, ed., *Rationes decimarum Italiae nei secoli XIII e XIV: Umbria,* in the series *Studi e testi,* vol. 161 (Città del Vaticano: Biblioteca apostolica vaticana, 1952), pp. 5–7. Another indication that the number of secular clergymen was small in this region, and not only in San Sepolcro, is evident in the number of canons in the cathedral chapter in Città di Castello. With responsibilities for worship in the cathedral as well as for the bishop's administration, including nearly fifty dependent rural churches, the number of canons

hovered around ten, for example eleven in 1288 and nine in 1399 (Muzi, *Memorie ecclesiastiche,* 2:180–87, 242–43).

14. Agnoletti, *Sansepolcro degli abati,* pp. 51–54.

15. See Luigi Pellegrini, "Gli insediamenti degli ordini mendicanti e la loro tipologia: Considerazioni metodologiche e piste di ricerca," *Mélanges de l'Ecole Française de Rome: Moyen âge—Temps modernes* 89 (1977): 564–67; for the events in San Sepolcro, see Agnoletti, *Sansepolcro degli abati,* pp. 63, 65. It has been impossible to compare the thirteenth-century church of San Sepolcro with the excellent study of the Paduan church by Antonio Rigon because San Sepolcro lacks notarial records in that period; he finds a whole panoply of lay religious groups in Padua in the notarial documents. See his "I laici nella chiesa padovana del duecento: Conversi, oblati, penitenti," *Contributi alla storia della chiesa padovana nell'età medioevale* 8 (1979): 11–81.

16. ASF, NA, P. 120, protocol of 1378, fol. 53v.

17. Agnoletti, *Sansepolcro degli abati,* p. 66; Agnoletti, *Memorie religiose,* p. 13; Muzi, *Memorie ecclesiatiche,* 5:51–52. Giovanna Casagrande has examined the "Registri della Cancelleria Vescovile" of Bishop Niccolò of Città di Castello and has concluded from these documents that the convents of Santa Maria della Strada and San Francesco di Pozzuolo were separate female Francescan houses; see her "Forme di vita religiosa femminile nell'area di Città di Castello nel secolo XIII," ed. Roberto Rusconi, in *Il movimento religioso femminile in Umbria nei secoli XIII–XIV,* Atti del Convegno internazionale di studio nell'ambito della celebrazioni per l'VIII centenario della nascità di S. Francesco d'Assisi (Florence: "La Nuova Italia" editrice, 1984), pp. 142–43.

18. See n. 24 below for the nuns in 1317; for 1343, see ASF, NA, S. 73, fol. 9r; for 1363, ASF, NA, P. 117, protocol of 1364, unfol., document of November 13, 1364; and for 1378, ASF, NA, P. 120, protocol of 1378, fol. 112r.

19. Casagrande, "Forme di vita religiosa," pp. 142–43.

20. AC, SS, cl. 32, reg. 202, fol. 148r.

21. ASF, NA, P. 121, fols. 124v, 176v.

22. See, for example, ASF, NA, P. 121, fols. 103r, 180v.

23. Brentano, "Il movimento religioso femminile a Rieti nei secoli XIII–XIV," in *Il movimento religioso femminile in Umbria,* pp. 74–75.

24. For the number of nuns in 1269, see Casagrande, "Forme di vita religiosa," p. 143, n. 76. The other totals of nuns in Franciscan houses are taken from a "Book of Memories" of the Fraternity of San Bartolomeo, in which the notary records the distribution of the bequests of Donna Nobile, widow of Guido dal Vierno; she made numerous bequests, particularly to the Franciscans. Donna Nobile bequeathed one lira to each of the 101 Franciscan nuns in San Sepolcro; she also made large bequests to the three Franciscan convents in San Sepolcro and bequests to other Franciscan houses from Assisi to Monte Verna. See AC, SS, cl. 32, reg. 202, fols. 148r–150r. The sizes of the female Franciscan houses in San Sepolcro are approximately the same as those in

Città di Castello in this period; see Casagrande, "Forme di vita religiosa," pp. 132–34.

25. ASF, NA, P. 115, protocol of 1356, fols. 1v–4r; ASF, NA, B. 1256, fol. 14v; ASF, NA, B. 1257, unfol., document of September 1, 1358.

26. See n. 24 above for the nuns in 1317; for 1380, see ASF, NA, P. 120, *filza,* unfol., document of June 6, 1380.

27. See above nn. 18, 22, and 26.

28. On Città di Castello, see Livario Oliger, "Documenta originis Clarissarum Civitatis Castelli, Eugudii . . .," *Archivium Franciscanum historicum* 15 (1922): 71–102. See also Roberto Rusconi, "L'expansione del francescanesimo femminile nel secolo XIII," in *Movimento religioso femminile e francescanesimo nel secolo XIII,* Atti del VII Convegno internazionale, Assisi (Assisi: La Società internazionale di studi francescani, 1980), pp. 265–313, and Mario Sensi, "Incarcerate e recluse in Umbria nei secoli XIII e XIV: Un bizzocaggio centroitaliano," in *Il movimento religioso femminile in Umbria,* pp. 101–2. For the ordering of the female religious life in the diocese of Città di Castello, see Casagrande, "Forme di vita religiosa," pp. 125–57. On the more general papal policy of regularizing houses of females, see Edith Pasztor, "I papi del Duecento e Trecento di fronte alla vita religiosa femminile," in *Il movimento religioso femminile in Umbria,* pp. 31–65.

29. Franco A. Dal Pino, *I frati Servi di S. Maria dalle origini all'approvazione (1233 ca.–1304),* 2 vols. (Louvain: Publications universitaires de Louvain, 1972), 1:870.

30. Ibid., p. 884; document III, 18 in ibid., 2:209–11.

31. Ibid., 1:977–79, 1198–99 and documents III, 115–17, 309, 310, 322–24 in ibid., 2:349–52, 431–33, 442–46.

32. Agnoletti, *Memorie religiose,* p. 60; Muzi, *Memorie ecclesiastiche,* 5:61.

33. Dal Pino, *I frati Servi,* documents III, 72, 322, 329, 333, 335, 346, 412, 542 in 2:256, 443, 451, 456, 457, 465, 508, 608; ASF, NA, P. 121, fols. 107v–109r; ASF, NA, P. 120, protocol of 1378, fol. 74v.

34. ASF, NA, P. 121, fols. 107v–109r; the testament of Carlino d'Arive provided several bequests to the friars and the convent of Santa Maria dei Frati as well as one hundred lire for construction of the church.

35. ASF, NA, P. 117, protocol of 1365, unfol., document of July 25, 1365.

36. Agnoletti, *Memorie religiose,* p. 28; Agnoletti, *Sansepolcro degli abati,* p. 72; ASF, NA, C. 715, fol. 38r.

37. Jacques Le Goff, "Apostolat mendiant et fait urbain dans la France médiévale: L'implantation géographique des ordres mendiants: Programme-Questionaire pour une enquête," *Annales: E.S.C.* 23 (1968): 335–52; Le Goff, "Ordres mendiants et urbanisation dans la France medievale. Etat de l'enquête," *Annales: E.S.C.* 25 (1970): 924–46. See also Anna Benvenuti Papi, "Ordini mendicanti e città: Appunti per un indagine, il caso di Firenze," in Domenico Maselli, ed., *Da Dante a Cosimo I* (Pistoia: Libreria Editrice Tellini, 1976), pp. 122–45. The bibliography on this question is voluminous. See the papers and bibliography from the Round Table held in Rome in 1977 under

the auspices of the Ecole française de Rome, *Les ordres mendiants et la ville en Italie centrale (v. 1220–v. 1350)* in *Mélanges de l'Ecole française de Rome: Moyen âge—Temps modernes* 89 (1977): 557–773.

38. This is, at least, the view of Chiffoleau, *La comptabilité,* pp. 186–204.

39. Muzi, *Memorie ecclesiastiche,* 4:3–6 and 5:53.

40. Ibid.; ASF, NA, P. 117, protocol of 1365, fol. 1r.

41. Mittarelli and Costadoni, eds., *Annales Camaldulenses,* 5:163, 398; Muzi, *Memorie ecclesiastiche,* 5:53; Agnoletti, *Sansepolcro degli abati,* pp. 73, 91–92.

42. Agnoletti, *Sansepolcro degli abati,* p. 41, n. 6.

43. Muzi, *Memorie ecclesiastiche,* 5:54, 61–65; ASF, NA, P. 114, fols. 136v–139r; Casagrande, "Forme di vita religiosa," pp. 130–31.

44. Largi, "Specchio," fol. 27r–v; Agnoletti, *Sansepolcro degli abati,* p. 77, n. 4.

45. ASF, NA, S. 181, unfol., no. 14, document of December 12, 1353; ASF, NA, P. 117, protocol of 1364, unfol., documents of October 10, 1364, and November 11, 1364; ASF, NA, P. 117, protocol of 1365, unfol., document of March 12, 1365; Agnoletti, *Sansepolcro degli abati,* p. 100.

46. See, for example, the comments of Casagrande, "Forme di vita religiosa," pp. 153–57.

47. On the *carcera* of Bona, see ibid., pp. 147–48. See also AC, SS, cl. 32, reg. 159, unfol., to the year of female recruitment.

48. ASF, NA, P. 114, fols. 136v–139r. On the general decline of the *carcere* and *carceri* across the fourteenth century, see Brentano, "Il movimento religioso femminile," pp. 75, 81.

49. Largi, "Specchio," fols. 26r–v, 125r. In 1287 the layman Jacomo di Domenico paid for the construction of the Casa di Misericordia, and in 1303 he bequeathed it to the Fraternity of San Bartolomeo. He gave a substantial amount of property, including land and several houses, to support the hospital, which was to be in perpetuity "a house of mercy and hospital for the poor." This Casa di Misericordia over time was renamed the hospital of Jacomo di Domenico al Fondaccio, Santa Maria di San Sepulcro, and Santa Maria del Fondaccio. The hospital was located in the southeast corner of San Sepolcro and existed concurrently with the hospital of Santa Maria della Misericordia, which has become well known for its altarpiece painted by Piero della Francesca. The hospital of Jacomo and the hospital of Santa Maria della Misericordia were separate institutions.

50. Fanfani, "La beneficenza," p. 43.

51. ASF, "Compagnie religiose soppresse" (hereafter CRS), San Sepolcro, L.XX.27, fol. 68bis.

52. See David Herlihy, *Medieval and Renaissance Pistoia: The Social History of an Italian Town, 1200–1430* (New Haven: Yale University Press, 1967), p. 76; David Herlihy and Christiane Klapisch-Zuber, *Tuscans and Their Families: A Study of the Florentine Catasto of 1427* (New Haven: Yale University Press, 1985), pp. 60–78; Enrico Fiumi, "La popolazione del territorio volterrano-

sangimignanese ed il problema demografica dell'età communale," in *Studi in onore di Amintore Fanfani* (Milan: Giuffrè, 1962), 1:251–90.

53. AC, SS, cl. 32, reg. 144, fols. 29r–46r.

54. See, for example, R. W. Southern, *Western Society and the Church in the Middle Ages* (Harmondsworth: Penguin, 1970), pp. 272–77.

55. The number of Franciscans may have been slightly more than the fifteen I have estimated, but I have no evidence for a larger number. Even doubling their number would not significantly change my conclusions because the data on the other houses, and especially the house of the secular clergy, indicate a radically low number of clerics.

56. See the discussion in Chapter 5 below.

57. Giuseppe Parenti, *La popolazione della Toscana sotto la reggenza Lorenese* (Florence: Rinascimento del libro, 1937), p. 132.

58. It should be kept in mind that these totals are estimates; doubtless the totals and proportions varied over the period under study here. The estimates are based on notarial records of clergy present as witnesses or at chapter meetings in 85 percent of the total of 200 males and females in this discussion.

59. Parenti, *La popolazione,* pp. 174–75.

60. Herlihy, *Medieval and Renaissance Pistoia,* p. 244; Herlihy and Klapisch-Zuber, *Tuscans and Their Families,* p. 153; Brentano, "Il movimento religioso femminile," pp. 80–81; Richard Trexler, "Le célibat à la fin du moyen âge: Les religieuses de Florence," *Annales: E.S.C.* 27 (1972): 1329–50.

61. Of the many studies, see the classic statement for France of Paul Adam, *La vie paroissiale en France au XIVe siècle* (Paris: Sirey, 1964).

62. Casagrande, "Forme di vita religiosa," p. 136; Rigon, "I laici nella chiesa padovana," pp. 11–81.

CHAPTER TWO
The Fraternity of San Bartolomeo and Commemoration of the Dead in San Sepolcro in the Thirteenth Century

1. Little is known of the economy in thirteenth-century San Sepolcro; most suggestive are two studies of Amintore Fanfani: *Un mercante del trecento* (Milan: Dott. A. Giuffrè editore, 1935) and "Le arti di Sansepolcro dal XIV al XVI secolo," in his *Saggi di storia economica italiana* (Milan: Società editrice "Vita e pensiero," 1936), pp. 85–107.

2. Gregory IX's letter appears in both Florence, Mediceo-Laurenziana, Plut. 66, cod. 25, fols. 11r–v, and Bercordati, "Cronaca di Borgo S. Sepolcro," fols. 15v–16r. See also the discussion of Agnoletti, *Sansepolcro degli abati,* pp. 57–58.

3. Muzi, *Memorie ecclesiastiche,* 4:78–79; Bercordati, "Cronaca di Borgo S. Sepolcro," fols. 16v–17r; Agnoletti, *Sansepolcro degli abati,* p. 62. For the dispute of the 1260s, see Mittarelli and Costadoni, eds., *Annales Camaldulensis,* 5:74.

4. Bercordati, "Cronaca di Borgo S. Sepolcro," fol. 18r; Muzi, *Memorie ecclesiastiche,* 4:80; Agnoletti, *Sansepolcro degli abati,* p. 69; and see the extended account in Alessandro Goracci, *Breve istoria dell'origine e fondazione della Città di Borgo San Sepolcro,* in *Collezione di storici e cronisti italiana,* 7 (Florence: S. Coen, 1844), 143–44.

5. Bercordati, "Cronaca di Borgo S. Sepolcro," fol. 19v; Coleschi, *Storia di San Sepolcro,* pp. 35–36.

6. Jean Delumeau, *Catholicism between Luther and Voltaire: A New View of the Counter-Reformation,* trans. Jeremy Moiser (London: Burns and Oates, 1977), pp. 154–74.

7. Giuseppina de Sandre Gasparini, *Contadini, chiesa, confraternità in un paese veneto di bonifica: Villa del Bosco nel quattrocento,* in *Fonti e ricerche di storia ecclesiastica padovana* (Padua: Istituto per la storia ecclesiastica padovana, 1979), esp. pp. 95–119, 129–44. For comments on funerals, see pp. 100, 108.

8. AC, SS, ser. 32, reg. 159. See Appendix I for an edition of the 1269 statutes, which henceforth will be cited by line and within the text. For a short description of the register, see Degli Azzi, "Inventario degli archivi," 141. The register is unpaginated and citations to it, other than the statutes, will be by archival notation and year. The register contains statutes, names of women members but lacking date, male entrants to the fraternity organized by month and year from 1278 to 1309, female entrants to the fraternity organized similarly from 1269 to 1309, and lists of the dead of the fraternity organized by month and year from 1269 to 1309. Within the yearly entrants and death entries, the yearly rectors are recorded. The quote at the beginning of 1269 reads: "In nomine domini amen. Iste sunt persone qui intraverunt in Fraternitate Sancti Bartholomei de Burgo tempore rectorie Kimbu et Ciacio et Forti, Rectores Fraternitatis predicte sub anno domini a navitatem eius millesimo ducentesimo sexagesimo nono, in primis de mense agusti."

9. Farulli, *Annali e memorie,* p. 14; Bercordati, "Cronaca di Borgo San Sepolcro," fol. 16v. For an analogous problem of supposed mendicant influence in the first lay confraternity in Rome, see Giulia Barone's comments on the myth that St. Bonaventure wrote the statutes of the lay Confraternity of the Gonfalone, "Il movimento Francescano e la nascità delle confraternite romane," in *Le confraternite romane,* pp. 75–78.

10. Muzi, *Memorie ecclesiatiche,* 3:152.

11. Largi, "Specchio," fols. 6v–7r: "Nel MCCLXVI a dì xii de genaio messere Nicolò, vescovo de Castello, conferma tucto como de sopra et [7r] ai rectori che potraranno un anno la maletta, confesati che siranno di loro pecchati, habbino plenaria remissione di tucti i loro peccati." I have never seen such an extraordinary indulgence elsewhere in the thirteenth century, though by the fifteenth century full remission of sin through a papal indulgence was not uncommon.

12. Penitence certainly remained an important practice in San Sepolcro as in all of Italy. Among the laity in San Sepolcro, several confraternities of flagellation were founded in the fourteenth century.

The bishops' grants to the fraternity may have been partially motivated by their competition with the Camaldolese abbot for spiritual authority within San Sepolcro. In addition to the privileges granted by the bishops and the Franciscans, the Augustinians bestowed on the members of the fraternity all the benefits an Augustinian friar would receive in this world and the next. See Largi, "Specchio," fol. 7r.

13. Ibid., fol. 6v. "Nel MCCLVII a dì viiii di settembre messere Pietro, vescovo de Castello, approvò la detta Congregatione et che i rectori overo balidori dela dicta Fraternità podèssero rescotere da omni persona le ragione, i beni guiditii, et legati, et altre cose che si lasciano ala Fraternità."

14. This judgment that the clerics were excluded from holding the office of rector is based on an examination of the names of the rectors from 1269 to 1309. The names of the rectors accompany the lists of entrants and the dead. For a list of rectors (in the 1310s renamed priors) from the fourteenth to the eighteenth centuries, consult the list in Farulli, *Annali e memorie,* pp. 85–92. For clerics in the fraternity, see AC, SS, reg. 159, for 1285; Frater Gilius, rector of the leprosarium and Bishop Jacobus of Città di Castello; in 1286 Giannes, the priest of the church in Monte Giovio, along with three other priests, joined the fraternity.

15. Appendix I, lines 7–9; Richard Trexler, "Charity and the Defense of Urban Elites in the Italian Communes," in Frederick C. Jaher, ed., *The Rich, The Well-Born, and the Powerful: Elites and Upper Classes in History* (Urbana: University of Illinois Press, 1973), pp. 64–109, discusses the shame-faced poor in fifteenth-century Florence. See also the numerous studies of Michel Mollat and especially as editor of *Etudes sur l'histoire de la Pauvreté,* 2 vols. (Paris: Publ. de la Sorbonne, 1974), 1:14–15, 35–45.

16. Appendix I, lines 53–62. The statutes specify that pennies should be distributed in the countryside, but money is not mentioned for the poor within the walls of San Sepolcro. Moreover, the statutes hold that the rectors should take the pennies from a *marsuppia*—purse—for the countryside. Again the *marsuppia* is not mentioned with regard to the town, though the *maletta*—box—is. I wish to thank John Henderson for pointing out this important distinction. Taking this distinction as the basis of the town-countryside relationship, we see an exchange system in which the townspeople contributed money to the fraternity, which the rectors distributed to the men and women of the countryside. One assumes that on market day the rural population returned this money through purchases from the merchants and craftsmen and rents to landlords. This system of charity exchange owes its logic to the high land rents characteristic of western Europe in this period of intense demand for land, which resulted from the press of an enlarged population. Among the many studies that demonstrate the high demand for land, see Herlihy, *Medieval and Renaissance Pistoia,* pp. 133–47.

17. See Huyghebaert, *Les documents nécrologiques.*

18. Fanfani, "La beneficenza," pp. 43–45.

19. AC, SS, ser. 32, reg. 159; the manuscript is unfoliated, but the lists of

members begin on fol. 2r. My judgment that all the names of the females lacking dates were written at the same moment is based on the following reasons: nearly all these names were written in the same hand but among the names of entrants from 1269 to 1309, the hand changes yearly as it does in the death entries; and each of the folios containing the names has thirty lines and two columns. These characteristics suggest that all the inscriptions were done at the same time. I believe that the summer of 1269 was the moment when the names of those who then belonged to the fraternity were recorded. The best evidence for this view is that the names of the entrants of August 1269 follow these names of females. Largi ("Specchio," fol. 5v) apparently believed that the 694 females and the inscribed men—the list was yet extant in 1438—all entered in 1268. Although that assumption would serve to swell the size of the fraternity and add to its corporate authority, I think it more likely that preparatory to recording the incoming men and women, as required by the statutes of 1269, the rectors inscribed the names of all members at that time. To do so would have been in the spirit of the instructions in the statutes.

That memorialization stands at the center of the fraternity's activities raises the possibility that only the names of the dead were recorded before 1269, that this list is a necrology, or a list of those—living or dead—for whom the fraternity was responsible. I have rejected these possibilities because (1) of the aforementioned identical hand; (2) crosses are drawn beside many of the names, indicating their deaths, and these crosses appear in no particular pattern; the names in the first folio do not, for example, have a higher percentage of crosses; and (3) the crosses have been drawn by different hands. Had the crosses been drawn by one hand or the same hand that inscribed the names, it would prove that the writer simply copied the names of both the living and the dead from earlier manuscripts. Rather, the various hands demonstrate that after the inscription of 1269, subsequent rectors noted the deaths from year to year by the use of the cross.

20. AC, SS, ser. 32, reg. 159, unfol., years 1285–89 for male entrants and 1274–75 for female entrants; see also Table 2.1. Throughout this chapter on the thirteenth-century fraternity, I have used the fraternal year August through July rather than the calendar year. I have chosen the years 1285–89 for males and 1274–75 for females because they are roughly comparable in total number and appear to have the greatest amount of information on the entrants. The year 1274–75 is the most successful year of female recruitment, following two years of relatively low recruitment, when an average of only thirty-two females joined. In the period 1275–79, the average yearly entrance rate was one hundred.

21. For Abbot Zeno's entrance, see AC, SS, ser. 32, reg. 159, unfol., to the year of male entrants; see also Agnoletti, *Sansepolcro degli abati,* pp. 72–74. On Bishop Jacopo, see AC, SS, ser. 32, reg. 159, to the year (1286) in the lists of the dead; for a short biographical sketch of Bishop Jacopo, see Muzi, *Memorie ecclesiastiche,* 2:165–77. Another bishop of Città di Castello died under the fraternity's protection in 1301–2; see AC, SS, ser. 32, reg. 159, to the year.

22. AC, SS, ser. 32, reg. 159, "Libro dei morti," to the year.

23. This 62 percent contrasts with the 75 percent conjectured by Fanfani, "La beneficenza," p. 43.

24. See Huyghebaert, *Les documents nécrologiques*. For Bede, see Molinier, *Les obituaire français du moyen âge,* pp. 24–25; for Guidinus, see Edward Hlawitschka, Karl Schmid, and Gerd Tellenbach, eds., *Liber memorialis von Remiremont,* in *Libri memoriales,* vol. 1, of the *Monumenta Germaniae historica* (Zurich: Weidmann, 1970), p. 66.

25. Meersseman, *Ordo fraternitatis,* 1:99–108.

26. De la Roncière, "La place des confréries," 76–77.

27. Weissman, *Ritual Brotherhood,* chaps. 2 and 3.

28. Augustine of Hippo, *De cura gerenda pro mortuis,* trans. M. H. Allies (London, 1914), pp. 58–59; see also the comments of Sister Mary Melchior Beyenka, *Consolation in Saint Augustine,* in Patristic Series, 83 (Washington, D.C.: Catholic University of America Press, 1950), pp. 71–76.

29. See Tables 2.1 and 2.2 in which the ratio of females to males was 52 to 48. This ratio was applied to the 694 females, yielding the 572 males estimated as being inscribed in 1269. Largi in 1437 examined a manuscript of membership and counted a total of 1,797 females and 1,486 males for the period from 1268 through all of 1283 ("Specchio," fol. 5v). My total of 1,785 females in this same period is slightly under Largi's, but we are in substantial agreement. His totals yield a female to male ratio of 55 to 45 that, if applied to the inscription year of 1269, would alter my figures slightly. I have chosen the 52:48 ratio because of the difficulty of sorting out males in the fraternity in 1269 from those entering in the period 1269 to 1283.

30. See Constable, "*Liber Memorialis* of Remiremont," pp. 261–77.

31. For the discussion of the population of San Sepolcro, see Chapter 1, at Table 1.1. above.

32. AC, SS, ser. 32, reg. 159, unfol., to the year 1288–89 of male entrants for the following discussion.

33. Fanfani, "La beneficenza," pp. 50, n. 2, and 51, n. 3. Fanfani has estimated, using data from the fourteenth century, that the *staio* of grain in San Sepolcro sold for thirty soldi on average.

34. AC, SS, ser. 32, reg. 159, unfol., to the 1288–89 year of male entrants. It was not unusual for confraternities to allow their less wealthy members to pay smaller amounts of dues; for example, see the statutes of the Confraternity of San Domenico of Capo Regio of Siena (1344–48) in Meersseman, *Ordo fraternitatis,* 2:661.

35. AC, SS, ser. 32, reg. 159, unfol., to the 1274–75 year of female entrants. In the computations regarding the 176 entrants, I have included the 11 females lacking any indication of marital status or guardian.

36. For this discussion, see AC, SS, ser. 32, reg. 159, "Libro dei morti," unfol., to the years. See also Tables 2.3–2.5.

37. For Benvenutus, see AC, SS, ser. 32, reg. 159, unfol., to the year (1285) of male entrants; Meersseman, *Ordo fraternitatis,* 1:498–504.

38. Cf. male and female entrants for 1285 in AC, SS, ser. 32, reg. 159, unfol., to the year.

39. ASF, CRS, La Compagnia di San Frediano, reg. 88, for dues paid from 1333. For an example of documents recording those derelict in their payments, see Florence, Archivio della Compagnia della Misericordia, regs. 380 and 385.

40. Consult Tables 2.1–2.2, which are based on the lists of male and female entrants in AC, SS, ser. 32, reg. 159.

41. This decade runs from July 26, 1269, to July 25, 1279, and I employ the phrase "decades of the 1270s" and analogous phrases for convenience.

42. This 39 percent includes estimates for missing data for two years.

43. Gabriele de Rosa, "Problemi della storiografia confraternite," in *Le confraternite romane,* p. 25.

44. De la Roncière, "Les confréries en Toscane," 59–60.

45. Saverio La Sorsa, *La Compagnia d'Or San Michele* (Trani, 1902), pp. 17, 19, 66–67, and see the statutes of 1294, pp. 185–86, 199–204, statutes XXIII–XXVI, XXVIII, XXXII, XXXVI.

46. De la Roncière, "Les confréries en Toscane," 60; De Rosa, "Problemi della storiografia," p. 24.

CHAPTER THREE
The Fraternity as Agent for the Poor, the Rich, and Dead Souls

1. Bercordati, "Cronaca di Borgo San Sepolcro," fol. 35v–36v; Coleschi, *Storia di San Sepolcro,* pp. 37–54.

2. Bercordati, "Cronaca di Borgo San Sepolcro," fols. 36v–37r.

3. Coleschi, *Storia di San Sepolcro,* pp. 53–72.

4. Ibid., pp. 53–72; Bercordati, "Cronaca di Borgo San Sepolcro," fols. 37r–41r.

5. Throughout these discussions I have dismissed the possibility that diminishing recruitment reflected the general decline in population and in the proportion of males to females in the general population by 1300. The discussions in Chapters 4 and 5 will demonstrate that males in the fourteenth and fifteenth centuries chose alternate forms of devotion and confraternities.

6. "Specchio," fol. 18r. Largi cataloged a register, no longer extant, with the signature of "C" in which the names of the priors were written and the names of "those who enter it." The "it" may refer to entrants to the fraternity or to the office of the priory. Largi stated that this register commenced in 1310 and continued until his day. Thus it follows register 159 of series 32 of the Archivio comunale of San Sepolcro, which recorded members and priors through 1309. If this register "C" contained the names of entrants through 1437 and not the names of priors, its relatively small size would demonstrate the decline in membership. In the same 128 years from 1309 to 1437 there were three "Libri dei morti"; see "Specchio," fols. 23v–24r.

7. Ugo Morini, ed., *Documenti inediti o poco noti per la storia della Misericor-*

dia di Firenze (1321–1525) (Florence: Ven. Arciconfraternità, 1940), pp. 2–6, 7–11, documents II (1329) and IV (1331).

8. Largi's abstracts of the bequests to the fraternity present several problems of organization and interpretation. First, the abstracts vary a great deal in the amount of information recorded; some, for example, simply state that the benefactor "instituted the fraternity," one presumes as universal heir, but often what was bequeathed is omitted. But the most difficult problem is that Largi did not note the date of every bequest, so that it is necessary in some instances to estimate dates of bequests from surrounding bequests that are dated. An aid in estimating the date of a bequest is that Largi informs his reader of the confraternal register from which he took his information. These "footnotes" often refer to three or four registers and their folio numbers; thus it is possible in many instances to determine the date of the bequests from other registers. In cases of registers that are not extant, it is possible to estimate the year of the bequest from information provided by Largi in which he specified the chronological limits of the registers and the number of folios they carried. Fortunately, it is not necessary to give precise years, but I have occasionally divided bequests lacking dates proportionally, if these bequests are at or near the chronological categories (decades or quarter-centuries) employed in this analysis of bequests to the Fraternity of San Bartolomeo.

9. Largi, "Specchio," fols. 25r–69v; most of the thirteenth-century bequests are found on fols. 25r–v and 66v–68v. Tables 3.1 through 3.7 are derived from fols. 25r–69v. My total of 1,033 bequests from Largi is less than Fanfani's ("La beneficenza," p. 43). I have subtracted Largi's cases of misnumbering and duplication of bequests.

10. One might expect to find the recording of dues in several extant registers of the fourteenth century, but neither these registers nor Largi noted dues from members. See, for example, AC, SS, ser. 32. reg. 202, which Degli Azzi described as follows: "Reg. cart., di cc. 269, di dare e avere dei Rettori della Fraternità di S. Bartolomeo per afito di beni e altri proventi: 1309–1323" ("Inventario degli archivi," 151). For Largi's catalog of registers extant in his day, see "Specchio," fols. 18r–21v.

11. See the discussion below of Donna Nobile's testament for an example of multiple bequests to several pious corporations.

12. Largi, "Specchio," fol. 23v. This "Libro dei morti" possessed the signature "E." Largi later stated, "I find in some places the notes of the dead are not entirely written, and there is also missing some book from 1317 to 1377; I want to search for it" ("Specchio," fol. 24r). He notes a journal of the deaths of 1317, when 242 individuals died, and then a "Libro dei morti," which begins in 1377 and records deaths through 1416. He also inventoried another book of the dead, which took up deaths as of 1416 and continued into his day ("Specchio," fol. 24r).

I have begun a study of this series of books of the dead. Degli Azzi described them as "Registri dei morti, ossia Obituari della Fraternità di San Bartolomeo: dal 1374 al 1727" ("Inventario degli archivi," 140). Register 143 in this series today has deaths from 1377 because the first folios of the register were lost.

13. Largi, "Specchio," fol. 17r. His discussion is headed "Dela casa dela Fraternita, libri et massaritie" and reads: "Omni congregatione et collegio licito et approvato bisogna residentia ove secretamente se tractino i facti necessarii. Et pero bisognando particular luocho aciò i Priori et homini de questa honesta Fraternità havuto conseglio compararo da Goro d'Acatta cardatore. Al Libro E a folio 16. . . .

"Una casa posta nel Borgo in lo quartieri de San Giovanni . . . in lagio di Ghiazzari, a lato oggi la casa de Sardo . . . con tre stantie, ciò l'entrata ove è la stala dei granari, di mano ritta uno spazzo da tenere massaritie, a mano mancha è l'audentia di Priori con un solayo d'assi al pe et de sopra un cielo d'assi. E a sommo le stale da omni mano sono doi granari ove se repongono grano et biado dela Fraternità et stanno le chiavi ale mani del Camarlengo."

14. Largi, "Specchio," fol. 17r. Largi cited register "E," folio 16, which, he said, had 226 folios and had entries from 1313 to 1368. The entry that marks the purchase of the residence is found on folio 16, and on that basis I estimate that the purchase occurred around 1320.

15. See above, n. 13.

16. Largi, "Specchio," fol. 5v. Largi asserted that the name change occurred in 1323 and that the number of priors increased from three to four. As early as December 22, 1313, however, the writer of the financial accounts referred to the three "priors." See AC, SS, ser. 32, reg. 202, fol. 83v. And in April of the following year, the same men are referred to as Rectors (ibid., fol. 94v).

17. Largi, "Specchio," fols. 5v–6r. "Adunavase la devota et magna brigata nella chiesa de San Bartolomeo del Borgo ove facivano celebrare messe, predicare et sermocinare, cantare lauda et cantici spirituali, sichè per fine ai nostri dì la prima domenica di ciascuno mese ancho se usava fare predicare a tucta la congregatione et ivi le donn il più solevano offerire loro promissioni como si fu omni sabato che sova fra i mercatante et artegiani per lo denaio de Dio; ali homini oggi tal predica ancho è intermessa."

18. AC, SS, ser. 32, reg. 202. The accounts begin on fol. 15r because the first folios are lost. Largi cataloged this reg. as "O" and described it as a "Libro del dare et del avere: Un . . . libro commenca coi fitti nel MCCCXIII perfine a folio 34. E poi seguinta ragioni de'testamenti et note et pagamenti et diverse ragioni perfine 1323. Sono folii 258" ("Specchio," fol. 19r).

19. See below, Chapter 4, at nn. 70–71.

20. AC, SS, ser. 32, reg. 202, fols. 148r–50r provides the basis for the discussion of the testamentary bequests of Donna Nobile.

21. The *quietatio* is a notarial form in which the parties acknowledge acceptance of an arrangement or payment as the fulfillment of an earlier contract.

22. Largi, "Specchio," fol. 35v, no. 160, and fols. 120v–121r for the discussion of Muccio's will and the fruit of his property for the following century. See also Fanfani, "La beneficenza," pp. 75–76.

23. Largi, "Specchio," fol. 22v.

24. Ibid., fols. 7v–13r.

25. For the totals of rents and grain paid to the fraternity in 1316, see ibid., fols. 22v–23v. The series of grain prices recorded by the notaries of the fraternity is found in AC, SS, ser. 32, reg. 171. Amintore Fanfani has studied the sixteenth-century series in his *Indagini sulla "rivoluzione dei prezzi"* (Milan: Pubblicazione dell'Università Cattolica del S. Cuore, 1940), pp. 59–77, 143–62. I wish to thank Richard Goldthwaite for this reference.

26. Largi, "Specchio," fol. 22v. Largi recognized that if the rents on the fraternity's land were lowered so as to secure reliable tenants the priors might grant the land cheaply to their friends. The priors, he said, would have to exercise "prudence" in selecting tenants and thereby avoid fraudulent practices.

27. AC, SS, ser. 32, reg. 143, to the date.

28. Ibid., fol. 17r.

29. AC, SS, ser. 32, reg. 9, fol. 141r. "Qui di sotto farò mimoria de tucta la cera che io Dom Agnilo trarò dell' armario in la quale metta tucta la cera che peritene ale mie mani della(?) corpi li quali se sotterano in le ghiese del Borgho, le quali ghiese secondo li statuti del Borgho deggono dare ala Fraternità uno cero d'onni corpo la quale se sotterà in esse ghiese. Trassi in prima a dì 25 di maggio, 1442, per fare doppieri quattro, facole cinque per li Priori et per lo Rectore, et per una facola per lo Notaio, et tre per li Manuali."

30. AC, SS, ser. 32, reg. 143, fol. 79v. "Fante forestieri fo morto al ponte d'Aste a dì ii d'octobre. Fo seppellito al Ospedale de San Niccolò. Prestamoli ai ceri." For Largi's statement, see "Specchio," fol. 24r: "E più se trova doi quaderni di morti, l'uno del MCCCC nel quale appare che i Priori prestavano ai morti il palio e i ceri e receivano[?] per morte X perfine in soldi XL. E tutto questo è scripto nel libro segnato X a suo luocho nel qual luoco fa memoria così fo ordinato se facesse."

31. AC, SS, ser. 32, reg. 163, fol. 93r.

32. The account of Don Ottaviano's candle was written, perhaps by Francesco de Largi as a *memoriale,* into one of the account books of the fraternity; see AC, SS, ser. 32, reg. 9, fol. 18r–v. "A tutti i successori se fa noto et manifesto che credemo essere asai utile che Dompno Optaviano, monacho de'Camaldoli, il quale fo abbate de Diciano, morì dì detto [March 21, 1414] in casa sua posta nella strada degli Abarbagliati e fo como e di consuetudine il corpo suo portato nella chiesa dela Badia del Borgho e quivi il sollempne uficio mortoro fatto, fo sepelleto. Et aspectato il sabbato havere il cero como se hane degli altri morti per l'abbate fo denegato volerelo dare. Il perchè mandamo il manoale a pregharlo c'el volesse mandare, il che non gionando, andammo noi Anthonio d'Aghumarello, Silvestro de Masso et Francesco de Largi al detto messer l'abbate e con agevole parole e [illeg.] il pregammo non volesse a noi torre le ragioni antiche e date ala Fraternità per lo statuto e per la consuetudine. E llo ne respose che non c'el volea dare e non volea dare perche diana[?] non essere ragione. E quivi moltiplicammo tanto in parole che forse

nè ala gravità del abbate del Borgo nè ancho al officio del priorato dela Fraternità stette bene. E cusì partitoci volendo le habandonate ragioni de questa casa un pocho sullevare, favellato prima al alcuno amicho de dette abbate deliberammo havere qui nella casa alcuno notevili citadini e con essi loro parlamentare e ragionare e conseghame quello che melglio da far fosse intorno a ciò, il perchè—18v—radunati nella casa in numero di beni XL. Fo a loro preposto la cagione perchè da noi chiamati erano che l'abbate non ce volea dare il cero de Dompno Optaviano e la ragione che assignava esso che diceva quello statuto non valea in pregiudicio di chi era nel [illeg.] loro. Per li citadini congregati fo variamente risposto messere Mastino de Catini disse a questo s'aguardosse ala consuetudine e che messer l'abate non fana bene pigliare questa pentata col comune, considerato che il cero si distribuisce per l'amore di Dio ai povari. Grigorio disse che sono morti degli altri simili e che se aguardesse quello era stato facto per altre volte di ceri degli altri preti, frati, monaci, che ello nolsapiva perchè nè ello nè alcuno di suoi fo mai di Priori dela Fraternità pur biasmando l'abate de non. E altri variamente dissaro e chi una e chi un'altra e furon di quelli che dissaro essere stato Priori che morendo uno frate di San Francesco nel convencto del Borgho ebbero il cero. Il perchè fo concluso che noi Priori andassimo al abbate et che noi narriamo a lui omni cosa facta e detta e che il pregammo volesse a noi dare il cero de Dompno Optaviano. Et però ristati alcuni deliberare fra noi del meglio pigliamo il partito già detto. E andammo al detto abbate e pregammolo come prima con dolci parole. E llo rischusandose dele parlo prima havente con noi e dicendo che gli uomini non sono sempre d'una dispostione, volentieri rispose volece il cero dare. E cusì fo fatto."

33. See above, n. 29. Largi, however, did not mention this privilege of the fraternity collecting one candle from each deceased person, nor is it found in the 1442 statutes. Largi did begin to compute the value of income from candle ends ("Specchio," fol. 132v).

34. Ibid.

35. Agnoletti, *Memorie,* pp. 5–7, 26–27. For the 1407 date and the locating of the Volto Santo in the Chapel of Sant'Antonio under the patronage of the fraternity, see AC, SS, ser. 32, reg. 163, fol. 105r.

36. Archivio della Fraternità dei Laici, Arezzo, "Libro dei morti," reg. 881.

37. For a discussion of the "Libri dei morti" and their purposes, see Carlo A. Corsini, "I Libri dei morti," in *Le fonti della demographia storica in Italia,* Comitato italiano per lo studio dei problemi della demographia storica (Rome, 1974), no. 7, vol. 1, pt. 2, pp. 851–64.

38. AC, SS, ser. 2, reg. 1, fols. 38r–v. The document recording these laws for plague years carries the date of July 24, 1417, but it is certain that the legislation was passed earlier. This redaction of 1417 was written by Largi while plague raged in San Sepolcro. The statutes may have been enacted in 1377, when the fraternity began to record all the burials of the town; see AC, SS, ser. 32, reg. 143, fol. 15r.

39. Ibid., ser. 32, reg. 143, to the year.

40. Ibid., ser. 2, reg. 1, fol. 39r.

41. I am preparing a study of these mortuary laws and the books of the dead of San Sepolcro. Among the many studies of sumptuary and mortuary laws see, for the region of San Sepolcro, G. Mischj, "Gli *Ordinamenta mortuorum* in Città di Castello," *Bollettino della R. Deputazione di storia patria per l'Umbria* 22 (1916): 41–53, and Giustiniano Degli Azzi, "Leggi suntuarie perugine nell'età dei comuni," ibid., 125–56. See also Curzio Mazzi, "Alcune leggi suntarie senesi del secolo XIII," *Archivio storico italiano,* ser. 4, 5 (1880): 133–44.

42. AC, SS, ser. 32, reg. 163, fols. 64r–65v.

43. Ibid., fols. 105r–v, 110r, 112r, for the period 1407–9. For the year 1416–17, see ibid., reg. 9, fol. 34r.

44. Ibid., reg. 163, fol. 110r, for an example. The cloth purchased by the priors was at times distributed to recipients other than the poor, such as to officials of the fraternity or to someone, not necessarily destitute, as a result of a bequest. See, for example, ibid., in which a prior on June 2, 1408, gave a "braccio del panno scharlatino" to Ser Meo de ser Achino, thereby fulfilling a bequest in Ser Achino's testament.

45. Ibid. From this and other purchases in 1407–8, I am assuming that wool cloth sold for one and one-half lire per *braccio*.

46. Ibid., to the year. See also the year 1450 for a continuation of this practice. For the division of the town into quarters with each prior representing a quarter, see Largi, "Specchio," fol. 4r.

47. For the cloth accounts of 1437, 1440, and 1450, see AC, SS, ser. 32, reg. 163, to the year. In this same register the cloth distributions for at least the years 1434, 1435, 1438, 1439, and 1441 to 1449 are missing, as are those for 1451 and 1452. If these years of no records of distributions reflect the failure of the priors to give cloth to the poor, it would partially confirm Largi's remark that of the charitable work of the fraternity in the past, there remained only the handing out of a small sum of money (a *quatrino*) on Saturday. See his "Specchio," fol. 6r: "Hora dele elimosine palesi niente altro se observa delo anticho e pietose rito se non solo il quatrino che omni dì de sabbato si da ala Casa a ciaschun poverello." For Largi's estimate of the amount of money spent on cloth annually, see ibid., fol. 133v. As discussed above, grain continued to be distributed.

48. AC, SS, ser. 32, reg. 173, fols. 77r–82v, 107r–114r, 89r–96v, 146r–147v, 104r–105r, 167r–v, 152r–153v, 174r–175r. I have recorded only those pious corporations with the largest amounts of land.

49. The statement is based on an assessment of the wealth of other possible landowners. The great families, the Pichi, Bercordati, and others, gained the preponderance of their wealth through trade and appear to have had relatively small quantities of land. Had the Malatesta retained power in San Sepolcro, they might have had as much land as the two wealthy confraternities and the abbot. The Malatesta in 1418, however, took property from several rebels and

gave it to the Fraternity of San Bartolomeo and the Confraternity of Santa Maria della Notte.

50. For Fanfani's estimate, see his "La beneficenza," pp. 50–51. He also attempted to determine the value of the 1,033 benefactions listed by Largi (ibid., pp. 51–52). And for Largi's account of the 1316 rents, see above, n. 25.

51. Herlihy, *Medieval and Renaissance Pistoia,* pp. 133–38.

52. Largi, "Specchio," fol. 133v. The total expenses include seventy-five *staia* of grain for which the fraternity was obligated; it is again valued at one and one-half lire per *staio*. This total also includes two entries of land listed, but not in the hand of Largi, in the 1440s and valued at twelve lire.

53. The estimate for expenses for administration and gifts to the clergy does not include some small expenses, for example, wages of servants and purchases of accounting books.

54. Largi, "Specchio," fol. 133v: "Bacinella omni sabbato per li poveri secondo l'usanza lire 5 per sabbato."

55. The list of the members of the New Council is found in AC, SS, ser. 2, reg. 1, "Riforme e Provvisioni della comunità di San Sepolcro, 1390 al 1398," fols. 7r–10v.

56. Ibid.

57. The priors of the fraternity are listed in Farulli, *Annali e memorie,* pp. 89–90.

58. Coleschi, *Storia di San Sepolcro,* pp. 73–74.

59. The members of the Conseglio dei Popoli are listed in AC, SS, ser. 2, reg. 2. The register is not foliated; the list is found at June 1442. The list of priors of the fraternity in the 1440s is taken from Farulli, *Annali e memorie,* pp. 91–92.

60. AC, SS, ser. 32, reg. 9, fols. 65v and 94v.

61. Ibid., fol. 42r, in June 1418. On August 12, 1419, Carlo Malatesta requested the fraternity to pay some of his debts (ibid., fol. 48r).

CHAPTER FOUR
The Confraternity of Santa Maria della Notte: From Processional Chanting to Administrative Devotion

1. See the text of the notarial act in Degli Azzi, "Inventario," 171–74.

2. Largi, "Specchio," fol. 25r, no. 7; fol. 25v, no. 22.

3. ASF, CRS, San Sepolcro, L.XX.2, chap. 1, fol. 2r–v. Citations to the statutes of the Confraternity of Santa Maria della Notte located in this register will henceforth be noted within the text by chapter number. The text of the statutes is found in Appendix II. The account of the founding of the confraternity in the early fourteenth century and its relationship to the clergy was written in 1441, but Largi claimed that his views were based on written records.

4. The most complete study of the *laudesi* is that of Meersseman, *Ordo*

fraternitatis, 2:21–79, and his bibliography. On the *disciplinati,* see below, Chapter 5, n. 3.

5. Lauro Martines, *Power and Imagination: City-States in Renaissance Italy* (New York: Knopf, 1979), pp. 58–61. Martines discusses the powerful effects of the *popolo's* gaining of political power on culture and society.

6. Meersseman, *Ordo fraternitatis,* 2:766–70; Florence, Archivio della Compagnia della Santa Maria della Misericordia, "Libri dei Quartieri," San Giovanni, fol. 1r.

7. For Florence, see the statutes of the two confraternities in Alfredo Schiaffini, ed., *Testi fiorentini del dugento* (Florence: Sansoni, 1926), pp. 35–72. And for the four *disciplinati* confraternities of the thirteenth century, see L. Scaramucci, "Considerazioni sui statuti e matricole di confraternite di disciplinati," in *Risultati e prospettive della ricerca sul movimento dei disciplinati* (Perugia: Convegno internazionale di studio, 1972), p. 135. See the comments on the early confraternities by Meersseman, *Ordo fraternitas,* 1:464–73.

8. I have accepted Largi's placement of the founding of the brotherhood in 1300, or soon thereafter, despite Agnoletti's assertion that it was founded in 1218; see his *Vescovi,* 1:47. But apparently Agnoletti has doubts about the early date because in his *Sansepolcro degli abati* (p. 96) he asserts that the confraternity was founded in the 1350s. The dating of this *laudesi* confraternity in the first decade of the fourteenth century is based on Largi's assertion (see chapter 1 of the confraternal statutes in Appendix II), the essential agreement of an eighteenth-century scribe of the confraternity who placed the founding in 1309 (ASF, CRS, San Sepolcro, L.XX.5, fol. 17r), that, on paleographic grounds, the earliest *lauda* of the confraternity is said to have been written about 1300 (see the comments of Guiliana Maggini and Luigi Andreini in the introduction to *Laudario della Compagnia di Santa Maria della Notte* [San Sepolcro: Cooperativa Culturale "Giorgio La Pira," n.d.], pp. 9–10), and that the year of the first recorded bequest to this confraternity was 1316 (ASF, CRS, L.XX.8, fol. 13r). Had the confraternity been founded in 1218, it would most likely have received bequests in the second half of the thirteenth century as did the Fraternity of San Bartolomeo, which was founded in the first half of the thirteenth century.

9. ASF, NA, P. 121, fols. 2v–3v. The name of this brotherhood varies in the documents. I have linked the *Laudesi* of Santa Maria Novella and the *Laudesi* who made processions through the town because in several testaments of the mid-fourteenth century and thereafter notaries denoted bequests to a confraternity that linked both of these elements. See, for example, the 1347 testament of a notary's widow who bequeathed five soldi to the "Laudesi di Santa Maria Novella que cantantur diebus festivis dominicis et festivis de Marie per Burgum" (ASF, NA, P. 121, fols. 1r–2r). I have assumed, therefore, that whenever documents refer to the "Laudesi di Santa Maria Novelle" or the "Compagnia della Laude de Santa Maria della Notte" they are denoting the Confraternity of Santa Maria della Notte.

10. ASF, NA, C. 714, *filza* of 1332–34, unfol., act of October 4, 1334.

11. ASF, NA, P. 121, fols. 20v–21v. I am assuming that if testators made bequests to a confraternity, the brotherhood was in existence, and if over several years and several tens of testaments no bequests were made, the brotherhood no longer existed.

12. ASF, NA, C. 713, *filza* 1 (1318–28), fol. 21v.

13. ASF, NA, P. 121, fols. 121r–v and 121v–122r. There are numerous bequests to the confraternity through 1364, but thereafter its existence cannot be confirmed from testaments until the fifteenth century. Among the bequests of the mid-fourteenth century, see ASF, NA, P. 121, fols. 1v–2r (1347), 11r–12r (1348), 95v (1350), 107v–108v (1356), 109r (1357), 117v–118r (1360), 133v–134r (1363), 167r–v (1364).

14. ASF, NA, F. 123, unfol., but recorded in the 1317 testament of Domina Palia, wife of Burgensius Domini; for 1348, see ASF, NA, P. 121, fol. 31r.

15. The citing of the confraternity of the *Laudesi* in San Bartolomeo in 1319 is found in the testament of Domina Clara, widow of Salvucius Orlandini, ASF, NA, F. 123, unfol. For 1348, ASF, NA, F. 123, unfol., to the year.

16. See the testament of Gratia di Piganelli in 1318, ASF, NA, F. 123, unfol.

17. ASF, NA, P. 121, fols. 43v–44r.

18. AC, SS, ser. 32, reg. 177, fol. 2r–v. These notarial authentications of elections stated that the confraternity required two-thirds of its members to be present for the election to be in accord with the statutes of the confraternity. This quorum is often found in statutes of other confraternities of the period. In estimating membership in the confraternities, I have assumed that the number of members present represented the minimum membership and represented two-thirds of the maximum membership.

19. Ibid., fol. 1v.

20. ASF, NA, P. 117, *fogli diversi,* act of October 10, 1365 (twenty-two men present); act of February 2, 1366 (twenty men present); ASF, NA, P. 117, protocol of 1366, unfol., act of August 10, 1366 (twenty-three men present); ASF, NA, P. 120, protocol of 1376, fol. 40v, act of February 25, 1376 (twenty-three men present); ibid., protocol of 1378, fol. 38v, acts of February 22, 1378 (twenty-three men present), and February 2, 1380 (twenty-six men present).

21. ASF, CRS, San Sepolcro, L.XX.5, fol. 17r.

22. Ibid., L.XX.27, fols. 2v–304r and L.XX.146, fols. 11r–15r.

23. Ibid., L.XX.2, fols. 3r–6r and L.XX.10, fol. 1r ff.

24. For Checcho's offices, see ibid., L.XX.27, fols. 2r–306r; L.XX.2, fols. 2v–3r; L.XX.10, fols. 1r–4r; L.XX.146, fols. 11r–79r. One of the two priors served as prior-treasurer and administered the confraternity's finances.

25. The problem of identifying family names in San Sepolcro is complicated by the practice there of employing the Latin ablative *de* to denote descent in the vernacular, whereas in many other parts of Tuscany the *de* in the Italian indicated an accepted family name. For the judgment that substantial social

status can be assumed from a family name, see, among others, Herlihy and Klapisch-Zuber, *Tuscans and Their Families,* pp. 347–52, and Samuel K. Cohn, *The Laboring Classes in Renaissance Florence* (New York: Academic Press, 1980), p. 23.

26. AC, SS, ser. 32, reg. 177, fol. 2r–v.

27. See above, n. 24.

28. ASF, CRS, San Sepolcro, L.XX.2, fol. 2r–v.

29. See above, n. 20. The membership may have been slightly larger than those who appeared at meetings for elections, but there should be little doubt that these forty-two names constitute the active members because they were taken from five meetings from 1366 to 1380.

30. Fanfani, "Le arti di Sansepolcro dal XIV al XVI secolo," *Saggi di storia economia italiana,* pp. 85–107. For the wool guild, see ASF, NA, P. 120, *filza,* unfol., act of December 30, 1376 (1375 modern style).

31. ASF, NA, P. 120, protocol of 1380, fol. 12r, and P. 120, *filza,* unfol. and undated, but of 1380 since the consuls are identical to those in the preceding act.

32. Ibid., protocol of 1380, fol. 189r, act of December 12, 1380.

33. Ibid., protocol of 1376, fol. 5v, act of January 1, 1376 for the apothecaries and ASF, NA, P. 116, *filza,* act of December 8, 1366 for the tailors. For the matricola of the guild of notaries, see ASF, NA, P. 117, *fogli diversi* for 1366. The *foglio* with the notaries' names is labeled P. 116.

34. On the legislative councils, see Bercordati, "Cronaca di Borgo San Sepolcro," fol. 38v; Coleschi, *Storia di San Sepolcro,* p. 56. For the New Council of the 1390s, see the register entitled "Riforme e Provvisioni della Comunità di San Sepolcro," AC, SS, ser. 2, reg. 1, fols. 7r–10v. The dating of the New Council is established by the fact that the notary Jacopo di ser Paolo di Ciuccio maintained the records through 1398. As chancellor, Jacopo recorded the names of the three hundred men of the New Council in 1391 and through 1398 added fifty-three others.

35. This procedure is possible because the vast majority of names on the council denote three generations.

36. AC, SS, ser. 2, reg. 1, fols. 42r–48v.

37. One other member of the confraternity, Paulus Mucii Casucci, is listed as a creditor in the 1393 list but not as a lender to the commune. He too was among the members of the legislative council in the 1390s.

38. AC, SS, ser. 2, reg. 2, unfol., but from June 1442.

39. See the preface of the statutes, Appendix II.

40. For example, see the rent of a piece of land owned by Bartolous, called Acerbo, son of the deceased ser Fini (whose brother belonged to the *laudesi* confraternity in 1376), to a confraternal member, Johannes olim Guido Peri dei Cipolli, for the substantial sum of thirty-six lire (ASF, NA, P. 120, protocol of 1376, fol. 41r). See Appendix II, *Capitolo* 20 of the statutes.

41. Pignani, "Compendio istorico," pp. 130–32.

42. See the comments of Maggini and Andreini, *Laudario,* p. 8. Agnoletti, *Vescovi,* I: 47, also mentions the thirteenth-century origin of the confraternity, but in his *Sansepolcro degli abati* (p. 96), he conjectures that the events described by Pignani occurred in the middle of the fourteenth century.

43. For the date of "Corsidoni," probably Carsidoni, as *gonfaloniere,* see Goracci, *Breve istoria dell'origine e fondazione della Città di Borgo San Sepolcro,* p. 247.

44. These expenses recur in the financial records of the confraternity. See ASF, CRS, San Sepolcro, L.XX.145, fols. 11r–79r. These wages for unskilled agricultural labor appear inexplicably high. Richard Goldthwaite has shown that in the first half of the fifteenth century skilled urban laborers often earned one lira per day and the unskilled received ten or thirteen soldi per day; see his *The Building of Renaissance Florence: An Economic and Social History* (Baltimore: Johns Hopkins University Press, 1980), pp. 317–31, 435–39.

45. ASF, CRS, San Sepolcro, L.XX.145, fol. 7r.

46. Ibid., L.XX.27, fols. 23r–34r.

47. Ibid., to the year.

48. AC, SS, "Fondo della Misericordia," reg. 14, fol. 4r–v. This "Fondo" has recently been rediscovered and provisionally numbered. Among the merchants who sold cloth to the confraternity were the brother of Francesco de Largi and Giubeleo de Niccolo de Carsidoni. The latter had been an active merchant in San Sepolcro since 1368 and served as a prior of the Fraternity of San Bartolomeo in 1418. See Fanfani, *Mercante,* pp. 11–24.

49. AC, SS, "Fondo della Misericordia," reg. 14, fol. 5r.

50. ASF, CRS, San Sepolcro, L.XX.27, unfol., to the year.

51. See, for example, the accounts of the priory of March through August 1431 in which Largi stated he placed eighty-three lire in a register of forced loans and adds in the margin that "Hane dato como appare al quaderno dele prestanze a più persone presta de voluntà della Compania" (ibid., to the year).

52. ASF, "Capitoli dei comuni soggetti," reg. 798, fol. 1r.

53. ASF, CRS, L.XX.27, to the year.

54. Largi's account of the confraternity's possessions is found in ASF, CRS, San Sepolcro, L.XX.27, fols. 114r–119v. For the measurements used in San Sepolcro, see Eugenio Battisti with Enzo Settesoldi, *Piero della Francesca,* 2 vols. (Milan: Istituto Editoriale Italiano, 1971), 2:216.

55. AC, SS, ser. 32, reg. 173, fols. 107r–114r for the land tax on Santa Maria della Notte, fols. 104r–105r for the Pieve, and fols. 77r–82v for the Camaldolese Abbey.

56. Agnoletti, *Sansepolcro degli abati,* p. 96.

57. For these financial records, see ASF, CRS, San Sepolcro, L.XX.27, fol. 23v–34r.

58. Ibid.

59. Largi may have changed the accounting procedures because of a charge of mismanagement of the monies of the confraternity leveled against him and

the priors. In 1439 Largi wrote a defense against a detractor who accused the priors of acting arbitrarily and with their eyes closed: "E anche acciochè mostrandese tucto chiaro sano di la lengua al detractore che pensa omni cosa de questa pietosa Compania si faccia inconsultamente a beneplacito e fa stello (?) e che questi optimi padri spendino a chiusi occhi, como se non se adsegnasse particularmente le ragioni de chi se deputa a spendere de tempo in tempo" (ASF, CRS, San Sepolcro, L.XX.145, fol. 1r–v). See also *Capitolo* XXX of the statutes (Appendix II), in which Largi hints at criticism of the confraternity for its choice of renters of the confraternal land.

60. The 238 testaments were those rogated by the notary Paolo di Ciuccio, ASF, NA, P. 121, fols. 1r–188v. In these testaments only the largest five bequests were tabulated, and doubtless there were many small bequests to the confraternity that escaped the survey. This loss may be balanced by the fact that, because Paolo often redacted the acts of the confraternity, a member might have been more inclined than the average citizen of the town to employ him.

61. ASF, CRS, San Sepolcro, L.XX.8. Largi divided the bequests into four series. These two are from series III (fols. 65r–72v), nos. 9 and 19.

62. Ibid. See ser. I (fols. 13r–39v), nos. 6, 20, and 30.

63. Ibid., ser. I, nos. 47, 49, 89, 103.

64. Ibid., ser. I, nos. 7, 13, 28, 50, 55, 72, 79, 85, 95; for the chapel, see ASF, NA, P. 121, fols. 132v–133r.

65. ASF, CRS, L.XX.8, ser. I, no. 88.

66. Ibid., ser. I, no. 72. Simone was listed as a member of the confraternity in 1345, 1346, 1366, and 1376. Simone's will appears in ASF, NA, P. 121, fol. 123r–v.

67. ASF, CRS, L.XX.8, ser. I, no. 46, and Largi's explanatory note on fol. 23r.

68. The number of small bequests by the testators of San Sepolcro dropped sharply not simply because of Largi's disinclination to count paltry bequests. An examination of the income of the confraternity in the six-month priory from March through August 1417 shows that the confraternity did not receive any bequests of money in that period. That Largi was computing income from bequests is evident from the following semester, when he recorded the payment of thirty-seven lire from a bequest. (ibid., L.XX.27, fol. 23r–40v).

69. Though it is extremely difficult to estimate the inflation of the second half of the fourteenth century, it should be clear that these figures surpass the influence of inflation. Since trends manifested in money are replicated in grain and property, the influence of inflation does not appear to be significant for my findings.

70. ASF, CRS, San Sepolcro, L.XX.145, fol. 1r.

71. See Appendix II, *Capitolo* XXIX of the statutes, in which Largi stated that if anyone took any of the possessions of the confraternity, the thief was to be expelled permanently from the brotherhood and labeled sacrilegious.

CHAPTER FIVE
Flagellant Confraternities: Purged Social Behaviors and Sacred Communities

1. Numerous chapels were founded in the churches of San Sepolcro in the century after the Black Death, but each was a private benefaction.

2. See note 51 in Chapter 1.

3. Research on the confraternities of discipline has been stimulated by the early studies of Meersseman, which appear in his *Ordo fraternitatis* under the chapter title "I disciplinati nel duecento," 1:451–512. Interest in these confraternities among Italian scholars led to two conferences in Perugia in 1960 and 1969. The papers of these conferences have been published as *Il movimento dei disciplinati nel settimo centenario dal suo inizio* (Perugia: Convegno internazionale, 1962) and *Risultati e prospettive della ricerca sul movimento dei disciplinati* (Perugia: Convegno internazionale di Studio, 1972). These volumes have been published by the Centro di documentazione del movimento dei disciplinati; in addition, the Centro has published several volumes entitled *Quaderni,* which include reports of research on the flagellants. See also the excellent survey by John Henderson, "The Flagellant Movement and Flagellant Confraternities in Central Italy, 1260–1400," *Studies in Church History* 15 (1978): 147–60. For Umbria, see Piero L. Meloni, "Per la storia delle confraternite disciplinate in Umbria nel secolo XIV," in *Storia e arte in Umbria nell'età comunale, Atti del Convegno di Studi Umbria,* 2 vols. (Perugia: A cura delle Facoltà di lettere e filosofia dell' Università, 1971), 2:533–87.

4. Meersseman, *Ordo fraternitatis,* 1:463–97.

5. Agnoletti, *Sansepolcro degli abati,* pp. 83–85.

6. Morghen, *Il passaggio,* pp. 33–37; Henderson, "Flagellant Movement," 149–51.

7. De la Roncière, "La place des confréries," 48; Meersseman, *Ordo fraternitatis,* 1:455.

8. "Capitoli dei disciplinati di Sant'Antonio," ed. Francesco Agostini in his *Testi trecenteschi di Città di Castello* (Florence: Presso L'Accademiá della Crusca, 1978), pp. 120–36.

9. Ibid., pp. 121–22, 129.

10. AC, SS, display case, testament of Guarnerottus, iudex filius olim Guarnerii, May 22, 1292.

11. See an edition of this bull in Gilles G. Meersseman, *Dossier de l'ordre de la penitence au XIIIe siècle,* in *Spicilegium Friburgense,* vol. 7 (Fribourg: Universitat verlag Freibourg, 1961), p. 75, and the discussion in Meersseman, *Ordo fraternitatis,* 1:381. The exact location of the translation of the "Regola dei Frati e dell'ordine di penitenza" has been debated and placed in San Sepolcro, Gubbio, and Città di Castello, but the most recent discussions point to this last city as the home of the translator; for these comments and the *volgare* edition of the "Regola," see Agostini, *Testi trecenteschi,* pp. 101–13. Meersseman's *Dossier* contains several documents that record the activities of the penitents in the

diocese of the bishop of Città di Castello in 1286, 1292, 1298–99, and 1301 (pp. 203ff.).

12. See Weissman, *Ritual Brotherhood*, pp. 50–58, who sees the flagellant confraternities as social organizations for gaining honor in the city of Florence. He regards the confraternities of Florence generally as organizations with the purpose of expiating the peculiar "agonistic" character of Florentine social life. Since confraternities appeared in all parts of Italy, not to mention western Europe, at approximately the same time, I see no reason to emphasize the peculiar nature of Florentine society. I see, instead, the specific juncture of a medieval Christian view of economics and politics with new economic and political practices and a new resolution of older ideals with new practices. This particular resolution had profound and long-lasting ramifications, several of which Max Weber identified as possible only in a society dominated by Calvinistic values; see Weber *The Protestant Ethic and the Spirit of Capitalism*, trans. Talcott Parsons (New York: Charles Scribner's Sons, 1958). In this chapter I have been influenced by Weissman's view that certain confraternities attempted to purge society of conflict and Trexler's view that at times specific social groups acquire a sacred character. For the latter, see his *Public Life in Renaissance Florence*, pp. 365–521.

13. Agnoletti, *Sansepolcro degli abati*, pp. 83–85.

14. ASF, NA, C. 714, unfol., testament of Gnolus olim Guidonis, June 6, 1338.

15. Agnoletti, *Sansepolcro degli abati*, p. 84.

16. ASF, NA, C. 714, unfol., act of June 22, 1338, testament of Gnolus olim Guidonis.

17. ASF, NA, P. 121, fols. 4v–83r, 125bis r–v.

18. Ibid., fol. 50r–v.

19. Ibid., fol. 47r–v, testament of Mucius olim Comandi, August 10, 1348.

20. Ibid., fols. 117v–118r, testament of Francischus Domini Ranierii de Mazettis, May 8, 1360, and see also fol. 53r–v, testament of Giovangeli Ughecti, August 16, 1348.

21. ASF, NA, N. 95, unfol., testament of Domina Bartola, widow of Petrus Cisci Vecce, October 1, 1362.

22. Agnoletti, *Sansepolcro degli abati*, pp. 84–85; ASF, NA, C. 714, unfol., testament of Nerus olim Raynerii Iancanelli, February 22, 1339.

23. Bercordati, "Cronaca di Borgo San Sepolcro," fol. 34v; Agnoletti, *Sansepolcro degli abati*, p. 89, holds that these flagellants of Santa Maria Maddalena banded together to provide the Christian charity of turning prostitutes to the "honest life" based on marriage or monastic vows. It is unclear whether this purpose taken from a sixteenth-century document can be attributed to the members in the fourteenth century.

24. ASF, NA, F. 132, *filza* 3, fol. 271r.

25. Bercordati, "Cronaca di Borgo San Sepolcro," fol. 34v; Agnoletti, *Sansepolcro degli abati*, p. 91, and for the identification of the *ecclesia* with the

disciplinati, see again the testament of Donna Sichina, who gave bequests to five *disciplinati* confraternities, ASF, NA, P. 121, fols. 1r–2r.

26. ASF, NA, P. 114, *filza* 1347–49, fol. 82v.

27. ASF, NA, C. 713, *filza* 1316–18, unfol., testament of Vannius Pieri Gualrade; ibid., F. 123, unfol., testament of Domina Clara, widow of Salvucius Orlandini, August 21, 1319.

28. ASF, NA, F. 123, unfol., testament of Tratia olim Pagnaelli, March 22, 1319.

29. Farulli, *Annali e memorie,* p. 141; Agnoletti, *Sansepolcro degli abati,* p. 88.

30. See, for example, ASF, NA, B. 1249, unfol., testament of Vannes olim Vollie, July 24, 1348.

31. Bercordati, "Cronaca di Borgo San Sepolcro," fol. 35r; ASF, NA, P. 121, testament of Mucius olim Comandi molendarius; on August 10, 1348, he bequeathed to the confraternity "unam capsam ad portandum cadavera seu corpora mortuorum."

32. Agnoletti, *Sansepolcro degli abati,* p. 89.

33. The earliest reference to this confraternity is in 1331 (ASF, NA, F. 123, *filza* 1, fol. 157v); for the continued existence of this group, see the 1347 testament of Domina Sichina, widow of the notary Fidele, prolific in notarial acts and notarial sons, ASF, NA, P. 121, fol. 1r–2r. For the 1345 citation, see Bercordati, "Cronaca di Borgo San Sepolcro," fol. 34r.

34. ASF, NA, P. 121, fol. 125bis-r–v, testament of August 8, 1348.

35. Robert Davidsohn, *Storia di Firenze,* vol. 7: *I primordi della civiltà fiorentina,* pt. III, *Il mondo della chiesa, spiritualità ed arte* (Florence: Sansoni, 1973), p. 183.

36. Van Engen, "Christian Middle Ages," 546–48.

37. For examples of discipline confraternities outside of San Sepolcro, see Meersseman, *Ordo fraternitatis,* 1:451–512; Henderson, "Flagellant Movement," 147–60; Scaramucci, "Considerazione sui statuti e matricole di confraternite di disciplinati," pp. 134–94.

38. See Appendix IV for the source of the testaments. The total of seven bequests may be somewhat underestimated because only the five largest bequests were tabulated. Compared to the other four confraternities of discipline that survived the Black Death, the Confraternity of Santa Croce received the fewest bequests. In all likelihood, it was one of the smaller groups among the flagellants.

39. AC, SS, cl. 32, reg. 152. See Appendix III for the transcription of the statutes (hereafter cited in the text by chapter number) and for the confraternal members named in these statutes. I assume the first set of additional statutes is from the early 1380s because it is located between the statutes of 1364 and 1392 and because not one member named in 1364 is found in these additional statutes, whereas one man from the year 1392 is listed. Also, the 1364 statutes advised reconsideration of the statutes every nine years, so I have estimated 1382 to be the most likely date of the first set of additions.

40. Meersseman, *Ordo fraternitatis,* 1:463–75, 476, 478, 480, 490; Morghen, *Il passaggio,* pp. 33–37.

41. This was not simply the case with the men of this Confraternity of Santa Croce. The testaments of San Sepolcro across the fourteenth century generally show a constricting of the vision of reform of Christian society. For this theme in European culture generally, see Morghen, *Il passaggio*.

42. Meersseman, *Ordo fraternitatis*, 1:390–408 for the offices and prayers of the Brethren of the Penitents.

43. For the Christocentric emphasis of the flagellants of Europe, see Henderson, "Flagellant Movement," 148–49.

44. See the testament of the priest Giovanni de Cescho, ASF, NA, P. 121, fol. 125bis r–v, August 20, 1348.

45. For examples of flagellation as voluntary identification with the passion of Christ, see Henderson, "Flagellant Movement," 148–49.

46. See Appendix III, chaps. 9, 14, 15, 21, 24, 29, 38–45, 47, 53, 55, 56, 58, 59, 60, and 62.

47. Agnoletti, *Sansepolcro degli abati*, p. 84.

48. AC, SS, cl. 2, reg. 1, fols. 38v, 39r.

49. ASF, CRS, San Sepolcro, A.CCCXLIII.35, fol. 42r, an example of a nonmember, as death approached, buying membership into the Confraternity of Sant'Antonio in 1430.

50. Ibid., fol. 76r, from 1449.

51. For the names of 353 men of the New Council, see AC, SS, cl. 2, reg. 1, fols. 7r–10v.

52. The political participation on the part of the twenty-two men of the Confraternity of Santa Croce may be slightly higher than that for all the confraternal members because these twenty-two were officeholders and might have been more active politically generally than the remainder of the members. But those particular leaders would not have been much more active in the council than any others because political participation was distributed widely among confraternal members.

53. Consult ASF, CRS, San Sepolcro, A.CCCXLIII.35, fols. 1r–77r in the years from 1382 to 1450 for numerous examples of entrants paying or promising to pay this initial fee. This register contains information on members, payments of entrance fees, names of those who guaranteed payment of the entrance fees if the individual did not pay at the moment of inscription, and finally the disposition of the confraternal cloak.

54. For example, in 1414, Andrea d'Antonio del Bianchuccio who entered the brotherhood with a priest's and Andrea's mother's promise to provide the entrance fees if Andrea could not. In that year and again in 1423 his mother promised to make the *vesta* for her son (ibid., fol. 14r).

55. Ibid., fols. 17r, 44v, for examples of debts paid to the confraternity after the member's death.

56. Ibid., fol. 34r.

57. ASF, CRS, San Sepolcro, A.CCCXLIII.1, unfol., to the year.

58. As in the case of other conclusions from this study of 351 testaments, these statements should be qualified by the understanding that only the five largest bequests to pious corporations were tabulated. Since some testators

gave to ten or more pious corporations, without doubt the number of gifts to the Confraternity of Sant'Antonio is low, but the limited size is also important. See Appendix IV for the sources of the testaments.

59. ASF, NA, P. 121, fol. 47r–v, August 10, 1348.

60. AC, SS, Fondo della Misericordia, reg. 236, fols. 89r–92r.

61. See, for example, ASF, CRS, San Sepolcro, A.CCCXLIII.5, fol. 24r.

62. ASF, CRS, San Sepolcro, A.CCCXLIII.33, fols. 7v–8r, 11r–v, 22r.

63. For a list of the "Men of the Company of Sant'Antonio," see ASF, CRS, San Sepolcro, A.CCCXLIII.34, fols. 42v–45r; and for examples of votes on the candidacy of entering men, see ASF, CRS, San Sepolcro, A.CC-CXLIII.33, fols. 16v–19v. On January 17, 1393, the votes on two prospective members were affirmative at nineteen to one and twenty-six to one (ibid., fol. 25r).

64. ASF, CRS, San Sepolcro, A.CCCXLIII.1, fols. 11r; for the limited number of members at meetings, see, for examples, fols. 12v, 14v, 25r.

65. For the members of the Confraternity of Sant'Antonio in 1393, see above, n. 63; for the members of the New Council in the 1390s, see above, n. 51. There is a possibility that the list of 198 confraternal members in 1393 included dead members of an earlier generation for whom the brothers continued to pray. I have rejected this possibility because, of those on a list of members in the 1350s and 1360s, only a few names reappear in the 1393 list; for the earlier period, see ASF, CRS, San Sepolcro, A.CCCXLIII.5, fols. 3r–50r.

That a few members from the 1350s and 1360s were still in the confraternity in 1393 indicates that many members entered in early adulthood and maintained membership until death. This impression is confirmed by a perusal of the membership of the confraternity in the fifteenth century; see ASF, CRS, San Sepolcro, A.CCCXLIII.35. In one flagellant confraternity in Florence in the fifteenth century, Weissman discovered that members joined in their early adulthood, represented all the social groups of the city in the first half of the fifteenth century, and the average period of membership was twenty years; see his *Ritual Brotherhood,* pp. 107–61.

66. The list of confraternal voters in the 1440s appears in ASF, CRS, San Sepolcro, A.CCCXLIII.1, fol. 25r. The members of the Council of the People in 1442 are found in AC, SS, cl. 2, reg. 2, unfol., June 1442.

67. I recognize that the existence of a large number of partially active members as in the Confraternity of Sant'Antonio places into question my method of arriving at a maximum number of members, since the number of flagellants of Sant'Antonio who attended meetings was only a small percentage of the affiliated members. I am attempting to demonstrate that a large percentage of males of San Sepolcro joined the confraternities of discipline, and my method tends to underestimate that percentage. I prefer to err against my view of high male participation. The method is simply a means of acknowledging that in a voluntaristic organization a certain percentage of members fails to attend meetings.

68. For the Confraternity of Santa Maria Maddalena, see ASF, NA, P. 114, *filza* for 1347–49, fol. 144r; Confraternity of Santa Maria della Misericordia, ibid., P. 119, protocol of 1352–77, fol. 151r–v; Confraternity of Santa Caterina, ibid., B. 1257, unfol., acts of February 3, 1359.

69. ASF, CRS, San Sepolcro, A.CCCXLIII.5, fols. 3r–50r.

70. A comparison of the lists of members attending meetings in the 1350s in the three confraternities cited above in note 68 did not reveal any individual in more than one confraternity or fathers and sons in the same confraternity.

71. ASF, CRS, San Sepolcro, A.CCCXLIII.35, fol. 1r.

72. The deaths of some members recorded in the group from 1382 to 1426 were noted, but all these deaths occurred after 1426 (ibid., fols. 1r–27v); for the later additions, see ibid., fols. 28r–43v.

73. In a sample of all entrants in the years from 1420 to 1429, twenty-four children were entered by one of their parents (ibid., fols. 17v–40r). Thus almost 16 percent of the sample were children. To arrive at the figure of 252 men, I have subtracted the 22 members who died in the years 1427–30 from the total of 321 and 16 percent of the remaining 299. This procedure overestimates the number of children in the confraternity because all those entering before 1415 would have been adults in 1430. Consequently, the estimate of 252 men in the confraternity in 1430 represents a minimum.

74. ASF, NA, M. 516, protocol of 1425–30, fol. 21v.

75. For the sources of income and expenses of the Confraternity of Sant'Antonio in 1392, see above, n. 62. The Confraternity of Santa Maria della Misericordia in the five-year period 1401–5 had a total income of 678 lire; see AC, SS, Fondo della Misericordia, *Entrata,* reg. 8, fol. 8v.

76. Another possibility is that the confraternity may have drawn members to itself because the other flagellant confraternities had more wealth or property, which resulted in compromising their corporate virtue. In this alternate construction the Confraternity of Sant'Antonio would have attracted members because its poverty implied greater spiritual power. I have rejected this construction on two grounds. First, the income of this confraternity and that of the Confraternity of Santa Maria della Misericordia were roughly equal around 1400 (ibid.). Second, in the testaments of the fourteenth century each of the flagellant confraternities received only a few bequests of property. Thus no one flagellant group received a great deal more property than any other with the exception of the Confraternity of Santa Maria della Misericordia. See Appendix IV for the testaments from which these observations are drawn.

Conclusion

1. The distinction between rural and urban has little importance in northern and central Italy because medieval Italians organized in concentrated aggregates, whether around a tower, on a fortified hill, or encircled within walls. Families seldom sought the isolated existence of a detached house. Doubtless

the *podere* of the countryside at times had only one family, but no one knows of their inclination, or lack of same, to join brotherhoods. The earliest known confraternity in Tuscany was founded in the eleventh century in the small rural commune of Sant'Appiano in Valdelsa (Meersseman, *Ordo fraternitatis,* 1:55–65).

2. See Le Goff, *Birth of Purgatory,* pp. 289–333.

3. Chiffoleau, *La comptabilité,* pp. 389–425.

4. See Becker, *Medieval Italy,* esp. chap. 1; Martines, *Power and Imagination,* pp. 62–66; Bernd Moeller, *Reichsstadt und Reformation* (Gütersloh: Gütersloher Verlagshaus, G. Mohn, 1962), pp. 15–18; Donald Weinstein, *Savonarola and Florence: Prophecy and Patriotism in the Renaissance* (Princeton: Princeton University Press, 1970), chap. 1, esp. pp. 34–36 and the bibliography cited there.

5. ASF, "Capitoli dei comuni soggetti," reg. 795, fols. 74v–75r.

6. Ibid., reg. 798, fol. 1r.

7. AC, SS, ser. 32, reg. 159, unfol., to the years of male entrants.

8. ASF, CRS, San Sepolcro, A.CCCXLIII.34, fols. 42v–45r. The samples drawn from the Fraternity of San Bartolomeo and the Confraternity of Sant'Antonio are so large, approximately 20 percent of the adult males of the town in both cases, that in all probability the samples represent faithfully the names of the men of the town.

9. Charles de la Roncière, "L'influence des Franciscains dans la campagne de Florence au XIVe siècle (1280–1360)," *Mélanges de l'Ecole française de Rome: Moyen âge–Temps modernes* 87 (1975): 27–103. De la Roncière's study has provided a model for my comparison of Germanic and Christian names, though he was concerned with the Franciscan influence in the spread of Christian names. See also the study of Benjamin Z. Kedar, "Noms de saints et mentalité à Genes au XIVe siècle," *Le moyen âge* 73 (1967): 431–46. I discovered this study after having written this conclusion; of profound importance is Kedar's relating of the appropriation of saints' names to the rise of the *popolo* to citizenship.

10. De la Roncière, "L'influence des Franciscans," 76–77.

11. See the note on testaments in Appendix IV.

12. See the testaments in ASF, NA, F. 123, 1317–20 and C. 714, 1329–41.

13. Meersseman, *Ordo fraternitatis,* 1:18, 29–31, 3:1291–1314; Weissman, *Ritual Brotherhood,* pp. 97–98. The flagellants were not unique in exempting non compliance; this provision is often found in confraternities and in the statutes of the Dominicans and Franciscans.

APPENDIX III

1. In the margin of this *capitolo* and in a hand different from that of the writer of the text there is a symbol to represent a bishop and barely legible the word *ratatre* or *ratarre* that appears to be a form of the verb *ritrattare.* At some point after the writing of the statutes, evidently, a bishop had this *capitolo*

"retracted"; this statute required members to obey reverentially the prior and not to reveal the secrets of the confraternity.

2. Though the marginal words are no longer legible it appears that a bishop, at some unknown moment though perhaps at the same time as in *capitolo* 14, canceled this statute.

3. Beginning with *capitolo* 24 and through 33, the titles of the individual statutes are not written or are not sufficiently clear to be readable. To avoid error, I have omitted the titles. The change in the existence and readability of the titles is related to a new hand that is first evident here on fol. 7r.

4. Beginning with statute 55 the hand of the text and titles changes again. In the following *capitoli* the titles are omitted through the end of the text.

5. Fols. 16v through 17v are blank.

Bibliography

Adam, Paul. *La vie parossiale en France au XIVe siècle*. Paris: Sirey, 1964.
Agnoletti, Ercole. *I vescovi di Sansepolcro*. Vol 1. Sansepolcro: Tipografia Boncompagni, 1972.
______. La Madonna della Misericordia e il Battesimo di Cristo di Piero della Francesca. Sansepolcro: N.p., 1977.
______. *Memorie religiose inedite di Sansepolcro*. San Sepolcro: Tipografia Boncompagni, 1970.
______. *Piccole storie di Sansepolcro e altrove*. San Sepolcro: Arti Grafiche, 1984.
______. *Sansepolcro nel periodo degli abati (1012–1521)*. San Sepolcro: N.p., 1976.
______. *Spigolature di Archivio*. San Sepolcro: Tipografia Boncompagni, 1971.
______. *Viaggio per le valli Altotiberine Toscane*. Sansepolcro: N.p., 1979.
Agostini, Francesco, ed. *Testi trecenteschi di Città di Castello*. Florence: Presso L'Academia della Crusca, 1978.
Ariès, Philippe. *Essais sur l'histoire de la mort*. Paris: Editions du Seuil, 1975.
______. *The Hour of Our Death*. Translated by Helen Weaver. New York: Knopf, 1981.
______. *Western Attitudes toward Death*. Translated by Patricia M. Ranum. Baltimore: Johns Hopkins University Press, 1974.
Augustine of Hippo. *Confessions*. Translated by R. S. Pine-Coffin. Baltimore: Penguin Books, 1961.
Banker, James. "Mourning a Son: Childhood and Paternal Love in the *Consolateria* of Giannozzo Manetti." *History of Childhood Quarterly* 3 (1976): 351–62.
Battisti, Eugenio, with Settesoldi, Enzo. *Piero della Francesca*. 2 vols. Milan: Istituto Editoriale Italiano, 1971.
Becker, Marvin B. "Aspects of Lay Piety in Early Renaissance Florence." In Charles Trinkaus and Heiko A. Oberman, eds., *The Pursuit of Holiness in Late Medieval and Renaissance Religion* pp. 177–99. Leiden: E. J. Brill, 1974.
______. "Individualism in the Early Renaissance: Burden and Blessing." *Studies in the Renaissance* 19 (1972): 273–94.
______. *Medieval Italy: Constraints and Creativity*. Bloomington: Indiana University Press, 1981.
Bellomo, Manlio. *Problemi di diritto familare nell'età dei comuni: Beni paterni e "pars filii."* Milan: Dott. A. Giuffrè Editore, 1968.

———. *Ricerche sui rapporti patrimoniali tra coniugi; Contributo alla storia della famiglia medievale.* Varese: Giuffrè, 1961.

Benvenuti Papi, Anna. "L'impianto mendicante in Firenze, un problema aperto." *Mélanges de l'Ecole française de Rome; Moyen âge–Temps modernes* 89 (1977): 595–608.

———. "Ordini mendicanti e città: Appunti per un'indagine, il caso di Firenze." In Domenico Maselli, ed., *Da Dante a Cosimo I,* pp. 122–45. Pistoia: Libreria Editrice Tellini, 1976.

Bercordati, Francesco. "Cronaca di Borgo San Sepolcro." Manuscript, seventeenth century. Archivio comunale, San Sepolcro.

Berliere, Ugo. "Les confréries bénédictines au moyen âge." *Revue liturgique et monastique* 12 (1926–27): 135–45.

Betazzi, Enrico. "Laudi della Città di Borgo S. Sepolcro." *Giornale storico della letteratura italiana* 18 (1891): 242–76.

Beyenka, Sister Mary Melchior. *Consolation in Saint Augustine.* Patristic Series, vol. 83. Washington, D.C.: Catholic University of America Press, 1950.

Boase, T. S. R. *Death in the Middle Ages: Mortality, Judgement and Remembrance.* New York: McGraw-Hill, 1972.

Bonanno, Claudio; Bonanno, Metello; and Pellegrini, Luciana. "I legati 'pro anima' ed il problema della salvezza nei testimenti della seconda metà del Trecento." *Ricerche storiche* 15 (1985): 183–220.

Brandileone, Francesco. *I lasciti per l'anima e la loro trasformazione: Saggio di ricerche storico-giuridiche.* Venice: Istituto veneto di scienze, lettere ed arti, 1911.

Brentano, Robert. "Innocent IV and the Chapter of Rieti." *Studia Gratiani* 13 (1967): 385–410.

———. "Localism and Longevity: The Example of the Chapter of Rieti in the Thirteenth and Fourteenth Centuries." In Kenneth Pennington and Robert Somerville, eds., *Law, Church, and Society: Essays in Honor of Stephan Kuttner,* pp. 293–310. Philadelphia: University of Pennsylvania Press, 1977.

———. *Rome before Avignon: A Social History of Thirteenth-Century Rome.* New York: Basic Books, 1974.

———. *Two Churches: England and Italy in the Thirteenth Century.* Princeton: Princeton University Press, 1968.

Brown, Peter. *The Cult of the Saints: Its Rise and Function in Latin Christianity.* Chicago: University of Chicago Press, 1981.

Brown, Theo. *The Fate of the Dead: A Study in Folk Eschatology in the West Country after the Reformation.* Folklore Society, Mistletoe Series. Ipswich: D. S. Brewer, 1979.

Bullough, Vern, and Campbell, Cameron. "Female Longevity and Diet in the Middle Ages." *Speculum* 55 (1980): 317–25.

Chaunu, Pierre. *La mort à Paris.* Paris: Fayard, 1978.

———. "Mourir à Paris (XVIe–XVIIe–XVIIIe siècles)." *Annales: E.S.C.* 21 (1976): 29–50.

Chiffoleau, Jacques. *La compatabilité de l'au-delà: Les hommes, la mort et la religion dans la région d'Avignon à la fin du moyen âge (vers 1320–vers 1480).* In Collection de l'Ecole française de Rome, vol. 47. Rome: Ecole française de Rome, 1980.

______. "Perché cambia la morte nella regione di Avignone alla fine del medioevo." *Quaderni storici* 50 (1982): 449–65.

______. "Pratiques funéraires et images de la mort à Marseille, en Avignon et dans le Comtat Venaissin (vers 1280–vers 1350)." *Cahiers de Fanjeux* 11 (1976): 271–303.

Christian, William A. *Local Religion in Sixteenth-Century Spain.* Princeton: Princeton University Press, 1981.

Cohn, Samuel Kline. *The Laboring Classes in Renaissance Florence.* New York: Academic Press, 1980.

Coleschi, Lorenzo. *Storia della Città di Sansepolcro.* Città di Castello, 1886. Reprint as *La storia di San Sepolcro* with Polcri Franco. San Sepolcro: C.L.E.A.T., 1966.

Constable, Giles. "The *Liber Memorialis* of Remiremont." *Speculum* 47 (1972): 261–77.

Corsini, Carlo A. "I libri dei morti." In *Le fonti della demografia storica in Italia,* Comitato italiano per lo studio dei problemi della demografia storica, no. 7, vol. 1, pt. 2, pp. 851–952. Rome, 1974.

Coste, Jean. "L'institution paroissiale à la fin du moyen âge: Approche bibliographique en vue d'enquétes possibles," *Mélanges de l'Ecole Française de Rome: Moyen âge–Temps modernes* 96 (1984): 296–326.

Dal Pino, Franco Andrea. *I Frati Servi di S. Maria dalle orgini all'approvazione (1233 ca.–1304).* 2 vols. Louvain: Publications universitaires de Louvain, 1972.

Davidsohn, Robert. *Storia di Firenze,* vol. 7, *I primordi della civiltà fiorentina,* pt. 3, *Il mondo della chiesa, spiritualità ed arte.* Florence: Sansoni, 1973.

Davis, Natalie Zemon. "Some Tasks and Themes in the Study of Popular Religion." In Charles Trinkaus and Heiko A Oberman, eds., *The Pursuit of Holiness in Late Medieval and Renaissance Religion,* pp. 307–36. Leiden: E. J. Brill, 1974.

"De beato Rainerio ordinis fratrum minorum Burgi S. Sepolcri in Umbria." Edited by Charles de Smedt, G. van Hooff, and Josephi de Backer. In *Acta sanctorum: Novembris . . . ,* 63, I. Paris: V. Palme, 1887, 390–402.

Delgi Azzi, Giustiniano. "Inventario degli archivi di San Sepolcro." *Archivi della Storia d'Italia,* 2d ser., 4 (1914): 77–194.

______. "Leggi suntuarie perugine nell'età dei comuni." *Bollettino della R. Deputazione di storia patria per l'Umbria* 22 (1916): 125–56.

De la Roncière, Charles. "La place des confréries dans l'encadrement religieux du contado Florentin au XIVe siècle: L'exemple de la Val d'Elsa." *Mélanges de l'Ecole française de Rome: Moyen âge–Temps modernes* 85 (1973): 31–77, 633–71.

______. "L'influence des Franciscains dans la compagne de Florence au XIVe siècle (1280–1360)." *Mélanges de l'Ecole française de Rome: Moyen âge–Temps modernes* 87 (1975): 21–103.

———. "Pauvres et pauvreté à Florence au XIVe siècle." In Michael Mollat, ed., *Etudes sur l'histoire de la pauvreté (Moyen Age–XVIe siecle),* 2:661–765. Paris: Publications de la Sorbonne, 1974.

Delisle, Leopold. "Monuments paleographiques concernant l'usage de prier pour les defunts." *Bibliotheque le l'Ecole des Chartres* 8 (1846): 361–411.

Delumeau, Jean. *Catholicism between Luther and Voltaire: A New View of the Counter-Reformation.* Translated by Jeremy Moiser. London: Burns and Oates, 1977.

Dini, Vittorio. *Il potere della antiche madri: Fecondità e culti delle acque nella cultura subalterna toscana.* Turin: Editore Boringhieri, 1980.

Duby, Georges. *The Early Growth of the European Economy: Warriors and Peasants from the Seventh to the Twelfth Century.* Translated by Howard B. Clarke. Ithaca: Cornell University Press, 1974.

———. *Medieval Marriage: Two Models from Twelfth-Century France.* Translated by Elborg Forster. Baltimore: Johns Hopkins University Press, 1978.

———. "The Nobility in Eleventh and Twelfth-Century Maconnaise." Translated by Frederic L. Cheyette in *Lordship and Community in Medieval Europe,* pp. 137–55. New York: Holt, Rinehart, and Winston, 1968.

———. *La société aux XIe et XIIe siècles dans la région maconnaise.* Paris: Librairie Armand Colin, 1953.

Duparc, Pierre. "Confréries du Saint-Esprit et communautes d'habitants au moyen-âge." *Revue historique de droit et étranger,* 4th ser., 36 (1958): 349–67.

Epstein, Steven. *Wills and Wealth in Medieval Genoa, 1150–1250.* Harvard Historical Studies, vol. 103. Cambridge, Mass.: Harvard University Press, 1984.

Falco, Mario. *Le disposizione "pro anima": Fondamenti dottrinali e forme giuridiche.* Turin: Fratelli Bocca, 1911.

Fanfani, Amintore. "La beneficenza in un comune toscana dal XIII al XV secolo." In Fanfani, *Saggi di storia economica italiana,* pp. 37–82. Milan: Società editrice "Vita e pensiero," 1936.

———. *Indagini sulla "rivoluzione dei prezzi."* Milan: Pubblicazione dell'Università Cattolica del S. Cuore, 1940.

———. *Un mercante del trecento.* Milan: Dott. A. Giuffrè editore, 1935.

Farulli, Pietro. *Annali e memorie dell'antica e nobile città di S. Sepolcro.* Foligno: N. Canpitelli, 1713.

Fiorani, Luigi, ed. *Le confraternite romane: Esperienza religiosa, società, committenza artistica.* In *Ricerche per la storia religiosa di Roma* 5 (1984).

Fiumi, Enrico. "La populazione del territorio volterrano-sangimignanese ed il problema demografica dell'età comunale." In *Studi in onore di Amintore Fanfani,* 1:251–90. Milan: Giuffrè, 1962.

Franceschini, Gino. "Alcuni documenti su la signoria di Galeotto Malatesta a Borgo San Sepolcro (1371–1385)." *Studi Romagnoli* 2 (1951): 39–56.

Francis of Assisi. *Writings and Early Biographies: English Omnibus of the Sources for the Life of St. Francis.* Edited by Marion A. Habig. 3d rev. ed. Chicago: Franciscan Herald Press, 1973.

Frugoni, Arsenio. "I temi della morte nell'affresco della chiesa dei disciplinati a Clusone." *Bullettino dell'Istituto storico italiano* 69 (1957): 175–212.

Galpern, A. N. "Late Medieval Piety in Sixteenth-Century Champagne." In Charles Trinkaus and Heiko A. Oberman, eds., *The Pursuit of Holiness in Late Medieval and Renaissance Religion,* pp. 141–76. Leiden: E. J. Brill, 1974.

———. *The Religions of the People in Sixteenth-Century Champagne.* Cambridge, Mass.: Harvard University Press, 1976.

Garufi, Carlo Alberto, ed. *Necrologio del Liber confratium di S. Mateo di Salerno.* Vol. 1. In *Fonti per la storia d'Italia,* 56. Rome: Tipografia del Senato, F. Donati, 1922.

Gasparini, Giuseppina. *Contadini, chiesa, confraternità in un paese veneto di bonifica: Villa del Bosco nel quattrocentro,* in *Fonti e ricerche di storia ecclesiastica padovana.* Padua: Istituto per la storia ecclesiastica padovana, 1979.

———, ed. *Statuti di confraternite religiose di Padova nel medio evo.* Padua: Istituto per la storia ecclesiastica padovana, 1974.

Geertz, Clifford. *The Interpretation of Cultures.* New York: Basic Books, 1973.

———. "Religion as a Cultural System." In Michael Banton, ed., *Anthropological Approaches to the Study of Religion,* pp. 1–46. London: Tavistock, 1966.

Gennep, Arnold van. *The Rites of Passage.* Translated by Monika B. Vizedom and Gabrielle L. Caffee. Chicago: University of Chicago Press, 1960.

Ginzburg, Carlo. *Indagini su Piero: Ill battesimo, il ciclo di Arezzo, la flagellazione di Urbino.* Turin: Giulio Einaudi editore, 1981.

Giorni, Bruno. *Monterchi.* Città di Castello: Tipografia Tappini, 1977.

Goldthwaite, Richard. *The Building of Renaissance Florence: An Economic and Social History.* Baltimore: Johns Hopkins University Press, 1980.

———. "I prezzi del grano a Firenze del XIV al XVI secolo." *Quaderni Storici* 10 (1975): 15–36.

Goody, Jack. *Death, Property, and the Ancestors: A Study of the Mortuary Customs of the LoDagaa of West Africa.* Stanford: Stanford University Press, 1962.

Goracci, Alessandro. *Breve istoria dell'origine e fondazione della Città di Borgo San Sepolcro.* 1636. Reprinted in *Collezione di cronisti italiani,* vol 7. Florence: S. Coen, 1844.

Gorer, Geoffrey. *Death, Grief, and Mourning in Contemporary Britain.* Garden City, N.Y.: Doubleday, 1965.

Gougaud, Louis. "La mort du moine." *Revue Mabillon* 19 (1929): 281–302.

Hands, Arthur Robinson. *Charities and Social Aid in Greece and Rome.* Ithaca: Cornell University Press, 1968.

Henderson, John. "The Flagellant Movement and Flagellant Confraternities in Central Italy, 1260–1400." *Studies in Church History* 15 (1978): 147–60.

———. "Society and Religion in Renaissance Florence." *Historical Journal* 29 (1986): 213–25.

Herlihy, David. "Deaths, Marriages, Births, and the Tuscan Economy." In Ronald Demos Lee, ed., *Population Patterns in the Past,* pp. 135–64. New York: Academic Press, 1977.

———. "Family and Solidarity in Medieval Italy." in David Herlihy, Roberto Lopez, and Vsevolod Slessarev, eds., *Economy, Society, and Government in Medieval Italy: Essays in Memory of Robert L. Reynolds,* pp. 177–88. Kent, Ohio: Kent State University Press, 1969.

———. *Medieval and Renaissance Pistoia: The Social History of an Italian Town, 1200–1430.* New Haven: Yale University Press, 1967.

Herlihy, David, and Klapisch-Zuber, Christiane. *Tuscans and Their Families: A Study of the Florentine Catasto of 1427.* New Haven: Yale University Press, 1985.

Hlawitschka, Edward; Schmid, Karl; and Tellenbach, Gerd, eds. *Liber memorialis von Remiremont.* Vol. 1, in *Libri memoriales,* 1, in *Monumenta Germaniae historica.* Zurich: Weidmann, 1970.

Huntington, Richard, and Metcalf, Peter. *Celebrations of Death: The Anthropology of Mortuary Ritual.* Cambridge: At the University Press, 1979.

Huyghebaert, N. *Les documents nécrologiqes.* In *Typologie des sources du moyen âge occidental,* 4. Turnhout: Brepols, 1972.

Kedar, Benjamin Z. "Noms des saints et mentalité populaire à Genes au XIVe siècle." *Le moyen âge* 73 (1967): 431–45.

Klapisch-Zuber, Christiane. *Women, Family and Ritual in Renaissance Italy.* Translated by Lydia G. Cochrane. Chicago: University of Chicago Press, 1985.

La Sorsa, Saverio. *La Compagnia d'Or San Michele.* Trani, 1902.

Lazzeri, Corrado. *Guglielmino Ubertini: Vescovo di Arezzo—(1248–1289)—e i suoi tempi.* Florence: Libreria editrice fiorentina, 1920.

Le Bras, Gabriel. "Les confréries chretiennes: Problemes et propositions." *Revue historique de droit français et étranger* 19 (1940–41): 310–63.

———. *Studi di sociologia religiosa.* Translated by Giuseppe Caputo and Liafranca Pellegnini. Milan: Feltrinelli Editore, 1969.

Le Clercq, Jean. "Documents sur la mort des moines." *Revue Mabillon* 65 (1955): 165–80; 66 (1956): 65–81.

Le Goff, Jacques. "Apostolat mendiant et fait urbain dans la France médiévale: L'implantation géographiques des ordres mendiants: Programme-Questionaire pour une enquête." *Annales: E.S.C.* 23 (1968): 335–52.

———. *The Birth of Purgatory.* Translated by Arthur Goldhammer. Chicago: University of Chicago Press, 1984.

———. "Ordres mendiants et urbanisation dans la France médiévale. Etat de enquête." *Annales: E.S.C.* 25 (1970): 924–46.

———. *Time, Work, and Culture in the Middle Ages.* Translated by Arthur Goldhammer. Chicago: University of Chicago Press, 1980.

———. "The Usurer and Purgatory." In *The Dawn of Modern Banking.* pp. 25–

52. Center for Medieval and Renaissance Studies, University of California, Los Angeles. New Haven: Yale University Press, 1981.

Lesnick, Daniel. "Dominican Preaching and the Creation of Capitalist Ideology in Late-Medieval Florence." *Memorie Domenicane,* n.s., 8–9 (1977–78): 199–247.

Lippens, P. Hugolinus. "De Litteris confraternitatis apud fratres minores ordinis initio ad annum usque 1517." *Archivium franciscanum historicum* 32 (1939): 49–88.

Little, Lester. *Religious Poverty and the Profit Economy in Medieval Europe.* Ithaca: Cornell University Press, 1978.

Lorcin, Marie-Thérèse. *Vivre et mourir en Lyonnais à la fin du moyen âge.* Paris: Editions du CNRS, 1981.

McManners, John. *Death and the Enlightenment: Changing Attitudes to Death among Christians and Unbelievers in Eighteenth-Century France.* Oxford: Oxford University Press, 1981.

———. "The History of Death." *Times Literary Supplement,* December 14, 1979, pp. 111–13.

Maggini, Giuliana, and Andreini, Luigi, eds. *Laudario della Compagnia di Santa Maria della Notte.* San Sepolcro: Cooperativa Culturale "Giorgio La Pira," n.d.

Magli, Ida. *Gli uomini della penitenza.* Rocca San Casciano: Capelli, 1976.

Martines, Lauro. *Power and Imagination: City-States in Renaissance Italy.* New York: Knopf, 1979.

Mazzi, Curzio. "Alcune leggi suntuarie senesi del secolo XIII." *Archivio storico italiano,* 4th ser. 5 (1880): 133–44.

Meersseman, Gilles Gerard. "Les confréries des disciplines de Saint-Dominique." *Archivum fratrum praedicatorum* 20 (1950): 21–63.

———. "Les confréries de Saint-Pierre Martyr." *Archivum fratrum praedicatorum* 21 (1951): 51–196.

———. *Dossier de l'ordre de la penitence au XIIIe siècle.* In *Spicilegium Friburgense,* vol. 7. Fribourg, Switzerland: Universitat verlag Freibourg, 1983.

Meersseman, Gilles Gerard, with Gian Piero Pacini. *Ordo fraternitatis: Confraternite e pietà dei laici nel medioevo.* 3 vols. Italia Sacra: Studi e documenti di storia ecclesiastica, vols. 24–26. Rome: Herder editrice e libreria, 1977.

Meloni, Piero L. "Per la storia delle confraternite disciplinate in Umbria nel secolo XIV." In *Storia e arte in Umbria nell'età comunale, Atti del Convegno di Studi Umbria,* 2:533–87. Perugia: A cura della Facolta di lettere e filosofia dell' Università, 1971.

Mirrors of Mortality: Studies in the Social History of Death. Edited by Joachim Whaley. New York: St. Martin's Press, 1981.

Mischj, G. "Gli *Ordinamenta mortuorum* in Città di Castello." *Bollettino della R. Deputazione di storia patria per l'Umbria* 22 (1916): 41–53.

Mittarelli, Giovanni Benedetto, and Costadoni, Anselmo, eds. *Annales Camaldulesis ordinis Sancti Benedicti.* 9 vols. Venice: Prostant apud Jo. Baptistam Pasquali, 1755–73.

Moeller, Bernd. *Reichsstadt und Reformation*. Gütersloh: Gütersloher Verlagshaus, G. Mohn, 1962.

Molinier, Auguste. *Les obituaires français du moyen âge*. Paris: Imprimerie Nationale, 1890.

Mollat, Michel, ed. *Etudes sur l'histoire de la Pauvreté*. 2 vols. Paris: The Sorbonne, 1974.

Monti, Gennaro Maria. *Le confraternite medievali dell'alta e media Italia*. 2 vols. Venice: La Nuova Italia, 1927.

Morghen, Raffaello. *Il passaggio dal Medioevo al Rinascimento nelle aspettative escatologiche del secolo XIV*. Rome: N.p., n.d.

———. "Raniero Fasani e il movimento dei disciplinati del 1260." In *Il movimento dei disciplinati nel settimo centenario dal suo inizio*, pp. 29–42. Deputazione di storia patria per l'Umbria. Spoleto: Arti grafiche Pametto Petrelli, 1962.

Morini, Ugo, ed. *Documenti inediti o poco noti per la storia della Misericordia di Firenze (1321–1525)*. Florence: Ven. Arciconfraternità, 1940.

La mort au moyen âge. Colloque de l'Association des Historiens medievistes françaises. *Recherches et documents*, vol. 25. Publications de la Société savante d'Alsace et des régions de l'Est. Strasbourg: Libraire Istra, 1977.

Il movimento dei disciplinati nel settimo centenario dal suo inizio. Deputazione di storia patria per l'Umbria. Perugia: Convegno internazionale, 1962.

Movimento religioso femminile e francescanesimo nel secolo XIII. Atti del VII Convegno internazionale, Assisi. Assisi: La Società internazionale di studi francescani, 1980.

Mueller, Reinhold. *The Procuratori di San Marco and the Venetian Credit Market*. New York: Arno Press, 1977.

Muzi, Giovanni. *Memorie civili di Città di Castello*. 2 vols. Città di Castello, 1844.

———. *Memorie ecclesiastiche di Città di Castello*. 5 vols. Città di Castello: F. Donati, 1843.

Novati, Francesco. "L'obituario della cattedrale di Cremona." *Archivio storico lombardo* 6, fasc. 2 (1880): 245–76; fasc. 3 (1880): 566–89; 8, fasc. 3 (1881): 484–506.

Oliger, Olivanio. "Documenta originis Clarissarum Civitatis Castelli, Eugudii . . . . *Archivium franciscanum historicum* 15 (1922): 71–102.

Les ordres mendiants et la ville en Italie centrale (v. 1220–v. 1350). In *Mélanges de l'Ecole française de Rome, Moyen âge–Temps modernes* 89 (1977): 557–773.

Orlandi, Stefano, ed. *"Necrologio" di S. Maria Novella: Testo integrale dall'inizio (MCCXXV) al MDIV*. 2 vols. Florence: L. S. Olschki, 1955.

Papi, Massimo. "Per un censimento della fonti relative alle confraternite laiche fiorentine: Primi risultati." In Domenico Maselli, ed., *Da Dante a Cosimo I: Ricerche di storia religiosa e culturale toscana nei secoli XIV–XVI*, pp. 92–121. Pistoia: Libreria Editrice Tellini, 1976.

Parenti, Giuseppe. "Fonti per la storia della demografia fiorentina: I libri dei morti." *Genus* 6–8 (1943–49): 281–301.

———. *La populazione della Toscana sotto la reggenza Lorenese.* Florence: Rinascimento del libro, 1937.

Pellegrini, Luigi. "Gli insediamenti degli ordini mendicanti e la loro tipologia: Considerazioni metologiche e piste di ricerca." *Mélanges de l'Ecole Française de Rome: Moyen âge—Temps modernes* 89 (1977): 563–73.

Pignani, Francesco. "Compendio istorico di memorie della città di San Sepolcro." Manuscript, 1758. Archivio comunale, San Sepolcro.

Pullan, Brian S. *Rich and Poor in Renaissance Venice: The Social Institutions of a Catholic State, to 1620.* Cambridge, Mass.: Harvard University Press, 1971.

Razi, Zvi. *Life, Marriage and Death in a Medieval Parish: Economy, Society and Demography in Halesowen, 1270–1400.* Cambridge: At the University Press, 1980.

Religion and Society in Early Modern Europe, 1500–1800. Edited by Kaspar von Greyerz. London: George Allen & Unwin, 1984.

Ricci, D. D. *La Fraternità di S. Bartolomeo.* San Sepolcro: S. Tipografica "La Resurrezione," 1936.

Ricci, Ivano. *Borgo San Sepolcro: Monografia storico-artistica.* San Sepolcro: Tipografica S. Boncompagni, 1932.

Rigon, Antonio. "I laici nella chiesa padovana del duecento: Conversi, oblati, penitenti." *Contributi alla storia della chiesa padovana nell'età medioevale* 8 (1979): 11–81.

Risultati e prospettive della ricerca sul movimento dei disciplinati. Deputazione di storia patria per l'Umbria. Perugia: Convegno internazionale di Studio, 1972.

Rosenthal, Joel. *The Purchase of Paradise: The Social Function of Aristocratic Benevolence, 1307–1485.* London: Routledge & Kegan Paul, 1972.

Rowell, Geoffrey. *The Liturgy of Christian Burial.* London: Alcuin Club/SPCK, 1977.

Rusconi, Roberto, ed. *Il movimento religioso femminile in Umbria nei secoli XIII–XIV.* Atti del Convegno internazionale di studio nell'ambito della celebrazioni per l'VIII centenario della nascità di S. Francesco d'Assisi. Florence: "La Nuova Italia" editrice, 1984.

Rush, Alfred Clement. *Death and Burial in Christian Antiquity.* Washington, D.C.: Catholic University of America Press, 1941.

Scaramucci, L. "Considerazioni sui statuti e matricole di confraternite di disciplinati." In *Risultati e prospettive della ricerca sul movimento dei disciplinati,* pp. 134–94. Perugia: Convegno internazionale di Studio, 1972.

Schiaffini, Alfredo, ed. *Testi fiorentini del dugento.* Florence: Sansoni, 1926.

Sella, Pietro, ed. *Rationes decimarum Italiae nei secoli XIII e XIV: Umbria. Studi e testi,* vol. 161. Città di Vaticano: Biblioteca apostolica vaticana, 1952.

Le sentiment de la mort au moyen âge. Edited by Claude Sutto. Montreal: L'Aurore, 1979.

Southern, R. W. *Western Society and the Church in the Middle Ages.* Harmondsworth: Penguin, 1970.

Stannard, David E. *The Puritan Way of Death: A Study in Religion, Culture, and Social Change.* New York: Oxford University Press, 1977.

———, ed. *Death in America.* Philadelphia: University of Pennsylvania Press, 1975.

Tenenti, Alberto. *Il senso della morte e l'amore della vità nel rinascimento (Francia e Italia).* Turin: Giulio Einaudi, 1957.

Toussaert, Jacques. *Le sentiment religieux en Flandre à la fin du moyen âge.* Paris: Plon, 1963.

Toynbee, Jocelyn M. C. *Death and Burial in the Roman World.* Ithaca: Cornell University Press, 1971.

Trexler, Richard. "Charity and the Defense of Urban Elites in the Italian Communes." In Frederic Cople Jaher, ed., *The Rich, the Well-Born, and the Powerful: Elites and Upper Classes in History,* pp. 64–109. Urbana: University of Illinois Press, 1973.

———. "Death and Testament in the Episcopal Constitutions of Florence." In Anthony Molho and John A. Tedeschi, eds., *Renaissance Studies in Honour of Hans Baron,* pp. 31–74. DeKalb: Northern Illinois University Press, 1971.

———. *Public Life in Renaissance Florence.* New York: Academic Press, 1980.

Van Engen, John. "The Christian Middle Ages as an Historiographical Problem." *American Historical Review* 91 (1986): 519–52.

Violante, Cinzio. "Sistemi organizzativi della cura d'anime in Italia tra Medioevo e Rinascimento: Discorso introduttivo." In *Pievi e parrochie in Italia nel Basso Medio Evo* (secc. XIII–XIV). Atti del VI convegno di storia della chiesa in Italia (Firenze, 21–25 settembre 1981). Vol. 1, pp. 1–19, in *Italia Sacra,* 35. Rome: Herder, 1984.

Volvelle, Michel. "Les attitudes devant la mort: Problemes de methode, approches, et lectures differente." *Annales: E.S.C.* 31 (1976): 120–32.

———. *La mort et l'occident de 1300 à nos jours.* Paris: Gallimard, 1983.

———. *Mourir autrefois: Attitudes collectives devant la mort aux XVIIe et XVIIIe siècles.* Paris: Archives Gallimard Julliard, 1974.

———. *Piété baroque et déchristianisation en Provence au XVIIIe siècle: Les attitudes devant la mort d'après les clauses des testaments.* Paris: Librairie Plon, 1973.

Weber, Max. *The Protestant Ethic and the Spirit of Capitalism.* Translated by Talcott Parsons. New York: Charles Scribner's Sons, 1958.

Weissman, Ronald. *Ritual Brotherhood in Renaissance Florence.* New York: Academic Press, 1982.

Wickham, Chris. *Early Medieval Italy: Central Power and Local Society, 400–1000.* Totowa, N.J.: Barnes and Noble, 1981.

Zanetti, Dante E. "La morte a Milano nei secoli XVI–XVIII." *Rivista Storica Italiana* 88 (1976): 803–51.

Index

Note: All lay and clerical corporations are indexed under either Churches, oratories and clerical houses; Confraternity; or Hospitals and Hospices and are alphabetized with *Santa* and *Santo* spelled out completely.